CHRISTIAN SPIRITUALITY
AND THE CULTURE OF MODERNITY

Christian Spirituality and the Culture of Modernity

The Thought of Louis Dupré

edited by

Peter J. Casarella and George P. Schner, S.J.

WILLIAM B. EERDMANS PUBLISHING COMPANY
GRAND RAPIDS, MICHIGAN / CAMBRIDGE, U.K.

© 1998 Wm. B. Eerdmans Publishing Co.
255 Jefferson Ave. S.E., Grand Rapids, Michigan 49503 /
P.O. Box 163, Cambridge CB3 9PU U.K.

Printed in the United States of America

03 02 01 00 99 98   7 6 5 4 3 2 1

Library of Congress Cataloging-in-Publication Data

Christian spirituality and the culture of modernity : the thought of
Louis Dupré / edited by Peter J. Casarella and George P. Schner.
p.   cm.
Includes bibliographical references and index.
ISBN 0-8028-4590-8 (pbk. : alk. paper)
1. Christianity — Philosophy — History. 2. Dupré,
Louis K., 1925- . I. Casarella, Peter J. II. Schner, George P., 1946- .
BR100.C536   1998
230 — dc21   98-4440
CIP

To Louis Dupré

Contents

Part 3: Retrospectives

List of Contributors

MICHAEL J. BUCKLEY, S.J.   Director of the Jesuit Institute at Boston College, and Professor of Theology. Has published *Motion and Motion's God* (Princeton: Princeton University Press, 1971); *At the Origins of Modern Atheism* (New Haven: Yale University Press, 1987); and numerous articles in philosophy, theology, and spirituality.

PETER CASARELLA   Associate Professor of Systematic Theology in the Department of Theology at the Catholic University of America. Has published "Nicholas of Cusa on the Power of the Possible," *American Catholic Philosophical Quarterly* 64 (1990): 7-34; "Experience as a Theological Category: Hans Urs von Balthasar on the Christian Encounter with God's Image," *Communio: International Catholic Review* 20 (1993): 118-28; and has a book manuscript in preparation entitled *Word as Bread: Language and Theology in Nicholas of Cusa*.

PHILIP CHMIELEWSKI, S.J.   Assistant Professor of Religious Social Ethics, Loyola University in Chicago. Has published *Bettering Our Condition: Work, Workers, and Ethics in British and German Economic Thought* (New York: Peter Lang, 1992).

PHILIP CLAYTON   Associate Professor, California State University (Sonoma). Has published *Explanation from Physics to Philosophy: An Essay in Rationality and Religion* (New Haven: Yale University Press, 1989) and *Theism and the Theology of Nature: God, World, Freedom* (Edinburgh: Edinburgh University Press, 1996).

KARSTEN HARRIES   Professor of Philosophy at Yale University. Has published widely on Heidegger, early modern philosophy, and the philosophy of art and architecture. He is the author of three books: *The Meaning of Modern Art* (Evanston: Northwestern University Press, 1968); *The Bavarian Rococo*

Church: Between Faith and Aestheticism (New Haven: Yale University Press, 1983); and *The Broken Frame: Three Lectures* (Washington, D.C.: Catholic University of America Press, 1990). With Christoph Jamme he has edited *Martin Heidegger: Politics, Art, and Technology* (New York: Holmes and Meier, 1994). *The Ethical Function of Architecture* (Cambridge: MIT Press, 1997) has just appeared.

THOMAS P. McTIGHE   Former Chair and Professor of Philosophy at Georgetown University. Has published "*Contingentia* and *Alteritas* in Cusa's Metaphysics," *American Catholic Philosophical Quarterly* 64 (winter 1990): 55-71, and numerous articles on medieval Neoplatonism, Boethius, Thierry of Chartres, Nicholas of Cusa, Galileo, and Descartes.

WILLIAM O'NEILL, S.J.   Associate Professor of Social Ethics at the Jesuit School of Theology at Berkeley and the Graduate Theological Union. Has published *The Ethics of Our Climate: Hermeneutics and Ethical Theory* (Washington, D.C.: Georgetown University Press, 1994); "Ethics and Inculturation: The Scope and Limits of Rights' Discourse," in the *Annual* of the Society of Christian Ethics, 1993; and "No Amnesty for Sorrow: The Privilege of the Poor in Christian Social Ethics," *Theological Studies* 55 (1994).

CYRIL O'REGAN   Assistant Professor of Religious Studies at Yale University. Has published *The Heterodox Hegel* (Albany: State University of New York Press, 1994).

ADRIAAN PEPERZAK   Holds the Arthur J. Schmitt Chair in Philosophy at Loyola University in Chicago. Has published *Philosophy and Politics: A Commentary on the Preface to Hegel's "Philosophy of Right"* (Dordrecht: Martinus Nijhoff, 1987) and *To the Other: An Introduction to the Philosophy of Emmanuel Levinas* (West Lafayette: Purdue University Press, 1993).

KENNETH SCHMITZ   Professor of Philosophy Emeritus and Fellow of Trinity College, University of Toronto, and presently Professor of Philosophy and Director of the S.T.D. program at the John Paul II Institute for Studies on Marriage and Family in Washington. Has published *The Gift: Creation* (Milwaukee: Marquette University Press, 1982); *At the Center of the Human Drama* (Washington, D.C.: Catholic University of America Press, 1994); and numerous articles in philosophy.

GEORGE P. SCHNER, S.J.   Associate Professor of Philosophy of Religion and Philosophical Theology at Regis College, Toronto School of Theology. Has edited a collection of essays entitled *Ignatian Spirituality in a Secular Age* and has published *Education for Ministry* (Kansas City: Sheed and Ward, 1993) and "The Appeal to Experience," *Theological Studies* 57 (1992): 40-59.

DAVID TRACY   Professor at the Divinity School of the University of Chicago. Has published numerous books and articles, among the most recent being *On Naming the Present* (Maryknoll, N.Y.: Orbis Books, 1994) and *Religion and Practical Reason* (Albany: State University of New York Press, 1994).

CHARLES TRINKAUS   Professor Emeritus of History, the University of Michigan. Has published *In Our Image and Likeness: Humanity and Divinity in Italian Humanist Thought* (London: Constable, 1970; paperback reprint, Chicago, 1996) and *The Scope of Renaissance Humanism* (Ann Arbor: University of Michigan Press, 1983).

JAMES WISEMAN, O.S.B.   Associate Professor and Chair of the Department of Theology at the Catholic University of America. Has published "'To Be God with God': The Autotheistic Sayings of the Mystics," *Theological Studies* 51 (1990): 230-51; "'Enveloped by Mystery': The Spiritual Journey of Henri Le Saux/Abhishiktananda," *Église et Théologie* 23 (1992): 241-60; and "'I Have Experienced God': Religious Experience in the Theology of Karl Rahner," *American Benedictine Review* 44 (1993): 22-57.

Preface

Editing a collection of essays multiplies many times the tasks necessary to bring to publication the solitary labors of the scholar. The thirteen other collaborators in this volume were gracious, patient, and conscientious partners in a task which took more than three years from the initial conversation which inaugurated the project. The two editors are grateful for the cooperation and encouragement they received from their colleagues.

Regis College and the Catholic University of America provided cordial environments in which to carry out the editing of the essays. A subvention was generously donated by the Catholic University of America at a key point in the preparations. The editors are also grateful to three assistants. In Toronto thanks goes to Deborah Knott, whose expertise — theological and philosophical, literary and grammatical — brought about the stylistic and technical unity of the final manuscript. In Washington thanks goes to Stephanie Brennan, Brian M. Doyle, and Alexander A. Merati, whose diligence in preparing the manuscript for publication proved equally invaluable in its last stages.

Without the kind support of William B. Eerdmans Jr. and the editorial assistance of his staff, this project would never have seen the light of day.

Thomas P. McTighe was not able to see this volume in its published form. We would like to mourn his passing and acknowledge his achievements here.

The hopes of the two editors and the efforts of all who contributed will be justly rewarded if this volume does indeed encourage conversation with the scholar whose work has inspired it and to whom we have dedicated it.

PETER J. CASARELLA
GEORGE P. SCHNER, S.J.

Introduction

Cacophonous late modernity encourages hastily scribed polemics, and its cease-less production of shifting paradigms impedes a serious study of its own origins. But not everyone succumbs. The contributors to this volume celebrate a man who took the time to assay our present situation by plumbing the spiritual foundations of the present crisis. Louis Dupré never separated painstaking scholarship from a simple grasp of the essential. His vast surveys of the spiritual legacy of the Christian West contain single utterances summarizing decades of reading and contemplation. (So much so that Trappist monks demanded their publication.) His probing into the genesis and maturation of the cultural epoch we call modernity not only enthralled a decade of Yale undergraduates but impels a new generation of scholarship reconsidering the configuration of premodern, modern, and postmodern.

We are often told today that the synthesis of God, the world, and human-ity has been torn asunder. We sense a profound regret that the system-building projects of modernity are impressive, albeit largely uninhabitable, edifices of thought. It seems that all the grand narratives of twentieth-century religious thought are likely to be consigned to the same dustbin to which Kierkegaard ironically relegated the Hegelian system. Even Hegel's own conviction regard-ing the rootedness of Western culture in a religious and even Christian un-derstanding of what is most real only provokes suspicion. The prominence of play, gesture, and sign points to an all-around erosion of confidence by philos-ophers and theologians that we can ever determine who we are essentially as persons.

Much on the present scene argues in favor of accepting this intellectual malaise as normative. Consider the highly problematic and much discussed notion of form. The ancients knew of no manifestation in the world that did not irradiate the essentially timeless order of things. All was form and form was all. First Jews, then Christian and Muslims introduced the idea that God brought form into the world in a single act of creation, and thereby sacralized a created order that depended for its existence upon a divine principle extrinsic to the temporal realm. Some Christian Neoplatonists continued to explore the identification of the Creator with the divine form *(forma formarum)*.

Modernity changes the picture considerably. With the advent of modernity, cosmic form as such is no longer either a metaphysical or theological principle. The epiphany of the finite world as a symbol of divine beauty is submitted to the arbitration of a subjective principle. A world whose "form" is still thought to manifest God and a self still called to "freedom" to labor for God's glory give way to "a new science" (Bacon) and the discovery of the individual. With Kant an infinitely greater Creator remains as a postulate of thought, yet form becomes a simply aesthetic phenomenon, one which completes the separation of its disclosive formal quality from its nonapparent content. Form becomes first and foremost the human capacity to receive and order sense data and make judgments about the world. Less consistent thinkers following in Kant's wake also turn to the subjective form of human experience but cannot agree as to what constitutes either its subjective or experiential quality. Most importantly, the formal quality of existence has now been detached from a synthetic and felt vision of God-self-cosmos that was taken for granted before the advent of modernity.

Modernity not only inaugurates a wholly new approach to a still-desired synthesis, but it thereby also initiates a process of rewriting the heritage of the past. The past as past is born with modernity's Cartesian dream of freedom from the prejudices that mark a commonsense perception of the world. As the modern project ages and its own ideals are subjected to criticism, so too with its firm control of the past. Critics of modernity's Promethean desire to distance itself from the past note the parasitic nature of modernity's hard-won secular emancipation.

Viewed from a putatively "postmodern" perspective (the distance of such a view from modernity's own roots is itself questionable), ancient and medieval anchorings of the world in the vision of a totalizing logos seem to be reoccupied by modern totalizations of selfhood, freedom, and history. The human will to power jettisons, then reabsorbs, the pretensions of a divine theophany. In this view, both ancients and moderns privilege presence over absence, speaking over writing, metaphysics over rhetoric, and a homogenizing system of doctrine over the playful textuality of biblical faith. This suppression of intrasystematic differences was predicated upon an exaltation of the status of the stabilizing ground of worldly essences and human freedom to an unspeakable realm beyond human experience and language. Modernity exploited the technical prowess of its new, more efficient thought mechanisms (e.g., historicism, modern philology, demythologizing). In the process the artificial being of an infinite

Word ("ontotheology") was disassembled only to be replaced by new, equally uninhabitable structures of human, all-too-human volition.

We today live, as George Steiner has said, in the age of the afterword. Popular wisdom maintains that the Word at the ground of appearances has quietly receded into the earth. Proclaiming the death of God today has little, if any, cultural force outside the ambit of fundamentalisms. Announcing the twilight of the idols moves no one to be shocked, for the claim for either the divinity's or humanity's decomposition no longer provokes. Heralding the revolutionary agenda of secularism has given way to poststructuralist bricolage. When its principles are applied consistently, poststructuralism aims not to replace either the high God of Christian faith nor the immutable Word of the metaphysical tradition. The *bricoleurs* are strategists who make critical use of the tools and materials of others without attempting to construct their own edifice. (And what, after modernity, could be more other than the past?) Kierkegaard's statement that he revels in the Hegelian system but cannot find a place for himself in it is an apt metaphor for the *bricoleurs*. Nietzsche's sense of the fragility of his age is equally desperate: "The ice that still supports people today has become very thin; the wind that brings the thaw is blowing; we ourselves who are homeless constitute a force that breaks open ice and other all too thin realities" (*The Gay Science*, n. 377). In light of Nietzsche's remark, one is tempted to think of the present-day *bricoleurs* as the metaphysically homeless with publishing houses only.

The situation depicted above is obviously bleak. If this diagnosis were accurate, then the proclamation of modernity's demise would be a true message for the present age. Detached irony and passionate (but seldom activated) calls to aid the victims of Western culture's homogenizing will to power would be the only reasonable strategies for our times.

Yet Louis Dupré has offered an alternative vision. His interpretation of the present age is suffused with an irenicism that eschews easy labels such as "modern" or "postmodern." Although he recognizes the pathology of intellectual "dis-ease" that accompanies postmodernism, he characterizes the current situation of Western culture as a time of transition, a sometimes difficult and unpredictable passage from high modernity to another, more mature but still modern culture. Dupré's stance toward modernity incorporates apology without cynicism, *apologia* without naïveté. His *Passage to Modernity* carries the subtitle *An Essay in the Hermeneutics of Nature and Culture*. It raises fundamental questions of interpretation about the loss of a synthesis of God-cosmos-humanity and even about the postmodern eclipse of the sense of loss. As such it represents a new genealogy of how we came into our present situation.

He has assayed the paradoxical hope that we may be able to recover those fragments of the premodern and modern syntheses that will position us to see a future which refuses the complacency of accepting metaphysical disintegration as the status quo. This is a real hope, for it allows us to reconstruct a synthesis out of the past and the present with a confidence that the wisdom embedded in them will point us toward the future. At the same time, it abhors restorationism. Modernity introduced a set of problems that were fundamentally new and proposed solutions that need to be tested and refined to find our way into the future.

All of the essays in this volume carry with them some element of that hope. After David Tracy masterfully introduces Louis Dupré's vision of modernity, there follow several essays by scholars who have entered into conversation with Dupré about the past and present of modern Western thought. These "more vigorous self-recoveries" (Emerson) bring us to the very heart of the book. Thomas McTighe, Adriaan Peperzak, and Charles Trinkaus investigate aspects of the medieval and Renaissance tradition that have contributed or could contribute to a revival of contemporary religious thought. McTighe initiates a conversation about the origins and meaning of the central Neoplatonic idea that unity is an "enfolding" of that which is unfolded diversely in a world of multiplicity. Peperzak places the contemplative strategies of both Plotinus and Bonaventure within the context of the cultural ambiguities that mark the shift from modernity to postmodernity. Trinkaus charts the transformation of the theme "the dignity of man" from the Renaissance of the twelfth century (William of Saint Thierry), through high Scholasticism (Thomas Aquinas), and into the Italian Renaissance (Lorenzo Valla). Philip Clayton and Michael Buckley, S.J., survey two often overlooked aspects of nineteenth-century thought on religion: Schelling's Spinozistic theological response to Hegel and the unprecedented and quintessentially nineteenth-century atheistic conception of God as an enemy of our human nature. Cyril O'Regan's probing synthesis of Martin Heidegger's and Hans Urs von Balthasar's views on modernity provides a fitting conclusion to this section of the volume.

The next four essays deal with some aspect of the contemporary discourse about religion and culture. Kenneth L. Schmitz develops a highly original defense of analogical negation, influenced both by Dupré's account of the *via negativa* and by Hegel. James Wiseman, O.S.B., offers some reflections on the confrontation of the Christian mystics with the experience of God's absence. He argues that the mystical account of divine absence as a terminal experience is a still-viable religious response to secularism. Karsten Harries has written a postscript to a seminar on art and religion which he taught with Louis Dupré at Yale University. His essay highlights their basic agreement about the complementarity of art and religion but also a sharp disagreement over the kind of genuine transcendence that is possible today.

Finally, no serious search for a future synthesis could proceed without elaborating a practicable language for speaking of the common good. Recent proposals in social ethics have been plagued by polarizations between adherents to an account of virtues inspired by either the Aristotelian *polis* or Thomistic *ecclesia* and defenders of modernity's legacy of the rights of an individual. The essay by William O'Neill, S.J., offers a new perspective. In evaluating some recent work of John Rawls and Jürgen Habermas on the relationship of public reason and the common good, he explores the hermeneutical bases for retrieving a postmodern conception of public reason and civic discourse. His own conclusions, O'Neill states,

> are far from a panacea, yet in the midst of the "negation and despair" of modernity, they hold the promise that we may yet, in Auden's words, "show an affirming flame."

These words are well chosen. They could even serve as an epigraph for the whole volume.

The final section of the volume contains three essays that focus on the thought of Louis Dupré. Out of his highly diverse collection of essays and books, we chose three foci. George Schner, S.J., presents Dupré's prodigious contribution to the philosophy of religion. Peter Casarella lays out Dupré's thought on religious belief in the modern world and considers how it might serve as the impetus for a program for Christian theology. Finally, Philip Chmielewski, S.J., surveys Dupré's studies of modern social critiques of culture in order to highlight his contribution to social ethics today. This is a fitting note on which to conclude because it shows how even in the realm of the practical cultivation of the human — family life, the workplace, and politics — Louis Dupré aims to restore what is worth saving of the culture of modernity.

This is not a Festschrift. Such volumes are written to celebrate scholarly achievements which have already reached their pinnacle. It would be premature to honor Louis Dupré's career as a fait accompli. Successor volumes to *Passage to Modernity* will no doubt engage scholars for many years to come. Nonetheless, the contributors to this volume felt that the time had arrived to take stock of his view of modern culture, necessarily from a variety of perspectives. Philosophy, theology, the history of ideas, social ethics, and the study of mysticism are all represented. Diverse confessional and nonconfessional beliefs stand side by side. It is our hope, however, that each essay contributes in some measure to the immensely enjoyable conversing that characterizes Louis Dupré's life and thought. Out of sincere gratitude for his example, we dedicate this volume to him.

THE EDITORS

PART 1

PROSPECTS

CHAPTER 1

Fragments of Synthesis? The Hopeful Paradox of Dupré's Modernity

DAVID TRACY

I. Dupré and the Contemporary Debate on Modernity

Louis Dupré has been one of the most trustworthy educators in our parlous times. More than any other contemporary philosopher of religion, Dupré has forced his fellow philosophers (and, for that matter, theologians) to pay serious attention to the philosophical and theological import of the spiritual traditions, especially the mystical traditions. From his earlier groundbreaking work, *The Other Dimension,* through his studies of mystical traditions (especially his beloved Ruusbroec) and his brilliant analyses of such thinkers as Kierkegaard, Hegel, Marx, Schleiermacher, and Duméry, to his constructive analyses of self-hood in modernity, Dupré has consistently instructed us all on the need to reconnect the spiritual traditions to the mainline philosophical and theological traditions. Moreover, he has achieved this work in Western traditions while remaining not merely open to, but informed by, the often greater success of non-Western (especially East and South Asian) traditions in keeping united the classic ancient syntheses of cosmos, the divine or ultimate, and the self.[1]

Dupré seems to possess a singular ability to rethink the contemporary dilemma both intellectually and spiritually by focusing his principal philosophical attention on the linked issues of transcendence and the self[2] in contemporary philosophies and theologies. More sharply than any contemporary philosopher

1. See, for example, Dupré's fine article "Mysticism," in *Encyclopedia of Religion,* ed. Mircea Eliade (New York: Macmillan, 1987), pp. 245-61.

2. See, especially, Louis Dupré, *Transcendent Selfhood: The Loss and Rediscovery of the Inner Life* (New York: Seabury Press, 1976), pp. 1-31, 50-79.

of religion, Dupré shows how the loss of transcendence and the "small soul" (Nietzsche) of the contemporary "self" are indissolubly linked philosophical and theological issues. That intellectual linkage for Dupré, moreover, is grounded in an even more basic difficulty: the uncoupling, in contemporary Western thought, of our critical intellectual (i.e., philosophical and theological) traditions and our spiritual traditions.

For over thirty years I, like many others, have followed and been genuinely instructed by Louis Dupré's unique and consistent project: to reunite what had been separated by modernity, both substantively — God, cosmos, self — and methodologically — the exercises and methods of our spiritual traditions and the theories and critiques of our philosophies and theologies. Dupré's work was already a substantial achievement before *Passage to Modernity*. Furthermore, his oeuvre (beginning with early Kierkegaard study and *The Other Dimension*) has become more, not less, relevant, since now many contemporary philosophers and theologians have joined Dupré's very early articulation of the kind of philosophical enterprise needed. For many thinkers are now forging their own rethinking of the relationships of our philosophical-theological and our spiritual, especially mystical, traditions. Indeed, the recent important debate between Jacques Derrida and Jean-Luc Marion on the phenomenon of "gift" and the reflections on the "Good" in the Dionysian tradition[3] are merely the clearest illustrations of a far more widespread philosophical and theological interest in rethinking the ordinarily marginalized mystical traditions as a resource that may be free of the ontotheological dilemmas of our intellectual traditions.

Dupré made this argument on the intellectual import of the mystical traditions long before more recent thinkers began to sense the importance of that largely uncharted route.[4] Moreover, several other thinkers who also see how Western modern thought has impoverished its notions of the self by developing dominating attitudes toward nature and effectively eliminating or at the best marginalizing any serious reflection on transcendence have now turned with fury against the modern project. Whatever their other crucial differences, both countermoderns (like Leo Strauss, Eric Voegelin, or Alasdair MacIntyre) and postmoderns (like Jean-François Lyotard, Michel Foucault, or Jacques Derrida) have forged powerful and, on the whole, persuasive if profoundly conflicting critiques of "modernity."

---

3. On "gift" in Derrida, see *Given Time: I. Counterfeit Money* (Chicago: University of Chicago Press, 1992); *Donner la mort* (Paris: Métailié-Transition, 1992); on the Dionysian tradition, see Derrida, "How to Avoid Speaking: Denials," in *Languages of the Unsayable*, ed. Budick and Iser (New York: Columbia, 1994). In Marion, see *L'Idole et la distance* (Paris: Grasset, 1977); *God without Being* (Chicago: University of Chicago Press, 1991); "Le phénomène saturé," in *La Phénomènologie et théologie*, ed. J. F. Courtine (Paris: Criterion, 1992).

4. See his early (1972) work here, *The Other Dimension: A Search for the Meaning of Religious Attitudes* (New York: Doubleday, 1972), pp. 484-547.

Dupré's recent entry into this charged debate on modernity provides, in my judgment, a new and important alternative to the usual debate. He sees as clearly as the countermodern and postmodern thinkers the seemingly hopeless impasse which modern thought, despite its remarkable achievements, now faces:[5] the devastating cultural and social consequences of an impoverished philosophical notion of the self aligned to a social condition of increasing possessive individualism; a pervasive mechanistic and scientistic understanding of nature united to a still dominative attitude expressed in an often unbridled technology; a marginalization of any philosophical concern with transcendence, either as a general and central philosophical category or as the religious-theological question of God, united to a marginalization and privatization of religion; a reifying of a once emancipatory Enlightenment reason as a modern rationality which either continues to build, at its worst, an "iron cage" (Weber) or, at the least, an increasing "colonization of the life-worlds" (Habermas).

In this situation Dupré presents an important alternative. He argues as very few other contemporary philosophers have (whether they be defenders or critics of modernity) that the contemporary debate needs to focus on a careful hermeneutical reading of early (fifteenth-to-sixteenth-century) modernity and not just modernity's later, hardened, even reified (eighteenth-century) Enlightenment version.

A good deal of contemporary thought (including my own) displays a kind of pervasive nostalgia for a lost premodern unity along with a radical hermeneutics of suspicion of all totality-systems (whether modern or premodern). So does Dupré's. And yet, Dupré's most recent and clearly major work, *Passage to Modernity: An Essay in the Hermeneutics of Nature and Culture*,[6] pays serious philosophical and theological attention to the missing link in most of the contemporary debate: the origins of modernity in the fifteenth, sixteenth, and early seventeenth centuries. In spite of my other differences with Dupré's reading of the contemporary debate, I have been enormously and thankfully instructed by Dupré's hermeneutical essay on early modernity. Indeed, in my judgment, Dupré's reading of modernity significantly changes the terms of the more familiar debates between moderns and postmoderns. One need not accept Dupré's reading of "postmodernity"[7] (indeed, I do not and consider it a serious

5. The formulations of these difficulties of "modernity" in the essay are my own, not Dupré's. Although I formulate the critique more strongly than Dupré usually does (at least in *Passage to Modernity*), the phrases are faithful to the spirit of his frequent criticisms of contemporary life, especially in *Transcendent Selfhood*.

6. Louis Dupré, *Passage to Modernity: An Essay in the Hermeneutics of Nature and Culture* (New Haven: Yale University Press, 1993).

7. It would be interesting to know what Dupré makes of the debate on postmodernity and negative theology in, for example, the following studies: *Derrida and Negative Theology*, ed. Howard Coward and Toby Foshay (Albany: State University of New York Press, 1992);

flaw in this otherwise amazing philosophical study) to see the import of his work. It is now possible to see that the understanding of "modernity" by both its defenders and its critics has been seriously misconstrued by ignoring, on the whole, the significance of the fourteenth-century nominalists and the fifteenth- and sixteenth-century humanists, as well as the major "early modern" formu- lations of Nicholas of Cusa and Giordano Bruno and, above all, the spiritual and religious resources that made early modernity not merely richer and more flexible than the eighteenth-century Enlightenment version but, above all, free of the set of problems that most contemporary versions of modernity share.

Of course, contemporary philosophical and theological thought was al- ready informed by the now classic works on early modernity by a great tradition of scholarship from Ernst Cassirer through Hans Blumenberg.[8] Moreover, Ernesto Grassi and other scholars of the humanist traditions in Italy have provided persuasive critiques of the widespread contemporary philosophical and theological ignorance of these humanistic traditions as philosophical re- sources relevant to the contemporary debates so influenced by Heidegger.[9] Furthermore, we are all now the inheritors of the explosion of first-rate scholar- ship in the formerly marginalized Neoplatonic traditions and, above all, the great spiritual and especially mystical traditions of our heritage. Though clearly an heir to this extraordinary scholarship on early modernity, Louis Dupré is singular among contemporary philosophers of religion for critically employing this classical history-of-ideas scholarship to provide a strictly philosophical hermeneutic of the "passage to modernity." Thereby Dupré allows both intel- lectual historians like Hans Blumenberg and all contemporary philosophers and theologians to rethink the philosophical import of early modernity for our contemporary problems.

As always, Dupré performs this hermeneutical-philosophical exercise with great modesty: he admits his (that is, our) intellectual and spiritual "poverty" (Emerson) on these central issues; he insists (as does any clearheaded interpreter of our situation) that the best we can hope for today is the recovery of some

---

Kevin Hart, *The Trespass of the Sign: Deconstruction, Theology, and Philosophy* (Cambridge: Cambridge University Press, 1988); *Shadow of Spirit: Postmodernism and Religion*, ed. Philippa Berry and Andrew Warnick (London: Routledge, 1992). My own readings of postmodernity and religion may be found in David Tracy, *Plurality and Ambiguity* (Chicago: University of Chicago Press, 1994); *On Naming the Present* (Maryknoll, N.Y.: Orbis, 1995).

8. See, especially, Ernst Cassirer, *The Individual and the Cosmos in Renaissance Philos- ophy* (Oxford: Oxford University Press, 1963); Hans Blumenberg, *The Legitimacy of the Modern Age* (Cambridge: MIT Press, 1983); Hans Blumenberg, *The Genesis of the Copernican World* (Cambridge: MIT Press, 1987).

9. Among others, see Ernesto Grassi, *Heidegger and the Question of Renaissance Humanism* (Binghamton, N.Y.: Medieval and Renaissance Texts and Studies, 1983). Grassi's important work here has also been influential in Dupré's fine philosophical retrieval of Renaissance philosophy.

intellectual and spiritual "fragments."[10] But note the shift in sensibility in Dupré's appeal to the familiar contemporary metaphor of "fragments" to describe our situation. The profound neoconservative thinker T. S. Eliot will appeal to the image of "fragments" as all we have left to shore up against our ruin as Eliot moves both poetically and philosophically from the contemporary *Waste Land* to the moving, fragmentary, premodern Christian theological resources of *Ash Wednesday* and the *Four Quartets*. Walter Benjamin, that brilliant dialectical revisionary Marxist oddly and uneasily united to a kind of revisionist kabbalist, also appealed to the metaphor of "fragments" with very different resources and readings than Eliot's (or Dupré's): the fragments in German baroque drama and the fragmentary character of the life of Baudelaire's *flaneur* and even the fragments of hope strongly embedded in kabbalistic readings of messianic Judaism or Franz Kafka's readings of modern life. Postmodern thinkers from Bataille to Kristeva also appeal to intense "fragments" now as expressions of excess and transgression, which may free us, however transiently, from the asphalt highway of modern rationality. For many postmoderns only the fragmentary and marginalized resources in our history — the avant-gardes, the mad, the hysterics, the mystics — will help us finally glimpse the emancipatory phenomena of "otherness" and "difference" in subjugated countertraditions to modernity and thereby free us from "more of the same" (Foucault).

These three distinct — even conflicting — appeals to "fragments" share with Dupré (as, indeed, with most of us) the sense that all we now possess are fragments of our heritage and, through those fragments, some modest hope. But Dupré provides a genuinely new vision of reasonable hope in his shifting of the usual terms of the debate: since the Enlightenment, modernity has been read in terms of too hardened a set of once flexible modern categories, too narrow, even dogmatic, a way of understanding the meanings of modernity by both its proponents and its critics. This misreading has been intensified in our period by the sometimes stridently defensive moves of the proponents of modernity and the equally strident outcries of many antimoderns and postmoderns. We may need to step back for a moment and examine, as calmly and deliberately as we can, the origins and the rich, flexible, still amazing passage our culture first took to the modern age. Then our fragments — both premodern and modern — may not simply shore us up against our ruin, nor merely help us undo the totality — thinking and totalitarian and colonizing temptations of Western modernity. Dupré offers another kind of hope: more modest, more willing to admit our present poverty, more honest in insisting, with most other critics of modernity, that fragments are all we any longer possess. At the same time, Dupré shows how these fragments — premodern and modern alike and,

---

10. Dupré, *Passage to Modernity*, p. 253. The full quotation from Emerson may also be found there.

in principle, the fragments of non-Western cultures and postmodern thinkers as well — may become possible "bricks of a future synthesis."[11]

An amazing and plausible vision. We must await Dupré's next constructive philosophical volume following the "hermeneutical" one to see more exactly what that envisioned "future synthesis" may prove to be. But on the basis of the remarkable philosophical-hermeneutical studies of *Passage to Modernity* we know already how central a category "synthesis" is to Dupré. His reading of the ancient and medieval syntheses of cosmos-self-God (or the divine) is, as I shall argue below, one of the best we have. He thereby shows new resources for contemporary thought from early modern thought: the humanists, like Ficino and Erasmus, as well as major novel thinkers like Cusanus and Bruno. He displays the usually overlooked cultural resources of early modernity: the Renaissance and even his remarkable anti-Benjamin, pro-Balthasar portrait of the baroque. Above all, Dupré shows how central (*pace* that fine tradition of intellectual historians from Burckhardt through Cassirer to Blumenberg) religion in fact was to early modernity, and thereby how necessary it is to rethink the relationships of spirituality, philosophy, art, and theology. Dupré's vision is a paradoxical and intriguing one indeed: "fragments" and "synthesis" are not usually coupled together.

To understand how Dupré manages to render persuasive this amazing appeal to "fragments" for a "synthesis," it is necessary to risk an interpretation of his interpretation. In my view, what modernity (in its dogmatic, reified Enlightenment form) broke was the premodern syntheses of form and content, feeling and thought, practice and theory. What Dupré's analysis helped me to see far more clearly than I ever did before is that none of these separations functioned in early modernity, even though the forms of both ancient and medieval substantive syntheses of God-cosmos-self were undone. And therein lies a tale (decidedly not a Whig history nor a grand narrative) that provides a more complex, more reasonable, and more hopeful vision for the present than the more familiar debates on "modernity": it may be possible to see, in early modernity, a way to rethink our options in the contemporary impasse on "late modernity," "countermodernity," and "postmodernity."

II. Modernity: Synthesis and Fragmentation

Since the critiques of Heidegger and Derrida there have been few more pejorative words in contemporary thought than the word "ontotheology." It is no small part of the intriguing character of Dupré's study that he returns a fully

---

11. Dupré, *Passage to Modernity,* p. 253.

positive meaning to this word.[12] For Dupré's book is, above all, a subtle and rich study of how the ancient as well as Jewish-Christian medieval synthesis of the cosmos, the divine, and the human rendered Western thought into a whole, in all its principal and very different religious, cultural, philosophical, and theological forms. For Dupré, what most basically happened in early modernity was the fragmentation of that synthesis. I cannot hope, in this short space, to do justice to the entirety of Dupré's rich, complex, and often somewhat cryptic study. I will, therefore, highlight only certain crucial aspects of his interpretation. The ancient organic Greek and Roman unity was, of course, originally threatened by the Jewish-Christian notion of a creator God transcendent to the cosmos (unlike the "gods").[13] Indeed, the greatest and, on the whole, most successful accomplishment of the Jewish, Christian, and Islamic medieval thinkers was the development of new syntheses designed to maintain the transcendent creator God's profound immanence in the cosmos and in humanity (through wisdom and grace). Until the late medieval period one or another version of an ontotheological synthesis of the cosmic, divine, and human realms held.

Then, on Dupré's reading, the nominalist crisis occurred. The nominalists separated an increasingly transcendent God defined by omnipotent will (and thereby by efficient, not formal, causality) from both cosmos and the human. The ancient and medieval ontotheological synthesis was shaken. Dupré seems, in fact, entirely ambivalent toward the nominalists and most of their successors (he reads postmodernity, for example, as basically neo-nominalism). On the one hand, the nominalist reflection on words and referents prepared the way for modern science to use concepts more freely and flexibly than otherwise might have been the case. On the other hand, nominalism fragmented the ancient synthesis which had formed the most basic ideal of Western culture. In Dupré's fascinating and complex reading of the late medieval nominalist crisis, the full ambiguity of modernity had already begun, therefore, as early as the late fourteenth century.

The daring character of Dupré's strategy asserts itself. First, it is not enough, in any critique of modernity, to focus only on the dilemma of one of the major elements in the modern period: neither the "self" (Taylor, Foucault, Kristeva, et al.), nor reason or logos (Derrida and other critics of Western logocentrism), nor God (the theologians, at least when they assume their proper role of articulating a *logos* on *theos*), nor the cosmos, narrowed to "nature" by

12. Dupré, *Passage to Modernity,* passim, esp. p. 5 where he clarifies his distance here from Heidegger, Derrida, and Rorty.

13. Dupré, *Passage to Modernity,* esp. pp. 22-63. See also the studies in *God and Creation: An Ecumenical Symposium,* ed. David Burrell and Bernard McGinn (Notre Dame: University of Notre Dame Press, 1990).

modernity (the ecologists and ecological science).[14] It is the fragmentation of *any* ontotheological synthesis that demands the most attention in order to understand what happened to any single element: God, cosmos-nature, self, reason.

Second, it is not sufficient, in any description of modernity, to move immediately to a discussion of the seventeenth-century scientific revolution and the political and intellectual components (perhaps all too easily understood, pro or con, in their doctrinal, eighteenth-century form) of the Enlightenment. One must first study the original "passage to modernity" from the end of the fourteenth to the early seventeenth century. An analysis of this rich period provides not only a way to understand how the fragmentation originally happened. That study also suggests several examples of a "usable past" for our contemporary needs: the humanists; the new threshold synthesis of Cusa and the early modern synthesis of Bruno; above all, the religious and spiritual forms and practices that underlay all these early modern movements and thereby allowed several new modern syntheses, not merely fragmentations of the old.

It may be the case that we late twentieth-century Westerners (whether we call ourselves late moderns or postmoderns) do find ourselves now without any synthesis at all — at least one that adequately correlates God-cosmos-humanity. Even contemporary defenders of the "unfinished project" of modernity like Jürgen Habermas and Karl-Otto Apel both insist on our "post metaphysical" status and render religion fundamentally "private," not "public," for the culture.[15] Contemporary critics of modernity from Heidegger through Derrida, moreover, read all Western thought from Plato through Hegel as ridden with an ontotheology. For them, that ontotheology is the fundamental problem of our intellectual tradition, not the need for a new synthesis. Although an analysis of the differing meanings of ontotheology would demand a separate study of the sometimes conflicting texts of Heidegger and Derrida, this much, after Dupré's study, seems clear: no serious critic of Western ontotheology should presume to speak of this central topic without addressing the crucial possibility which Dupré's study of early modernity shows.[16] The ontotheology which has afflicted us with a mechanistic cosmos, an isolated self, and a God who is either dead or so removed from cosmos, self, and history alike as to function as *deus otiosus* may prove to be a specific product of the

14. This is the principal topic of part 1 of Dupré, *Passage to Modernity*, "From Cosmos to Nature," pp. 15-93.

15. See here the fine study by Franklin I. Gamwell, *The Divine Good: Modern Moral Theory and the Necessity of God* (San Francisco: Harper, 1990), esp. pp. 127-213.

16. Dupré's study is here allied to Jean-Luc Marion's studies of Descartes: among others, see *Sur la théologie blanche de Descartes* (Paris: Presses Universitaires de France, 1981); *Sur le prisme métaphysique de Descartes* (Paris: Presses Universitaires de France, 1986).

dilemmas of modernity, not a necessary outcome of the Western turn to theory with the Greeks.[17]

The stakes here are high, as Dupré himself insists in his narrative of early modernity:

> Only when the early humanist notion of human creativity came to form a combustive mixture with the negative conclusions of nominalist theology did it cause the cultural explosion that we refer to as modernity. Its impact shattered the organic unity of the Western view of the real.[18]

As Dupré unfolds his interpretation of the humanists on human creativity, however, it becomes clear that the humanists, on the whole, kept some form of the synthesis alive, either by grounding poetic (for example, Dante) or rhetorical (for example, Petrarch) understandings of human creativity in the divine Word creating *ex nihilo*, or by retrieving some new form of Neoplatonism (Ficino) which allowed for radical immanence, or by any number of other humanistic intellectual strategies (from Erasmus through Montaigne).[19] Each thinker found a way to free early modern humanist thought from the more radical fragmentation of the nominalists without retreating on the modern breakthrough in creativity, individuality, and expressivity.

Moreover, like Hans Blumenberg before him, Dupré focuses on two outstanding thinkers of this period, Nicholas of Cusa (1401-64) and Giordano Bruno (1548-1600).[20] Unlike Blumenberg, Dupré shows that Cusanus, with his amazing pre-Copernican but already nongeocentric view of the cosmos allied to his equally original notion of God's infinity, is not merely a premodern thinker but a genuinely threshold figure. For Cusa, in fact, reconfigured the ontotheological ancient and medieval synthesis in genuinely new (that is, modern) ways. He managed this originality while still maintaining a synthesis of God-self-cosmos, and in that sense held to a fundamental continuity with the classic ancient and medieval Neoplatonic tradition. He is the threshold thinker of early modernity. Moreover, Bruno (more indebted to Cusa, in fact, than to Copernicus) worked out his extraordinary immanentist, panentheistic synthesis of God (no longer, to be sure, a creator God), cosmos, and humanity by developing a philosophical vision which was both creative-expressive (that is, poetic) and genuinely religious, even hermetic.

17. For a good study of how the question of God is thus affected, see Michael Buckley, *Motion and Motion's God* (Princeton: Princeton University Press, 1971), and *At the Origins of Modern Atheism* (New Haven: Yale University Press, 1989).

18. Dupré, *Passage to Modernity,* p. 3.

19. Dupré, *Passage to Modernity,* esp. pp. 93-119.

20. Dupré treats both Cusanus and Bruno at several crucial points in his narrative. Among the most significant are Dupré, *Passage to Modernity,* pp. 59-62, 186-202 (Cusa); pp. 61-66, 125-26, 183-85 (Bruno).

Dupré succeeds in giving a more subtle and judicious reading of the syntheses of both Cusanus and Bruno than Blumenberg does, precisely because he focuses attention on the character of their new ontotheological syntheses as syntheses related to yet different from the older syntheses, rather than simply stressing their relationships (implicit for Cusanus; explicit for Bruno) to the forthcoming Copernican world-picture. A good part of Dupré's success in this portrait of both Cusanus and Bruno, moreover, lies in his attention to the crucial religious components of both Cusanus and Bruno. The understated subtlety of Dupré's interpretation is clear when one compares them not only (as above) to Blumenberg's famous portrait of "The Cusan and the Nolan"[21] but also to such well-known studies of Cusanus as Ernst Cassirer's or Karl Jaspers's.[22] Neither Cassirer nor Jaspers, in their otherwise admiring portraits of Cusanus, seem to know what to make of his religious, even mystical, dimension. For Cassirer, Cusa's work, brilliant as it is, becomes a kind of "mystical" precursor to Kant's later, clear reflections on the limits and antinomies of reason.[23] Jaspers seems puzzled that so fine an analyst as Cusa of the "symbolic ciphers" of both authentic existence and thought could still prove so christological in focus.[24] The neo-Kantian teleology in the implicit grand narratives[25] of modernity in both Cassirer and Jaspers, or even the more cautious, more complex, neo-Copernican grand narrative of modernity in Blumenberg, lack the complexity and subtlety of Dupré's portrait of Cusanus principally by their failure to provide an adequate account and analysis of the religious, even mystical, elements in Cusa as other than somehow dispensable elements on the route to either Copernicus or Kant.

Nor does Dupré exaggerate the import of these religious, even mystical, elements. As clearly as Frances Yates, for example, Dupré disowns the bizarre nineteenth-century rationalist reading of Bruno.[26] Unlike Frances Yates, how-

---

21. Blumenberg, *Legitimacy of the Modern Age*, pp. 457-597; and on Bruno and Copernicanism, Blumenberg, *Genesis of the Copernican World*, pp. 353-86. It is also important to note that Dupré makes his argument for the importance of religion and theology for understanding early modernity without falling back into the "secularization" hypothesis of Karl Löwith, which is criticized by Blumenberg in *Legitimacy of the Modern Age*, pp. 3-125.

22. Cassirer, *Individual and the Cosmos;* Karl Jaspers, *The Great Philosophers* (New York: Harcourt, Brace and World), pp. 116-273.

23. For a useful study of Cassirer's neo-Kantian position, see John Michall Krois, *Cassirer: Symbolic Forms and History* (New Haven: Yale University Press, 1987).

24. Jaspers, pp. 193-95.

25. This emphasis on the "grand narratives" of modernity is Jean-François Lyotard's well-known argument in *The Postmodern Condition* (Minneapolis: University of Minnesota Press, 1984).

26. See Frances S. Yates, *Giordano Bruno and the Hermetic Tradition* (Chicago: University of Chicago Press, 1964).

ever, Dupré does not make the "hermetic" elements in Bruno so pervasive to his thought that the uniquely modern (even Copernican) factors in Bruno are underestimated by a "hermetic-mystical" reading of this remarkable early modern thinker. Dupré's readings of Cusa and Bruno persuade precisely by his insistence on the fuller complexity of both thinkers — both their novelty (hence modernity) and their equally genuine (and religiously inspired) commitment to the classical Western ideal for some ontotheological synthesis. On Dupré's fine reading, both Cusanus and Bruno become plausible heuristic models for the kind of serious modern thought that wants to rethink rather than destroy the ancient ontotheological synthesis even, perhaps especially, in the contemporary period. They are fragments now themselves, serving in our day, as Jaspers saw with clarity, as "ciphers" of a possible transcendence. More importantly, as Dupré shows, the efforts of both Cusanus and Bruno can serve as heuristic fragments-ciphers of hope for some synthesis beyond our present fragmented impasse.

III. Form and Forms:
Foundation and Expression of the Synthesis

What Hans Urs von Balthasar argued, on theological grounds, for theology, Louis Dupré argues for philosophy: no interpreter can understand the Western intellectual tradition without focusing on the phenomenon of form in that tradition. Indeed, the central ideal of Western thought from its beginning in Greece (or even before classical Greece, as argued by Mircea Eliade) was the idea of the real as, in essence, its appearance in form. As Dupré interprets this centrality of form (the principal leitmotif of his study of modernity), form grounds the ancient and medieval ontotheological synthesis.[27] For the ancients, the essence of the real and our knowledge of it consist ultimately of form. Form, moreover, shows forth the real in harmonious appearance: whether in sensuous image as in Greek sculpture; in mathematics as in Pythagoras; in the forms of tragedy which render some aesthetic harmony even to chaos and strife; above all, through the ancient philosophical turn to reflective form in the soul or mind. The real appears in an orderly way and thus becomes (even in tragedy) harmonious appearance. This aesthetic, that is, form-focused, understanding of the real provided the ultimate grounding for any harmonious synthesis of the cosmic, the divine, and the human realms among the ancients. It is a difficult thought to comprehend for us late twentieth-century heirs of the fragmentation

---

27. Dupré, *Passage to Modernity*, esp. pp. 150-93, for Dupré's most extended analysis of the form principle — an analysis whose richness I merely suggest in this summary.

of all syntheses. It is even more difficult for us as inheritors of a hermeneutics of suspicion that every form may merely mask indeterminacy and every appearance or manifestation may always already hide a strife involving both disclosure and concealment.

Nevertheless, both critics and proponents of classical, medieval, and much modern thought (Bruno to Hegel) cannot grasp Western thought without dwelling on the centrality of form. For the premoderns, what appears or manifests itself through form is not our subjective construction but the very showing forth, through form, of the real. For the Greeks real being begins with intelligible form, that is, with a multiplicity, chaos, strife rendered somehow orderly and harmonious through form. The Jewish and Christian thinkers accepted the centrality of form but could not accept the necessity of form in Greek and Roman thought. The Greek gods need the form principle; indeed, the form is divine and the divine is form for the Greeks. For the Jew, Christian, and Muslim, God creates form. But as long as God is not understood as exclusively a purely transcendent will and as long as God's actions are not read exclusively through efficient causality, form survives, indeed prevails: now through the creator God's formal, immanent causality. For Christian thought, moreover, the doctrine of the Word grounded this reality of form in the central Christian doctrines of Christology and Trinity.

This principle of reality manifested *as real* in and through harmonious form in-form-ed the Western philosophical ontotheological tradition from Plato through Hegel. For Plato,[28] with all his constant rethinking of "form," especially in *Parmenides,* form in some manner resided within the appearing objects of which it constituted the intelligible essence. As determining factor of that intelligibility (and thereby reality), form also surpassed the objects. For Dupré, in all Greek philosophy (including Aristotle, despite his critique of Plato on form) being is defined in terms of form. Moreover, form's dependence is to be understood primarily, not exclusively, in terms of participation. The same is also true, it might be added, of archaic and Greek religion as manifestation (Eliade) or, as Hegel nicely named Greek religion, the religion of beauty. The same centrality of form, as Balthasar so brilliantly shows,[29] is true of any form of Christianity faithful to the incarnational principle and to a properly theological understanding of Word as Logos, that is, manifestation in and through form. Above all, there is a profoundly Neoplatonic and even Hegelian tone to Dupré's reading of the centrality of form for all Western thought. Indeed, for

---

28. Dupré, *Passage to Modernity,* pp. 167-68.

29. Hans Urs von Balthasar, *The Glory of the Lord: A Theological Aesthetics,* vol. 1, *Seeing the Form,* trans. Erasmo Leiva-Merikakis, ed. Joseph Fessio, S.J., and John Riches (San Francisco and New York: Ignatius Press and Crossroad, 1982), esp. pp. 429-685.

Hegel, as Dupré justly observes, all content attains its truth in and through form.[30]

In my judgment, Dupré could (and perhaps should) render his own constructive philosophical position explicitly hermeneutical in harmony with his brilliant historical-hermeneutical readings of the centrality of form in Western thought. On the basis of this first volume alone, it is sometimes difficult to know exactly where Dupré himself stands on the philosophical issues his study of modernity clearly involve. To be sure, the subtitle to his book is "An Essay in the *Hermeneutics* of Nature and Culture" (my emphasis). And yet it is difficult to tell how far to take this hermeneutical turn in Dupré. In one sense of the term (a sense Dupré explicitly endorses) there is clarity: we need a sound hermeneutics (that is, description in the philosophical, not only history-of-ideas nor social history, sense) of the passage to modernity before we can attempt a worthwhile philosophical critique of modernity. Granted, but still the question recurs: Does Dupré's excellent "essay in hermeneutics" function only as a study of how central "form" and "manifestation" are to the Western ideal of some synthesis of the cosmic, the divine, and the human realms? Or does Dupré's philosophical essay not also show how central a hermeneutical understanding of truth itself is to his entire philosophical enterprise?

Hermeneutics, after all, has articulated a position on truth very like that implicit in Dupré's hermeneutical-historical study in *Passage to Modernity*.[31] At one point, indeed, Dupré interprets the ancients as holding that truth does mean "to be justified" (as for the moderns), but that justification can be found principally in the sense that truth means participation in being (not construction of it) as manifested through form. This ancient sense is also the one argued by modern hermeneutics: first by Hans-Georg Gadamer in his insistence in *Truth and Method* that truth is fundamentally disclosure, and it is best rendered through form *(Dar-stellung,* not *Vor-stellung);* second and most carefully by Paul Ricoeur in his contemporary argument that truth is primordially manifestation, and only derivatively correspondence or even coherence, allied to Ricoeur's further hermeneutical question of how the world of possibility of the manifestation is rendered through the forms of composition, genre, and style.

---

30. Dupré, *Passage to Modernity,* p. 44.

31. This hermeneutical notion of truth is also in harmony with Dupré's analysis of "correspondence," "coherence," and "disclosure" models (the latter in Gadamer's sense) in his article "Truth in Religion and Truth of Religion," in *Phenomenology of the Truth Proper to Religion,* ed. Daniel Guerrière (Albany: State University of New York, 1990), pp. 19-43. This discussion needs to be explicitly related to the discussion of form in *Passage to Modernity* and then to Gadamer's relationship of disclosure and form in *Truth and Method* (New York: Crossroad, 1988) and Paul Ricoeur on the role of form as composition, genre style in *Interpretation Theory: Discourse and the Surplus of Meaning* (Fort Worth: Texas Christian University Press, 1976).

Any philosopher who argues, on contemporary grounds, in favor of a hermeneutical understanding of truth as primordially manifestation through some
form (as I also have in other writing) cannot but be heartened by Dupré's
extraordinary reading of the centrality of form in the Western philosophical
tradition.

   At the same time, we cannot but wonder why Dupré does not also develop,
in terms of contemporary hermeneutics, what seems to be his own constructive
(and not merely descriptive) position: truth as primordially manifestation-
through-form. Perhaps we must await the next volume for this development.
And yet, for this reader at least, this is somewhat disappointing. For the hints
Dupré does give of what I can only surmise as his hermeneutical position on
truth are indeed fascinating. Consider, for example, Dupré's implicit critique
of Heidegger in his own anti-Heideggerian reading of manifestation (note that
he does not use the Heideggerian formula of disclosure-concealment); Dupré's
interpretation of form in both Plato and the Renaissance (on the former, Dupré
is with Gadamer against Heidegger; on the latter, he is with Grassi against
Heidegger); his critique of Heidegger's notion of ontotheology as too general a
thesis to allow for the profound differences between the ancient and medieval
ontotheological synthesis and that modern ontotheological subjectism which
Heidegger so brilliantly exposes.[32] Consider, as well, Dupré's subtle insistence
that, although Jacques Derrida is both correct and helpful in his analysis of the
logocentric character of Western Greco-Christian thought,[33] still Derrida misreads the full complexity of that thought by failing to distinguish between the
ancient understanding of logos as participatory in being itself from the modern
understanding of logos as exclusively found in the human subject which gives
all other being its meaning. The latter, purely modern understanding demands,
to be sure, theoretical Western logocentric culture. But that is a necessary, not
a sufficient, condition for Derrida's understanding of logocentrism. The sufficient conditions for the modern form of logocentrism can only be found in the
crisis of the original ontotheological synthesis from the late medieval nominalists forward. If I am correct in this reading, Dupré agrees more with Gadamer
and Ricoeur than with either Derrida or the more radical side of Heidegger on
this crucial issue of truth as manifestation through form. Hence the philosophical underpinnings of Dupré's hermeneutical-historical enterprise are implicitly
hermeneutical and should be explicitly so in order to clarify how his hermeneutical-historical argument already (that is, even before the further analyses
of volume 2) bears a contemporary, strictly philosophical significance.

   Dupré here does not agree with Hegel, despite his profoundly Hegelian
affinities. Dupré does want his work to allow the "fragments" of our culture's

---

32. On Heidegger, see Dupré, *Passage to Modernity*, esp. pp. 5-8, 111, 118, 162.
33. Dupré, *Passage to Modernity*, p. 24.

religious and philosophical and theological traditions to become once again "building blocks" for a new (and needed) ontotheological synthesis. However, Dupré also clearly disowns any Hegelian ambition to find a form that would encompass all forms (the speculative proposition, the *Begriff*) arrived at (phenomenologically) through a journey through all the principal forms of art, religion, and philosophy. One will have to await the further constructive developments of Dupré's position to see the fuller outline of his own proposed new synthesis. But this much is true: Dupré advances some hope for a future, relatively modest ontotheological synthesis (perhaps like Whitehead's?). But he offers no hope at all for the "mad and secret dream of Hegel" (Karl Rahner): an ultimate ontotheological synthesis, indeed system, rendered in and through the ultimate form, the dialectically achieved speculative proposition. Like Gadamer and Ricoeur, Dupré has long since abandoned this Hegelian rejection of finitude without forsaking his profound debts to Hegel throughout his entire oeuvre, including *Passage to Modernity*.

Like contemporary hermeneutical thought, therefore, Dupré is a thinker fully aware of finitude, with finite fragments trying to build a new, modest ontotheological synthesis. No ultimate system, no all-inclusive speculative proposition, no grand narrative can be allowed. Instead, Dupré leaves his attentive reader with something more valuable: a series of reflections on how different the ontotheological synthesis of the premoderns was from what many now name modern "ontotheology"; a stern and persuasive reminder of how form served, and could still serve, as the central ideal of our culture in manifesting and rendering intelligibility, truth, and reality; a welcome insistence on how early modernity cannot be understood without understanding the religious elements that pervaded and sometimes grounded modernity's new intellectual and cultural synthesis from Cusanus and Bruno through the humanists, the Reformers, and the baroque. Dupré has written an intriguing narrative encompassing the many forms of early modernity worthy of retrieval: many early modern images, symbols, hymns, and myths; the Renaissance retrieval of rhetoric and poetics; the forms Cusanus and Bruno forged by developing formal, not efficient, causality to show the nondualistic relationship between the finite and the Infinite; new forms for the use of light as form in Duccio and Giotto; form as individuating in Dante; Ficino's aesthetical philosophy; Erasmus's narrative theology; Luther's dialectical theology so expressive of modern unresolved tensions and oppositions; Ignatius of Loyola's rendering a form for ancient spiritual exercises now translated into a modern method; and, most surprising of all, Dupré's brilliant defense of the moving, transient, elusive modern form of baroque culture.

Throughout Dupré's careful interpretations of all these forms (and more) lies his pervasive analysis of the centrality of form itself to our culture. Dupré leaves his reader with something far grander than one more grand narrative of modernity or one more now-familiar critique. Dupré leaves one amazed again at the newness of modernity and thinking again about our culture's original passage to modernity. He persuades us to take that passage again as not merely our fate but our destiny. At least, modernity could become that if we would make the effort to understand its rich, complex terms, not the dogmatic terms for the modern of the eighteenth, nineteenth, or most of the twentieth century. Like the best historians, Louis Dupré in *Passage to Modernity* helps one see afresh an entire period. Like very few philosophers, Dupré also helps one to think through anew the most central issues of philosophy (form, nature, culture, the self, transcendence) by rethinking our culture's history. No small accomplishment that.

PART 2

CONVERSATIONS

CHAPTER 2

A Neglected Feature
of Neoplatonic Metaphysics

THOMAS P. McTIGHE

I

There is a feature of the Neoplatonic metaphysics whose importance has not received sufficient attention. I refer to the notion according to which a unity is conceived as an "enfolding" within itself of its corresponding multiplicity, and conversely the multiplicity is regarded as an "unfolding" of its unity. As is well known, this conception of the relationship of a unity to its multiplicity figures prominently in the philosophy of Nicholas of Cusa, where it is expressed by the couple *complicatio-explicatio.* No one, of course, questions the importance of this couple in Cusanus's writings or in those of Thierry of Chartres from whom Cusanus derived it. But is not the use of the couple simply a special feature of their own brand of Neoplatonism, and even at that merely a kind of metaphor,[1] but hardly a controlling metaphysical schema? In response to these questions, I want to claim that the *complicatio-explicatio* couple is neither a feature peculiar to these two thinkers, nor is its function simply that of a metaphor. My thesis is that use of the couple is critical to the Neoplatonic tradition stretching from Plotinus and Proclus through Boethius to Thierry of Chartres and Nicholas of Cusa.

To be sure, the doctrine of enfolding-unfolding has not been entirely ignored by students of classical Neoplatonism. Many have alluded to it in

1. The terms are of course originally metaphorical. The root "plic" is from the Greek, *plekein,* meaning to coil or weave; hence *complicare,* "to coil up," and *explicare,* "to uncoil." See M. de Gandillac, "*Explicatio-Complicatio* chez Nicolas des Cues," in *Concordia Discors,* ed. Gregorio Piaia (Padua: Editrice Antenore, 1993), p. 86. This article by one of the most outstanding Cusanus scholars is useful as a dossier of texts but disappointing in its lack of analysis.

27

passing, particularly to the "unfolding" side of the couple.[2] Gersh, for example, notes the importance of *anelittein* in Proclus,[3] and Armstrong says Plotinus "is fond of the word, *exelittein*," though he seems to regard the idea it expresses as dangerously subversive of Plotinus's metaphysics.[4] But there has been no systematic treatment of the use of the couple in the Neoplatonic tradition. In this paper I would like to make a beginning at such an enterprise. The order I shall follow is this: after a brief account of the use of the couple in Cusanus and Thierry, I shall try to elucidate its presence in Boethius, and from there move to an analysis of the enfolding-unfolding schema in the Greeks. Boethius is most directly indebted to Proclus. But I should like to concentrate the most attention on Plotinus, not only because he is at the beginning of the Neoplatonic tradition, but, more especially, because the thesis of a connection between the Christians and Plotinus on the issue of enfolding-unfolding has recently been challenged. A response to this challenge allows us to go to the very heart of the question on what is good and bad Neoplatonism in this matter.

II

Let us consider Nicholas of Cusa first. From the very beginning in his first philosophical work, *On Learned Ignorance,* he makes extensive use of the *complicatio-explicatio* couple, and he continues to use it in his subsequent writings. A *complicatio* is a unity, and a unity signifies "what unifies all things."[5] Thus a *complicatio* enfolds within its simplicity that which is unfolded into otherness or diversity. Correspondingly, the condition of unfolding *(explicatio)* is defined as *omnia . . . in pluralitate esse* (all things existing in multiplicity).[6] Thus every unity-multiplicity correlation is an instance of enfolding-unfolding. For ex-

2. Thus Willy Theiler, *Die Vorbereitung des Neuplatonismus,* 2nd ed. (Berlin: Weidman, 1964), pp. 96-97; Heinrich Dörrie, *Das Reallexikon für Antike und Christentum* (Stuttgart: Heiresmann, 1962), vol. 5, cols. 488-91; Hans Joachim Kramer, *Der Ursprung der Geist-metaphysik* (Amsterdam: P. Schippers, 1964), pp. 338-43; Pierre Hadot, *Porphyre et Victorinus* (Paris: Études augustiniennes, 1968), vol. 1, p. 228; Jean Trouillard, *La Purification plotinienne* (Paris: Presses Universitaires de France, 1955), pp. 67-75; Stephen Gersh, *Kinesis Akinetos* (Leiden: E. J. Brill, 1973), p. 105; Arthur Hillary Armstrong, *The Architecture of the Intelligible Universe in Plotinus* (Cambridge: Cambridge University Press, 1940), p. 62; Werner Beier-waltes, *Plotin. Über Ewigkeit und Zeit* (Frankfurt: Klosterman, 1967), p. 257; René Ferwerda, *Les images de Plotin* (Groningen: J. B. Wolters, 1965), pp. 86-87.

3. Gersh, p. 105.

4. Armstrong, *Architecture,* pp. 62-63.

5. Nicolai de Cusa, *De Docta Ignorantia,* ed. Paul Wilpert and Hans Gerhard Senger (Hamburg: Felix Meiner, 1979), II, 3, no. 105 (hereafter cited as *DDI*).

6. *DDI* II, 3, no. 108.

ample, motion and rest are related to each other as the unfolded to the enfolding. Motion is rest *seriatim ordinata* — rest unfolded into ordered succession. Motion is, as it were, a succession of othered, differentiated states of rest.[7] The same is true of time. Its unity is *nunc* (now), that is, *praesentia* (presence) enveloping in it all the moments, past, present, and future, of unfolded time. Indeed, in all cases, an identity stands to its diversity as enfolding to unfolding.[8]

The overarching *complicatio-explicatio* (hereafter: C-E) schema is, of course, the relationship of God to creatures. "Therefore there is *one* enfolding." And that one enfolding is God, "the enfolding of all things, even of contradictories."[9] In the infinite unity of God (the Maximum as Cusa commonly refers to him in *On Learned Ignorance*), "enfolded diversity and enfolding identity are not opposed."[10] In a well-known formula Cusanus summarizes this relationship: "God, therefore, is that which enfolds all things in that all things are in him. God is that which unfolds all things in that he is in all things."[11]

Cusanus uses the typical Neoplatonic analogy of number to exhibit the relationship of unity enfolding to multiplicity unfolded.[12] The number three, for example, does not, qua three, possess a positive nature such as Aristotle would claim. Three does have, indeed, a positive nature, namely, unity or the monadic one, and so do four and two, and so forth. In other words, all numbers are enfolded within the monadic unit, their essence. In the monadic unit, no additive, multiplicative, or other relations obtain.[13] Every number is every other number in the simplicity of the monad. Numbers in their diversity are the monadic unit unfolded. Three, we could say, is a lot of "ones." In *On the Game of Spheres*, using the number two as an example, Cusanus says, "*Alteritas* ("otherness") does not belong to the essence of two, although the fact that it is two (and not, say, three or five) is due to the presence of contingency."[14] This is exactly the case with finite things. God is the true essence of all things as the monadic unit is the essence of all numbers. This does not mean that finite things qua finite are not without

---

7. *DDI* II, 3, no. 106.

8. *DDI* II, 3, no. 106.

9. *DDI* I, 24, no. 67.

10. *DDI* II, 3, no. 107. The Wilpert-Senger edition has *diversitas explicata*. Jasper Hopkins is right, I believe, in reading it as *diversitas complicata*. See his *Nicholas of Cusa on Learned Ignorance*, 2nd ed. (Minneapolis: Arthur J. Banning Press, 1985), p. 193 n. 32.

11. *DDI* II, 3, no. 107.

12. *DDI* II, 3, no. 108.

13. See Nicholas of Cusa, *De Coniecturis* II, 1, no. 75, in *Nicolai de Cusa opera omnia iussu et auctoritate Academiae litterarum heidelbergensis* (Hamburg: Felix Meiner, 1972), vol. 3, p. 74. This edition will be cited hereafter as h.

14. Nicholas of Cusa, *De Ludo Globi*, bk. II, in *Nikolaus von Kues. Philosophisch-theologische Schriften*, ed. Leo Gabriel (Vienna: Herder, 1967), vol. 3, p. 308. On the role of otherness and contingency in Cusanus's thought, see my "*Contingentia* and *Alteritas* in Cusa's Metaphysics," *American Catholic Philosophical Quarterly* 64 (1990): 55-71.

determinations (i.e., formal diversity); indeed, all diversity is a matter of contingency and hence without any positive cause.[15] This reduction of determinateness to contingency is a necessary consequence of the C-E couple.

A corresponding consequence is the rejection of a doctrine of divine ideas. "God alone is absolute, all other things are contracted."[16] Nothing mediates between the divine enfolding and the unfolded multiplicity of finite individuals. "Therefore there cannot be many distinct exemplars. . . . For only one infinite Exemplar is sufficient. . . . In it all things exist."[17] Can such a doctrine be regarded as authentically Neoplatonic, that is, one which is in continuity with the Neoplatonism of Plotinus and Proclus? Of course, the rejection of levels of being which mediate between the Absolute and the world of sensible singulars marks a profound divergence of Cusanus from the Greeks. But this feature aside, is the denial of plural exemplars and the C-E doctrine which is its metaphysical basis merely an aberrant form of Neoplatonism?

III

What is the source of Cusanus's doctrine of C-E? His philosophy, original enough in its own way, is nonetheless almost a mosaic of ideas from early and late forms of Neoplatonism, for example, Proclus, Pseudo-Dionysius, Scotus Eriugena, and Meister Eckhart, to name the most outstanding. But the immediate source of the C-E couple is rather Thierry of Chartres. Indeed, many features of Cusanus's thought, often to the point of a near word-for-word reproduction, are traceable to the influence of Thierry's three commentaries on Boethius's *On the Trinity*.[18] These are the *Commentum, Lectiones,* and *Glosa*.[19]

In each of these the relationship of God to creatures is conceived in terms of enfolding to unfolding, expressed, however, not in the rambling, discursive manner of Cusanus but in the terse style of a twelfth-century *lectio*. Thus in the *Glosa* God is described as the *rerum universitas* (totality of all things). But neither

15. *DDI* II, 2, nos. 98-99.

16. *DDI* II, 9, no. 150.

17. *DDI* II, 9, no. 148.

18. Compare, e.g., chaps. 7 and 8 of Cusanus's *Idiota de Mente* with Thierry's *Commentum* II, nos. 2-9. On Cusanus's appropriation of Chartrian themes, see my "Thierry of Chartres and Nicholas of Cusa's Epistemology," *Proceedings of the Patristic Mediaeval and Renaissance Studies Conference* 5 (Villanova: Villanova University Press, 1980): 169-76.

19. The *Commentum, Lectiones,* and *Glosa* are to be found in Nikolaus M. Häring's excellent edition, *Commentaries on Boethius by Thierry of Chartres and His School* (Toronto: Pontifical Institute of Mediaeval Studies, 1971). All citations of the commentaries are to this volume.

things nor their exemplars are in God as a kind of collection, each retaining its determinate status, but "as enfolded in a certain simplicity."[20] Thierry's general rule is: "Enfolding always precedes unfolding as unity precedes plurality."[21] Thus "God is the unity enfolding in Himself the totality of things in a certain simplicity."[22] And "the unfolding of this *complicatio* is all things that were, that will be and that are [now]."[23]

The consequence of this notion of God as enfolding is precisely the same for Thierry as for Cusanus — the denial of plural exemplars, divine ideas. They are, as Thierry says (the plural is, of course, wrong), "collapsed" *(relapsae)* in the divine form. Hence they constitute neither an internal nor an external multiplicity. They are the simple one.[24] Thus, the divine form is all forms in the simplicity of the divine enfolding.

But what, then, is the status of finite determinateness? The consequence of the unfolding side of the doctrine is much the same as in Cusa. Thierry calls a finite form (e.g., humanity) *forma haec* (this form). The adjective *haec* does not designate individuation, but rather the given form, for example, *humanitas*. So one can ask concerning *forma haec* two questions: Why is it *forma* and why is it *haec?* The answer to the first question is as follows: A *forma haec* is a *forma* due to the integrity, completeness *(perfectio)*, and equality of beings which is the divine form. That it is *haec* — humanity and not some other determination — is due to matter.[25] Hence, if there were no existing human beings, humanity as humanity (the *haec* in *forma haec*) would cease to be. But the form in itself *(forma quantum in se)* can never perish, since, of course, it is God.[26]

But again, what is one to make of this doctrine that the Absolute is a simplicity enfolding within itself all determinations and that all subordinate diversity is that Absolute "outered," as it were? Is the doctrine's central feature, namely, the C-E couple itself, entailing, as it does, a denial of plural exemplars, simply a Christian deformation of Neoplatonism?

In a recent article, Norris Clarke makes just this claim. His thesis is that the Chartrian doctrine of the identity of all forms or ideas in God is authentically Christian metaphysical doctrine, but it is not "authentically Neoplatonic doctrine."[27] The reason is that "the ideas in the divine *Nous* (mind) for all classic

20. *Glosa* II, no. 12, p. 271.
21. *Lectiones* II, no. 6, p. 156.
22. *Lectiones* II, no. 4, p. 155.
23. *Lectiones* II, no. 5, p. 155.
24. *Commentum* II, no. 45, p. 82.
25. *Commentum* II, nos. 46-47, p. 83.
26. *Commentum* II, no. 49, p. 84.
27. W. Norris Clarke, "The Problem of the Reality and Multiplicity of Divine Ideas," in *Neoplatonism and Christian Thought*, ed. Dominic J. O'Meara (Albany: State University of New York Press, 1982), p. 120.

Neoplatonism are already unfolded in their distinct intelligible multiplicity and, hence, in their plurality of being."[28] A few pages earlier, speaking specifically of Plotinus's *Nous,* Clarke describes it as "an intelligible (hence, real) diversity in unity."[29] He then goes on to convict the Chartrians (as well as Scotus Eriugena) of the "conversion of Neoplatonic realism into a latent idealism."[30] In the end, however, the Chartrians are not entirely to blame, for "they are trying to cope with the rich but enigmatic heritage of Pseudo-Dionysius."[31]

Is Clarke correct in claiming that Thierry's is a deformed, inauthentic Neoplatonism which is mediated by that of Pseudo-Dionysius? I think he is wrong on both counts. It is neither inauthentic nor derived from Dionysius. The issue turns on Clarke's expressions "real diversity" and "really multiple." To be sure, he stresses a real diversity within the spiritual unity of *Nous* itself. Nonetheless, he keeps insisting that there is in Plotinus what he calls a "strong dosage of Platonic realism,"[32] a realism which Christian Neoplatonists like Thierry have jettisoned. But is there such a "strong dose" of realism in Plotinus's account of *Nous* and its intelligibles? Are the ideas unfolded into a real diversity on the level of *Nous* itself? I want to respond to these questions with the claim that once the enfolding-unfolding correlation in Plotinus is understood, the answers must lie in the negative. If this is the case, then the relationship between unity and multiplicity as structured by Thierry and Nicholas, far from being a deformation, may turn out to be a creative continuation of a basic theme of classical Neoplatonism.

There is one further point to raise about Clarke's account which is useful for making the transition to the thinker who introduced the C-E couple into the Christian tradition. It was not Pseudo-Dionysius from whom Thierry derived the notion of the enfolding of all forms in the divine simplicity. Thierry mentions Pseudo-Dionysius only a few times, and never in relation to the C-E structure. No, the source for Thierry is the very author whose tractate he is commenting on, Boethius. In his commentaries Thierry effected in a remarkably creative way a juncture of the *On the Trinity* account of form and the metaphysics of C-E from the *Consolation of Philosophy.*[33]

---

28. Clarke, p. 120. The Plotinian ideas are said to be "really multiple or distinct" (p. 112).

29. Clarke, p. 112.

30. Clarke, p. 121.

31. Clarke, p. 121.

32. Clarke, p. 111.

33. It is interesting to note that a contemporary of Thierry, Gilbert of Poitiers, makes no effort in his own commentary on Boethius's tractate to introduce the ideas of the *Consolation.* It should be no surprise, then, that he arrives at a quite different theory of being — a metaphysics of form and essence, not a unity metaphysics. See the useful summary of Gilbert's thought in Étienne Gilson, *History of Christian Philosophy in the Middle Ages* (New York: Random House, 1955), pp. 140-44.

Boethius has long been recognized as an agent for the transmission of Greek ideas and language into the Christian world. One more such idea, hitherto unrecognized, should be added to the list — the enfolding-unfolding couple. This schema is central both to the metaphysics and the theory of knowledge of Boethius. Only a brief summary of its function is possible here.[34] The central text is IV, Prose 6 of the *Consolation*. Here Boethius is describing the relationship between providence and fate. It is immediately clear, however, that he is outlining the relationship between God and the world of finite things. A summary statement toward the end of Prose 6 shows this to be the case: "As discursive thinking is to intellectual intuition, as that which is generated is to that which is, as time is to eternity, as the circle is to its center, so is the moving sequence of fate to the stable simplicity of providence."[35] Here we have a series of unity-multiplicity correlations. The unity of intuition, being, eternity, and providence is contrasted with the multiplicity of discursive thinking, becoming, time, and fate. All these are analogized to the relationship of the center to the circle. This geometrical image is very significant, for along with the arithmetical image we have noted in Cusanus, it is common to Neoplatonists, both before and after Boethius. Unfortunately, Boethius does not elaborate on the image. It may be, in fact, that he could rely upon his readers to recognize its import immediately. In any case, we shall see that it signifies, as it does in Plotinus and Proclus, a relationship of enfolding unity to unfolded multiplicity.

Boethius in Prose 6 speaks of a *modus* (limit, manner, mode) which, considered from the point of view of God, that is, Providence, is pure undifferentiated simplicity. The same *modus,* considered from the point of view of its multiplicity, the other side of the coin, so to speak, is fate.[36] Providence is described as enfolding *(complectitur)* within its simplicity all things, "however diverse, however endless." This diversity is present *pariter* (together, equally, at the same time). Thus in the absolute unity of God all differentiation, all opposition, is overcome. Here, perhaps, is the distant origin of Nicholas of Cusa's coincidence of opposites. Fate is, by contrast, described as the temporal "un-

---

34. For a more extended account see my "Eternity and Time in Boethius: His *Complicatio-Explicatio* Method," in *History of Philosophy in the Making*, ed. Linus Thro, S.J. (Washington, D.C.: University Press of America, 1982), pp. 35-62. See also the remarks of Fernand Brunner in the discussion appended to his article "Deus Forma Essendi," in *Entretiens sur la Renaissance du 12e siècle*, ed. Maurice de Gandillac and Edouard Jeauneau (Paris, 1968), p. 105.

35. Boethius, *The Consolation of Philosophy*, IV, Prose 6, p. 80. All references to the *Consolation* are to the edition of Ludwig Bieler, *Corpus Christianorum. Series Latina* (Brepols: Turnhout, 1957), vol. 94.

36. *Consolation*, IV, Prose 6, p. 79. This matter of consideration (*conspicitur* and *refertur*) is an important theme in all Neoplatonism. See the very suggestive remarks of Annick Charles in "Analogie et pensée serielle chez Proclus," *Revue Internationale de Philosophie* 23 (1969): 69-88; see esp. pp. 85-87.

folding" of order. It is the unfolded multiplicity of what is one *(adunata)* in the divine mind.[37] Earlier in the *Consolation,* Boethius spoke of the procession *(procederet)* of things from God as an unfolding *(explicarent)* into space and time of what abides *(manens)* in the absolute simplicity of God.[38]

Eternity and time are also related to each other as enfolding to unfolding. Boethius's famous definition of eternity describes it as a possession *(possessio).* The language he uses in V, Prose 6 makes it clear that the possession is one of enfolding. Eternity enfolds *(complectens)* within its presence *(praesentia)* the infinite extent of past into future. It is, therefore, an inclusive simplicity enfolding within itself all moments of temporal progression. Indeed, the very resolution of the culminating problem of the *Consolation,* namely, the reconciliation of divine foreknowledge and human freedom, turns on this equation of eternity with enfolding.[39] Unfortunately, Boethius devotes only a few lines to the discussion of time. But what he says makes it clear that in falling away *(deficit)* from immobility into motion, and in declining *(decrescit)* from the simplicity of the eternal now to the infinite succession from past into future via fleeting present, time is an unfolding.[40]

If, then, God for Boethius is simplicity enfolding within himself all multiplicity, can there be any room for a theory of plural divine ideas? Space does not allow for a careful sifting of the evidence, but I think it can safely be maintained that Boethius, in fact, rejects such a theory and that, therefore, Thierry of Chartres is faithful to his master on this point.[41]

IV

I pose once again my question: Is the metaphysics of C-E entailing a rejection of divine ideas bad Neoplatonism? Well, if it is, Plotinus himself is not a very good Neoplatonist. For he has a fairly well developed theory of enfolding-unfolding

37. *Consolation,* IV, Prose 6, p. 79.

38. *Consolation,* III, Prose 12, pp. 101-2. There is a possible echo of Proclus's very important notion of *mone* in Boethius's *manens ipse.* For the Proclean notion see J. Trouillard's excellent account in *L'Un et l'âme selon Proclos* (Paris, 1972), pp. 91-109.

39. *Consolation,* V, Prose 6, pp. 101-2.

40. *Consolation,* V, Prose 6, p. 102.

41. Boethius's example of "man" whose shape, species, and *simplex forma* are respectively the object of sense and imagination, reason and *intelligentia* seems to gainsay this claim. It implies that there is a plurality of simple forms, one of which is that of "man." However, an examination of the rest of Prose 5 and Prose 6 shows, I believe, (a) that *intelligentia* is the divine, not human, mode of knowing and (b) that the *simplex forma* is God in whom all plurality is enfolded. Thus Thierry is accurately reflecting Boethius's thought when he asserts that *omnes formae . . . sunt in formam quodam modo divinam relapsae* (*Commentum* II, no. 45, p. 82).

that, far from traducing his basic metaphysical options (as Armstrong claims),[42] is eminently consistent with them. Unities are inclusive simplicities which enfold within their indistinction a subordinate diversity which, in turn, is unfolded into multiplicity. Plotinus's equivalents for *complicare* and *explicare* are *perilambanein* and *exelittein*.[43] The latter term was seldom used before him (by Plato not at all, by Aristotle three times), but, as H. Dörrie says, it becomes for Plotinus "one of the coined words of his basic philosophical posture."[44] Theiler suggests a possible Posidonian origin for this term. *Perilambanein* may have been suggested by a passage in the *Timaeus* (30c and 31b).[45] This language is applied to the relationship of the One to *Nous*, of *Nous* to the Soul, and also of eternity to time.

Early on in the treatises numbered 5 and 6 according to Porphyry's order, Plotinus states two general principles. The one pertains to enfolding, the other to unfolding. In VI, 5, 9 the point is made that a genuine unity *(hen ontos)* cannot be a composition of many things, a mere sum or whole of parts. Rather, such a unity must contain in potency that nature which is *the very opposite of itself*, namely, multiplicity.[46] Here Plotinus is discussing *Nous*, but Dodds is, I think, correct in regarding this remark as stating a general principle, applicable not only to *Nous*, but even to the One.[47] Multiplicity is truly in or within such a unity, not as a diversity of parts but in potency. This condition, "in potency," is one of enfolding or envelopment (*periechonta* is Plotinus's word). In general, then, enfolding is the condition of possessing a multiplicity in a nonmultiple way. A genuine unity is, to borrow an expression from Lewis Ford, a kind of "inclusive simplicity enfolding within itself its very opposite, its subordinate diversity."[48]

Before going on to the unfolding side of the Neoplatonic couple, it is worth pausing to reflect on the immense significance of the notion of enfolding

---

42. See n. 4 above.

43. *Periechein* is often used as a synonym for *perilambanein*. Plotinus uses *anelittein* only once, whereas in Proclus it seems to be the accepted technical term to signify the unfolding into multiplicity.

44. Dörrie, col. 490.

45. See Janin Berthier et al., eds., *Plotin. Traité sur les nombres* (Paris: J. Vrin, 1980), p. 47.

46. All citations of the *Enneads* are to the Loeb Classical Library edition, Arthur Hilary Armstrong, ed. and trans., *Plotinus*, 7 vols. (Cambridge, 1966-88). Armstrong's translation, it goes without saying, is a notable contribution to Plotinus scholarship. But Martin Jougin is right in noting that his varying translations of *exelittein* (unroll, unfold, spread out, explicate) fail to reflect the systematic function which the term has in the *Enneads*. See Jougin's translation of Gilles Deleuze, *Spinoza et le problème de l'expression* (Paris: Les Editions de Minuit, 1968). The English translation is *Expressionism in Philosophy: Spinoza* (New York: Zone Books, 1990), p. 415 n. e.

47. Eric R. Dodds, ed., *Proclus: The Elements of Theology*, 2nd ed. (Oxford: Clarendon Press, 1963), p. 259.

48. Lewis S. Ford, "Boethius and Whitehead on Time and Eternity," *International Philosophical Quarterly* 8 (1968): 42.

for all Neoplatonists. From one end of the history of Neoplatonism to the other, the idea that a unity pre-contains its subordinate multiplicity perdures. As Kurt Flasch says of Cusanus's One, "It is not an empty One; it is that in which all multiplicity is found."[49] Interestingly, the text which Flasch cites in support of his claim is from Cusanus's *De Principio* (On the origins), a work which amounts to a commentary on selected portions of Proclus's *Commentary on the Parmenides:* "omnis multitudo ab aliqua sibi convenienti unitate continetur. . . ." [Every multiplicity is held together by some unity appropriate to it].[50] In fact, Cusanus's language is lifted almost verbatim from William of Moerbeke's Latin translation of this work.[51] Proclus himself repeatedly speaks of multiplicity as originally "hidden" *(kryphios)* in its appropriate unity.[52] And in his *Elements of Theology* where he is speaking of *Nous,* he enunciates the general principle: "A multiplicity which is concentrated (*suneptugmenon* — literally, folded up) precedes a divided [multiplicity]. . . ."[53]

This notion of a unity containing within itself without prejudice to its unicity its subordinate multiplicity is, I believe, a genuine innovation of Neoplatonism. All Neoplatonic metaphysics originates in the Platonic thesis (one might call it Plato's "ontological law") that, as Cusanus often puts it, Plato posited one before every multiplicity. The one of Plato, however, is never regarded as pre-containing its subordinate multiplicity. A Platonic Form, beauty, for example, does not enfold within its essential unity the many beautiful things. The same holds true for "the unwritten teachings" concerning the One and the Indeterminate Dyad, which were for the Neoplatonists an important source of their own metaphysical doctrines. Aristotle's account of the generation of the Forms nowhere characterizes the One as enfolding within itself the plurality of forms to be generated.[54] Rather, the multiplicity is the result of the defective imaging of the One on the part of the Dyad, the underived multipliability principle.[55] For Plato, then, no unity pre-contains its subordinate multiplicity.

---

49. Kurt Flasch, *Die Metaphysik des Einen bei Nikolaus von Kues* (Leiden: E. J. Brill, 1973), p. 259.

50. Nicholas of Cusa, *De Principio* h, vol. 10, fasc. 2b., no. 30, p. 43.

51. See the notes of Joseph Koch to the German translation of the *De Principio,* Maria Feigl, trans., *Über den Ursprung* (Heidelberg: F. H. Kerle Verlag, 1967), p. 95 n. 117.

52. E.g., in his *Platonic Theology* III, 9, in *Proclus. Theologie platonicienne,* ed. Henri-Dominique Saffrey and L. U. Westerink (Paris: Les Belles Lettres, 1978), vol. 3, p. 39.

53. *Proclus: The Elements of Theology* (ed. Dodds), prop. 171, p. 150. In my translation I have followed J. Trouillard's French version ("concentrée") rather than that of Dodds ("implicit") (p. 151). See Trouillard, *Proclus. Elements de Theologie* (Paris: Editions Montaigne, 1965), p. 163.

54. Aristotle, *Metaphysics* I, 6, 988a8-16, and bks. XIII and XIV, passim.

55. Cf. Leonard J. Eslick, "The Material Substrate in Plato," in *The Concept of Matter in Greek and Medieval Philosophy,* ed. Ernan McMullin (Notre Dame: University of Notre Dame Press, 1965), pp. 39-54.

The thesis of enfolding is therefore a quite significant innovation of Plotinus and the later Neoplatonists.

Surprisingly, it is an innovation which has been overlooked by the commentators. Even where, as noted above, the role of unfolding *(exelixis)* in Neoplatonic metaphysics has been remarked, its correlative has been little noted. And more to the point, when enfolding has been considered, it has been misunderstood. E. R. Dodds's example is instructive. In the course of explaining Proclus's doctrine of the "henads," Dodds makes a comparison with Plotinus. He claims that one of the motivations for this curious doctrine of henadic unities is to cope with a problem inherited from the founder of Neoplatonism; namely, "the yawning gulf which Plotinus had left between the One and reality." According to Dodds, Plotinus was so acutely aware of this gulf that "he practically confesses that plurality cannot be got out of unity unless it is first put into it." As evidence Dodds cites a text we have already seen — VI, 5, 9. Apparently he is referring to Plotinus's remark that the One somehow possesses the very opposite of itself, multiplicity. But if the One is the power of all *(dunamis panton)*, it must be potentially all *(dunamei panta)*, and that is "to infect the One with at least the seeds of plurality." By contrast, Proclus's henads, though they "import plurality into the first hypostasis," do so in such a way "as to leave intact the perfect unity of the One."[56]

Never mind that Dodds himself does not explain how Proclus pulls off this trick. Is he right that the doctrine of *perilepsis* (embracing, enfolding) (for that is what "having the opposite nature to itself" is expressing) is a kind of afterthought, born of desperation in the face of "the yawning gulf"?[57] But why not see it as a creative response to the problem left over from the Plato of the unwritten teachings; that is, how does one derive multiplicity from the One if the idea of an underived principle of multiplicity is to be rejected? In point of fact Dodds maneuvers Plotinus into a dilemma with equally unacceptable alternatives. Either the One retains its purity as absolute unity at the expense of a yawning gulf. Or the One possesses within itself all subsequent reality, but at the expense of being infected with the seeds of plurality.

This dilemma is, however, entirely of Dodds's contrivance. To be sure, the explanation of *how* the many emerge from the One is a problem for all Neoplatonists. This is especially the case once an underived dyadic principle is jettisoned. Witness Plotinus's efforts to account for the emergence of the first multiplicity by fusing the doctrine of the Dyad with an inchoate *nous* generated

56. Dodds, p. 259.
57. [Prof. McTighe is referring to a passage in *Enneads*, VI, 5, 9, in which Plotinus states: "[the One] must appear as in some way having the opposite nature to itself *(ten enantian auto phusin echon)*, that of multiplicity, in its power . . ." — Ed.]

from the One and bending back in contemplation of the One.[58] Proclus no less than Plotinus faces the "how" problem, that is, the mechanics of the production of multiplicity. As with poor Saint Denis, martyred and his head under his arm, so with the Neoplatonists: *c'est le premier pas qui coûte.* But all this aside, Plotinus has no difficulty with the principle that the multiple qua multiple arises from the One because it is already pre-contained as a non-multiple in the One. The doctrine of enfolding-unfolding is a centerpiece of his metaphysics.

The text of VI, 5, 9, far from being a confession, is in fact a very clear statement of this doctrine. One final text of Plotinus dealing explicitly with this issue is worth considering. Like VI, 5, 9, it too has been misinterpreted, this time by J. Rist. Commenting on a passage in V, 3, 15, Rist says: "Here Plotinus considers and rejects a theory that the many are in the One potentially and in an indistinct manner *(hos me diakekrimena).* . . ."[59] This is a truly remarkable claim, for the text says exactly the opposite, as a look at the whole of section 15 will show.

The previous section (14) ended with the statement that though the One gives *logos* (discursive reason) *nous* (mind) and *aesthesis* (sense perception), it is not itself these; it is higher than them. Section 15 then begins by posing the very dilemma to which Dodds saw no answer. Is it "by having them or by not having them? But how did he give what he does not have? But if he has them, he is not simple; if he does not have them, how does multiplicity come from him?" Plotinus then describes the first multiplicity which comes after the One, namely, *Nous. Nous* reveals itself as a *hen panta,* i.e., "all things by participation in the One." Thus the One is the principle of all things. There follows then the crucial passage the sense of which Rist has exactly reversed:

> But how is it that One is the principle of all things? Is it because as principle it keeps them in being making each one of them exist? Yes, and because it brought them into existence. But how did it do so? By possessing them beforehand. But it has been said that in this way it will be a multiplicity. *But it had them in such a way as to not to be distinct:* They are distinguished on the second level in the rational form.[60]

58. See, e.g., Armstrong, *Plotinus,* V, 3, 11, vol. 5, pp. 108-10; cf. John Rist, "The Indefinite Dyad and Intelligible Matter in Plotinus," *The Classical Quarterly,* n.s., no. 12 (1962): 99-107.

59. John Rist, *Plotinus: The Road to Reality* (Cambridge: Cambridge University Press, 1967), p. 44. On Rist's curious reversal of the meaning of this text, see John Bussanich, *The One and Its Relation to Intellect in Plotinus* (Leiden: E. J. Brill, 1988), pp. 22-23.

60. Armstrong, *Plotinus,* vol. 5, pp. 124-27. Armstrong's translation of *to logo,* "in the rational form," is not very helpful. Plotinus is saying that the *panta* are differentiated not at the level of the One but at the level of *Nous.* Clearly he is referring to the intelligibles, the Forms. What, then, would it mean to say that they are differentiated "in the rational form"? Bréhier's version *(par le fait du Verbe)* is of no more help. See *Plotin. Ennéades,* ed. and trans.

These lines can, in effect, be read as an exposition of what Plotinus meant by his characterization of the One as a *perilepsis panton* (an enfolding of all). Note the progression of thought. How is it that the One can be said to be the principle of all things? A first answer: It (the One) accounts for their being and continued existence. But this, though true enough, is insufficient. The deeper reason for the origin of multiplicity is that its principle already possesses that multiplicity. At this point Plotinus repeats the objection made at the beginning of the section: If the One possesses all things, it will not be truly one. It will (shades of Dodds!) be a multiplicity. Not so, answers Plotinus. The One does, indeed, have all things, but *hos me diakekrimena* (in an indistinct manner). The multiple are in the One in a nonmultiple way. Distinction, or differentiation, occurs for the first time at the level of *nous*. In short, subordinate multiplicities emerge from unity because unity for Plotinus and his Neoplatonic successors is never an empty one.

Now to the unfolding side of the Neoplatonic couple. The general principle of unfolding is stated in *Enneads* IV, 8, 6: "It is inherent in every nature to produce what comes after it," which production is for a unity to be unfolded *(exelittesthai)* into a diversity. And here, as in so many other instances where it is a case of describing unfolding, Plotinus uses the very significant image of the seed. The seed contains within itself in indistinction the multiplicity to be unfolded into the different parts that constitute the mature living being. This image and the geometrical image of the circle are central to Plotinus's exposition of the enfolding-unfolding schema. In sum, then, unfolding is a kind of devolution[61] of a unity into multiplicity. This pluralization does not, of course, entail the destruction of the antecedent unity. The latter remains, as Plotinus says, in its proper place or "seat."

Let us now consider the first two hypostases — the One and the *Nous* — in terms of the enfolding-unfolding structure. In VI, 8, 18 the first hypostasis is described as *perilepsis panton kai metron* (the enfolding and measure of all). The One is the primal enfolding or envelopment. The first unfolding from the One is, of course, *nous* and being. The latter are said to depend upon what there is of the intellectual in the nature of the One. They are witnesses to the presence of the intellectual in the One, although the latter is itself not intellectual since it is absolutely one. The unfolding of the second hypostasis from the One is analogized to the unfolding of the radii from the center of the circle.

Émile Bréhier, 2nd ed. (Paris: Les Belles Lettres, 1954), vol. 5, p. 70. Now *contre* Clarke (see nn. 27-32 above), the intelligibles for Plotinus are not a plurality of separate and really distinct essences. They are, as he so often puts it, *homou panta* (all together). Thus it seems to me that *diekekrito to logo* means that they are distinct "by reason" or "rationally," i.e., by a rational as opposed to a real distinction. Cf. the use of *logo* in VI, 7, 40, line 17.

61. The term is from Hans Jonas, "Delimitation of the Gnostic Phenomenon," in *Le Origini dello Gnosticismo* (Leiden: E. J. Brill, 1967), pp. 90-108.

The circle, Plotinus says, receives in some way its form from the center because it "touches" the center. It does so by virtue of its radii, whose tips are, as it were, anchored in the center. But the unity of the center is not merely an additive totality, the sum of all the tips. The center is "more than" the tips. The center is all the tips, indeed all the radii, in indistinction. The center, as Plotinus puts it, contains them in potency.

So it is with the One. It, too, contains in potency all that comes after it.[62] The One cannot be a mere featureless blank as Schelling's absolute was made out to be by Hegel. Though Plotinus never explicitly says so, the One is not only *dunamis panton,* but also *dunamei panta* (power of all). The One is not every thing, if by "every thing" actual multiplicity is meant, but it is everything — *ekeinos panta* (potentially all), according to the celebrated expression of V, 2, 1. The One, therefore, is not, to use another of Lewis Ford's expressions, an "exclusive simplicity"[63] seated in lonely isolation above all things. It is rather an inclusive simplicity. In other words, if there is enfolding there must be the enfolded. The One is no exception.

One other feature of the circle-center image is significant. The center, Plotinus says, is unfolded into the many radii, but does not unfold itself.[64] The One, then, undergoes no internal unfolding. Its absolute unity forbids it.

Turning now to the second hypostasis, *Nous.* It, too, is an inclusive simplicity enfolding a subordinate multiplicity, which latter is, in turn, unfolded at the level of soul. But the relationship of enfolding and unfolding in *Nous* is considerably more intricate than that of the One. The *quaestio vexata* here is: How is nous characterized as *hen polla,* both one and many? Surely the authors of the recent team study on the treatise on numbers are correct when they speak of "one of the most obscure features of Plotinus' thought, we mean, the architecture or, simply, the organization of the intelligible."[65] Let us see if any clarification comes from considering this architecture from the point of view of enfolding-unfolding.

---

62. Clearly here potency does not mean, as it does for Aristotle, passivity and lack. Cf. V, 3, 15: "The One is the potency of all things. But in what way . . . ? Not in the way in which matter is said to be in potency: for matter is passive" (Armstrong, *Plotinus,* vol. 5, p. 127). A further clue to its meaning is to be found in the use of the genus-species relationship as an analogy for the relationship of *Nous* to beings (V, 9, 6) and to particular intellects (VI, 2, 20). In both cases *Nous* is said to enfold *(periechein, emperiechein)* the two multiplicities as a genus enfolds its species. In VI, 2, 20 the genus is said to be the potency of the species, all of which are in the genus "quietly" *(esucha).* That is, they are there in the genus, not in the Aristotelian sense of potency, but actually there, though without their subsequent multiplicity. Potency has the sense of "latent act." In short, to describe the One as potency of all is equivalent to characterizing it as a *perilepsis.*

63. See n. 48 above.

64. VI, 8, 18; Armstrong translates *"exelichthen ouk exeleligmenon"* as "spread out without having been spread out" (Armstrong, *Plotinus,* vol. 7, p. 287). See n. 46 above.

65. Berthier, p. 67.

From the earliest to the latest treatises Plotinus describes *Nous* in terms of *perilepsis.*[66] In V, 9, 14 Plotinus writes, "We must admit as a principle this nature *(Nous)* which enfolds all things in the intelligible." In III, 8, 11 *Nous* is described as radiant with beauty "enfolding the nature of real beings." In III, 5, 9 Plotinus relates the god Poros to the rational principle in the soul and Kronos to *Nous.* The former is said to be more diffused and unfolded *(haplotheis),* whereas "that which is in *Nous* is contracted together."[67] An even clearer description of the second hypostasis as an enfolding of all intelligibles in an inclusive simplicity is given in VI, 6, 7: "For in general it is necessary to conceive intelligible things in a unique nature *(mian phusin)* and to conceive a unique nature possessing them all and in some way enfolding *(perilabousan)* them." This enfolding unity is, Plotinus continues, the very opposite of the sensible world where each thing is separate *(choris)* from the others. By contrast the intelligible world is *homou en heni panta* (all together in one), a formula constantly under the pen of Plotinus when it is a case of describing this world.

To illustrate the unity signified by *homou panta* (all together), Plotinus uses once again the image of the circle with its plural radii originating in a unique center.[68] The image, he says, is a useful one, but always in need of correction. In a circle the radii are separated, spatially distinct. In the intelligible world, however, it is a case of "undifferentiated powers and essences."[69] Hence these — the intelligibles — are to be compared not to the radii but to their tips anchored in the center. Each of these tips is itself a kind of center, and they are unified all together in the unique center. Thus the plurality of centers is not a real diversity internal to the unique center. The plurality, the real diversity, is in the manifestation of the unique center via the radii. Such are the intelligibles. They do not form a real diversity within *Nous.* Like the multiple centers in the unique center, the intelligibles are *homou panta.* Plotinus goes on to say that the radii may continue to serve as an analogy — not for the envelopment of multiplicity in *Nous's* simplicity — but for "the things which are touched by the intelligible nature," that is, soul and the sensible world. Clearly, then, there cannot be a real diversity of intelligibles in *Nous.*[70] It is necessary to say that

66. The noun form is, however, used only once (VI, 8, 18), where, as we have seen, it is applied to the One.

67. The translation is that of Armstrong, *Plotinus,* vol. 3, p. 199. Cf. Bréhier, *Ennéades,* vol. 3, p. 85, where *sunespeiramenon* is translated as *"enroulée sur elle-même."*

68. Armstrong, *Plotinus,* vol. 6, p. 337.

69. Armstrong, *Plotinus,* vol. 6, p. 337: *"adiastatoi dunameis kai ousiai,"* translated as "unspaced powers and substances." The translation in the text is mine.

70. Against Clarke's claim that the intelligibles are "really distinct," cf. the perceptive remarks of Bréhier (*Ennéades, Notice* to V, 9, vol. 5, pp. 157-58). It is significant that Proclus regularly criticizes Plotinus for merging the intelligibles *homou en heni panta* (all together in the one). See, e.g., his *Platonic Theology,* ed. Saffrey and Westerink, I, 10, p. 42.

the many are in the enfolding unity of *Nous,* but they are not there qua multiple. The distinct is in the indistinct according to the mode of the latter.

Whence, then, comes the distinction of the intelligibles? In the early treatise (V, 9) Plotinus uses the same language that is used in the later treatise on numbers. "Being and *Nous* are a unique nature *(mia phusis).* So, too, are beings, the act of being and *nous;* and so, too, are intellections, the form and shape of being and its act." But here there is a very significant addition: "It is we in our thinking who separate them, so that some are before others. For the *Nous* which divides and the undivided *Nous,* which separates neither beings nor being, are different."[71] In short, the division of the intelligible into multiple intelligibles is effected not at the level of *Nous,* the second hypostasis, but at the level of our *nous,* the highest part of the soul.

The process of dividing the undivided is precisely one of unfolding. In the very late Treatise I, 1, 8, Plotinus once again raises the question: What relationship do *we* have to *Nous* and its intelligibles? And by *Nous* here is meant not the highest part of the soul, but *Nous* itself, the second hypostasis. The intelligibles, Plotinus says, are possessed in two ways: "in the soul they are unfolded *(aneiligmena)* and separated; in *Nous* they are all together *(homou ta panta)."*[72] Thus the relationship of *Nous* to soul is one of enfolding unity to unfolded multiplicity. The intelligibles in *Nous* are not unfolded into a real diversity. A text from V, 1, 11 makes clear the relationship of the three levels of thinking: discursive reason, *Nous* in us *(noun en hemin),* and *Nous* itself. Discursive reason asserts: "this is just" or "that is beautiful." This is possible because *nous* in us distinguishes out an immutable justice *(to dikaion)* and beauty. But in *Nous* itself these are all together enfolded in indistinction.

This, however, is not the whole story. Recall what Plotinus said of the One: it is unfolded but does not unfold itself. Not so in the case of *Nous.* In V, 3, 10 Plotinus states a kind of general principle: "that which unfolds itself *(exelittei heauto)* is multiple." The context makes it clear that this principle is applied to *Nous,* the second hypostasis. And in III, 8, 8 *Nous* is said to have "unfolded itself *(exeilixen auton)* wanting to possess all things." And once again the familiar image of the circle appears, though here its thrust is, I believe, quite different from that of VI, 5, 5. *Nous* unfolds itself as a circle unfolds itself into circumference, center, and radii. But here it is clear that the radii symbolize not an unfolding into an outer subordinate diversity, but an unfolding of diversity interior to *Nous* itself. Of course, Plotinus immediately qualifies this conclusion.

71. V, 9, 8. The translation is mine. For the Greek text and Armstrong's translation see his *Plotinus,* vol. 5, pp. 306 and 307. The late treatise VI, 2, 3 (Armstrong, *Plotinus,* vol. 6, p. 120) expresses the same notion of *Nous* as a *mia phusis* which we divide in our discursive thinking.

72. This is the sole use of *anelittein.*

For *Nous* is universal, possessing all things, and is not merely a heap of jux-taposed things. Still, the fact remains that *exelixis* (unfolding) has been intro-duced into *Nous* itself. Can it be that Clarke is right after all when he claims that "the ideas in the divine *Nous* for all classic Neoplatonists are already unfolded in their distinct intelligible multiplicity and, hence, in their plurality of being"?[73]

But how can it be that the intelligibles are both an enfolding *homou en heni panta* and really diverse? No, it must be that the *exelixis* in question here is a new and different form of unfolding, not to be confused with the unfolding into a subordinate diversity. A text from Proclus, which cites Plotinus on this very matter, offers some clarification. In the *Platonic Theology*, where he is describing *Nous*, Proclus characterizes it typically as an identity fixed in eternity all at once *(homou)* as to its being, powers, and acts. But besides this identity there is also difference. Hence, there is in *Nous* a kind of "leading on toward multiplicity" such that *Nous* can be said to have unfolded the intelligible *(to noeton anelixas echei)*. Then he goes on to say: "Thus the soul unfolds *Nous*, whereas *Nous* has unfolded itself, as Plotinus rightly says somewhere in treating of the degrees of the intelligible."[74] Thus, Proclus, citing Plotinus for support, clearly distinguishes two types of unfolding. Let us call the one from *Nous* to soul a vertical unfolding. The other, a kind of lateral unfolding within *Nous* itself, could be called a horizontal unfolding. Now, I think, Proclus is correct. These two unfoldings obtain in Plotinus as well. But just what is this horizontal unfolding?

Stephen Gersh, who comments on the Proclus text to his own ends, makes in passing a helpful suggestion.[75] He rightly notes that the two unfoldings cannot be of the same sort, for in the enfolding which I have called "vertical," the multiplicity — in his words — "has an added dimension." Hence it must be that "the *anelixis* takes place in an analogous way at higher levels in the system."

Now what Gersh asserts of Proclus is, I believe, true of Plotinus. The unfolding into plurality of what is indistinct at the level of *Nous* cannot be directly equated with the kind of unfolding described in V, 3, 10 and III, 8, 8. In short, one cannot conflate horizontal and vertical unfolding.

Gersh's suggestion, however, of an analogous similarity, though a trifle vague, is near the mark. The two unfoldings do resemble each other in this single respect: each involves the generation of a multiplicity. But there the similarity ceases. For in both Proclus and Plotinus the higher, horizontal un-folding entails the presence of a multiplicity within simplicity, a division or

---

73. See nn. 27-32 above.
74. *Platonic Theology*, ed. Saffrey and Westerink, I, 19, p. 93.
75. Gersh, p. 105 n. 4.

differentiation with the undifferentiated. In the commentary on the *Timaeus,*
Proclus puts this point in a striking way: "In *Nous* there is division, since
otherness is there, but it is a division in the primal sense and as it were in a
secret and indivisible way."[76] Plotinus in IV, 8, 6 uses the same language: "Act
(energeia) always manifests a hidden and indivisible power, a true reality. . . ."

There is another passage where Plotinus describes what I have called
horizontal unfolding. It is in VI, 6, 9 where Plotinus gives an account of the
triad of being, life, and *nous* in the second hypostasis in terms of number. He
asks the rhetorical question: "Is it not possible to say that being *(to on)* is number
unified; that beings *(onta)* are number unfolded *(exeleligmenos);* that nous is
number moved in itself and that life *(to Zoon)* is number enfolding *(perie-
chon)?*" Here it is clear that unfolding and enfolding are simultaneous moments.
The unfolding here is not a devolution into a subordinate diversity, nor is it the
unfolding of a real diversity of distinct intelligibles. It is a case, once again, of
the distinct within the indistinct. This is the sense of number used here. Number
is regarded as essential *(ousiodes),* that in which all beings have their foundation,
source, root, and principle.[77]

V

The Neoplatonic *perilepsis* or *complicatio* is, to use Lewis Ford's expression, an
"inclusive simplicity." Perhaps we can better understand its special character if
we compare it briefly to other versions of inclusive simplicity that have appeared
in the history of philosophy. There is, for example, a Whiteheadian type, described and approved by Ford himself, in which the subordinate diversity retains
its diversity within the simplicity and so is, as Ford says, "available for analysis."[78]
He tries, unsuccessfully in my opinion, to foist this thesis onto Boethius's
doctrine of eternity and time.[79] But neither for Boethius nor any other Neoplatonist does the subordinate diversity retain its diversity within its antecedent
enfolding unity. Diversities are "available for analysis" only at the level of the
diversity, and then only according to the exigencies of the lower level. Thus in
Plotinus the *eide* (forms) are "analyzable" not as folded together *(homou ta
panta)* in *Nous,* but as unfolded *(aneiligmena)* in the soul's discursive thinking.[80]
In Cusanus's epistemology *ratio* (discursive reasoning) and *intelligentia* (the

76. Proclus, *Procli Diadoche in Platonis Timaeum Commentaria,* 3 vols., ed. E. Diehl
(Leipzig: B. G. Teubner, 1903-6), vol. II, p. 247.

77. See the excellent analysis of section 9 in Berthier, pp. 53-58.

78. Ford, p. 52.

79. See my article cited in n. 34.

80. See above, p. 42.

power of the intellect) are similarly related; they stand to each other respectively as *explicatio* to *complicatio*. In mathematics, for example, the numbers with which reason operates are plural and diverse. Reason asserts that two plus three equals five. In *intelligentia,* however, these numbers are identical with each other.[81] In short, Neoplatonic enfolding unities allow for no internal discrimination. Correspondingly (a crucial point, as we shall shortly see) unfolding is a devolution to a multiplicity *external* to the enveloping simplicity.

By way of conclusion, another example of an inclusive simplicity worth considering at some length is that of Spinoza, more precisely, the Spinoza of Gilles Deleuze.[82] According to Deleuze's very striking interpretation, the Dutch philosopher makes effective use of the Neoplatonic *complicatio-explicatio* schema — the version of Cusanus, not that of Plotinus. Deleuze characterizes Spinoza's philosophy as an "expressionism." It brings to full power, he argues, a dimension of Renaissance thought according to which "expression" is regarded as a basic category. This doctrine of expression which is embedded in Spinoza's account of the relationship of substance to its attributes is explainable, claims Deleuze, as a fusion of Cusanus's doctrine of *complicatio-explicatio* and the Scotistic doctrine of formal distinction. The appropriation of the former enables Spinoza to explain how attributes express substance. They "unfold" substance in the way in which multiplicity unfolds, according to Cusanus, its antecedent complicative unity. The deployment of a distinction akin to that of Duns Scotus enables Spinoza to explain how the attributes of thought and extension are really and not merely mentally distinct within the absolute simplicity of substance. Clearly, then, the success of Deleuze's interpretation will turn on how he reconciles Cusanian enfolding simplicity with the Scotistic formal distinction among the attributes.

Deleuze's account begins by emphasizing that expression is not to be confused with emanation. Spinozistic attributes are immanent to substance, and substance is immanent to its attributes. Hence for attributes to express substance is not for them to emerge outside of substance as, say, *nous* emerges from the One of Plotinus. "The unity of substance and the distinction of attributes," says Deleuze, "are correlates that constitute expression. The distinction of attributes is nothing but the qualitative composition of an ontologically single substance."[83] Thus Spinoza's version of Neoplatonism replaces Plotinian emanation with immanence. It does, however, retain the schema of enfolding-unfolding, but as radically transformed by such Renaissance thinkers as Nicholas of Cusa.[84] The expression of substance by its attributes is correlated with

81. "[T]hey coincide in the unity of intelligence." Nicholas of Cusa, *De Coniecturis* II, 1, h, vol. 3, no. 75, p. 74.
82. See n. 46 above. All references are to the English translation.
83. Deleuze, p. 182.
84. Deleuze, p. 19. According to Deleuze, in Renaissance thinkers such as Cusanus, "Neoplatonism developed to the point where its very nature changed. . . ."

"the double movement of complication and explication: substance 'complicates' its attributes, each attribute explicates the essence of substance. . . ."[85]

The attributes of substance are, however, really distinct.[86] And here precisely is the problem. How, as Deleuze puts it, does one "reconcile the ontological unity of substance with the qualitative plurality of its attributes"? Or, to put it another way, how can really distinct attributes perdure as distinct within a Cusanian type of *complicatio*? Deleuze's answer is that Spinoza rejects the "indistinct distinctions, undivided divisions" of the early Neoplatonists in favor of the Scotistic "formal, that is to say, real distinction."[87] The Spinozistic attributes of thought and extension are distinct within substance in the way in which for Scotus the divine attributes are distinct within the divine essence.

For Scotus divine attributes such as goodness and wisdom are formally distinct, that is, formally nonidentical quidditative contents within the divine essence.[88] This is a real, that is to say, an objective and not merely mental, distinction. But it is a real distinction that obtains among quidditative contents, *(realitates* or *formalitates)* and not *res* (things). Thus within the absolute simplicity grounded in divine infinity, attributes are formally nonidentical. Formal nonidentity and actual ontological unity are not incompatible. For Scotus it is God's infinity that assures identity in being without suppression of the formally distinct attributes. Infinity can function thus because it is a modality of being and not one more formally distinct quidditative content. It is, in short, a kind of inclusive unity or identity that maintains its unicity without prejudice to the distinctions among its contents.

Now the contours of Deleuze's interpretative fusion of Neoplatonism and Scotism emerge. Spinoza's attributes are not emanations from the unitary substance. They are internal to substance which enfolds (complicates) them. But the attributes all the while being internal to substance are at once really distinct from each other and expressive of substance. They "explicate" the essence of substance. As Deleuze puts it, "The first expression, prior to any production, is as it were the constitution of substance itself."[89]

But how can attributes maintain their distinctions within substance if, as Deleuze claims, substance is a kind of Cusanian *complicatio,* an enfolding of these attributes? Is not enfolding an ontological condition in which the plural, the diverse, are present without their plurality, their diversity? Deleuze's re-

85. Deleuze, p. 185.
86. Whether they are in fact real and really distinct is of course much debated by commentators of Spinoza.
87. Deleuze, p. 182.
88. This brief account of Scotus's theory of the distinction of the divine attributes relies, as does that of Deleuze, on Étienne Gilson, *Jean Duns Scot. Introduction à ses positions fondamentales* (Paris: J. Vrin, 1952), pp. 243-54.
89. Deleuze, p. 185.

sponse is to claim that this is true of the Neoplatonism of Plotinus and his Greek successors. They "were constrained by various requirements: distinction had to be produced from the indistinct or the absolutely One. . . . Such requirements explain neoplatonist efforts to define the status of indistinct distinction, unplurifiable pluralities."[90] It is not true, however, of thinkers like Cusanus in whom Neoplatonism has undergone "a change in its very nature." Immanence replaces emanation. Deleuze takes this to mean that the unfolding of the antecedent complicative unity is immanent to that unity and not an emanation from it. As he puts it, "Substance expresses itself in formally distinct . . . attributes; each attribute expresses the essence of substance. Here again we find the double movement of complication and explication: Substance 'complicates' its attributes, each attribute explicates the essence of substance. . . . This first expression, prior to any production, is as it were, the constitution of substance itself."[91]

Here, indeed, is the core of Deleuze's account of Spinoza's Neoplatonism: the double movement of enfolding-unfolding constitutes substance itself. What Deleuze's interpretation of Spinoza requires is a *complicatio* which contains within itself items that are formally distinct, namely, the attributes of thought and extension. To that end he must collapse *explicatio* (distinction and expression) into the unicity of Cusanus's *complicatio*. In other words, real identity, simplicity, and unity of substance *(complicatio)*, and formal nonidentity of attributes *(explicatio)*, are internal to and constitutive of substance. Immanence, expression, and the Cusanian *complicatio-explicatio* are all one and the same.

Now it would be one thing if Deleuze were claiming that this telescoping of *explicatio* into *complicatio* was Spinoza's creative use of the Cusanian schema for his own ends. It is quite another to claim, as Deleuze clearly does, that all this is faithful to Nicholas's new and improved Neoplatonism. For it most certainly is not. Deleuze consistently misreads Cusanus's thesis that the multiple, the explicated, is *in* its antecedent unity *(complicatio)* to mean that the multiple is present there *as* multiple. But, of course, he must so misread if the formally distinct Spinozistic attributes are to be interpreted not as emanations from but as immanent to substance. The fact is that Deleuze seems to have been misled by the translation of the much cited text from Cusanus's *On Learned Ignorance:* "God, therefore, is that which enfolds in that all things are in him. God is that which unfolds all things in that he is in all things."[92] Deleuze's English translator is faithful to his French: "God is the universal complication . . . ; and is the univeral explication. . . ."[93] Now as thus translated the text does say that God

90. Deleuze, p. 182.
91. Deleuze, p. 185.
92. *DDI* II, 3, no. 107.
93. Deleuze, p. 175.

is at once both *complicatio* and *explicatio.* But what does this mean? Deleuze takes it to mean that Cusanus is substituting "a co-presence of two correlative movements"[94] for Plotinian emanation. And he is clearly taking *explicatio* here to mean expressive plurality. In other words, God is simultaneously enfolding unity and unfolded plurality. This may be good Spinozism, but it is most definitely not the Neoplatonism of Nicholas of Cusa.

Deleuze has been further misled by an ambiguity in the term *explicatio.* In the first place note that Cusanus uses the participial, not the noun, form — *complicans, explicans.* The second half of the text is saying that God is "that which unfolds." It is *not* saying that God is "that which is unfolded." The noun form is ambiguous. It can mean either the process of unfolding which pertains to God and which is the sense here; or it can mean that which is unfolded, that is, the finite, the multiple, which is the sense that Deleuze wrongly gives it. He may very well be right that Spinoza's substance is a kind of inclusive simplicity in which the attributes are present without prejudice either to the unicity of substance or the distinctness of the attributes. But the effort to explain how this is the case by invoking Cusanus's *complicatio-explicatio* schema is doomed to failure. Cusanus's immanence — the immanence of creatures to God and of God to creatures — is not the immanence of Spinoza. Over and over Cusanus emphasizes in *On Learned Ignorance* and succeeding works that the many, the diverse, are internal in a nonmultiple way to the divine *complicatio:* "in which the many are present without multiplicity since they are present in enfolding oneness."[95] This same notion of multiplicity existing nonmultipliably in enfolding unity is even more vividly conveyed in the first book of *On Learned Ignorance.* Infinite unity, God, is described as enfolding all things in its simplicity "where there is no otherness or diversity, where a man does not differ from a lion or heaven from earth; yet they are most truly there *(verissime ibi)* — not according to their finitude but in an enfolded way the maximal unity itself."[96]

Deleuze's claim that the Renaissance Neoplatonism of Cusanus marks a transformation in the very nature of Neoplatonism is therefore completely unfounded. In respect to this central metaphysical schema according to which a subordinate multiplicity is truly present within its antecedent unity as enfolded in its indistinction, Nicholas of Cusa differs not one whit from the earlier Neoplatonists. Cusanus asserting that in the Absolute "enfolded difference is not opposed to enfolding identity"[97] and Plotinus claiming that for the One to be truly one it must contain "the nature which is its very opposite, viz., multiplicity," are at one in their commitment to this central feature of Neoplatonism,

94. Deleuze, p. 175.
95. *DDI* II, 3, no. 108.
96. *DDI* I, 24, no. 77.
97. *DDI* II, 3, no. 107.

the enfolding-unfolding schema. Finally, the idea of enfolding is, *pace* Dodds, far from being a confession of desperation. And the idea of unfolding is not, *pace* Armstrong, merely a Stoic adulterant making for bad Neoplatonism. Rather the schema is one dimension of the creative advance which the Neoplatonists make beyond the metaphysics of their master, Plato.

CHAPTER 3

Plotinian Motifs in Bonaventure's
Itinerary of the Mind to God

ADRIAAN PEPERZAK

Marked by the shift from modernity to postmodernity, our epoch shares the ambiguities of both. The hybris of an emancipation that burdened humanity with a superhuman responsibility for the well-being of the entire world; greedy concentration on human, all-too-human needs; generous proclamations of universal human rights and deficient attempts at concretizing them; a humanistic moralism in conjunction with the greatest mass murders of history; a highly ambivalent relationship to religion and faith; a combination of blatant ignorance and repressions with fine scholarship about our past; an exaggerated veneration of science and technology; ruthless exploitation and romantic divinization of nature; the "museolization" of works and entire cultures, with the ensuing relativisms, skepticisms, and cynicisms; a nostalgia for simple forms of life, close to animals and flowers in an unspoiled nature . . . ; these and other features of modernity have marked our ways of living our lives and thinking our thoughts. At the same time we participate in this epoch's agony and in a longing for otherness. The death of modernity has filled us with "postmodern" anxiety: a desert seems to have replaced the spiritual wealth of the modern and premodern Occident. Nostalgia is tempting. How could we give up our attachment to that wealth? Our memory, filled with the highlights of our Greek and Roman, Christian and humanistic civilization, does not want to be repressed by total immersion in postmodern — or even posttheological, postphilosophical, postoccidental — "museolity." Since education has made us feel at home in three thousand years of Western civilization, we cannot but resist the skepticism that seems to follow naturally from a dying culture. Rather than being objects for destruction or deconstruction, the achievements of our past awaken awe and gratitude, inviting us to comparable attempts at realizing meaning. We participate hermeneutically in the unrepeatable but inspiring lives and works of our history and celebrate their ways of coping with human existence. Despite our separation, we celebrate exemplary figures in a hopeful kind of *memoria*. Perhaps we may even link such celebrations to a sacramental memory in which *the* Meaning comes to light and life.

The following pages sketch how Saint Bonaventure received and transformed some Neoplatonic motifs in writing his *Itinerary of the Mind to God*. More specifically they compare Plotinus's conception of the ascent to the One with Bonaventure's description of approaching God through speculation. Although Bonaventure never studied any works of Plato or Plotinus themselves, he was obviously inspired not only by the *liber Scripturae* (book of Scripture), as old as revelation, and the *liber naturae* (book of nature), as old as creation, but also by the books that transmitted a (Neo-)Platonic, Stoic, and Aristotelian heritage to him, thus giving him a chance to transform pagan wisdom into an element of his Christian contemplation. Perhaps his way of "receiving" and "reducing" a past more than a thousand years old gives us a better example of remembering than any variety of destruction.

I. Plotinus's Travel Guide to God

In order to see how philosophy functions according to Plotinus in discovering the meaning of human life, I turn to the famous and central treatise *Enneads* VI, 9 [9], entitled "On the Good and the One." One can read this treatise as a more or less well-organized travel guide for the soul in its search for what it most desires. Although *eros* appears rather late (in section 9), the allusions to Diotima's discourse on its nature and workings (Plato, *Banquet* 201d-212c) are spread out over the entire treatise. The soul *(psychē)* is driven by a necessity (9, 27: *ex anagkēs*) to seek her origin and father; the deepest desire, which constitutes or coconstitutes the *psychē*, is directed to the first and ultimate (the *archē* and *telos*) of the universe *(ta panta)*. The beloved is none of all the things or persons of the world; it cannot be found in any being, not even in the totality of beings. It is neither all beings together nor their being as such *(to on hēi on)*. The Intellect *(Nous)* itself cannot still the soul's desire because as a totality of thinking thoughts it encompasses the entire cosmos of being *(ousia)* and is thus multiple. Eros flees plurality and points to an extremely simple unity, the unity of the One "before" and beyond all beings and ideas, a unity to which the soul responds by trying to become as simple and one as it was when it was born from that unique and simple One. The soul's journey is a progressive self-transformation; at the same time it is the discovery of the soul's true nature. The encounter with the One demands and grants it the greatest possible simplicity.

It reveals what the soul has always been, although this fact has become obscured by its falling down into the dispersion of worldly existence. United with a body, entangled in material change and history, obsessed by all kinds of wants and sorrows, the soul is estranged from its original state. The journey is a return; therefore it requires a conversion from dispersion and a systematic exercise of unification.

The stages of the return to the One can be distinguished according to the hierarchy of the universe: from material things to the *psyche* itself, from the *psyche* to the *Nous,* and from this to the One. The levels of progressive simplification through which the soul proceeds show a progressive spiritualization. The greatest obstacle lies in being tied to the material world through corporeality. *Askesis,* virtues, meditation, abnegation, and purification are necessary for becoming what one is in one's origins and most authentically. As separation from corporeality, death is welcome, on the condition that the soul has prepared itself by practices that express its most intimate desire.

Chief among these practices is the practice of philosophy. Scholars like A. J. Festugière, Pierre Hadot, A. Hillary Armstrong, and others have shown that philosophy in the Hellenistic epoch is not identical with the modern project of scientific and autonomous rationality. It is much more religious and ethical, intimately connected as it is with the existential search for meaning and ultimate wisdom. It cannot be dissociated from a specific way of life, the particular orientation and tone of a *bios,* including the basic attitudes and *tropoi* of the thinking that is part of such a life. These insights have important consequences for our concept of philosophy and its history. The relations of philosophy with science, moral practice, religion, beliefs, and faith have to be revised, and postmodern as well as medieval criticisms of theoretism will appear to have ancient precedents. Yet we must concede that the philosophical spirituality proposed by Plato and his followers heavily emphasized, and probably overemphasized, the role of *theoria,* and that this emphasis, which in modern times developed into an extreme scientification, has marked the history of our culture.

Plotinus, in treatise VI, 9 [9], shows that thinking as theoretical practice is an indispensable guiding principle in the human search for meaning, but he also insists that theory is not enough. First, no theoretical endeavor would be possible if it were not driven by *eros.* Second, and more important, theory does not reach far enough to get in touch with the desired end. One cannot approach the One without passing through the discursivity of *episteme* and ideality, but since the *kosmos noetos* is a totality composed of many ideas, knowledge of it is unable to realize the simplicity of a union with the absolutely one. The exclusion of all plurality from the Origin itself is responsible for the fact that theory alone cannot satisfy our deepest desire. To settle in the noetic realm of ideas and arguments does liberate us from the dissemination that typifies the world of *aisthesis* and *aistheta,* but with regard to the One, which can only be "seen" or "touched" through an immediate contact, thinking — or, more generally, "speaking and writing" — can do no more than awaken the mind from its immersion in *logoi* and point out the conditions of the ultimate union. Instruction *(didaxis)* and reflection *(dianoeisthai)* prepare the soul, but to go the whole way in order to experience the vision is a further-reaching task *(ergon)* of the person who is longing for it (VI, 9, 4).

The threefold way from *aisthēsis* to *noēsis* and from *noēsis* to contact with the One can be represented as an ascent. To describe this ascent, Plotinus borrows many metaphors from Plato's *Republic, Banquet,* and *Phaedrus.* However, another mode of spatializing — and one that perhaps is closer to the truth — describes the search as a turning inward. The One beyond being is present *(paresti)* within the soul, at the center of its center. It has always been there, even if most people neither know nor notice it. To approach the One is to free the core of your soul from all its additions and complications. You must divest yourself of the many things, thoughts, and elements that surround and obscure the One. To become *eudaimōn* is to become simple in union with the One, which is also the Good. Plotinus's guidance urges his readers to open their souls to the presence of God who has never left them, although their turning away from him to earthly things caused them to forget their origin and destiny.

The urge for unity suppresses every attachment to multiplicity and demands an affective distance from corporeal and material realities insofar as these tend to seduce us to a scattered way of life. Intersubjective and social relationships, friendship and love do not play a direct role in the discovery of our destiny except as conditions for the authentic practice of thinking on the way to insight. God can be found within our soul, but to get in touch with him, one must practice detachment with regard to the entire universe of beings, including the manifold of ideas, souls, and communities. The ascension is therefore a solitary task (4, 23: *monos anabebēkōs*). The recommended kind of life does not find enjoyment in the things here below *(bios anēdonos tōn tēide);* it is a flight of the single *psychē* alone to the One alone *(phygē monou pros monon:* 11, 50-51, cf. 9, 52-54). The meaning of human existence lies in its becoming *angelic:* a soul at home in the spiritual cosmos of being and thought, but reaching out beyond this dimension, since even spirit is still too diverse and complex.

The most beautiful and fecund aspect of Plotinus's spirituality lies in his conviction that neither morality nor philosophy in the purely theoretical sense of this word fully responds to the desire that drives us. Emphasizing that the words "seeing" *(thea)* and "intuition" *(noein)* fail to describe the soul's union with the One, since they still presuppose some duality, he does not fall into the theoretism that has been a strong temptation for the entire history of Western civilization. However, his interpretation of transcendence as a super- and supranoetic return to the undivided Principle through detachment from all multiplicity has exacted a high price for which we still are in debt. Plotinus's spiritualistic turning away from matter, which — as dispersion — is the cause of evil (I, 8, 14), seems to preclude finding the One in devotion to singular and corporeal beings. Love for the One who — despite its admirable generosity — is uninterested in the totality of beings and thoughts (which, for their part, are totally dependent on it) demands distance from everything else. The One is present everywhere: in all thoughts and souls, including the cosmic soul that encompasses all individual souls and things. The order and beauty of the visible universe, which Plotinus defends against the Gnostics, testify to the generosity of their unique Source; yet the experience of its presence in them cannot coincide with service or grateful enjoyment of human or other beings. Though nothing that exists is bad (except the dispersion of a materialistic existence), all ideas, bodies, souls, and spirits point to the only One that can be loved without restriction. The search for union with this Beloved leads through its resemblances, but to what extent does the Good send us back to involvement in the corporeal, sensual, and historical world of human life? Once the union with the Good has made the soul a god, politics seems below one's dignity, although it is possible that intimacy with the Good expresses itself by telling others about it and giving them indications about the way to reach it (VI, 9, 7). True communion between humans ultimately depends on each one's own approaching of the unique Source. Instead of concentration on the material conditions of a just society, it is the attempt to become wholly spiritual which gathers us into a community (cf. I, 4, 3-4).

It is obvious that death will have a very different meaning according to whether it is seen as a flight from the world or as a total destruction for which in the end no other meaning can be found than that of an extreme opportunity for selfless love. Salvation through spiritualization is radically different from a redemption that transforms the entire human constitution by turning a deviated heart back to the God whose outgoing love remains highly interested.[1]

II. Bonaventure's Guidance for the Encounter with God

Many Platonic and Plotinian elements can be found in the fifth chapter of Bonaventure's *Itinerary of the Mind to God*, although this chapter contains only two explicit quotes from Greek philosophy (nn. 4 and 6) as well as an allusion to the *Liber de Causis* (*propositio* 17 in n. 7). The quotes are not from Plato or

---

1. I want to thank Kevin Corrigan and Eric Perl for their observations on an earlier version of this text. If my picture still fails to do justice to Plotinus's attitude toward the corporeal and social universe, the responsibility is entirely my own.

Plotinus but from Aristotle's *Metaphysics* (II, 1, 993b9-11) and his *Topica* (V, 5, 134b24-25). The subject of chapter 5 is very similar to the Plotinian treatise VI, 9. However, whereas Plotinus identifies the One *(to hen)* with the Good *(to agathon)* and clearly separates it from Being, which belongs to the *Nous,* Bonaventure presents the unicity *(unum)* of God as an aspect of God's being *(esse),* contrasting this to God's goodness *(bonitas),* which in chapter 6 will be shown to be another name for God as Trinity.

Chapters 5 and 6 taken together describe the penultimate station of the mind's ascent to God. They must be situated in relation to the preceding four chapters and the final, seventh, chapter, which describes the rest that comes after the traveling. Chapter 1 stipulates the conditions of the journey. It shows how typically Christian the whole journey and its stages are, but also how much in conceptual and structural analysis and terminology their description owes to (Neo-)Platonic predecessors.

Following the Greek tradition as expressed, for instance, in Aristotle's *Ethics* and in the Stoic treatises on "well-being," the first chapter begins by stating that the goal of the journey lies in *beatitudo.* This word translates the Greek *eudaimonia,* but, as we will see, it also evokes the paradise of Genesis 2 and a *peace* that surpasses all human powers of acquisition. (The coincidence of these meanings in Bonaventure's text already indicates how much the Greek *eudaimonia* and the Roman *beatitudo* have been transformed in their encounter with the biblical *eirēnē, pax.*) Plotinus, too, pointed out that the union with the One cannot be conquered by the soul's own forces; after having settled in the *Nous* and looking up from there, one must wait until the union overwhelms one's ethical and theoretical possibilities, but the character of the One, of the soul, and of their relation, as Plotinus depicts them, is different from their parallels in Bonaventure's travel guide.

Bonaventure defines *beatitudo* as "nothing other than the enjoyment of the utmost good" *(nihil aliud est quam summi boni fruitio,* n. 1), a formal definition that seems to fit many ethics. However, since the utmost good is "above us" *(supra nos),* its enjoyment can be reached only through an ascent. The mind must therefore transcend the possibilities of its own being. This transcendence is neither a corporeal movement nor a liberation from corporeality. The ascent is a "cordial" *(cordialis)* one: a task for the human heart, not for reason or intellect or behavior alone. As the phenomenological center of the human *compositum,* the heart is the core that mobilizes human interests and provides them with passion for what really matters.

Since human beings are not able to surpass themselves by their own forces, they must look up to God's grace. According to Plotinus, no soul can even begin its ascent unless it is driven by *eros,* which, like all good things, comes from the Good itself; through its union with the soul, the Good shows that it always already has been present. The union is nothing other than the full unfolding of

an original but hidden and inhibited unity. The natural, necessary, and anony-
mous character of this presence differs from Bonaventure's more dramatic
conception of God's gracious dealings with the contingencies of human history,
but it is not so easy to determine this difference without doing injustice to
Plotinus.

The normal human response to grace is an attitude of looking up, which
Bonaventure calls *oratio* (prayer). By stating that "prayer" is the basic condition
for approaching God, he declares that thinking, in order to point in God's
direction, must emerge from a pretheoretical turn of the heart that can be
characterized by the words "humble" and "devout" (*petunt ex corde humiliter
et devote*, n. 1). "Prayer is the mother and origin of all upward-action" (*oratio
. . . est mater et origo sursum-actionis*, n. 1), including philosophy and theology.
Theory is thus rooted in the dimension of the heart, or — as I would like to
translate — theory is born from and oriented and nurtured by spirituality. The
necessity of *oratio* for the authenticity of all God-talk does not imply that
philosophers or theologians cannot do their work successfully without saying
a host of prayers. Without excluding these, "prayer" means first of all a specific
mind-set or turn of mind (a *tropos*) through which humans respond in an
appropriate way to the infinity of the One who is interested in finite beings that
are interested in God.

The relations and proportions involved in this mutual interest must be
clarified according to two perspectives, which traditionally have been contrasted
as *nature* and (sacred) *history*. According to the first perspective, the situation
of the human mind can be determined with the help of the parallelism between
macrocosmos and *microcosmos* (n. 4), which was introduced into philosophy by
Plato's *Timaeus* and became very popular in the course of the twelfth century.

III. Creation

Typical modes of feeling, knowledge, and practice relate the human mind to
the three main dimensions of the universe: the dimension of things outside us
(extra nos), the dimension of our own interiority *(intra nos)*, and the dimension
of what surpasses us *(supra nos)*. Corporeality enables us to know and handle
the world through the senses; having a will and intellect opens us up to the
aeviternal dimension of the spirit; transcendence to the suprarational enables
us to enjoy God in a relation of affection that surpasses all kinds of discursivity
and behavior.

Bonaventure's originality here lies in the doubling of each of these levels
through the application of a distinction between a seeing *per speculum* (through
the mirror) and a seeing *in speculo* (in the mirror): each level of reality mirrors

some other reality in two different ways. The schema itself can be understood as a development of Platonic and Neoplatonic speculations about *mimesis* (imitation), but it is profoundly transformed in a Christian context.

Finite realities, such as the human mind, a tree, or a mountain, can be taken as points of departure for the ascent insofar as each of them, in its own way, mirrors God as the creator — and therefore also, in some sense, shows God to be the "formal cause" *(causa formalis)* of all things. In concentrating on the tree (or the mountain or the mind), we can discover certain traits in it that suggest an essential reference to its first cause, and thus, by way of conclusion, direct the mind to God. Having found God *per speculum,* the mind can then enjoy its discovery by realizing that the reference of finite realities to God entails a certain presence of God *in* those realities, not only behind them or deep down, concealed at the bottom of or underneath their being, but also *in and as* their ultimate and primordial truth and "essence." God's infinite being then becomes visible, audible, touchable as displayed (be it in a finite, limited manner) in the mirror of finite entities *(in speculo).*

Bonaventure's retrieval of Platonic *topoi* transposes into the language of speculative theology the Franciscan experience of a world that shows and bespeaks God. Corporeality is not an obstacle to meeting with the One. The phenomena invite us to decipher their phenomenality; or, as Bonaventure repeats again and again, they "preach" *(praedicare),* "clearly indicate" *(manifeste indicare),* "insinuate" *(insinuare)* and show *(ostendere),* "evidently proclaim" *(evidenter proclamare),* "declare" and "clarify" *(manifeste declarare)* God's presence in all beings and lead us by the hand *(evidentissime manuducere)* to God. All these expressions are found in chapter 1, which treats the "lowest" level of micro- and macrocosmos. A human mind which discovers the omnipresence of God's self-manifestation is awakened by the "shouts" of the phenomena.

Nothing in this universe is despicable, and the Good does not demand any separation or destruction. What we must flee from is not matter but instead a wrong manner of concentrating on and relating to God and the universe. If goodness lies in corresponding appropriately to all that exists, evil is a mode of turning away from it toward its negation, a manner of existence that distorts the proportions of the original creation. And here we meet with the typically Christian explanation of why the mind has so much difficulty in following the path that leads to God through appropriate behavior toward the universe.

IV. History

Instead of materiality or multiplicity, the great and unique obstacle lies in the noncoincidence of human factuality with what we originally and "naturally" —

through creation — are. Our basic orientation is deviated; human desire is inclined to betray itself by preferring finite satisfactions over the enjoyment of the *summum bonum* (highest good). To climb the "ladder" of the universe would be easy if we were pure and innocent, spontaneously looking up toward the complete and perfect good. However, our orientation has become bad through greed and arrogance, and a lifetime of bending one's tendencies straight is necessary for becoming genuinely what one was meant to be from the outset. It is the heart that generates and encompasses theory and practice, and the deviation of this heart, not the body or materiality, is the source of guilt. The negations and abnegations imposed by our search for the ultimate should not be shaped by contempt for corporeality, but rather by respect for the true proportions that rule the universe and promise *beatitudo* to those whose behavior and reflection take them into account.

The hierarchical model of the microcosmos develops certain Greek analyses of the human psyche, but Christian faith integrates it into a history of sin and redemption. The entire microcosmos, including its most spiritual levels, is curved and crooked *(curvatus)* because of its turning away from the real good and the light of truth. Since the root of this deformation lies in a self-willed or consensual deviation from God's presence, a return to the lost straightforwardness can only come from a more benevolent force than human reason and will. Grace is this force, but it is powerless if it is not welcomed by will and reason, imagination and the senses that attach us to the world. The first expression of this cooperation is purification. What Plato and Plotinus said about the role of "justice" *(dikaiosynē)* in the discovery of the truth is integrated into Bonaventure's theory of a union of grace and human effort. He, too, sees justice as the necessary condition for acquiring true knowledge, and he agrees with Plotinus in making a distinction between the highest form of science and the wisdom of a nondiscursive union with the One. But Bonaventure's conception of wisdom is one of an affectionate and communicative kind of embrace rather than that of a vision. This preference is intimately linked to his belief that justice and wisdom in their belonging together have been perfectly revealed and realized in the charitable way of life that was accomplished by Jesus the Christ. The encounter of the One who is the Good and the acceptance of grace cannot bypass the historical reality of a person who lived the ultimate truth of goodness by unreservedly giving himself for others (n. 7).

V. The One (Chapter 5)

Chapters 5 and 6 outline the highest level of contemplation before entrance into the promised land of well-being and bliss. The mind looks here to that which is above us *(supra nos):* the light that enlightens our mind, presupposed in all former discoveries as the condition of their possibilities. Appealing to Psalm 4:7 and a text of Saint Augustine (83 *Quaestiones,* qu. 51, 2, 4), Bonaventure states that this light is the eternal Truth itself insofar as it "forms our mind immediately." In it we experience all things, but we could not enjoy it if it were not *"signatum"* (marked, sealed, signed) on our mind.

The light of the eternal truth has two aspects. The first aspect manifests God as *esse;* the other becomes manifest by a consideration of his goodness. The divine names "being" *(esse)* and "good" *(bonum)* are thus disclosed as the ultimate discursive possibilities to recognize God. Bonaventure compares the contemplation of God's *esse* and the contemplation of his goodness *(bonum)* with the "two Cherubim of Glory that stand over the Ark, overshadowing the Mercy Seat" *(propitiatorium,* Exodus 25): the first mode of contemplation *(per nomen primarium esse)* concentrates on the *essentialia Dei,* the other *(in nomine quod est bonum)* considers what is proper to the three persons in God. As the contrast between *per* and *in* in the titles of chapters 5 and 6 suggests, these modes differ in degree of proximity to God. Although both Cherubim seem equally holy, being *(ipsum esse)* is the radical principle through which all other aspects of God's essence *(essentialia)* are discovered, but *bonum* is the *"most principal (principalissimum)* foundation for the contemplation of the emanations," that is — as we will see — of the communicative structure of God.

The parallels and differences with Plotinus's *theoria* are obvious. There the One is discovered *through,* not *in,* the knowledge of being *(Nous, ousia, to on);* the ascent leads from the knowledge of being to the experience of the Good "beyond being," which shows its goodness by overflowing into emanations. Bonaventure does not separate being from the good but synthesizes both names by subordinating God's "being" *(esse)* to his goodness, which is revealed in God's trinitarian structure and movement. He thus integrates a certain plurality into God, the plurality that is indispensable for love.

Since his treatment of being *(esse)* in chapter 5 seems to be a synthesis of Neoplatonic and Aristotelian ontotheology, whereas the disclosure of God's trinity obviously depends on Christian faith, one could expect that the first of the Cherubim with whom Bonaventure compares the two highest kinds of contemplation would represent the summit of Greek philosophy, whereas the second Cherub would then symbolize the biblical tradition, in which there is little speculation and even less ontology but a lot about God's communication and compassion. This is not the case, however. Almost all of chapter 5 is a rigorously philosophical analysis of the concept of being *(esse)* which shows how much Bonaventure has learned from Greek ontology. However, his summary of that ontology is framed by two quotes from the Bible and presented as a speculative summary of its faith in one, unique God. The first Cherub represents the Old Testament, while the second stands for the New Testament.

Bonaventure's presentation is thus not meant to be a synthesis of Greek wisdom and Judeo-Christian faith. Although his whole deduction of God's *essentialia* (chap. 5, nn. 3-6) is purely philosophical and not supported by biblical texts, Bonaventure offers his retrieval of Greek ontotheology as a speculative translation of God's self-revelation in Exodus 3:14. The truths contained in the expression "Ego sum qui sum" [I am who am] were revealed to Moses long before Parmenides inaugurated the ontological language which permits us to conceptualize them. "He, who is" *(Qui est)* is equated with being itself *(esse ipsum)*, and this is shown to be the pure actuality of being, which is the first that is "thought," or rather the preconceptual a priori of all thought (*quod primo cadit in intellectu,* n. 3), the first, unique, most simple, most perfect, eternal, infinite, creative, most present, immutable origin and end, the center which is also the circumference, etc. Since all these "names" can be shown to include one another, God is the One in the most extreme and absolute sense of pure simplicity and one-ness. While the self-revelation of God to Moses as told in Exodus 3:14 opens the analysis of *esse,* the beginning of the Shema Israel closes its first, fundamental part (n. 6). Bonaventure concludes his analysis with these words:

> If "God" is the name of the primary, eternal, most simple, most actual, most perfect *esse,* it is impossible to think that he is not or that he is not one,

but then he immediately connects through the word "therefore" *(igitur)* a Latin translation of Deuteronomy 6:4: *Audi igitur Israël, Deus tuus Deus unus est.* "Listen [therefore] Israel, your God is One God."

VI. The Good (Chapter 6)

Although Bonaventure places his consideration of the Good beside *(juxta)* the "ontological" Cherub of chapter 5, there is a difference of degree: being *(ipsum esse)* is the radical principle *(principium radicale)* for the contemplation of God, but the *good (ipsum bonum)* is the most fundamental principle *(principalissimum fundamentum)*. Although "being" is the name through which all other predicates of God are known, it is somehow included in, and to that extent also subordinate to, the good, as Bonaventure points out in note 2. For stating the identity of the One and the Good, he could have appealed to the Neoplatonic tradition, but again he sees himself more inspired by the New Testament than by philosophy. Yet he builds a logical argument by showing the necessary connection between God's being and his goodness through an Anselmian formula. If God is the good, he is the best, namely, "that better than which nothing can be thought." "Since it is absolutely better to be than not to be," the good (or the best) "cannot be thought not to be" (n. 2). Being is therefore contained in the good. And since being is absolutely one, God's goodness entails his one-ness.

The great admirer of Dionysius here clearly takes a distance from negative theology. Far from dismissing ontology as failing to name God, Bonaventure suggests that it can explain the Jewish and Christian faith in God's unity, and that it is an essential part of the contemplation of his goodness. By the same token Bonaventure bridges the abyss Plato and Plotinus maintained between the Good and the *kosmos noētos* of the *Nous*.

An even greater difference from Neoplatonic thinking shows up in Bonaventure's view on the emanations. The goodness of the One is not only the source *(pēgē)* and origin *(archē)* of the ideal, essential, psychical, and material universe that flows from it, but it multiplies the One within itself. Appealing to the Pseudo-Dionysian dictum "bonum est diffusivum sui," understood as a résumé of the gospel's testimony about God's love, Bonaventure infers without much ado that the supreme good *(summum bonum)* must be diffusive and self-diffusive to the utmost degree. To be good is to be communicative and self-communicative. Its absolute mode (neither a degree nor a mode) is realized in God's communication of his own essence within the unity of this same essence. Goodness is love, and infinite love is the sharing of God's substance with another, who thereby is generated in one and the same God. Since love between two persons is not complete without a third, God and his "Son" together "breathe" the Spirit as the third person within the same essence.

Surprisingly for modern minds, Bonaventure does not seem to consider the trinitarian structure of God a strange truth too difficult for philosophers to swallow. He presents it as a logical consequence of God's absolute goodness. It is clear, however, that his understanding of goodness, quite different from that of Plotinus, would not have been possible without faith in God's love, a love which he explains here as extreme self-communication. What Bonaventure finds really surprising, incomprehensible, and admirable is not so much God's unicity and God's trinity taken separately, but rather their simultaneity and mutual inclusiveness. He even warns the reader: see that "you do not deem yourself to comprehend the incomprehensible" (n. 3). Instead of promoting insight into the tri-une nature of God, he affirms it as an inevitable but incomprehensible certainty. The combination of incomprehensibility and certainty forces the thinker into a change of attitude; the ontological approach yields to another kind of relation to God. Instead of seeing or comprehending, affections come into play. At the summit of the intellectual contemplation the traveler is urged to achieve a radical shift: admiration is now more appropriate than the most rigorous form of ontotheology. In the end, theory is shown not to be an overcoming of amazement, as the beginning of Aristotle's *Metaphysics* had suggested, but the preparation of a more sublime surprise and wonder. However, the theological concentration on God's being one *and* threefold in love is not the end stage of the journey to which the mind is invited. Once the traveler has identified with both Cherubim by contemplating the wonderful essence and personal relationships of God, the mind must direct its eyes to the "Mercy Seat" (*propitiatorium,* Exod. 25:20) on top of the ark in order to admire something even more wonderful than the "superadmirable *(supermirabilem)* union of God and man in the unity of Christ's person" (n. 4). This is the center and synthesis in which the union of God's being and his trinity expresses itself as the perfect union of the Creator and his creation: Christ is the human icon in which the Word of the Origin has become the open book in which all essential truths can be found. Whoever has become able through the stages of the journey to read this book has found the perfect source of illumination. After this discovery no other progress can be made, except by an ongoing intensification of appropriate affections.

By emphasizing and repeating that admiration should take over when reason and intellect have exhausted their capacities for truth, chapter 6 has prepared the reader to enter the end station of the road, which is somewhat similar to but also very different from the *extasis* that crowns Plotinus's post-theoretical union with the One. Discursivity has made room for a suprarational kind of mood characterized as *peace.* Only at the end of the road can the full meaning of this word be experienced. The mind enters into this peace through an "excess"; the speculative attitude, maintained throughout the six stages of the road, undergoes a final conversion (n. 2). Bonaventure's excess is not the Plotinian unification in which the mind loses its self-consciousness. "To be perfect, this transition must leave all intellectual operations behind, while the tip of affection *(apex affectus)* entirely is transformed into God" (n. 4). The supratheoretical disposition needed is composed of faith, hope, devotion, admiration, exultation, appreciation, praise, and jubilation. Bonaventure's phenomenology of emotions, virtues, spiritual senses, gifts of the spirit, and *"beatitudines"* should be brought in at this point to get a better idea of the mind-set and the kind of life that are demanded as a response to the central mystery (the *"propitiatorium"*) in which God is most adequately manifested. This mystery is the simultaneously divine and human fact of Jesus the Christ as crucified. The final meaning of human existence, introduced in chapter 1 under the name of *beatitudo,* is now revealed in a dying man, who is God. The *theōsis* of human mortals is realized in God's mortality. Encountering God is not an escape from corporeality, but the acceptance of mortality as a symbol and concretization of absolute generosity and self-communication. The journey of the mind to the *eudaimonia* of peace is a passage (a *pascha*) through the Red Sea under the guidance of the cross. Death is necessary, not in order to free the soul from its imprisonment in corporeality, but rather to pass over into the dominance of grace.

CHAPTER 4

From the Twelfth-Century Renaissance to the Italian: Three Versions of "the Dignity of Man"

CHARLES TRINKAUS

"Let us make human beings in our image, according to our likeness. . . ." (Gen. 1:26). Saint Augustine's explanation of why Moses, the supposed author of these words, used the plural to announce the creation of human beings laid the basis for the medieval and Renaissance discussions of the dignity of the human person: the plural form *faciamus* (let us make) indicates that the entire Trinity of Father, Son, and Holy Spirit participated in this notable divine action. And inquiring into what was meant by *ad imaginem et similtudinem nostrum* (in our image and likeness),[1] Augustine concluded that the human soul was made according to God's image, and this image was, as Augustine later argued in *On the Trinity*,[2] itself a lowercase trinity of memory, intellect, and will.

There was no simple agreement on these three faculties, and a variety of such triads were asserted by many different authors. Although there were some earlier

---

1. Augustine, *De Genesi ad litteram* III, 19, 20 (Migne, *Patrologia Latina* 34:291-93; hereafter cited as *PL*); VI, 12 (*PL* 34:347-48); VII, 2 (*PL* 34:356-57). See Trinkaus, *In Our Image and Likeness: Humanity and Divinity in Italian Humanist Thought* (London: Constable; Chicago: University of Chicago Press, 1970), chap. 4, "The Dignity of Man in the Patristic and Medieval Traditions," here pp. 181-82 esp. n. 8.

2. The second part of *De Trinitate*, books VIII to XV, is a long exploration of the interrelationships of the variously articulated images of the Trinity and the Trinity itself. The specific attributes of Memory, Intellect, and Will are designated in X, xi, 17, and the trinity in humankind is elaborated through books IX to XII. See Migne, *PL* 42:982-83, and *Oeuvres de Saint Augustin*, ed. P. Agaësse, S.J., and J. Moingt, S.J. (Paris: Desclée de Brouwer, 1955), vol. 16, pp. 152-57.

examples, the twelfth century, no doubt because of its own accelerated pace of learning, included a number of references to these human qualities as dignities. Robert Javelet has shown the richness of twelfth-century thought for discussions of the many ways humankind could be imagined to image the Creator or move through piety and the moral virtues to closer likeness to God.[3] Further, these varied reflections of the nature of the deity, at least clouded over by the fall, could easily be transformed through sin into either the image of Satan or of the animals, above which humankind was held to excel because of its divine image.[4]

With the coming of Scholasticism, this way of thinking of humanity fell into disfavor (probably because of the influence of Aristotle's more systematic and empirical treatise *On the Soul*), only to be revived by Petrarch and the Italian humanists and Platonists in the late fourteenth century and thenceforth.[5] It will be the object of this paper to examine these three phases in the history of Western anthropological thinking in a concrete but limited way, focusing on one salient example from each of the three phases: twelfth-century Renaissance, high Scholasticism, and Italian Renaissance. Admittedly an extensive variety of examples could be gathered for any of the three, and I must be content to rely on the assumed archetypal character of my selections. They are: William of Saint-Thierry's *On the Nature of the Body and the Soul*;[6] Thomas Aquinas's *Summa contra gentiles* II, 46-90, supplemented by references to his *Sententia libri de anima* (commentary on Aristotle's *On the Soul*) and *Summa theologiae*;[7] and Lorenzo Valla's *Retractatio totius dialectice cum fundamentis universe philosophie*, parts of book 1 on the soul.[8] Common sense will recognize that in the space at my disposal I must be even more restricted in my exposition, but I do hope to bring out some general observations.

3. Robert Javelet, *Image et ressemblance au douzième siècle de Saint Anselme à Alain de Lille*, 2 vols. (Strassbourg: Éditions Letouzey & Ané, 1967).

4. Cf. Augustine, *De Trinitate* XII, xi, 16 (Migne, *PL* 42:1006-7); *Oeuvres*, 16:240-43.

5. Trinkaus, chap. 4, esp. pp. 188-90ff. I have probably stated this too strongly as far as scholastic discussion of the image of God in human beings is concerned. There was, however, a tendency to stress the intellect as the primary attribute of the divine image in human beings and to play down the others.

6. William of Saint-Thierry, *De natura corporis et animae*, in Migne, *PL* 180, cols. 695-726.

7. Thomas Aquinas, *Sententia libri de anima*, vol. 45/1 of *Opera omnia* (Rome: Commissio Leonina; Paris: Libraire Philosophique J. Vrin, 1984); Aquinas, *Summa contra gentiles*, bk. 2 (Rome: Comissio Leonina and Libreria Vaticana; Desclee & Cie.); English translation of book 2 by James F. Anderson, vol. 2 of *Summa contra gentiles* (Notre Dame: University of Notre Dame Press, 1975). The other books have other translations in volumes 1, 3, 4 of the Blackfriars edition. Thomas Aquinas, *Summa theologiae*, trans. Edmund Hill, O.P., vol. 13 (London: Eyre & Spottiswoode; New York: McGraw-Hill, 1964).

8. Lorenzo Valla, *Retractatio totius dialectice cum fundamentis universe philosophie*, ed. Gianni Zippel (Padua: Editrice Antenore, 1982).

I. William of Saint-Thierry: Dignity as Ascetic Domination

William of Saint-Thierry (ca. 1085–ca. 1148), the counselor of Saint Bernard, abbot of Saint-Thierry from 1119 to 1135, was well known for his criticisms of Abelard, of William of Conches, and of Gilbert of Poitiers, all bearing on theological errors arising from misapplications of the new, predominantly Neo-platonic, and still pre-Aristotelian philosophical interests.[9] William's own work *On the Nature of the Body and the Soul* in its first book on the body is a remarkably clear and compact account of human physiology, itself deriving from Constantinus Africanus's translation of the *Pantegni* of Haly Abbas, an advanced work of Arabic medicine. Its humoral theory and detailed description of the bodily organs and their functioning must surely be accounted up-to-date, and the dominant medical physiology until at least the sixteenth century. But my interest is in his second book on the soul,[10] and in the ways in which his understanding of human dignity is developed in the context of a discussion of the interworking of the soul and the body.

Before he arrives at this second book, William has also discussed the physiology of the five senses,[11] how they are connected with the four humors,[12] and how certain natural philosophers vainly seeking to locate the dignity of human nature in some part of the human body find it in our erect stature, which shows we have something in common with heaven, or in the unity and beauty of the members, or in the weight, measure, and number of our composition. These physical thinkers say that if a person is laid on the ground with his arms and legs extended, a circle inscribed from the umbilicus as the center will find these equal. In number, besides the limbs, there are 241 bones in the body, seven equal nerves leaving the brain, and thirty-two equal and one unequal from the *nucha*.[13]

9. There are only scattered references to William of Saint-Thierry in *A History of Twelfth-Century Western Philosophy*, ed. Peter Dronke (Cambridge: Cambridge University Press, 1988). Eugenio Garin quotes his *De natura corporis et animae* in two brief paragraphs of his *La "Dignitas Hominis" e la letturatura patristica* (Turin: G. Giappichelli Editore, 1972), pp. 39-40.

10. William of Saint-Thierry, *De natura, Liber Primus "Physica Humani Corporis,"* in Migne, *PL* 180, cols. 695a-708c; *De natura, Liber Secundus "Physica Animae,"* in Migne, *PL* 180, cols. 707d-726c.

11. William of Saint-Thierry, *Liber Primus*, in Migne, *PL* 180, cols. 704-7.

12. William of Saint-Thierry, *Liber Primus*, in Migne, *PL* 180, col. 707. The humors also differentiate the four ages: adolescence up to the twenty-fifth or thirtieth year is sanguine; youth to the thirty-fifth or fortieth year is choleric; senectitude to the fifty-fifth or sixtieth year is melancholic; senility from then on "is naturally the driest and coldest, but accidentally moist on account of indigestion and abundance of phlegm."

13. William of Saint-Thierry, *Liber Primus*, in Migne, *PL* 180, col. 708ac. I do not know what *nucha* or *nux*, "nut," refers to, unless it is the spinal cord.

The soul, according to the doctors of the church rather than the physical philosophers, is a spiritual and proper substance created by God that is life-giving, rational, and immortal but convertible into good and evil. It is properly a substance because it is the only spirit that can assume a body so that it can mourn or rejoice through its passions.[14] It gives life to its body as such and the power to live well and the opportunity for future goods. Though intending to make a sharp differentiation between the physical and the spiritual, William keeps trying to relate aspects of the latter to bodily organs. Life as such is conveyed through the brain, the heart, and the liver, the good life through the senses. Lungs and stomach are necessary to keep the body alive and the humors in balance. The creation is compared to the working of a sculptor who first blocks out the essentials and then adds the refinements:[15]

> Thus we are born as the cattle, and the image of the Creator cannot shine in us continually without great and daily labors, but man is led by some long trail through the material and cattle-like properties of the soul to his perfection. . . . But though plants and trees seem in some way to live and brute animals to have souls, yet it is settled that all these, though in some way living, do not have a soul nor rise up in this to the dignity of the human condition.[16]

While insisting that the soul is a spirit that cannot be located in any part of the body, William shows a persistent interest in the ways in which the soul and the conformation of the human body combine to engage in modes of action befitting human dignity. For instance, the spirit of man utilizes the senses to learn and make judgments:

> Reason, sitting like a queen in the central fortress of the city, with the gates of the senses open in all directions, receives and distinguishes by face and habit the natives and foreigners entering and locates each in its place of knowledge, and distinguishes genuses from each other and assigns them to their own houses of memory.[17]

Like an organist composing with a range of sounds, nature adapts the parts of the body to the uses of reason in a harmony.[18] For example, there are many uses of hands in war and peace, but if we were without hands our form would

---

14. William of Saint-Thierry, *Liber Primus*, in Migne, *PL* 180, cols. 707-708d.

15. William of Saint-Thierry, *Liber Primus*, in Migne, *PL* 180, cols. 709-710c.

16. William of Saint-Thierry, *Liber Secundus*, in Migne, *PL* 180, col. 710cd.

17. William of Saint-Thierry, *Liber Secundus*, in Migne, *PL* 180, col. 711c. This same metaphor was used for similar purpose by Scotus Eriugena, Bonaventura, and Nicolaus Cusanus (and possibly others). See Pauline Moffitt Watts, *Nicholas Cusanus: A Fifteenth-Century Vision of Man* (Leiden: E. J. Brill, 1982), pp. 212-13 and n. 48.

18. William of Saint-Thierry, *Liber Secundus*, in Migne, *PL* 180, col. 712bc.

have to be shaped like a quadruped in order for us to eat, with a long neck for seeing food on the ground, the nostrils extended beyond the mouth, with hard, heavy, thick lips for cutting food like dogs and other carnivorous animals,[19] and

> thus it would happen if hands were missing from the body that the voice articulately shaped to the mouth would be lacking and the formation of the mouth would not be adapted to the use of sound and it would be necessary for man either to bleat or to moo or bark or utter some other bestial growl. Now indeed while the hand serves the mouth, the mouth is the handmaid to reason and through this to the soul in spiritual and incorporeal matters.[20]

As a learned musician who lacks the proper voice to express some passion makes it public by the foreign voices of flutes and lyres, so the soul, the inventor of different thoughts, although it lacks corporeal words because it is incorporeal, is able to show the force of the intellect through the bodily organs. For an additional function of the gift of reason is that the hand can speak by means of writing:

> Thus both hand and mouth serve reason: the hand by writing for future and absent persons, the mouth by easily and promptly saying whatever internal reason suggests.[21]

William proceeds to address the question of what is meant by dignity. The human person who is made in the image of God does not stay in the stability of the deity but acts through the instruments of the senses. In this we are far from God in whose image we are created because it would be absurd to understand the reception and multiformity of the operation of the receiver to consist in the simplicity of deity, for that would be identity, not image. Dignity therefore does not imply deification:[22]

> Man's erect figure extended toward heaven and looking upwards does signify the imperial and regal dignity of the rational soul and shows the dominion passed on to him by the Creator over all the creatures looking downward. And it shows he has much in common with supernal beings if he guards the dignity of the inborn image so that the soul rules by reason and allows nothing to be chosen which is not useful. But those are lacking in this dignity who, making reason which is naturally the mistress the slave to natural desires, are servilely gratified by lust which exists through the senses. . . . For, as it is said, what are matters of nature in animals are vices in man.[23]

---

19. William of Saint-Thierry, *Liber Secundus*, in Migne, *PL* 180, cols. 712cd-713a.
20. William of Saint-Thierry, *Liber Secundus*, in Migne, *PL* 180, col. 713a.
21. William of Saint-Thierry, *Liber Secundus*, in Migne, *PL* 180, col. 713ab.
22. William of Saint-Thierry, *Liber Secundus*, in Migne, *PL* 180, cols. 713d-714b.
23. William of Saint-Thierry, *Liber Secundus*, in Migne, *PL* 180, cols. 714b and 714d.

Our dignity, then, consists in our rule over nature and is lost if instead we serve nature.

Elaborately and eloquently William argues this,[24] and introduces a basic theme of the genre, the topos that we are born nude and helpless, not as the other animals are, armed with tooth and claw:[25]

> And in what way, someone might ask, would such a creature be said to possess empire over all? In all ways very well. First because human reason has the power of harming its subject while guarding against it prudently or destroying it potently or driving it back into its own servitude. For what seems to be a lack in our nature is an occasion for domination of those who are subject to it. And a man might indeed disdain empire while he is in no need of the service of subordinates. But now thanks to this condition the utilities of this life are distributed through the individual beings which are subjugated to us so that empire by which God elevates human nature over them is necessary for us.[26]

He sees in this rule of humankind over the animals that we have a royal nature and have been created "for rule over others through similitude to the king of the universe as if we have been chosen as a kind of animated image of Him," like the portraits of human kings and potentates clad in purple.[27]

William's treatise has many more things to say about the dignity of human nature, especially of its psychological, moral, and intellectual qualities, and of its ascent in seven steps to the beatific vision itself. But I must end with the following quotation:

> Just as nothing exists without God, the Creator, namely the Holy Trinity itself, so nothing at all can exist which is not one and threefold. Certainly every soul, as has been said, subsists in three individual parts: memory, intelligence and will.[28]

The concern in *On the Nature of the Body and the Soul* with the physiological, neurological, and spiritual working of the body, and with the organically articulated interworkings of the soul in the body, is both impressive and perplexing. It is less perplexing if it is seen from the perspective of a Cistercian ascetic for whom the concern to manage one's bodily urges was no doubt constant. The emphasis on human domination of the subhuman world of corporeal nature, zoological and natural, was also keyed into the monastic moral system,

---

24. William of Saint-Thierry, *Liber Secundus,* in Migne, *PL* 180, cols. 714d-715c.
25. William of Saint-Thierry, *Liber Secundus,* in Migne, *PL* 180, cols. 715d-716c.
26. William of Saint-Thierry, *Liber Secundus,* in Migne, *PL* 180, col. 716cd.
27. William of Saint-Thierry, *Liber Secundus,* in Migne, *PL* 180, col. 717a-c cit. b.
28. William of Saint-Thierry, *Liber Secundus,* in Migne, *PL* 180, col. 722ab.

as was the aspirational treatment of the soul's spiritual powers of rationality, concupiscibility, and irascibility, all three of which could be directed upward toward God or downward toward the destruction of human dignity in corporeality.

II. Thomas Aquinas: Soul as Intellect

Thomas Aquinas, whose commentary on Aristotle's *On the Soul* is thought to have been written about 1267, a century and a quarter later than William of Saint-Thierry's work, viewed the problem of human dignity and the soul very differently. His major concern can best be grasped within the context of Aristotle's *On the Soul* and Averroës's *Commentarium magnum*. Thomas interpreted Aristotle as holding that the intellective soul (to be distinguished but not separated from the sensitive and the nutritive soul) was the form of the human.[29] As such the power of intellection, called the possible intellect, was not a separate substance which entered into the soul of an individual through images within the fantasy, as Averroës argued,[30] something that would deny the individuality of a human's thinking. Further, the possible intellect was not a power within a human that came from a blending of bodily elements as Alexander of Aphrodisias had held,[31] nor was it a temperament or harmonizing of the humors as Galen taught.[32] And finally the intellect, when engaged in thought, was not the agent intellect, something outside of the human person that entered on occasion, as Avicenna held.[33] The emphasis and the length of discussion based on Aristotle's *On the Soul* that Thomas devoted to these arguments in the *Summa contra gentiles* was important, for he was attempting to disprove two kinds of notions, each of which would have been contrary to doctrines necessarily following from the Christian religion as Thomas conceived it and subversive of his efforts to support the Catholic faith by rational philosophical demonstration. The first notion of the soul as a separate substance would have imposed an intermediary spiritual being governing the terrestrial world between divine providence and hu-

---

29. The discussion of this question occurs in Aquinas, *Summa contra gentiles*, bk. II, chaps. 57-59. These three chapters are devoted to refuting Plato's conception of the soul as separate from and utilizing the body, and to affirming Aristotle's position that the soul, as intellect, is the form of a man consisting of soul and body.

30. Aquinas, *Summa contra gentiles*, II, chap. 60, pp. 159 and 161; Anderson, pp. 185 and 190-91.

31. Aquinas, *Summa contra gentiles*, II, chap. 62, pp. 162-64; Anderson, pp. 193-96.

32. Aquinas, *Summa contra gentiles*, II, chap. 63, p. 164; Anderson, pp. 197-98.

33. Aquinas, *Summa contra gentiles*, II, chap. 74, pp. 176-78; Anderson, pp. 227-32.

manity, such as, for example, the world soul, or *anima mundi,* or a sphere for the possible intellect, or the agent intellect as Averroës or Avicenna would have called it.[34] The second notion of the soul as composed of bodily elements, furnished by Alexander and by Galen, would have denied the possibility of the immortality of the human soul, something that Pietro Pomponazzi in fact did do in the great immortality controversy of the high Renaissance.[35]

In his *Summa theologiae* I, Q. 93, Thomas follows the Augustinian tradition of considering the human person as created in the image and likeness of God, and therefore having a trinitarian soul of memory, intellect, and will, or some similar combination of powers or qualities.[36] However, in *Summa contra gentiles* he argues that it was necessary for the perfection of the universe that we were created as an intellectual substance:

> Hence the complete perfection of the universe required the existence of some creatures which return to God not only as regards likeness of nature, but also by their action. And such a return to God cannot be made except by the act of the intellect and will, because God Himself has no other operation in his own regard than these.[37]

Thus Thomas does regard the human intellect and will as likenesses of God. But he explicitly excludes memory as confined to actual terrestrial events and

34. Aquinas, *Summa contra gentiles,* II, chap. 73, p. 176; Anderson, p. 227.

35. Cf. Martin L. Pine, *Pietro Pomponazzi: Radical Philosopher of the Renaissance* (Padua: Editrice Antenore, 1986), chap. 1, "The Nature of the Soul," pp. 56-123.

36. Aquinas, *Summa theologiae,* vol. 13, Q. 93, "*De homine facto ad imaginem Dei,*" pp. 48-85. There is controversy over whether Thomas in this question is closely following Augustine, *On the Trinity,* or is adapting Augustine's interpretation to an Aristotelian metaphysic. In a recent publication D. Juvenal Merriel, *To the Image of the Trinity: A Study in the Development of Aquinas' Teaching* (Toronto: Pontifical Institute of Mediaeval Studies, 1990), argues that Thomas closely follows Augustine and that it is erroneous to interpret Q. 93 of the *Summa theologiae prima* as conforming to an Aristotelian metaphysics. Much of his book is in refutation of Marie-Joseph Serge de Laugier De Beaurecueil, O.P., "L'homme image de Dieu selon S. Thomas D'Aquin," *Études et recherches: Cahiers de théologie et de philosophie* 8 (1952): 45-82; and 9 (1953): 37-96. De Beaurecueil argues that Thomas superimposed on his Augustinian source a notion of human dignity that was more in conformity with Aristotle's intellectualist conception of the dominance of *mens* in the human soul and with Pseudo-Dionysius Areopagitica's vision of hierarchy. Though neither scholar utilizes the *Summa contra gentiles,* the chapters cited from this work indicate Thomas's concentrated concern with the intellect, both agent and possible, as the form of the human. In *Summa theologiae,* Q. 93, a. 6, "Whether the image of God is in man only in regard to the mind," Thomas says: "although in all creatures there is some likeness to God only in the rational creature a likeness to God is to be found in the mode of an image; but in all other creatures it is in the mode of a vestige" (*Summa theologiae,* 13:66).

37. Aquinas, *Summa contra gentiles,* II, 46, 3, p. 139; Anderson, p. 140.

as part of the imaginative faculty.[38] Thomas does not speak in terms of the "dignity of man" here, but this does not mean that he would exclude such a notion. In arguing for the separation of the intellect from the corporeal in his *Sententia,* he says:

> And this happens because the human soul on account of its nobility surpasses the capacity of corporeal matter and cannot be totally included within it, hence there remains for the soul some action in which corporeal matter does not communicate, and on account of this power of the soul for such action it does not have a bodily organ and in this sense the intellect is separate.[39]

I certainly do not regard the above as all that could be said concerning Thomas's conception of human beings and their power, but I intend it to show how Thomas relied on Aristotle for support of his doctrines. I also do not mean for this to stand for the full range of scholastic thought, whether of the thirteenth or fourteenth century, but only to indicate the kind of thinking that Lorenzo Valla was attempting to criticize.

III. Lorenzo Valla: "Born for Eternity"

Just as in the case of William of Saint-Thierry and of Thomas Aquinas, Lorenzo Valla (1407-57) does not represent every current of the religious and moral thought of his age, but his conceptions were surely among the most bold and confidently held ones. Renaissance humanists were in general critical of scholastic thought, but again for very specific reasons. In many ways their movement represented a sympathetic revival of twelfth-century culture where literary and rhetorical concerns were commonly linked to theological ones.

Well-known examples of Renaissance humanist or Platonist statements on the theme of the dignity of humanity as image of God were written by Petrarch, Manetti, Ficino, Pico, and others.[40] Although Lorenzo Valla clearly

---

38. Aquinas, *Summa contra gentiles,* II, chap. 60, p. 158; Anderson, p. 183. It is interesting that in *Summa theologiae,* Q. 93, a. 7, ad 3, Thomas argues, citing Augustine, *On the Trinity* 14, 7, that Augustine places the image of the divine Trinity in intelligence and will when they are actually engaged, rather than in what they are in the habitual retention of the memory: "Ex quo patet quod imaginem divinae Trinitatis potius ponit in intelligentia et voluntate actuali quam secundum quod sunt in habituali retentione memoriae." He adds: "licet etiam quantum ad hoc aliquo modo sit imago Trinitatis in anima, ut ibidem dicitur" (*Summa theologiae,* 13:74). Thomas paraphrases, subtly changing Augustine rather than directly quoting him here.

39. Aquinas, *Sententia libri de anima,* bk. III, chap. 1.

40. Trinkaus, part II, "The Human Condition in Humanist Thought: Man's Dignity

thought along such lines, he does not seem to have written a specific treatise on this theme. However, he did write on this theme in the first book of his *Retractatio,* his revised version of his *Repastinatio dialectice et philosophie,* both versions generally known as his *Dialectical Disputations.*[41] Strangely, the attention of scholars has been concentrated on the last two books (2 and 3) of this work, which deal with the meanings of terms and the modes of argumentation, branches of dialectic as such.[42]

Book 1, however, deals with the fundamentals *(primordia* or *praedicamenta)* of philosophy and is a deliberate attempt to displace the influence of Aristotle and his transmission through Boethius upon Christian thought, namely, scholastic theology and philosophy. Valla seeks to do this by demonstrating not only that Aristotle's statements are needlessly complex and confusing but also that his doctrines are totally unsuitable for Christian theology. If

---

and His Misery," and part III, "Four Philosophers on the Condition of Man: The Impact of the Humanist Tradition."

41. I will use Gianni Zippel's edition of both the earlier and the combined second and third redactions: Laurenti Valle, *Repastinatio Dialectice et Philosophie,* ed. Gianni Zippel, Thesaurus Mundi 21 (Padua: Editore Antenore, 1982). Volume I comprises Zippel's *Introduzione* and the text of the combined later redactions of 1448 and 1453; volume II, consecutively paginated, comprises the first redaction of 1439 and the indices. This reversal of the chronological order of the redactions is curious but justified by Zippel on the grounds that the second, 1448 version is the one that circulated in the only incunabular and early printed editions, including the *Opera omnia* of Valla of Basel 1540 and 1543, the so-called *vulgata.* The first redaction of 1439, existing in two manuscripts: Bibliotheca Vaticana, Cod. Urbinatis 1207 and Perugia, Archivio della Badia di San Pietro, Cod. 53, seems not to have been known to scholars until Gianni Zippel called attention to it in his "Note sulle redazione dalla 'Dialectica' di Lorenzo Valla," Convegno di Studi per il V Centenario della morte di Lorenzo Valla, in *Archivio storico per le Province Parmensi,* Quarta serie, IX (1957): 301-14. It was used as one of the basic texts for my chapter on Valla in *In Our Image and Likeness* of 1970 (written in November 1965), and another early usage was in Salvatore Camporeale, *Lorenzo Valla: Umanesimo e teologia* (Florence: Instituo nazionale di Studi sul Rinascimento, 1972). In returning to Lorenzo Valla in this and other recent articles, I have concentrated on the second/third redaction as edited by Zippel. I have come to the conclusion that these later redactions are at least in part (especially book 1) a commentary and correction of the 1439 redaction, which apparently had wider diffusion in the fifteenth century than the survival of but two manuscripts would indicate. This would account for the title: *Retractatio.* Book 1 is far more than a simple reedition and minor correcting of the earlier 1493 version, such as the 1453 redaction is of the 1448 one. It was thus possible for Zippel to edit a combined version of these later redactions, indicating in footnotes the insertions of version three into version two. This text will be cited as Zippel, page numbers, and line numbers.

42. See for example the cogent discussion of Valla's logic as presented in books 2 and 3 by John Monfasani, "Lorenzo Valla and Rudolph Agricola," *Journal of the History of Philosophy* 28 (1990): 181-200. A notable exception is Salvatore I. Camporeale's paper, "Lorenzo Valla 'Repastinatio, Liber Primus': Retorica e Linguaggio," in *Lorenzo Valla e l'umanesimo italiano,* ed. Ottavio Besomi and Mariangela Regoliosi (Padua: Editrice Antenore, 1986), pp. 217-39, as well as his *Lorenzo Valla, Umanesimo e teologia,* cited above.

this makes Valla sound in some way reminiscent of William of Ockham, so be it. I am not the only scholar to have suggested that Ockham may well have been one of Valla's unacknowledged sources, overtly critical though he was of Ockham's late medieval contemporaries and followers.[43] I will deal here much too sketchily with three chapters of book 1: "On 'Spirit' and on 'God' and 'Angels'" (chap. 8), "On the 'Soul'" (chap. 9), "On 'Virtues'" (chap. 10).

Valla was one of the Renaissance thinkers who held that reality had to be seen through the refracting medium of other human perspectives, in his case the collective perspective of the usages of a given language.[44] God and Christianity could be known through the Word, or language of God, namely, the Scriptures. But, says Valla,

> when apt words in divine matters are lacking, we may accommodate our speech as best we are able and compare God to things created by Him, with Paul saying: "The invisible things of the world are seen by the intellect through those which are visible."[45]

Following on that principle, Valla declares God, the divine Trinity, to be similar to the sun, which contains the three actions of vibration, lighting, and heating and their respective qualities. But these must be seen as the actions and qualities of a single essence. Thus "God the Father, potent and living" may be compared to the "sun, potent and living"; "God the Son, wise" to the sun, bright and shining; "God the Holy Spirit, loving" to the sun, hot and burning. Thus the trinitarian God would be one essence with three qualities.[46]

> And from this is the reason why the Greeks, if I am not mistaken, spoke of three *hypostases:* because they understood that beyond those three (if they may be so-called) "properties" of the Father and the Son and the Holy Spirit there existed below [*subesse*] something "substantial" which I call "essence," if only it may be thus called.[47]

We do not find the meaning of this matter in the Old or the New Testament. And we should let what God wanted to be hidden to remain hidden, "lest with Aristotle's gigantic arrogance, who wished nothing to seem to be unknown, we

---

43. E.g., see Zippel's *Introduzione*, p. lxxxvii n. 1; p. xci; p. ciii; p. civ with n. 2. I am quite aware that Ockham was also a student of Aristotle, as any scholastic was. It is his criticism of the ontologizing of abstract terms that makes Ockham comparable to Valla.

44. Another such thinker was Nicholas of Cusa, who is perspectival metaphysically and cosmically. Cf. Hans Blumenberg, *The Legitimacy of the Modern Age*, trans. R. M. Wallace (Cambridge: MIT Press, 1983), pp. 509-12 and nn. 42, 43.

45. Zippel, 52.1-5.

46. Zippel, 52.15-25.

47. Zippel, 52.25–53.4.

dare to scale heaven and tear it open."[48] This is what he is able to touch upon concerning God "so that the faculty of quibbling in such words as 'substance,' 'essence,' 'subject,' 'matter' might not be granted to anyone when we are speaking about God."[49]

The use of such terms in theology is trouble enough. Even worse are Aristotle's own conceptions of god. Aristotle's god, because it is a living being, or animal, and because it is bound together with the Ptolemaic cosmos (which he calls a many-headed hydra), is a "monster."[50] Moreover, Aristotle considered the world eternal and uncreated. But if human beings existed forever, how is it that the arts invented by them are only three thousand years old? If there were no human beings, there was no world, for no one is so lacking in intelligence as not to know that the world was created for us.[51]

Aristotle also continually confuses gods and demons:

And although he takes away action from the gods, he nevertheless attributes contemplation to them, as if to contemplate was not to act, and contemplation not action. . . . Thus, while he wishes to render men similar to the gods, he makes the gods similar to men. What? Does that great God do nothing but contemplate, has he no business himself, does he not show himself to another, does he do nothing to benefit us, does he bother neither the living nor the dead? Then what piety would there be, what religion, what sanctity, what reward of the virtues and punishment of the vices after this life? Finally, what greater relationship does he have with us than with the animals, if the same mortality is the end of both? These things are nothing to the Aristotelian god, but neither with Aristotle are there any souls after death of the body.[52]

Valla's God is instead highly providential. Moreover, though he does not talk in terms of God having absolute and ordained powers, as the scholastics of the *via moderna* and their predecessors did, he goes far beyond their limitation of God's omnipotence, that God cannot violate the law of contradiction. Valla says:

Aristotle denies that only God can cause it to happen that what has been done would not have been done: as if he could bring it about that what was to be done would not be done, or would have already been done, so that future time would be past or present and the present past or future. Or as if there would not be other things besides time and easier to do than that, as making the sweet not to be sweet and the bitter not to be bitter. . . . It ought not to be said that God cannot do these things which, when it piously and wisely

48. Zippel, 53.13-22.
49. Zippel, 53.23-25.
50. Zippel, 54.1-5, 56.4-14.
51. Zippel, 56.24–57.9.
52. Zippel, 58.9-23.

pleases him that these things should be done or be such, they should not be able to take away from him as though they were evil. For ultimately God can do those things which are of his wisdom and goodness to do.[53]

In effect, this is to argue that God cannot be restricted to the laws of nature as Christian Aristotelians, including Thomas, were suspected of doing by Bishop Étienne Tempier in the condemnations of 1277.[54]

When Valla begins his discussion of soul, he finds Aristotle inept for having attributed soul to plants and trees and hairs and horns rather than life, or *viriditas* (greenness), in the case of plants. As a result

> if trees, plants and herbs are to be said to live, certainly they ought not to be said to live by soul lest there be as many souls in my body as hairs, and more in the body of beasts in which there are more hairs which would be ridiculous to say.[55]

Aristotle also combines a rational and irrational soul, of which the first is neither generated nor corruptible, and the second is created from seeds making the soul similar to a centaur or a satyr or a triton: "Thus our soul would be biformed or bianimate, preposterously with the front part beastly and the rear divine."[56] Valla quotes several passages from Aristotle indicating how the rational soul rules the irrational and how the two are necessary for each other, and finally a long and complicated passage from the beginning of book 2 of *On the Soul*, about which he asks, "Who does not see that because of these obscure circumlocutions and confusions of words and of meanings Aristotle reasons most stupidly about the soul?"[57] Thomas gives a painstakingly careful explanation of the same passage in his commentary, citing other works of "the Philosopher."[58] Valla continues:

> The souls of the dead which reveal themselves to some by aspect or voice (as is affirmed by Homer and all maguses) could admonish [Aristotle] that they neither die, nor are born from bodies, nor lack affects, nor are compacted from two parts or natures as an animal of which the body is the vessel of the soul. For a part of the soul cannot be called the vessel of another part, unless perchance he wishes it to be the casing of a corporeal vessel; for I do not understand what he is saying, whether the rational part is part of God or lives

---

53. Zippel, 153.19-30. Cf. Aristotle, *Physics* II, 8, 198b18.

54. Cf. Edward Grant, "The Condemnation of 1277, God's Absolute Power, and Physical Thought in the Late Middle Ages," *Viator: Medieval and Renaissance Studies* 10 (1979): 211-44.

55. Zippel, 60.20-24.

56. Zippel, 62.5-7.

57. Zippel, 64.20-21. Cf. Aristotle, *De anima* II, 1, 412a6-21, 412b6-8.

58. Aquinas, *Sententia libri de anima*, pp. 67-73.

when the body is dead. If every thing generated dies or is corrupted, as he says, therefore either the soul of man dies or it is not generated, both of which are false.

Does Aristotle think the soul is a quality or a substance? If a quality, of what? If a substance, it would depart into nothing and likewise be made from nothing, both of which all schools of philosophy would deny.[59]

Valla then states his own position: the soul of animals is a substance produced by no natural cause but is made, created, or generated by divine nod from nothing, *ex nihilo*. Made from nothing, it will return to nothing. The animal soul does not differ from the human because, as Aristotle claims, the human participates in reason and in that sense in the divine, while animals lack reason, so that humans are called "a rational mortal animal"; the animal, "an irrational mortal animal." Both conceptions are wrong. Human souls and animal souls, says Valla, are composed of memory, intellect, and will. Memory is the first power, that of retaining in the soul what is received. The next power is intellect, or "reason," the office of which is to examine the things perceived and retained in the memory and carry a judgment. The third power, which does not exercise its function unless the memory holds and reason judges, is the will. Its function is to love and hate, which animals cannot do unless they judge, so that they also must have reason. The Aristotelians claim this is not reason but instinct, cleverly also denying memory and will in animals. But instinct is derived from will and gives an impetus to the will in humans and animals alike. Because animals also have these three powers, for this reason they are called *animalia* or ensouled.[60]

God made both human beings and beasts living souls and gave both the breath of life. But God himself breathed the breath of life into Adam and Eve and formed them with his own hands. This was not said about the animals. When God said, "Let us make human beings in our image, according to our likeness," this meant that God had breathed an eternal soul into the human being.[61] Here, then, is Valla's explanation of our dignity:

> Therefore it is by this that we differ from animals, that we are created eternal in the image and likeness of God, otherwise similar to the animals, just as the stars to mortal lights. Due to this we are erected toward heaven in soul and body and look upon the sublime; we are extended toward this sublimity not only in soul but also in body because God Himself (as I have said) fabricated us especially by his own hands; and therefore, because we are born for eternity, we understand eternal and celestial things, therefore we are

59. Zippel, 64.21–65.8.
60. Zippel, 65.25–68.19.
61. Zippel, 68.20–69.5.

capable of more, we wish for more and greater, we desire more, fear more, enjoy and suffer more.[62]

He is ready to concede that if reason is defined as the force of mind for understanding and loving divine things, human beings alone are capable of reason (as contemporary ecclesiastics hold), following philosophers rather than the Scriptures. And also Aristotle, Cicero, Quintilian, and Lactantius may be cited as granting limited reason to animals. But the Greeks call them *aloga*, from the word *logon*, meaning both speech and reason. This leads him to suspect that animals were called *aloga* from the beginning because they lacked speech, and afterward, because of the ambiguity of the word, the adjective *aloga* was used by captious philosophers to mean they lacked reason.[63]

The three powers of the soul transferred into bodies produce motion, resourceful use of humors, and heat. The heart as seat of the soul is constantly moving, and it sustains and provides heat and motion to the members as the sun does to the world. Neither the soul nor God remain quiet and do not move; therefore, it is insulting of Aristotle to name God the "prime mover." The three powers of the soul also make use of the five senses: the first for receiving objects, the second for judging them, the third for taking pleasure or pain from them, there being no *sensus communis,* another rejection of Aristotle's psychology.[64]

This leads directly into his discussion of the virtues, our final topic. Out of the first two powers of the soul, memory and reason, come the arts and the disciplines based either on knowledge or opinion and engaged in distinguishing the true and the false. In these powers are also all deliberation and judgment of future things, all invention and the first of the four cardinal virtues, prudence, or wisdom, the daughter of practice and memory.[65]

But Valla, as we shall see, plays down the cardinal virtues and definitely regards prudence as having nothing to do with morality as such, since it can be employed for both good and evil ends. Justice, fortitude, and temperance are all subordinate aspects of the one basic moral virtue which is Christian charity. Out of the final power of the soul, the will, come the affects, which he lists, following, I believe, Augustine's *City of God* 14, as

> fear and desire concerning the future, pleasure and distress in the present, although there is something of pleasure in desire and much distress in fear; also in past things there is delight and distress when we remember them.[66]

62. Zippel, 69.6-15.
63. Zippel, 69.16–70.27.
64. Zippel, 71.20–73.4.
65. Zippel, 73.13-24.
66. Zippel, 73.24–74.4. Cf. Augustine, *On the City of God* XIV, 5 and 6. The idea, as Augustine points out, is also Platonic and Stoic. He cites Cicero, *Tusc. Disp.* 4, 6, 11, obviously well known to Valla.

In the first version of the *Repastinatio,* which I used in *In Our Image and Likeness,* Valla was unclear as to whether the affects coming from the will engaged in virtue or vice in accord with the judgments of prudence, or whether they were independently committed good acts or bad depending on the degree of courage or timidity that had prompted them. Failure or omission to act out of weakness would have been deemed a vice.[67] Here in the *Retractatio* he says: "If the affects follow the leader reason, they are virtues, if not vices. From this nothing should be said to be done well or badly except by affect, and nothing else merits praise or vituperation than affect."[68] The word "virtue," he understands, can be used to indicate successful actions such as those of a physician, a teacher, a ruler, a shoemaker noting the form of a foot. Not knowledge of the law but justice is a virtue, not knowledge of divine and human things but to live according to the precept of wisdom: "praise is not for knowing the good but for willing it, not for knowing evil but not willing it."[69] Valla forcefully renounces the primacy of the intellect over the will: "And therefore those who constitute the intellect as the lord and ruler of the will err."[70] The intellect does not teach the will but rather the soul as a whole receives and holds knowledge, then inquires and judges, then loves and hates, "nor does the soul itself so rule itself that in one part is the mistress in another the maid, because if reason was able to rule over the will, certainly the will would never have sinned."[71]

Continuing, he asserts that prudence, which is in the intellect, is not a virtue, and proceeds to cite Cicero, Aulus Gellius, Jeremiah, Paul, and Plato on how prudence can mean malicious or evil intention.[72] He also argues against Aristotle's notion that virtue is a habit. Rather, a virtuous wish can suddenly occur by some impetus or "flight." And it can be as suddenly lost. On the other hand, knowledge and learning are acquired step-by-step.

> We speak more suitably of stages than what Aristotle does by "disposition" and "habit" since they [the Aristotelians] are scarcely able to distinguish between these two and between "first disposition" and "ultimate" (if any such ultimate may be said to exist). There are many and almost infinite steps and "first disposition" would be some habit and in so far as it is habit a disposition to further ones; thus all will be confused.[73]

---

67. Trinkaus, p. 159; Zippel, 413.22–414.11. In *In Our Image and Likeness,* I used the first version. He retreats to a more conventional view in later versions.

68. Zippel, 74.5-8.

69. Zippel, 74.21-22: "neque scire bonum laus est sed velle, nec nescire malum, sed nolle." Cf. Trinkaus, p. 48, for similar sentiments in Petrarch.

70. Zippel, 75.8-9.

71. Zippel, 75.13-17.

72. Zippel, 75.20–77.10.

73. Zippel, 78.20–79.17; cit. 79.2-10.

After a long section that subtly criticizes Aristotle's conception of virtue as the mean between extremes by demonstrating how it makes virtue a matter of prudence rather than of goodwill, and hence an intellectual and not a moral virtue,[74] Valla comes to the theological virtues. Only charity makes us good, for faith "is to believe God omnipotent, all-wise, and all-benevolent, and hope is to believe that such will be in you," both matters of the intellect,

> while charity, which is to love God and to love man on account of God, is an affect. Moreover when charity is involved in a battle it is called "fortitude" which is the only virtue called by its proper name, as *arete* in Greek and *virtus* in Latin not from man . . . but from power and powers from which *vir* perhaps, descends, for *vis* is converted from Greek *'is;* hence Greek *dunamis* (power), which is *vis* or *vires* or *potentia* (potency) or *potestas* (power), is usually translated as *virtus*.[75]

Why, then, is fortitude the same as charity? Were not the apostles who received the Holy Spirit, who is the charity of the Father and of the Son, rendered most brave from faintheartedness so as to undergo martyrdom?[76] In this way Valla reconciles the ancient idea of military virtue with Christian charity. Similarly he argues that justice is a mode of bearing love to others.[77] Moreover, virtue involves dominating one's passions, "from which it happens that virtue is nothing if it lacks an adversary."[78] Both virtue and vice seek a reward. Christ said "you will receive a hundred-fold and you will possess eternal life" when Peter asked, "what will there be for us?"[79] Hence God should be loved as the efficient cause of all the good things of this world and of beatitude in the next. We love the joy of loving. "When life has ceased we will know God with face revealed, as we ourselves are known, then there will be perfect charity" such as the seraphim enjoy.[80] Valla explicitly affirms what he had argued in *De vero bono* (On true good), that the pleasure of loving is beatitude, happiness, and the end,[81] not virtuous activity of the soul, as Aristotle claimed.

74. Zippel, 79.18–85.2.
75. Zippel, 85.8-20.
76. Zippel, 85.20–86.6.
77. Zippel, 86.24–87.14.
78. Zippel, 87.24–88.14.
79. Zippel, 88.23–89.9; Matt. 19:27, 29.
80. Zippel, 90.2–91.2; cit. 90.25-28.
81. Lorenzo Valla, *On Pleasure. De Voluptate*, ed. Maristella Lorch, trans. E. Kent Hieatt and Maristella Lorch (New York: Abaris Books, 1977), bk. III [XIII] [2], pp. 274, 275.

IV. Conclusion

It is possible that William of Saint-Thierry could have known Aristotle's *On the Soul,* as some of his interest in the relation of intellect to more organic modes of soul and in the mind/body problem might suggest, but this is unlikely. Thomas Aquinas, on the other hand, adheres as closely to Aristotle as Christianity permits. Although his discussion of how human beings are made in the image of God in *Summa theologiae* I, Q. 93, seems explicitly to follow Augustine's *De Genesi ad litteram* and *On the Trinity,* his stress is on the soul as intellect. Valla is also closely preoccupied with Aristotle, but as an object of criticism, and with Thomas indirectly. He differs from Aristotle and Thomas in making the tripartite soul of memory, intellect, and will common to both humans and animals. The difference between human and animal is ~~not~~ that in the human an intellectual soul is added to the animal's more corporeal nutritive, and sensitive souls, as Aristotle and Thomas held. The difference lies rather in that the soul of a human being, unlike that of an animal, is rendered eternal by God's direct creation of it in God's image and likeness, which is also the cause and the condition of the dignity of the human being.

Significantly Valla is basing his positions on a combination of philological analysis of the Greek terms of the New Testament and comparison of them with the Latin *and* a literal acceptance of the truth of the Scriptures once the original, correct meaning of its language is ascertained. In this lies his humanism and his criticism of Scholasticism, which was his original intention in the first version of the *Repastinatio* of around 1439. The final version of the early 1450s, as well as the middle version of the late 1440s, have been transformed into a critique of Aristotle based on his reading of the Greek texts, but the positions taken remain (with a few modifications toward the more orthodox and more customary) essentially those of the original version. These revised versions are also a confirmation of the views of his *De vero bono* which have been found difficult to interpret because they were voiced by three interlocutors in a dialogue. It is as well a further use of the methodology of his *Collatio Novi Testamenti,* the pioneering work of Renaissance and Reformation biblical criticism.

CHAPTER 5

The *Other* Theistic Logic:
Reflections on Schelling's Spinozism

PHILIP CLAYTON

In one sense, the following project is possible in its present form only if Louis Dupré is right about modernity. In *Passage to Modernity* Dupré has argued that the alleged passage from modern to "postmodern" thought is much less discontinuous than the passage from premodern to modern thought.[1] Major changes took place in the early Renaissance, changes that represented a decisive break with the realism of the Middle Ages. Here indeed a new way of thinking was born, one in which once-basic beliefs lost their sheen of certainty and in many cases ceased to be credible at all: God's continual intervention in the world; a purpose or direction to a history that is both led by God and points toward God; a semantics of direct realism; an anthropology that deduced human value from *Heilsgeschichte*. Out of Dupré's Yale seminars and lectures on the "Shape of Modernity" from the early 1980s, one phrase comes continually to mind, a phrase which served as a sort of litany in those classes (and which I have quoted to my own seminars repeatedly in the years since): With the advent of modernity, the human subject became the sole source of meaning and truth in the world. Each new philosophical development — Kantianism, naturalism, positivism, "postmodernism" — continues in one form or another the paradigm of modernity.

1. Louis Dupré, *Passage to Modernity: An Essay in the Hermeneutics of Nature and Culture* (New Haven: Yale University Press, 1993). The debts to Professor Dupré in the following pages, and in my other works, are too numerous to list. Perhaps above all, I owe to him a sense of what Christian philosophy really is: not a type of thinking that presupposes Christian theses as settled truths, and thus *closes* itself to insights from other realms of experience, but a philosophy that lives from an openness to acts of God — hence not absolute system but the thinking of freedom.

A recent *Review of Metaphysics* article makes a similar point.[2] In addition to an insightful "reading" of the claims of postmodernists and a painful critique of Rorty, Dupré shows that the main presuppositions of postmodernity — voluntarism and a nominalist theory of meaning — are in fact defining characteristics of modern thought. Both reflect a sense of *radical contingency:*

> The origin of this sense of radical contingency lies in the breakup of that ontotheological synthesis which had given classical, medieval, and early humanist culture its remarkable coherence as well as its confidence in knowing itself integrating with all reality. When this synthesis began to unravel in the fifteenth century, language and reality, power and dependence, immanence and transcendence separated into oppositional poles.[3]

This means that thinkers like Derrida are not inaugurating a new phase (or a new fashion) of intellectual activity, but are continuing to struggle with the same loss of foundations that has preoccupied philosophers since Descartes (and before). And they are no further from, or closer to, the metaphysical project than any other modern thinker. Appropriately, Dupré ends with the famous Kantian line, "Dieser Dämon (sc. metaphysics) läßt sich ja niemals beschwören" [This demon (metaphysics) will never be exorcised].

I believe that Dupré's thesis has important implications for one such "demon," reflection about God. For most philosophical theologians today presuppose something very different: that changes *within* the modern period have made *our* setting for thought about God qualitatively different from that of a Descartes or Spinoza; the concept of transcendence is supposedly no longer available to us, whereas it was to the early modern thinkers. One weakness of their thesis is clear already from the confusing array of turning points and alleged grounds that are advanced. Some say the situation changed with the development of modern physics; others appeal to Kant's *Critique of Pure Reason;* and others to the writings of "philosophers of suspicion" (Paul Ricoeur) such as Feuerbach, Marx, Nietzsche, and Freud. At any rate, we are told, at some point a transition took place, such that we late moderns face an impossibility unknown to our forebears, an impossibility that forces us away from talk of transcendence and into "the adventures of immanence."[4]

Dupré has shown convincingly that talk of a radical change is a myth — however much we have learned about the difficulties faced by language about God. It is not my goal here to exegete or explore the Dupréan thesis directly.

2. See Louis Dupré, "Postmodernity or Late Modernity? Ambiguities in Richard Rorty's Thought," *Review of Metaphysics* 47 (1993): 277-95.

3. Dupré, "Postmodernity or Late Modernity?" p. 294.

4. So Yirmiyahu Yovel, *Spinoza and Other Heretics,* 2 vols. (Princeton: Princeton University Press, 1989), vol. 2, *The Adventures of Immanence.*

Instead, I propose *applying* it as a working methodological hypothesis for theistic metaphysics. If Dupré is right, then there does not exist as great a separation between early modern reflection on God and our standpoint today as is sometimes claimed. Perhaps, then, these writings have more to offer us — stripped of some of their confidence, of course, "problematized," pluralized — than our positivist century has as of yet acknowledged. The difficulties of (re)appropriating the Spinoza tradition today are daunting, and there is no promise of success. But, as Dupré reminds us, we are no closer to exorcising the "demon" of the quest to think the transcendent than were the founders of modernity. I therefore suggest using his argument as an encouragement to wrestle again with the texts and ideas that lie somewhat closer to the birth hour of modernity.

I

There has always been an "other" side to Christian theism, a side that resists the sharp separation between God and world of classical or orthodox theology. To use what can be no more than labels, we could call the two strands the Aristotelian and the Neoplatonic. "Aristotelian" or classical theology gives one the ability to speak of God as the highest being, the creator *ex nihilo* of a world distinct from himself. One finds, of course, an other, a Platonic side to classical theology, such as in the acknowledgment that all existing things, insofar as they exist, participate in the being of God. But any possible heretical implications of this participation in Being are held in check by the Aristotelian structure. The discreteness of the forms requires a clear set of distinct ideas and species, and the dependence of form on matter for individuation preserves distinct individuals.

By contrast, Neoplatonism represents the "other" theistic logic, no longer held in check by the careful analytical constraint of the forms. Because it begins with concepts such as the One or the infinite, it has tended to emphasize the God-infusedness of the world as an emanation of God rather than the separateness of the world, and the *via negativa* rather than the knowledge of the divine. This tendency of thought — for to speak of a "school" would be misleading — finds its greatest expression in the mystical philosophy of Plotinus, and then again and again in the history of medieval thought. Separate studies would be required to trace its various lines of influence and to chronicle its diverse forms in the individual thinkers I have in mind: in John Scotus Eriugena,[5] in Meister Eckhart,

---

5. For one impressive example, see Werner Beierwaltes, "Eriugena. Aspekte seiner Philosophie," in his *Denken des Einen. Studien zur neuplatonischen Philosophie und ihrer Wirkungsgeschichte* (Frankfurt: Klostermann, 1985).

in Nicholas of Cusa,[6] in Giordano Bruno;[7] but also in "mainline" early modern philosophers such as Descartes[8] and Leibniz.[9]

Our theme is one such "other theistic logic" in the modern period. Separate stories would have to be told about the "other theism" in Descartes, Malebranche, Pascal, the Cambridge Platonists, Leibniz, and others. Our narrative focuses instead on just one figure, the Plotinus of modernity, Baruch de Spinoza; on just one metaphysical/theological question, the relationship of God to world; and in particular on just one of the many philosophers influenced by his thought, Schelling.

Spinoza's basic insight was that a substance cannot be dependent on any other substance; hence objects in the world cannot be separate substances that depend on God as their creator. In one sense his famous equation, *deus sive natura* (God or nature), merely spelled out the consequences from Descartes's own theory of substance. According to Descartes's *Principia*, a substance is that which requires nothing else in order to exist; yet

> there is only one substance which can be understood to depend on no other thing whatsoever, namely God. In the case of all other substances, we perceive that they can exist only with the help of God's concurrence.[10]

Descartes did not of course draw a monistic moral from this view, perhaps because that would have destroyed the realm of clearly and distinctly perceived entities on which knowledge of the world is to rest. Unfortunately, there is no detailed or adequate treatment in Descartes of how these two perspectives are to be united. His failure to unite the two ontological approaches (independent things versus omni-dependence on God) set the stage for the developments in ontology over the next several centuries. In the tradition running by way of Malebranche to Spinoza, Descartes's halfhearted substantivalism was gradually

6. See the special issue of the *American Catholic Philosophical Quarterly* 64 (1990), edited by Louis Dupré and devoted to the thought of Nicholas of Cusa.

7. Werner Beierwaltes has drawn attention to the Neoplatonic aspects in Bruno's work in his *Identität und Differenz* (Frankfurt: Klostermann, 1980), pp. 194ff., 200ff., and in his chapter "Actaeon," in *Denken des Einen*, pp. 424-35.

8. See Philip Clayton, "Descartes and Infinite Perfection," *American Catholic Philosophical Association Proceedings* (1992): 137-47; cf. my *Das Gottesproblem. Gott und Unendlichkeit in der neuzeitlichen Philosophie* (Paderborn: Ferdinand Schöningh Verlag, 1996), chap. 2. An English version will appear as *Toward a Pluralistic Metaphysics: Models of God in Early Modern Philosophy* (under consideration).

9. See, e.g., George McDonald Ross, "Leibniz and Renaissance Neoplatonism," *Studia leibnitiana Supplementa* 23 (1983): 125-34. G. Rodier claims *"une profounde influence"* in *Revue de Métaphysique et de Morale* 10 (1902): 552-64; but I do not find Ross's references to Leibniz's own writings sufficient to defend this strong thesis.

10. René Descartes, *Principia*, pt. 1, art. 51, in *Oeuvres de Descartes*, ed. Charles Adam and Paul Tannery (Paris: J. Vrin, 1964-76), vol. 8A, p. 24.

discarded and the independence criterion for substance was given unlimited sway: only one substance exists; all other so-called substances become modes of the One.

Clearly, this claim presented a problem for Christian orthodoxy: if God is the one substance, there is no room for the creation of a world outside of God. As Schulz describes the dilemma, "Seen from Spinoza's perspective, Christian doctrine represents the futile attempt, on the one hand, to posit God as almighty and, on the other hand, to define man in opposition to him as a nature which, in spite of its dependence on God, is in fact relatively self-sufficient."[11] To the Neoplatonist (leaving out for the moment all historical nuancing, and treating him or her as an ideal type), classical theism always seemed to stop short of acknowledging the final implications in the doctrine of God. The really highest ontological principle must be the absolute One, above all distinctions and divisions; and everything that exists must emanate from and participate in that One. Only evil or nonbeing (if it even makes sense to speak of such things as existing) would be excluded from the highest principle. Likewise, for the Spinozist the highest principle must be pure substance. But substance, rigorously conceived, must be totally independent; and it cannot be that *more than* one thing is independent in this fashion. Since nothing else than the One Substance can be a substance, everything else must exist as modes of that substance, and hence as ontologically dependent on it. All that exists is the One and its modes; all other "things" — and, what for Spinoza amounts to the same thing, all other conceptual distinctions — have only relative truth or being. For both Spinoza and Plotinus, the motivation for monism emerges out of the same impulses that theism is trying to express, that is, out of reflection on the nature of the highest (being).[12]

By speaking of Spinozism as the "other" theism, I imply both that it was clearly distinguished from orthodox, acceptable theism and that it played in

11. "Von Spinoza her gesehen stellt die christliche Lehre den unsinnigen Versuch dar, Gott einerseits als allmächtig anzusetzen und andererseits ihm gegenüber den Menschen als ein Wesen zu bestimmen, das bei aller Abhängigkeit doch relativ selbständig ist" (Walter Schulz, *Der Gott der neuzeitlichen Metaphysik* [Pfullingen: GüntherNeske, 1957], p. 66).

12. With this parallel I do not maintain that Spinoza's is a fundamentally Neoplatonic position, though this has been argued. For an (only partially successful) case for Spinoza's Neoplatonism, see Paul Oskar Kristeller, "Stoic and Neoplatonic Sources of Spinoza's *Ethics*," *History of European Ideas* 5 (1984): 1-15. The connection I intend is much closer to what Beierwaltes has in mind when he says that the main characteristics of Plotinus's *"All-Einheits-Lehre"* are "Paradigmen für spätere All-Einheits-Lehren . . . , ob sie nun mit Plotin geschichtlich verbindbar sind oder nicht" (Beierwaltes, *Denken des Einen*, p. 64). It is in this sense also that Beierwaltes develops his fruitful parallels between Plotinus and Schelling, both in this work (pp. 64-72) and in *Platonismus und Idealismus* (Frankfurt: Vittorio Klostermann, 1972). It is certainly no coincidence that Schelling devoted a whole dialogue to Bruno, on the Neoplatonic aspects in which see Beierwaltes, *Identität und Differenz*, pp. 176-240.

the eighteenth century an increasingly influential role as orthodoxy's Other. The former claim is indisputable. The (apparently) monistic nature of the *Ethics* — hence "pantheistic," hence "fatalistic," hence "atheistic" — turned it into an increasingly hated whipping boy for almost a hundred years after Spinoza's death. Indeed, there is something symbolic in Spinoza's being ousted from his synagogue at age twenty-four for teaching that "God had a body": it was clearly the first of many orthodox (mis)interpretations of Spinoza's monism. Already by the time of Pierre Bayle's famous article on Spinoza, the longest article in the thirteen-volume *Dictionnaire,* Spinozism had become the evil other to orthodoxy. According to Bayle; it is "the most absurd and monstrous hypothesis that can be imagined, and the most contrary to the most evident notions of our mind."[13] At the same time, Bayle admits that "few people are suspected of adhering to his doctrine; and among those who are suspected of it, few have studied it; and among the latter, few have understood it, and most of them are discouraged by the difficulties and impenetrable abstractions that attend it."[14]

What, then, of the *influence* of Spinozism? At first, European thinkers dismissed Spinoza with charges that he was evil, satanic, and so forth.[15] There were few serious studies of his work before (roughly) the 1760s,[16] when Jacobi, the great defender of orthodoxy, became worried about pantheistic tendencies in Lessing's thought and published his conversation with Lessing, in which the latter allegedly identified himself with Spinoza's views: Jacobi: "Then you would indeed be more or less in agreement with Spinoza"; Lessing: "If I am to call myself by anybody's name, then I know none better."[17] Over the following forty years, despite stiff resistance from orthodox thinkers such as Jacobi — or perhaps *because* of them — the "Spinozistic option" gradually lost its horror and became a position that one could take out in public. Prepared by the work of Moses Mendelssohn (especially in the *Morgenstunden*) and by the Sturm und Drang movement, the major culminating steps are associated with the names Schleiermacher (in the *Speeches*), the later Fichte, and especially the later Schel-

13. Pierre Bayle, "Spinoza," *Dictionnaire historique et critique de Pierre Bayle,* nouvelle édition (Paris: Desoer Libraire, 1820), vol. 13, pp. 416-68. See same entry, vol. 5 of *Mr. Bayle's Historical and Critical Dictionary: The Second Edition* (London, 1738).

14. Bayle, "Spinoza," French 13:418, English 5:217.

15. For a detailed account of the early criticisms, see Han-Ding Hong, *Spinoza und die deutsche Philosophie* (Aalen: Scientia, 1989), and the classic study by Max Grünwald, *Spinoza in Deutschland* (Berlin: Verlag von S. Calvary, 1897).

16. See my *Toward a Pluralistic Metaphysics,* chap. 7.

17. See Gérard Vallée, ed., *The Spinoza Conversations between Lessing and Jacobi: Text with Excerpts from the Ensuing Controversy,* trans. G. Vallée, J. B. Lawson, and C. G. Chapple (Lanham, Md.: University Press of America, 1988), p. 85. I have examined the *Spinozastreit* in detail in "The Temptations of Immanence" (paper read to the American Philosophical Association Central Division, May 1994, publication forthcoming).

ling. Each deserves a treatment of his own; I limit myself here to the work of Schelling.

II

There is no question about the strong influence of Spinoza on Schelling.[18] Schelling's opus represents, more than anything else, the attempt to rethink Spinoza's ontological insights in light of Kant's critique of reason and the subsequent idealist focus on the constitutive activities of the human subject.[19] Notwithstanding the absence of a polished system on the model of Hegel — or perhaps *because* of its absence — Schelling manages to express many of the desiderata of a panentheistic theory of the highest principle or God. This project appears in three major guises in the course of his career: first in the form of his early transcendental idealism, which he understood as overcoming Fichte's subjective idealism by transforming it into a transcendental system; later through his doctrine of divine potencies; and finally in his late attempt at developing a "Christian pantheism."[20]

Schelling's Kantianism is expressed *(inter alia)* in his dualism, in the no that he opposes to the pan-rationalism of the ontotheologians. In my view, and in that of his major defenders,[21] he has been the most successful philosopher in the Western tradition in thinking God or infinite substance *as subject*. This idealist emphasis, he claims, contrasts sharply with the *Ethics*, which "determined the absolute as an absolute *object*" (*SW* 1:242 n). Schelling's goal was to

18. Schelling speaks of him as "the sole son and heir of true science throughout the entire modern period" (*SW* 8:340), in whom are "scattered the seeds of higher developments" (10:40). Spinozism represents "realism in its most sublime and perfect shape" (4:110). The parenthetical references are to F. W. J. von Schelling, *Sämtliche Werke*, ed. K. F. A. Schelling, 14 vols. (Stuttgart, 1856-61); hereafter cited as *SW*. For recent accounts of Spinoza's influence on Schelling, see Manfred Walther, ed., *Spinoza und der Deutsche Idealismus* (Würzburg: Königshausen and Neumann, 1991), esp. the essays by Ehrhardt and Dietzsch.

19. In her important recent book, Birgit Sandkaulen-Bock (*Ausgang vom Unbedingten. Über den Anfang in der Philosophie Schellings* [Göttingen: Vandenhoeck & Ruprecht, 1990]) argues that Schelling (after his break with Fichte's idealism) attempted to accomplish a systematic completion of Kant's critique by means of a combination of the philosophical resources of Spinoza and Jacobi, and that the repeated failures of this project led him through a long series of new starts and repeated failures right up to the late philosophy.

20. *SW* 14:66. On the last see Horst Fuhrmans, "Der Gottesbegriff der Schellingschen positiven Philosophie," in *Schelling-Studien. Festgabe für Manfred Schröter zum 85. Geburtstag*, ed. Anton Mirko Koktanek (München: R. Oldenbourg, 1965), pp. 9-47.

21. Above all in the classic work by Walter Schulz, *Die Vollendung des deutschen Idealismus in der Spätphilosophie Schellings* (Stuttgart: W. Kohlhammer, 1955).

escape from Spinoza's "pure realism" (and from Fichte's "pure idealism") in order to conceive God as genuinely personal.

As a direct consequence of this goal, Schelling turned away from both determinism and fatalism, the "system of necessity" into which Spinoza had fallen.[22] This correction of Spinoza explains, in no small part, his greatest publication, the *Freiheitsschrift* of 1809, in which the concept of freedom rose to a position of centrality. The human agent is able to act freely, even in light of knowledge of the absolute, as long as freedom is understood correctly (*SW* 7:384) and an adequate theory of subjectivity is in place. Spinoza had not properly distinguished between empirical necessity and a special internal necessity, whereas Schelling, along with the other idealists, sharply separated them. In particular, the creation of the world can be understood as a free act as long as the Absolute is pervasively subject *and* is determined by its nature alone. For the same reason, as *The Ages of the World* tries to show (*SW* 8:269ff.), universal history can also be understood as an open process of genuine or novel development. If God is to be free, the creation of the world cannot be a necessary result of God's nature. And if God is free, his actions cannot be known in advance. God, too, is in a process of continual and nonpredictable development. Schelling speaks of a *"Werden Gottes":* God is aware of himself only in becoming (*SW* 7:403), such that "the eternal movement, within which nature is only the beginning, is really only a progressive actualization of the highest, from which every step that follows comes closer to the actualized divinity."[23]

Unfortunately, Schelling did not abandon his early idealist roots as fully as he should have; the problem is not that his philosophy of freedom moved him too far from Hegel but that he stayed too close. Even in his late work Schelling still thought he could identify the "Begriff des bloß unzweifelhaft Existirenden" [the notion of a being whose existence is simply beyond doubt], an idealist analog to necessary being, and demonstrate its divinity (*SW* 13:159). I suggest instead that his own insight into the centrality of freedom, thought through to its end, should have led him to abandon the dream of a "purely

---

22. *SW* 10:47. Schelling writes, "Spinoza calls God *causa sui*, but in the narrower sense that he *is* by the mere necessity of his nature, therefore *only is* without being able to be retained as ability to be (as *causa*); the cause has vanished completely in the operation and stands simply as *substance*" (*SW* 10:35). Spinoza's God is *das Seiende* but not *das Sein* (11:372). "Had [Spinoza] posited the living substance instead of the dead, blind one, then that dualism of attributes would have offered a means of actually comprehending the finiteness of things" (10:44).

23. The argument is that "die ewige Bewegung, von der die Natur nur der Anfang ist, eigentlich nur eine fortschreitende Verwirklichung des Höchsten ist, von der jede folgende Stufe der verwirklichten Gottheit näher ist" (Schelling, *Die Weltalter. Fragmente, in den Urfassungen von 1811 und 1813*, ed. Manfred Schröter [München: Biederstein Verlag, 1946], p. 234).

rational" philosophy.[24] Of course, the freedom argument is only one of many reasons to leave behind the paradigm of a self-grounding philosophy. The problem is that a *Letztbegründung* (final grounding) for philosophy would have to be either deductive or dialectical. But a deductive philosophy would be linear, and hence excluded from letting its conclusions feed back to (and perhaps alter) its starting points, and purely formal, and hence unable, even in principle, to thematize the relationship between its premises and the *thinking* of its premises; and finally, arbitrary, because it could not ground its own starting points, since they would remain external to philosophy itself.[25] Hence a self-grounding philosophy would have to be dialectical and self-referential, in the sense of a system of thought that emerges from (or, just *is*) a necessary movement of Reason as present already in its first concepts (Being-Nothing-Becoming) and that lifts itself upward in an unbroken movement to its highest concept, Absolute Spirit.[26] But neither Hegel nor his reconstructors have been successful either in finding any such all-inclusive starting point or in demonstrating, either empirically or a priori, the necessary movement of reason that such a dialectic would demand.[27]

The failure of the dream of self-grounding philosophy provides the hermeneutical lens for a modern-day (re)reading of Schelling. Not so much his continuous wrestling to create an absolute system recommends him to us today, but rather his *criticisms* of such a project (whether or not he himself fully took them to heart). Schelling was his own greatest critic, remaining dissatisfied with each of his drafts of a "system of transcendental idealism." This awareness of the intrinsic difficulties with *system*, along with the stress on freedom both divine and human, makes Schelling an indispensable guide to theistic metaphysics today.

In works like the *Freiheitsschrift* — but equally in his critical attitude toward his own work — Schelling models *philosophia negativa*. According to

24. For a clear sense of how much Schelling remained indebted to this idea, see his "Darstellung der reinrationalen Philosophie," the "philosophische Einleitung in die Philosophie der Mythologie," in vol. 9 of the *Sämtliche Werke*.

25. So Wolfgang Cramer, "Philosophie als Letztbegründung. Das Absolute," chap. 6 of *Das Absolute und das Kontingente. Untersuchungen zum Substanzbegriff* (Frankfurt: Klostermann, 1959), pp. 57-68, e.g., p. 60. Obviously, I am drawing from Cramer's line of argument exactly the opposite conclusion to the one he hopes the reader will draw.

26. This, of course, is the claim made in Hegel's *Logik*. The demands of a truly dialectical philosophy as they arose out of Hegel's interaction with his critics are brilliantly presented in the recent major study by Bernd Burkhardt, *Hegels "Wissenschaft der Logik" im Spannungsfeld der Kritik. Historische und systematische Untersuchungen zur Diskussion um Funktion und Leistungsfähigkeit von Hegels "Wissenschaft der Logik" bis 1831* (Hildesheim: Georg Olms Verlag, 1993).

27. At any rate, I presuppose this in what follows; a full defense of this claim is clearly not possible here.

the "Darstellung der reinrationalen Philosophie" [the presentation of a purely rational philosophy], his philosophy should be called negative, "inasmuch as it — no matter how important or even indispensable — knows nothing at all with regards to that which is alone worthy of knowing, for it posits its principle only by cutting it out [from the whole], i.e. as a negative principle."[28] In Schelling's later period the moment of negation is at its strongest. At several points he even speaks of an abandoning of all knowledge. For example, philosophy's "first step is not a knowing but rather expressly an unknowing, an abandoning of all knowing. . . . By letting go of knowing, humans make room for that which is real knowledge, namely for the absolute subject, of which I have shown that it is precisely knowledge itself."[29] In the following paragraphs Schelling describes this experience (or *Anschauung*) as *"Ekstase,"* referring to Plato's famous phrase, "There is no other starting point for philosophy than wonder *(das Erstaunen)*" (*SW* 9:230). In fact, already in *The Ages of the World* Schelling is willing to speak of a *"nichtwissenden Wissen,"* an unknowing knowing:

> [The absolute subject] can only be known by means of an unknowing knowing. For all knowledge refers first of all to an object; where there is no object, there is also no knowledge — or, if there is knowledge, only an unknowing knowledge. Exactly this is the point of that old expression: only when it is not sought will it present itself; if one tries to objectify it, it will disappear; only through non-recognition or non-knowing will it be known *(ignorando cognoscitur)*; if one attempts to comprehend it, it will elude the seeker.[30]

God is the "Lord of Being" or "incomprehensible Being" (*SW* 14:337); hence God can be "known" only in negation and silence. In a well-known passage that holds up the philosophy of the Hindu Brahmans as a model, Schelling writes of the "overcoming of oneself" *(Selbstentschlagung)* and the "absolute unknowing of itself" that is the correct response in the face of "purest Being," that is,

---

28. It is negative "indem sie, so wichtig, ja unentbehrlich sie ist, doch in Beziehung auf das allein Wissenswerthe nichts weiß; denn sie setzt das Princip nur durch Ausscheidung, als negative . . ." (*SW* 11:562).

29. "[Der Philosophie] erster Schritt ist nicht ein Wissen, sondern vielmehr ausdrücklich ein Nichtwissen, ein Aufgeben alles Wissens für den Menschen . . . indem Er sich des Wissens begibt, macht er Raum für das, was das Wissen ist, nämlich für das absolute Subjekt, von dem gezeigt ist, daß es eben das Wissen selbst ist" (Münchner Vorlesungen, 9:228).

30. "Eben darauf zielte der andere Ausdruck, daß es nur vermöge eines nichtwissenden Wissens gewußt werde, denn alles Wissen bezieht sich zunächst auf einen Gegenstand, wo also kein Gegenstand ist auch kein Wissen oder wenn Wissen nur nichtwissendes Wissen. Eben dahin zielt auch jener alte Ausdruck: nur wenn es nicht gesucht werde stelle es sich dar, suche man es aber gegenständlich zu machen, so entfliehe es, nur durch Nichterkennen werde es erkannt (ignorando cognoscitur), wolle man es aber mit ihm zum Wissen bringen so entziehe es sich dem Wollenden" (Schelling, *Die Weltalter. Fragmente*, p. 214).

that Being *(das Seyn)* from which the understanding can win nothing, the Being that it only brings to expression by being silent and only comprehends by not wishing to comprehend. For this Being cannot be comprehended in the same way as the objects in other forms of knowledge, that is, by one's moving out of oneself. Instead, it can be grasped only by means of a holding in oneself, a remaining still within oneself.[31]

At his most extreme, Schelling even speaks of a complete negation of the finite (cf. *SW* 1:440; 6:161) in light of the "boundless Nothing" *(bodenloses Nichts,* 13:7f., 1:243f.; but see 6:155).

III

Yet what is fascinating in this thinker is that he combines a sense for transcendence and the breakdown of language with a clear awareness that the reflective "demon" cannot be exorcised, even when it threatens to drive us finally from metaphysics to metaphor, mythology, and the limits of silence. Schelling's late *positive* philosophy is characterized by the implicit goal of responding to reality as it actually presents itself to us, rather than deducing its attributes a priori. (The necessary failure of the deductive project is the subject of what he calls *negative* philosophy.) Since the goal of this philosophy is a knowledge of God, one has to look to, and hence leave room for, a revelation of God. Thus Schelling's positive philosophy has been described as "a philosophy of revelation."[32] He correctly sees that the task of theistic metaphysics is to do justice to both religion and thought, to both *religiöse Philosophie* and *philosophische Religion* (*SW* 13:134). As Pöltner writes,

> Schelling intends to abrogate neither religion nor thinking. On the one hand, God in his divinity is supposed to burst upon thought; thought should be brought before *God* and not before a mere idea of reason. On the other hand, God is supposed to become present *to thinking,* which means that this presence should occur as the achievement of reason in its independence.[33]

31. "das Seyn, dem der Verstand nichts abgewinnen kann, das er nur ausspricht, indem er schweigt, und nur erkennt, indem er es nicht erkennen will. Denn es wird nicht erkannt wie der Gegenstand in anderem Erkennen, indem man aus sich herausgeht, sondern vielmehr im an-sich-Halten, im selbst-still-Stehen" (*SW* 13:251).

32. Thomas Buchheim, *Eins von Allem. Die Selbstbescheidung des Idealismus in Schellings Spätphilosophie* (Hamburg: Felix Meiner, 1992), p. 17.

33. "Schelling will weder der Religion noch dem Denken Abbruch tun. Es soll auf der einen Seite dem Denken Gott in seiner Göttlichkeit aufgehen, das Denken soll vor Gott — und nicht vor eine bloße Vernunft-Idee gebracht werden. Auf der anderen Seite soll Gott

I have argued that the "other" theism, the Spinozism on which Schelling relied, teetered on the margins of orthodoxy. This "both inside and outside" status is *philosophically* significant, insofar as it suggests that late-model Spinozists like Schelling brought to expression temptations that were inherent within orthodox theism itself, which means within the philosophical categories on which it relied. If I am right, theism in the context of modern philosophy tends of its own weight toward conclusions that are (broadly speaking) Spinozistic. In particular, the notion of God, taken in its most stringent form, tends toward Spinoza's *hen kai pan,* the one and all, and hence tends to challenge the independent existence of objects and persons in the world. There is something pantheistic about theism itself.

But how exactly is this pantheism to be understood? It's not sufficient to define it as "God is everything," a phrase which means everything and therefore nothing.[34] Schelling discusses three possible interpretations of Spinoza's pantheism that are *not* adequate: (a) everything is God; (b) every individual thing is God; (c) all things are nothing. Yet, Schelling shows, each of these positions is problematic: in *(a)* God must be *more than* the sum of all existing things (and clearly Spinoza and Schelling meant this "more than" when they interpreted God as the infinite ground of finite things). Schelling called *(b)* "the most common" view of God (*SW* 10:45), since it leads to a fetishism where every object becomes an object of religious adoration and the "moreness" of God is denied. And *(c)* attempts to express the starting point, "God is everything," as a negative pronouncement, the denial of any real existence to things; as such it represents the opposite of *(a)*.[35]

What emerges as the most viable understanding of the pantheistic insight in the period from Spinoza to Schelling, when all the inadequate options have been eliminated, is *all-in-God*, or what has come to be called pan*en*theism. Beierwaltes explains this view in connection with Plotinus and Schelling as

> the insistence on the transcendence or the absolute difference of the One in contradistinction to everything else that comes from or exists "outside" of it;

---

dem Denken gegenwärtig werden, d. h. diese Gegenwart soll als der Vollzug der selbständigen Vernunft geschehen" (Günther Pöltner, "Der Gottesbegriff beim späten Schelling," in *Wahrheit und Wirklichkeit. Festgabe für Leo Gabriel zum 80. Geburtstag,* ed. Peter Kampits et al. [Berlin: Duncker and Humblot, 1983], pp. 101-10, quote p. 102).

34. This is a point that Dupré has made in lectures for a number of years.

35. See Schelling's *Freiheitsschrift, SW* 7:340-45, and the commentary in Martin Heidegger, *Schellings Abhandlung Über das Wesen der menschlichen Freiheit,* ed. Hildegard Feick (Tübingen: Max Niemeyer Verlag, 1971), pp. 82-90. As always, matters are more complicated than a brief argument indicates. For a discussion of early texts that point more toward *(a)*, see Horst Fuhrmans, *Schellings Philosophie der Weltalter. Schellings Philosophie in den Jahren 1806-1821. Zum Problem des Schellingschen Theismus* (Düsseldorf: L. Schwann, 1954), pp. 66ff.

and at the same time the equally decisive contention that this principle is *in* everything and everything only exists *through* it.[36]

From shortly after 1800, in always changing forms, Schelling's philosophy represents a continual struggle to express this insight in a manner that is systematic while not usurping the freedom of the highest personal being.

How is this God to be understood? We might say that Schelling accepted Spinoza's thinking on the Absolute (at least as interpreted by Jacobi) as far as it went, and took this to be the *first* pole of God, God in his aseity. In the early works, where the positive connection to Spinoza is the strongest, one finds the fullest treatment of the theory of the Absolute. But from early on Schelling *also* reads Spinoza through the lenses of the freedom problem; namely, that the very success of the Spinozistic system seems to eliminate any place for an absolute subject. A free God would have to be freely self-unfolding, and hence involved in a process of becoming.[37] As of the *Freiheitsschrift* Spinoza's God becomes the free unfolding of himself into a world. Still, the framework remains panentheist because of the insistence that there are individual substances within the one divine substance. They are "inseparable but distinguishable" (*SW* 7:358), or, put differently, they have "derivative absoluteness" (7:347). The distinguishability stems from our *finitude,* that is, from *the contingency of all that exists.*

Methodologically, this midcourse correction of Spinoza turned Schelling in the direction of romanticism and mysticism, earning him the title of "the philosopher of German Romanticism."[38] On the one hand, one finds (as in Spinoza) a thoroughgoing naturalism; on the other, the subject-object identity that characterizes idealism allowed him to speak of God in vitalistic and teleological terms. Substance became a living force, manifested by all of nature. By moving from Spinoza's mechanism to an organic philosophy, Schelling was able to view mind and body as "different degrees of organization and development of living force."[39]

36. "[Panentheismus heißt] das Insistieren auf der Transzendenz oder absoluten Differenz des Einen gegenüber allem Anderen, was aus und 'außer' ihm ist, zugleich aber die ebenso entschiedene Behauptung, daß das Prinzip in Allem ist, was durch es allerest ist" (Beierwaltes, *Denken des Einen,* p. 64).

37. One is thus tempted to present Schelling's *"Kehre"* around 1805 as analogous to Hartshorne's movement away from the God of perfection to a process notion of God.

38. On the interaction with romanticism see, classically, Fuhrmans, *Schellings Philosophie der Weltalter,* pp. 75-151, e.g., esp. p. 79. On the interaction with German mysticism see Robert F. Brown, *The Late Philosophy of Schelling: The Influence of Boehme on the Works of 1809-1815* (Lewisburg, Pa.: Bucknell University Press, 1977), and Thomas Franklin O'Meara, O.P., *Romantic Idealism and Roman Catholicism: Schelling and the Theologians* (Notre Dame: University of Notre Dame Press, 1982), esp. pp. 78ff.

39. Frederick Beiser, "Introduction: Hegel and the Problem of Metaphysics," in *The Cambridge Companion to Hegel,* ed. Beiser (Cambridge: Cambridge University Press, 1993), pp. 1-24, quote p. 6.

The pantheistic side remains: "everything that exists is, insofar as it exists, God" (*alles, was ist, ist, insofern es ist, Gott; SW* 6:157). But now the teleology is expressed through a panentheistic correction: "By 'the Absolute' Schelling understands that which transcends, encompasses, and enfolds within itself everything that is actual, the ideal as well as the real."[40]

Clearly, such a God must *be* in becoming. God is *"ein werdender Gott"*; in him there is "an eternal becoming" (*SW* 7:432). In the process of "external-ization" (*Entäußerung,* 10:124) it is possible to say that "God creates himself" (*Gott macht sich selbst,* 7:432). Yet, since we find negativity in the world, there must also have been "something negative in God" (8:73). Hence Schelling comes to speak of "the dark ground" (*der dunkle Grund,* 7:360) or the "foundation" (8:25) or "what is Real and without consciousness" in God (7:435) or even of "Nature — within Gott" (7:358). Because God includes or contains the finite, he is "a suffering God" (*ein leidender . . . Gott,* 4:252) — as well as being "the existing God" (7:435) or "God as subject" (8:25) or "the conscious God" (8:62). The same freedom that brings this dark side also holds out the hope of a final positive culmination of the process (7:429, 408; cf. 9:221): at the end of the whole process God will have "evolved out of himself to that which is most perfect in act" (*zum actu Vollkommensten,* 8:65). I interpret Schelling as begin-ning with the (at least potential) subjectivity of God: *because* God is subject, and *as* subject, he can function as Ground, which is the most foundational designation of God's relation to the world.

Under Schelling's construal of the problem, freedom becomes *the major problem* for theistic metaphysics. The more we are able to *explain* who God is and how and why God created, and the better our theories are, the more God's freedom threatens to elude us. One limit case would be randomness, the claim that there is absolutely no rhyme or reason to what proceeds from God.[41] Consistently construed, this limit case would entail pure mystery — and of course the failure of the philosophical project in which Schelling and others were engaged. The other limit case, again, is Hegel: the world issued forth with necessity *via* a purely conceptual *(begriffliche)* self-development, and with ne-cessity it will lead to the fullness of Absolute Spirit.

I suggest that Schelling has formulated a particularly successful middle position between these two limit cases. The "ground of being" is pure essence;

---

40. "Unter dem Absoluten versteht Schelling das, was alles Wirkliche, die ideale wie die reale Welt, übergreift, umgreift und in sich befaßt" (Wilhelm Weischedel, *Der Gott der Philosophen, Grundlegugn einer philosophischen Theologie in Zeitalter des Nihilismus* [Frank-furt: Wissenschaftliche Buchgesellchaft, 1971], vol. 1, p. 252).

41. A position often associated with Søren Kierkegaard, e.g., in *Fear and Trembling* or *Concluding Unscientific Postscript.* But is it not already a conceptual determination — and hence a limitation and an explanation, an understanding — to construe God as infinite subjectivity?

it specifies God's basic nature without determining all of his actions. The transition from essence to a created realm of existing beings cannot be a logical or rational step, a requirement of the System à la Hegel or of the nature of God.[42] Even to say that God's nature as Love requires God to create is to remove the freedom that an adequate theory of God must preserve. Rather, Schelling insists,

> God created beings outside himself not because of a blind necessity of his nature but with the greatest freedom. More precisely, on the basis of mere divine necessity, since it applies only to his own existence, there would be no creatures. Therefore, through freedom God overcomes the necessity of his nature in the creation; freedom is placed above necessity, not necessity above freedom. (*SW* 8:210)

There's nothing in the Ground as such that would require a world; the existence of the world cannot be derived from the infinite as an inevitable correlate of its existence. So the criticism that creation is necessary is not difficult to avoid. However, sidestepping it still leaves, at first blush, *two* options instead of one: the creation of the world could be a free act — an intentional product of God's will or agency — or it could be a chance event, an unexplained (and inexplicable) chance by-product of a nonpersonal infinite (à la Spinoza), without a source in volition.

Schelling, along with the other German idealists, realized that the knowledge of an absolute must coincide with the being of that absolute. Hence he rejects Spinoza's unity as "only the dead unity of mere *Sein*, to which the processes of life and development (which grow out of antithesis) remain entirely foreign"[43] in favor of the model of God as a self-unfolding subject. It is not necessary to move all the way to a controlling theory of self-consciousness, according to which the subject *necessarily* externalizes itself into an other and then synthesizes self and other; indeed, to do so is again to subordinate the self to a structure of necessity and thus to lose freedom as its distinguishing feature. Thus the mediating conclusion: if God possesses the attribute of thought, as Spinoza insists, then God must ultimately be construed primarily as subject and not merely as object.[44]

42. These claims will be problematic for the Hegelian, who insists that — at least with regard to a philosophy of the Absolute — there *can* be no separation between essence and being (cf. *"die Untrennbarkeit von Wesen und Sein"*).

43. Brown, p. 248, citing Schelling, *SW* 8:340.

44. Incidentally, note that God's freedom does not have to be construed as full libertarian freedom; it can remain neutral between libertarian and compatibilist accounts of freedom. The argument does require that we construe it as the freedom of a subject rather than as the chance motions of an object (as in the physics of chaos). Still, this requires only that we attribute mental spontaneity to God, the power of *self*-motivated thought. It could still be that the *content* of this thought will turn out to be determined by the nature of the being in question, that is, God will have compatibilist but not libertarian freedom.

The focus on freedom also provides some parameters for what is required if self-revelation is to be possible:

> Now a free being is free in the sense that it does not have to reveal itself. To reveal itself is to act, and all acting is a self-revelation. In order to be a free being, it must be free either to remain with its mere ability [to act], or to make the transition to action. If this transition were made with necessity, [God] would not be what he really is, namely free. (*SW* 8:306)

At this point, however, we must distance ourselves again from the unconvincing idealist logic of the early Schelling. It is not that a philosophy of self-consciousness *requires* an affirmative and a negating moment within God, and hence that the infinite God *had* to create a finite world or that an all-good being had to "fall" into an evil state. Rather, it is that *if an ultimate principle is to be (adequately) thought* at all — and it is not, and perhaps could never be, clear that it can be thought — then it must be thought out of the unity of the finite and infinite. "Until our doctrine acknowledges such a power in God, or until it grasps the absolute identity of the infinite and finite" (*SW* 8:74), there is no place to speak of the personality of God. Schelling's enduring insight is to see that, given that necessity claims are suspect, *freedom* provides the best means for pointing toward the relationship of infinite and finite. "Freedom," he argues in *Ages*, "is the affirmative concept of unconditioned eternity" (*SW* 8:235). We must now consider the structure, and then the content, of the stance presupposed by this starting point.

Schelling (in *Ages*) conceived the infinite or unconditioned as nonbeing, as irrational will.[45] This is correct in the sense that the unconditioned cannot be limited from the start by the specific connotations of objective being or substance ontology, and in the sense that it is better interpreted as subject (or potential subject) than as object in the Spinozistic sense.[46] "Irrational will" also correctly suggests that the subsequent development of the world cannot consist of necessary steps according to some transcendent dialectic. Yet, as I have argued, Schelling tends to fall into the same difficulty that Hegel had, although on the other side. Where Hegel remained bound by necessity, Schelling is often unable to rise above the irrationality of his starting principle. As Bolman saw, "The

---

45. *SW* 8:220f.; cf. the excellent summary in Paul Tillich, *Die religionsgeschichtliche Konstruktion in Schellings positiver Philosophie, ihre Voraussetzungen und Prinzipien* (Breslau, 1910), pp. 17f.

46. Thus Schelling's phrase *"das absolute ich."* Usually he refuses to speak of it as an *actual* subject: the absolute is neither subject nor object, knower or known. Among many supporting passages see Schelling's "Fragment einer Abhandlung zur Strukturtheorie des Absoluten," published by Barbara Loer in *Das Absolute und die Wirklichkeit in Schellings Philosophie* (Berlin: Walter de Gruyter, 1974), p. 32.

problem of positive knowledge for Schelling was how to make the indefinable definable, the unutterable utterable. When he proceeds to ascribe freedom to this indefinable object, he merely expresses the conviction [typical of claims to] positive knowledge that that object may come to be defined."[47] On this question, then, we should be agnostic; although the first principle is better understood as will than as object, it is simply unclear whether its origin is irrational or whether its development can be reconstructed in a rational fashion.[48]

IV

There is space in closing only to hint at the broader narrative in the history of modern theistic metaphysics of which Schelling's Spinozism is a part.[49] Early modern metaphysics was saddled with a (premodern?) doctrine of the intrinsic perfection of being, which dominated philosophy from Descartes through Leibniz and his followers. The Kantian critique, as well as internal difficulties with this line of thought, spelled its final demise. The particular importance of Spinoza is to have introduced a metaphysical framework that dispensed with the assumption of being as perfection.[50] In this respect, Schelling stands clearly in the Spinozistic tradition; as Pöltner notes, "Schelling understands ontological contingency primarily not — as was the case for broad segments of the tradition — as frailty, imperfection (because of limitation) or as the inadequacy *(Mangelhaftigkeit)* of [finite] being, but rather as the manifestation of absolute freedom and omnipotence."[51]

Schelling vacillated between metaphysics as self-grounding system, as philosophical theology, as *"Theosophie,"* and as *via negativa.* He was preoccupied throughout his career with a single pattern of thought or figure, which "opposes

47. Cf. the Frederick de W. Bolman translation of *The Ages of the World* (New York: AMS Press, 1942, 1967), p. 124 n.

48. One could, however, imagine the following wager: if the ultimate principle, and hence the ultimate nature of reality, is irrational, then we can have no justified knowledge of reality anyway. So if we wish to pursue knowledge of what is, we must assume that it is (to some degree) knowable; we will therefore *treat* it *as* such. This doesn't mean, of course, that we *know* it to be such, just that our project presupposes it, and perhaps someday we will know which assumption was right.

49. The argument is presented in detail in my *Toward a Pluralistic Metaphysics.*

50. See Philip Clayton, "The Theistic Argument from Infinity in Early Modern Philosophy," *International Philosophical Quarterly* 36, no. 1 (March 1996): 5-17.

51. "Schelling versteht die ontologische Kontingenz primär nicht — wie dies traditionellerweise auf weite Strecken hin geschehen ist — als Hinfälligkeit, Unvollkommenheit (weil Beschränkheit) oder als Mangelhaftigkeit des Seienden, sondern als die Manifestation absoluter Freiheit und Allmacht" (Pöltner, p. 104).

to the immanence of reason a transcendence that is able to become immanence."[52] To the bitter end, however, he thought he could express this insight
as system, and hence as reflecting necessary ontological (or pre-ontological)
structures. But given the difficulties that we encountered above with the notion
of self-grounding system, I do not think we can declare him successful in this
attempt. How then *should* metaphysical reflection be characterized, if it lies
somewhere between the ideal of a completed system à la Hegel and the overcoming of all metaphysical inclinations, the possibility of which we questioned
in discussing Dupré's work in the opening pages?

There is time just for one concluding example that helps to answer this
question: Schelling's late trinitarian speculations. Consider first the contrast
with Hegel's dialectical theory of the Trinity. The latter theory, especially in the
religion chapter of the *Encyclopedia,* is a masterful philosophical achievement;
it also comes closer to meeting the conditions of orthodoxy than any other
philosophical doctrine of the Trinity since the formulation of the creeds themselves. Its very success, however, is its weakness, for *if* Hegel were indeed successful at showing the Father, Son, and Spirit to be necessary moments of the
self-explication of (what would finally become) *Absoluter Geist* (absolute Spirit),
then he has removed what must be equally a condition of a successful theological
account of the Trinity: true freedom — God's free self-explication and self-
revelation.

At first it looks like Schelling's account faces the same danger. His three
moments are those of the three potencies: "that which is able to be without
mediation or assistance" (*das unmittelbar Seynkönnende; SW* 13:207), "pure
being" (13:210), and "that which remains by or of itself" (13:235) — or, more
simply, "*Subjekt,*" "*Objekt,*" and "*Subjekt-Objekt*" (13:235). The first of these
alone would not be God, for it would be pure potency and would lack actuality.
Hence in the potency there must also be a possibility which represents the *real*
possibility of being; thus the second moment, that of pure existence. But this
second moment cannot be external to the first. So the *potentia universalis* has
to be the unity of the two, or "*Subjekt-Objekt.*" The unity of the three is "the
complete, self-contained, and in this sense absolute Spirit" (*SW* 13:239).

I suggest, however, that such speculations take on a completely different
status in the context of a process of reflection that is embedded within a negative
philosophy. For in this case there *can* be no necessary development (or *Entäußerung*) of an a priori structure into an existing world, as in Hegel's philosophy. Rather, only a pure act of freedom can accomplish the transition from
system to reality.[53] No system of thought could know or predict this develop-

---

52. See Sandkaulen-Bock, p. 179.
53. This is the main theme of Heidegger's masterful treatment of Schelling's *Freiheitsschrift* (n. 35 above).

ment a priori (or at least could not know if it had); reason's job — as "positive philosophy" — can only be to recognize what has already come to be through the pure freedom of its decision. If God were only the triune structure or *potentia universalis*, Schelling realizes, he would be already "posited with a relation to the world, and indeed one that is of his very essence" (*SW* 11:293). In this case God's *transcendence* would remain unthought. Instead, God is "the true subject" and "the absolute *Prius*" (see 13:159). Where Hegel offers a necessary externalization, a dialectical unity of being and thought, Schelling insists on a negative moment: reason "sets" or posits Being "as that which is absolutely outside or external to itself" (*ein absolutes Außer-sich*, 13:163). In Pöltner's words, "Incomprehensible Being appears as blind facticity, as *factum brutum*, because it is defined by reason in a purely negative fashion as its other."[54]

Schelling has seen correctly that reason must be in some sense *"verlassen,"* left behind: "the great, the final, and the actual crisis consists in the fact that God, the One who was found last of all, will be removed from the idea [because he transcends it], and that the 'science' of reason will thereby be left behind (or rejected)."[55] Here, finally, is Schelling's greatest contribution: to take on the rigorous demands of metaphysical reflection, to grant that the metaphysical project is unavoidable; to hold one's results, however tentatively, as true; and yet at the same time to acknowledge that the object after which one is searching partially recedes beyond even one's most perceptive conceptual grasp. One cannot help but notice that in this final point, Schelling is again true to his Spinozistic heritage — this time to the Spinoza of the closing pages of the *Ethics:*

> Our mind, insofar as it knows both itself and the body under a form of eternity, necessarily has a knowledge of God, and knows that it is in God and is conceived through God. . . . That is, the mind's intellectual love towards God is part of the infinite love wherewith God loves himself.[56]

---

54. Pöltner, p. 109.

55. "Die große, letzte und eigentliche Krisis besteht nun darin, daß Gott, das zuletzt Gefundene, aus der Idee ausgestoßen, die Vernunftwissenschaft selbst damit verlassen (verworfen) wird" ("Darstellung der reinrationalen Philosophie," *SW* 9:566). There are a number of parallels to the later Fichte that might be explored. Fichte writes of God's appearance, "Die Erscheinung ist darum schlechthin ein Freies: durch und an Gott, ein bloßes, reines Vermögen, zu erscheinen und sichtbar zu machen so Sich wie Gott. Dieses ist ihr [der Seele] ideales Sein durch Gott" (F. W. J. Fichte, *Werke*, ed. I. H. Fichte [Bonn: A. Marrus, 1845-46; reprint, Berlin: W. de Gruyter, 1962ff.], X, 383). At the end of his comparison of the two thinkers, Buchheim writes of Schelling, "Selbstsein ist Verhältnis nicht als Reflexion, sondern als Oeffnung-zu" (Thomas Buchheim, "Die reine Abscheidung Gottes. Eine Vergleichbarkeit im Grundgedanken von Fichtes und Schellings Spätphilosophie," *Zeitschrift für philosophische Forschung* 42 [1988]: 95-106, quote p. 106).

56. Spinoza, *Ethics*, trans. Samuel Shirley (Indianapolis: Hackett, 1982), book V, props. 30, 36.

CHAPTER 6

Modernity and the Satanic Face of God

MICHAEL J. BUCKLEY, S.J.

The religious intellect must recognize that in the nineteenth century it confronts a unique situation, unprecedented both in the depth of its challenge and in the extension of its claims. During that period, the denial of the reality of God rose to achieve an articulate and influential presence within the intellectual culture of western Europe. This denial was no longer the persuasion of this or that idiosyncratic figure such as Diagoras of Melos or Theodore of Cyrene in pre-Christian antiquity; nor did it constitute the mentality of a peculiarly enlightened cast such as the d'Holbachian circle in Paris in the eighteenth century. During the nineteenth century, "the eclipse of God" advanced much farther, descending massively upon modernity and upon the world that it embraced as non-European nations fell under the influence of Western thought. This eclipse circumscribed an absence of religious faith or of any living theistic affirmation, together with an attendant sense of alienation, indifference, or hostility toward religious doctrines, presence, and institutions. This atheism or secularism or agnosticism together with its cognate indifference or contempt for the religious was unique within the history of the world in the public acceptance it secured during that century, in the ascendancy within particular subcultures it gained, and in the rapidity of increase it enjoyed among intellectuals and the formative sources of culture. It came to shadow all ranks of society in Europe, from workers to bourgeoisie to intellectuals, gathering strength to spill into the twentieth century with an ideational force unmatched since the Protestant Reformation.

During this steady devolution of religious affirmation, not only did the judgment about the validity of religious belief fall under suspicion and question, but the nature or content of religious ideas themselves did as well. The religious culture of Europe was being reconfigured because the notion of "God" was being reconfigured. God was coming to be seen now as the alienation of the human species in favor of an imaginary subject or as the structure of the human society now writ large or as the projection out of fear and longing of oedipal necessities. Each of these reconfigurations lent new shapes to political economy or theology, literature, philosophy, and rhetoric. Emerging as the psychological dynamic that explained religious ideas were such terms as *Vergegenständlichung* and *Entäusserung*, objectification and alienation, and the face of God changed, as in some way the hermeneutics of suspicion registered the human interests that had created it.[1]

But there was another, very different historical development in modernity's disclosure of the profound projection within religious belief. The initial grammars of religion revealed that the human was the truth of the divine. The second wave of interpretation would tear off this mask and see beneath it not the human but the antihuman. God is revealed as — to borrow a term from Spanish mysticism — *el enemigo de natura humana*, the enemy of human nature. The discovery of this equation between the divine and the diabolical was both the product of the nineteenth century and one of the fundamental reversals of the sacred in the history of religion. This discovery the following essay attempts to outline in a series of very broad brush strokes. To do so, it proposes: (1) to indicate something of the dialectic that lies at the origins of modern atheism, the paradoxical sources of modern atheism;[2] (2) to examine the radical shift in fundamental thinking that took place in the nineteenth century — in what Hobbes called the "First Grounds of Philosophy"; (3) to trace the effect that this produced in the basic evidence advanced for the reality of God; (4) to outline some classic moments in the massive rise in atheistic consciousness that these philosophical and theological arguments dialectically occasioned; (5) to identify the "god" that emerges from these counterpositions.

---

1. See Michael J. Buckley, "Atheism and Contemplation," *Theological Studies* 40 (1979): 680-99. Eugene Kamenka maintains that "the psychological use of the word 'projection' in English originated in George Eliot's translation of the *Essence of Christianity*. She used it to render Feuerbach's (Hegelian) terms *Vergegenständlichung* (objectification, reification) and *Entäusserung* (alienation)." See Eugene Kamenka, *The Philosophy of Ludwig Feuerbach* (London: Routledge & Kegan Paul, 1970), p. 167 n. 43. It should be noted, however, that Ralph Waldo Emerson, some ten years before Eliot's translation, makes the world "a projection of God in the unconscious," and consequently it is "to us, the present expositor of the divine mind." *Nature*, in *The Complete Essays and Other Writings of Ralph Waldo Emerson*, ed. Brooks Atkinson (New York: Random House, 1940), vol. 7, p. 36.

2. I have elsewhere suggested this pattern of internal contradiction at the origins of modern atheism and would like in this paper to follow it as it was transposed in the nineteenth century, the golden age of atheism. Cf. Michael J. Buckley, S.J., *At the Origins of Modern Atheism* (New Haven: Yale University Press, 1990). This initial section is little more than a précis of the findings of that work. For a brilliant and incisive cultural critique of the project and of the revolution that was modernity, see Louis Dupré, *Passage to Modernity: An Essay in the Hermeneutics of Nature and Culture* (New Haven: Yale University Press, 1993).

I. At the Origins

The ideational origins of modern atheism lie remarkably with the strategies employed against it. It was generated and shaped by the attempt to provide for the affirmation of the existence of God by using the new sciences as the fundamental and irrefragable basis for such an affirmation. Thus Isaac Newton maintained that the "main Business of natural Philosophy is to argue from Phaenomena without feigning Hypotheses, and to deduce Causes from Effects, till we come to the very first Cause, which certainly is not mechanical."[3] By the beginnings of the eighteenth century, design in nature furnished the comprehensive warrant for the illation to the affirmation of God. Only a divine cause could account for design in the universe, from the solar system to the structure of organic bodies. The inference from design to designer would serve as the principal foundation for later discussions of the divine nature, moral theology, and the possibility of divine revelation. Hundreds of studies came out under the inspiration of so great a genius as Newton, physico-theologies giving the grounding for the assertions of God by arguing from design in nature. Theologians were generally enthusiastic.

But few noticed what such an approach omitted. It bracketed all religious experience as cognitively irrelevant, as implicitly empty. While it formulated a "natural theology" that found patterns in the physical universe and then argued to a supreme geometer/architect/παντοκρατωρ — to omnipotent intelligence and power — it found nothing in the history of the human involvement with God in Christianity or Judaism that bore seriously upon this issue. The single phrase that captures the great enterprise and influence of Isaac Newton was "universal mechanics," a mechanics that provided not only the foundations of mathematics, but the rational basis for all theology and religion. Such a universal mechanics, Newton argued, while all-embracing, must have principles or warranted sources of explanation that were finally not mechanical.

Superseded by this universal mechanics was the attempt of some sixty years before to provide a rational basis for religion. Descartes, followed by Malebranche, had formulated a first philosophy that found the warrant for God in the content of ideas that confronted the thinking subject. For Descartes, mechanics was a limited, not a universal, discipline, and everything it studied was to be explained by only mechanical principles. He had saved mechanics from theology by laying the grounds for the affirmation of the existence of God in a first philosophy that was not mechanics, but an independent metaphysics. Thus the disciplines were distinct and mechanics was limited, but it was autonomous.

---

3. Isaac Newton, *Optics, or a Treatise of the Reflections, Refractions, Influctions, and Colours of Light,* ed. Duane H. D. Roller (New York: Dover, 1952), Query 28, p. 369.

Now, the combination of these two strategies in the eighteenth century was powerful enough to ground or justify an articulate, confessional atheism. This theological failure of physics, of course, did not motivate atheism; it did legitimize it. Denis Diderot and Paul d'Holbach took the imperial idea of a universal mechanics from Newton and its confinement to only mechanical principles from Descartes in order to frame a universal mechanics with principles that were rigorously mechanical. The ground for affirmation or denial of transcendence was to be physics or mechanics, but its principles must be commensurate. These principles, or really, this comprehensive principle, the source of all natural phenomena, was matter in motion. It was more than adequate for universal explanation.

Figures in sympathy with Diderot were persuaded that in dynamic matter they had found something far more engulfing than God to explain the universe. For what confronted the human subject in the world of nature was much more than design; there were also horrors, tragedies, and catastrophes that equally called for understanding. Dynamic matter could offer a capacious explanation, one that did not have the obvious difficulties of Newton's great architect. For the argument from design could explain only order in the universe but had to fall silent or wax convoluted before disease and the terrible physical evils that permeated the world. Blind and dynamic matter suffered no such embarrassment. It could explain both design and monsters. If natural theology was to argue from the physical universe, matter in motion dealt much more adequately with the entire range of physical phenomena. Out of so fecund a principle, everything that was — the designed and the monstrous — had equally and mindlessly evolved. Everything could be reduced to and explained by dynamic matter, matter and its inherent movement.

Atheism as a justified idea — prescinding from the multitude of social and cultural developments that gave this idea its time — emerged from a change in physics, but a physics that had been made to bear the burden of natural theology. And so with Denis Diderot and Paul d'Holbach, "atheism" shifted from a charge that one made against one's enemies to a personal confession of beliefs. Atheism moved from invective and accusation to signature.

Why were theologians and atheists to struggle on this common front of nature and design? Not simply because the philosophers and theologians yielded pride of disciplinary place to mechanics, but because it offered the most serious or promising way of dealing with the physical universe, identified for all the world as creation. Newton did not pay deference to Locke; Locke paid deference to Newton. But why build an apologetics upon the physical universe? In part, because of the focus of "fundamental thinking" at the time.

Fundamental thinking designates that disciplined reflection within an intellectual period which explores the foundation for all subsequent sciences and arts, the area from which the basic terms for thinking are derived and all other human inquiries explained and justified. Fundamental thinking explores what one must understand "before" — as the grounding for all other disciplined inquiry — although one often comes upon that "before" long after other disciplines have been pursued. One often comes upon the first last.[4] In the seventeenth and eighteenth centuries, the focus of fundamental thinking was on the reality that confronted or surrounded the thinking subject, whether as the content of ideas as with Descartes or all the phenomena of the physical universe. Thus Thomas Hobbes, from that intellectual era, would insist that "The First Grounds of Philosophy" must deal directly with the physical universe and so combine the geometry that studied simply the motion of things, as in Galileo's mechanics, and the physics that bore upon the general properties of bodies. After this foundation is laid in a grasp of the nature of things, one can go on to study the human person and political society or the state.

II. The Shift in Fundamental Thinking

In the writings, the enormously influential writings, of John Locke, one can find the beginnings of an intellectual revolution against this priority of investigation into the nature of things or into the Cartesian content of ideas. With Locke, a sea change began in fundamental thinking. One has only to open to Locke's "Epistle to the Reader," the preface to his masterpiece, *An Essay concerning Human Understanding*. This "Epistle" was necessary, thought Locke, to understand how the essay itself came about. Many before and after Locke had embarked upon a similar journey in inquiry. But Locke made the understanding of understanding the foundation of all exploration and inquiry. A turn to the subject had already been initiated by Descartes, but he grounded his first philosophy not upon the processes of understanding, but upon the content of ideas. In contrast, Locke would study the processes themselves. Richard Rorty has noted quite correctly: "We owe the notion of a 'theory of knowledge' based on an understanding of 'mental processes' to the seventeenth century, and especially to Locke."[5] The necessity that an analysis

---

4. The concept of "fundamental thinking" is derived from Richard McKeon's formulation and use of "general selection characteristics of the philosophic communication of a period" as well as from the distinctions that he drew within general selection and brought to bear so perceptively upon the history of thought. See Richard P. McKeon, "Philosophic Semantics and Philosophic Inquiry," in *Freedom and History and Other Essays: An Introduction to the Thought of Richard McKeon,* ed. Zahava K. McKeon (Chicago: University of Chicago, 1990), pp. 251-52.

5. Richard Rorty, *Philosophy and the Mirror of Nature* (Princeton: Princeton University Press, 1980), p. 3. Rorty distinguishes Locke's contribution from that of Descartes: "We owe the notion of 'the mind' as a separate entity in which 'processes' occur to the same period, and especially to Descartes" (pp. 3-4).

of the processes of thought form the prior foundation for statements about the processes of things distinguishes John Locke:

> Were it fit to trouble thee with the History of this Essay, I should tell thee that five or six Friends meeting at my Chamber, and discoursing on a Subject very remote from this [the principles of morality and revealed religion], found themselves quickly at a stand, by the Difficulties that rose on every side. After we had awhile puzzled our selves, without coming any nearer a Resolution of those Doubts which perplexed us, it came into my Thoughts that we took a wrong course; and that, *before* we set our selves upon Enquiries of that Nature, it was necessary to examine *our own Abilities, and see, what Objects our Understandings were, or were not fitted to deal with.* This I proposed to the Company, who all readily assented; and thereupon it was agreed, that this should be our *first Enquiry.*[6]

This is very different "fundamental thinking" from that found in Descartes or Newton or Hobbes. In the early months of 1671, during these important conversations at Exeter House, Locke was transferring the focus of foundational thought from the exploration of that which confronts the thinking subject — such as issues about "the principles of morality and revealed religion" — to the processes of thinking themselves.[7] The "Epistle to the Reader" insisted upon an antecedent epistemological foundation, upon a consideration of the potentialities for human knowing and their commensurate "objects," before attempting to deal with problems that immediately touch the nature of things. "First inquiry" should be epistemological. What Locke modestly "proposed to the Company, who all readily assented" in the country home of Lord Ashley, soon to be first earl of Shaftesbury, was actually a sweeping change within modernity.

The emphasis that Locke gave to the processes of thought gathered force in the years that followed and ran full steam into the works and subsequent influence of Immanuel Kant. His three *Critiques* were to transpose all fundamental reflection into this new key: "I do not mean by this a critique of books and systems, but of the faculty of reason in general, in respect of all knowledge after which it may strive independently of all experience. It will therefore decide as to the possibility or impossibility of metaphysics in general."[8] Before one

---

6. John Locke, *An Essay concerning Human Understanding,* ed. Peter H. Nidditch (Oxford: Clarendon, 1975), "Epistle to the Reader," p. 7 (emphasis added).

7. One of these friends, James Tyrrell, records in the marginalia he appended to his copy of the essay that the conversation had been "about the principles of morality and revealed religion." For this, as also for the dating and location of these conversations, see Maurice Cranston, *John Locke: A Biography* (New York: Macmillan, 1957), pp. 140-41.

8. Immanuel Kant, *Critique of Pure Reason,* trans. and ed. Norman Kemp Smith (London: Macmillan, 1963), "Preface to First Edition," p. 9.

launches into metaphysics or natural theology or universal mechanics, one must analyze the knowing of the knower to determine what could be known; otherwise human inquiry yielded only transcendental illusion. Before one explores morality and ethics, one must analyze the practical intellect or *Wille* and the human ability to determine itself freely to choose. Before one deals with the beautiful and the sublime, with taste and genius, one must understand the reflexivity or harmony that is possible between the imagination in its representations and the understanding in its judgment. Again, Kant did not originate this flood; he augmented and sanctioned it for the century that was to follow. Under his blessings, these waters became holy. Disciplines bearing such names as epistemology or criticism or phenomenologies of spirit or cognitional theory became foundational in nineteenth-century modernity. One had to look at human capacities, at the various potentialities for knowledge and choice and even taste, in order to determine what the proper objects of these potentialities are. When this was established, one could bring these powers to bear upon questions of inquiry and decision without the dangers of irresolvable contradiction and conflicts. One must gauge the human first.

The foundational importance of the self-appropriation of the knowing subject carried persuasion also in theology, entering emphatically into the inquiries of the greatest Protestant theologian of the nineteenth century, Friedrich Schleiermacher. Here one finds a primordial dependence of all discussion of theological subjects or the propositions of religion upon the prior assessment of immediate consciousness, variously formulated as either the feeling and intuition of the infinite or the feeling of absolute dependence.

Kant and Schleiermacher, as Fred Lawrence has so well maintained, represent two distinctly different kinds of foundational consciousness.[9] Kant tethered reason, understanding, or judgment to consciousness as a perception of objects; like Rousseau, Schleiermacher rooted them in the perception of feelings, the feeling of feeling, that he sometimes referred to as "sentiment." What Kant was for philosophy, Schleiermacher was for theology. Both gave a foundational priority to human subjectivity — not in the sense of an arbitrary imposition of meanings, but in the sense of the subject as agent, possessing its own internal structure of mind or spirit, whose capacities must be determined as the fundamental security for subsequent affirmations. For both, the human subject came first; the human subject would measure the things that it would engage. Not nature, but human nature had become fundamental.

---

9. Fred Lawrence, "The Fragility of Consciousness: Lonergan and the Postmodern Concern for the Other," *Theological Studies* 54 (1993): 58-62.

III. Theistic Argumentation in a New Key

As this revolution swept through modernity, Kant and Schleiermacher transposed the arguments for the reality of God into a new key. They formulated disciplines for so much of the philosophy and theology that would follow them, disciplines that were to shift the issue of God to human subjectivity for its fundamental point of departure. Kant provided critiques, while Schleiermacher explored "religion." In both God emerged as a necessity to deal with human life and experience. God was an entailment of the human.

The *Critique of Practical Reason* laid the foundation for ethical reasoning and for the metaphysics of morals in the centrality of human freedom. The living of a human life, the entire ethical enterprise, presupposed human nature as free. Freedom — which was to dominate the nineteenth century's inquiries into the human — identified with the subjectivity that was human nature and was itself the originator of the moral life:

> By "nature of man" we here intend only the subjective ground of the exercise (under objective moral laws) of man's freedom in general; this ground — whatever is its character — is the necessary antecedent of every act apparent to the senses. But this subjective ground, again, must itself always be an expression of freedom (for otherwise, the use or abuse of man's power of choice [*Willkür*] in respect of the moral law could not be imputed to him nor could the good or bad in him be called moral). Hence the source of evil cannot lie in an object determining the will [*Willkür*] through inclination, nor yet in a natural impulse; it can lie only in a rule made by the will [*Willkür*] for the use of its freedom, i.e. in a maxim.[10]

Freedom in Kant is both potency and act. It is the transcendental power to choose, the independence of *Willkür* from determination by external objects and by the impulses of past or present. It is the reflexive self-legislation of *Willkür*, shown in its selection of maxims by which to govern its exercise and in its selection of objects upon which its actions will devolve. One is free in transcendental freedom because one is one's own master, coerced in the process of choice by no external master. Secondly, freedom is also actualization or autonomy. Autonomy occurs when one chooses in accordance with the universal law, living free from external determination and realizing in actuality the moral potentiality of the human. Heteronomy occurs when one renounces one's power as a free being by choosing to act dependently upon the determinations of desires. In this sense, human life is the movement from freedom to freedom,

---

10. Immanuel Kant, *Religion within the Limits of Reason Alone,* trans. Theodore M. Greene and Hoyt H. Hudson, with a new essay by John R. Silber (New York: Harper and Row, 1960), bk. 1, pp. 16-17.

the freedom of *Willkür* to the freedom of autonomy, the freedom of potentiality to the freedom of actuality, and the path to this freedom of autonomy constitutes the ethical enterprise itself.[11]

For the internal coherence of human freedom, i.e., for human life to make sense morally, one must postulate the existence of God. The austere ethical imperative is to do one's duty, and duty dictates that one strive for the highest human good. This object conjoins virtue (dictated by duty) and happiness (which objectively ought to be united with virtue). The virtuous deserve to be happy. If this highest human good is imperative, it must be possible, and for this "possibility we must postulate a higher, moral, most holy, and omnipotent Being which alone can unite the two elements of this highest good."[12] Without God, the ethical or moral life is a movement into absurdity. One would be morally commanded or directed toward the impossible, toward a conjunction of happiness and virtue that only happenstance effects in human life — and even this rarely. Morality is only rationally coherent if the object of morality is itself seriously possible. Thus what human beings cannot effect must be within the power of another. There must be that omnipotent intelligence that can make possible the object of command, the "highest good." "Morality thus leads ineluctably to religion, through which it extends itself to the idea of a powerful moral Lawgiver, outside of mankind, for Whose will that is the final end (of creation) which at the same time can and ought to be man's final end."[13] In this way, God alone makes rational morality possible for human beings, and Jesus Christ is the exemplification of this morality.

For Schleiermacher, "religion" becomes the foundation for dogmatics and indeed for his greatest work, *Die Glaubenslehre*, and the basis of all religion is the consciousness of the infinite, or what in his more mature work he would call "the feeling of absolute dependence." Kant had deliberately excluded experience from the exercise of human freedom because "the philosopher, as teacher of pure reason (from unassisted principles a priori [in ethics]), must confine himself within the narrower circle, and, in so doing, must abstract from all experience."[14] For Schleiermacher, there is no parallel refusal of experience in

11. See John R. Silber, "The Ethical Significance of Kant's Religion," introduction to Kant, *Religion*, pp. lxxx-xcvi.

12. Kant, *Religion*, "Preface to the First Edition," pp. 4-5.

13. Kant, *Religion*, "Preface," pp. 5-6. The classic treatment of the existence of God as a postulate of pure practical reason is, of course, in book II of Kant's *Critique of Practical Reason*, chapter 5, "The Existence of God as a Postulate of Pure Practical Reason." See Immanuel Kant, *Critique of Practical Reason*, ed. Lewis White Beck (Indianapolis: Bobbs-Merrill, 1956), pp. 128-36.

14. Kant, *Religion*, p. 11. This translation has been modified, since the German reads: ". . . von aller Erfahrung abstrahieren muß. . . ." Immanuel Kant, *Die Religion innerhalb der Grenzen der bloßen Vernunft*, ed. Karl Vorländer (Hamburg: Felix Meiner Verlag, 1990), p. 13.

favor of illation. On the contrary, one appeals to the fundamental experience that underlies all inference and even differentiated thought. Whether that immediacy be termed "intuition" or "feeling," it denotes a fundamental awareness, a self-consciousness given in every act of cognition. Now this self-consciousness is inseparable from God-consciousness — as doubt in Descartes is inseparable from existence:

> To feel oneself absolutely dependent and to be conscious of being in relation with God are one and the same thing; and the reason is that absolute dependence is the *fundamental* relation which must include all others in itself. This last expression includes the God-consciousness in the human self-consciousness in such a way that, quite in accordance with the above analysis, the two cannot be separated from each other. . . . God is given to us in feeling in an original way.[15]

God is an illation of ethics in Kant, making duty's object, the highest good, seriously possible; God is a given of the primordial experience of self-consciousness in Schleiermacher.

Through the influence of both thinkers, a critically important shift was taking place in modernity that would resituate fundamental thinking about the divine reality, a shift that Tennyson would both celebrate in *In Memoriam* and comment upon at the end of his life. He saw that the heady days of the religious use of nature were passing, or at least diminishing. Charles Lyell's *Principles of Geology* (1830-33), with its demonstrations of the great age of the earth and the successive and massive extinction of species, had left "Nature red in tooth and claw / With ravine." Tennyson found that nature "shriek'd against his creed," leaving those who depended upon Nature's witness convinced that they must regard "life as futile, then, as frail."[16] The nineteenth-century thinker must turn elsewhere:

> Yet God *is* love, transcendent, all-pervading! We do not get *this* faith from Nature or the world. If we look at Nature alone, full of perfection and imperfection, she tells us that God is disease, murder and rapine. We get this faith from ourselves, from what is highest within us, which recognizes that there is not one fruitless pang, just as there is not one lost good.[17]

---

15. Friedrich Schleiermacher, *The Christian Faith*, ed. H. R. MacIntosh and J. S. Stewart (Edinburgh: T. & T. Clark, 1928), introduction, n. 4, p. 17 (emphasis added).

16. Alfred, Lord Tennyson, *Tennyson: In Memoriam*, ed. Susan Shatto and Marian Shaw (Oxford: Clarendon Press, 1982), section 56, lines 15-16, 25, p. 80.

17. This remark is cited by his son and introduced with the remark: "After one of these moods in the summer of 1892, he [Tennyson] exclaimed. . . ." See Hallam, Lord Tennyson, *Alfred Lord Tennyson: A Memoir* (New York: Macmillan, 1897), as cited in *Alfred, Lord Tennyson, In Memoriam*, ed. Robert H. Ross (New York: Norton, 1973), p. 119. For the

"This faith from ourselves, from what is highest within us. . . ." Nature, for all the physics and universal mechanics it evokes, stills carries its history of destruction and deaths. It cannot establish the warrant for the existence of God. One must rather go to the inferences entailed by the critique of practical reason or to the experience fundamental to religion. For all of their contrasts and even contradictory procedures, what both critique and the analysis of religion have in common is what they both take as foundational: the radically human — in contradistinction with subhuman nature. The Kantian critique recognized that ethics engages an activity that is uniquely human, the way human beings should decide and act and live; Schleiermacher saw that human passivity is engaged by religion, the manner of human experience, preconceptual "feelings," change worked by the influence of an object, which reveals its existence to one in the inner consciousness.

> The same is true for religion. The same actions of the universe through which it reveals itself to you in the finite also bring it into a new relationship to your mind and your condition; in the act of intuiting it, you must necessarily be seized by various feelings. In religion, however, a different and stronger relationship between intuition and feeling takes place, and intuition never predominates so much that feeling is almost extinguished.
>
> On the contrary, is it really a miracle if the eternal world affects the senses of our spirit as the sun affects our eyes? Is it a miracle when the sun so blinds us that everything else disappears, not only at that moment, but even long afterward all objects we observe are imprinted with its image and bathed in its brilliance? Just as the particular manner in which the universe presents itself to you in your intuitions and determines the uniqueness of your individual religion, so the strength of these feelings determines the degree of religiousness.[18]

Nature does not provide the warrant for God; the warrant for God is found in human nature, either active in its choices or passive in its immediate experience or feeling.

So profound and pervasive is this shift to human nature as foundational for dealing with the reality of God that both Kant and Schleiermacher can cite it as the linchpin of their fundamental works. Kant's four books on religion become the study of human nature:

---

influence of Charles Lyell's *Principles of Geology* (1830-33) and its demonstrations of the great age of the earth and the successive extinction of species, see Eleanor D. Mattes, *In Memoriam: The Way of a Soul* (New York: Exposition Press, 1951), pp. 55-61, 73-86, 111-25, as excerpted in *Alfred, Lord Tennyson*, ed. Ross, pp. 120ff.

18. Friedrich Schleiermacher, *On Religion: Speeches to Its Cultured Despisers*, trans. Richard Crouter (Cambridge: Cambridge University Press, 1988), Speech II, pp. 109-10.

> In order to make apparent the relation of religion to human nature (endowed in part with good, in part with evil predispositions), I represent, in the four following essays, the relationship of the good and evil principles as that of the two self-subsistent active causes influencing men.[19]

The purpose of Schleiermacher's *Reden* is stated: "I wish to lead you to the innermost depths from which religion first addresses the mind. I wish to show you from what capacity of humanity religion proceeds, and how it belongs to what is for you the highest and dearest." Precisely for its engagement of the human in such depths, this inquiry is not for all, maintains Schleiermacher, but only for "you" who are capable of "raising yourselves above the common standpoint of humanity, you who do not shrink from the burdensome way into the depths of human nature in order to find the ground of its actions and thought."[20]

And how does one move "into the depths of human nature"? Through the differentiation among three disciplines and the recognition and prosecution of religion as one of them. For metaphysics finds its essence in thinking; morality, in acting and doing; but religion, in intuition and feeling. In Schleiermacher, God emerges as the active source of these feelings; God is even given a nominal definition in terms of the feeling of absolute dependence: "the *Whence* of our receptive and active existence, as implied in this self-consciousness, is to be designated by the word 'God,' and that this is for us the really original signification of that word."[21] The original human awareness of God is simply of that which is the codeterminant in this feeling. Thus to feel oneself absolutely dependent and to be conscious of being in relation to God is one and the same thing. In this sense, God is given to immediate human awareness, i.e., in feeling, in "an original way." Indeed, this can be recognized as "an original revelation of God to man or in man."[22]

One can only remark about the radical contrast this offers to the major and most influential thinkers of the seventeenth and eighteenth centuries. In these previous centuries, heady with the emergence of the universal competence of the new mechanics, nature or design or the content of ideas or things had provided the evidence for asserting the divine existence. Now the battleground is confined to human nature and its entailments. This recasting of the foundations of religion provides the theological point of departure for the nineteenth century: What is it to be human, and how does this warrant necessitate the affirmation or denial of God?

---

19. Kant, *Religion*, p. 10.
20. Schleiermacher, *On Religion*, p. 87.
21. Schleiermacher, *The Christian Faith*, p. 16.
22. Schleiermacher, *The Christian Faith*, pp. 17-18.

IV. The Humanistic Foundations of the Emergent Atheism

The dialectical reversal of theistic positions that obtained in early modernity repeated itself analogously within the changed coordinates of the nineteenth century. In these earlier centuries, the strategies to rationalize the divine existence furnish the weapons to attack. The positive generated its own commensurate self-contradiction. In the nineteenth century, philosophy and theology had moved to ground religious affirmation on the entailments of human nature; now they will be contradicted on the same ground in the struggle that Henri de Lubac so aptly called "the drama of atheistic humanism."[23]

One must begin with the originating genius of this movement, Ludwig Feuerbach — a Bavarian theological student become philosopher under the instruction of Hegel, only to become atheist — the man whose writings were so successful, so influential that Marx saluted him as the great precursor of dialectical atheism and Freud held him as his favorite philosopher.[24] Atheism came as the climax of his intellectual development, and he summarized the steps of his growth in this way: "God was my first thought; Reason my second; Man, my third and last thought."[25] Respect for the character of nineteenth-century fundamental thinking dictated that Feuerbach begin the *Essence of Christianity* with an analysis of the essential nature of the human person as self-consciousness, i.e., consciousness of species. He could deduce his conclusions about the source and object of religion from the phenomenon that human beings have religion while brutes do not, and that this must derive from this species-consciousness. In his third edition he placed his central thesis at the very beginning: "The essence of the human being [self-consciousness] in differentiation from the beasts is not only the ground or cause, but also the object of religion."[26] The figure of God, the object of religion, is a projection of the human essence. God is the human writ large as species.

Feuerbach argues to this cardinal fact of projection, that the true sense of

23. Henri de Lubac, *The Drama of Atheistic Humanism,* trans. Edith M. Riley (New York: Sheed and Ward, 1950).

24. See Kamenka, *The Philosophy of Ludwig Feuerbach,* pp. vii-viii, 16, 27, 117-18; Peter Gay, *Freud: A Life for Our Time* (New York: Norton, 1988), pp. 28-29, 532. On March 7, 1875, Freud wrote to Edward Silverstein: "Among all philosophers, I worship and admire this man (Feuerbach) the most." See Gay, p. 28.

25. Cited from Ludwig Feuerbach's *Philosophical Fragments* by Kamenka, p. 39.

26. Ludwig Feuerbach, *Das Wesen des Christentums,* ed. Werner Schuffenhauer, 3rd ed. (Berlin: Akademie-Verlag, 1973), p. 29 n. 3. This sentence appears in the third edition, done in 1849 while Feuerbach still lived. The celebrated English translation, *The Essence of Christianity,* trans. George Eliot from the 2nd rev. ed. of 1843 (New York: Harper, 1957), was first published in London in 1854. The German original of this addition to the third edition reads: "Das Wesen des Menschen im Unterschied vom Tiere ist nicht nur der Grund, sondern auch der Gegendstand der Religion."

theology is anthropology, from three dimensions of human nature: human consciousness, linguistic predication, and the history of human alienation — consciousness, language, and history.

(1) The nature of human self-consciousness: the object that is essentially known reveals the subject to itself. When such an essential object does not have its independent existence guaranteed by sense perception, it is nothing more than the essential nature of the subject. (2) The essential humanity of the divine attributes — such as wise, blessed, provident: What is predicated of God is taken from human experience and is true of human beings alone. Now the truth of the subject is found in its predicates. Since the divine predicates are human, their subject is also human. (3) Commensurate alienation: what human beings ascribe to God has been historically subtracted or alienated from the human essence. One can trace this through the history of religions or theology. That God may be enriched as good and holy, the human person must be seen as poor and sinful.[27]

That such projection of the human into an alien subject should take place is to be understood as a stage in human self-appropriation through otherness. If one fixates at this stage, however, one formulates the illusions that are theology. But the developments of cultural history have reached a time of further progress. Philosophy, now the interpreter of the truth of religion, is called to reappropriate these "divine" attributes for the human, to restore to human beings their grandeur. One does not eliminate the divine predicates, but only the imaginary divine subject of these attributes. The attributes are true not of this supernatural illusion, but of the human actuality. What is "God" in this state of illusion? The alienation of the human from itself: "a perversion, a distortion; which, however, the more perverted and false it is, all the more appears to be profound."[28] Feuerbach's inquiries mount what is basically a philosophical grammar in the medieval sense of "grammar" as a *scientia interpretandi* or *ars interpretandi*, a science or a technique for the understanding of the meaning of fundamental symbols.[29]

Karl Marx accepted Feuerbach's critique of religion, but modified it in two ways: he insisted upon the social-economic sources of the origin and fixation of this projection; and he rejected Feuerbach's strategy of reflexive assimilation or hermeneutical recognition in favor of the destructive and trans-

---

27. This is the burden of the initial chapter of *The Essence of Christianity*. These three basic argument are repeated in Feuerbach's other works. See Feuerbach, *The Essence of Christianity*, pp. 1-32.

28. Feuerbach, *The Essence of Christianity*, p. 231.

29. For the medieval sense of "grammar," see Michael J. Buckley, S.J., "Towards the Construction of Theology: A Response to Richard McKeon," *Journal of Religion* 58, Supplement (1978): S58-S59, esp. n. 15. It was Rabanus Maurus who recaptured for the Middle Ages the definition of Marius Victorinus and brought it to bear upon the world of symbols.

formational activity of the "revolutionary principle." He changed Feuerbach's human person from a contemplative interpreter to a practical agent whose transitive activity is to change social structures. One does not simply interpret alienation; one destroys it — in the social order. Marx moved materialism from a reflexive principle to a revolutionary principle. This shift is what Marx refers to in his classic eleventh thesis against Feuerbach: "The philosophers have only *interpreted* the world, in various ways; the point, however, is to *change* it."[30] Grammar was not enough, and if grammar was the discipline most analogous to Feuerbach's enterprise, rhetoric seems most apt for Marx.

The human being is sensuous and practical, and for this emphasis Marx changes the meaning of this last term, collapsing the distinction between Aristotle's πραξις and ποϊγιησις — so that "practical" now contains the "poetic" activity that creates a new world. The human being is not an abstract essence, but economic and social and essentially called to a much greater factive activity than Feuerbach understood. The failure of Feuerbach's materialism was that it did not grasp human activity's revolutionary and transitive (not contemplative) character, that it essentially passes into the external world and into the lives of other human beings, that it inescapably forms community, and that this practical activity constitutes all reality, all objects.

Truth is not discovered; it is constituted by this activity. Human beings make their world true. Anything else is scholasticism! To realize this human dynamism in practice is to come into possession of one's humanity. This realization of what it means to be human carries with it an enormous responsibility for the world and for the lot of human beings. The philosopher must not simply realize this alienation that religion entails, but must destroy it in its social and economic roots. "Once the earthly family is discovered to be the secret of the holy family, the former must then itself be criticized in theory and revolutionized in practice."[31] Religious critique has a priority over economics and politics; it is the presupposition of all other criticism. Marx's *Contribution to the Critique of Hegel's Philosophy of Right* insists that only this critique can restore the human essence to the human being, make the human being free enough to drive this criticism deeper into the criticism of right and of politics for "religion is only the illusory sun which revolves round man as long as he does not revolve round himself."[32] Hence to restore the revolutionary principle to the human

---

30. Karl Marx, "Theses on Feuerbach," in *Marx and Engels on Religion*, introduction by Reinhold Niebuhr (New York: Schocken Books, 1964), p. 72 (emphasis added).

31. Marx, "Theses on Feuerbach," Thesis no. 4, p. 70.

32. Karl Marx, *Contribution to the Critique of Hegel's Philosophy of Right*, in *Marx and Engels on Religion*, pp. 41-42. "The abolition of religion as the illusory happiness of the people is required for their real happiness. The demand to give up the illusions about its condition is the demand to give up a condition which needs illusion. The criticism of religion is therefore in embryo the criticism of the vale of woe, the halo of which is religion" (p. 42).

means a critique of fundamental human alienation, religion, and only "the criticism of religion ends with the teaching that *man is the highest essence for man,* hence with the *categoric imperative to overthrow all relations* in which man is debased, enslaved, abandoned, despicable essence."[33]

In a stunning reversal of Kant and Schleiermacher, God is now the one who alienates men and women from their humanity, both speculatively as in Feuerbach and ideologically in the economic and social structure in which human beings live. It is not ethics that God makes possible; it is alienation and exploitation.

Marx had realized this as early as his doctoral dissertation. Long before he elaborated a dialectical humanism, he had abridged and made his own the words of Prometheus from Aeschylus's *Prometheus Bound* (l. 975): "ᾳ᾿Απλω λογω, τους παντους εχθαιρω θεους." Prometheus becomes the hero of philosophy, and his declaration is truncated by Marx to become the maxim for humanity and the mission of philosophy. Philosophy must take from Prometheus "its own motto against all gods, heavenly and earthly, who do not acknowledge the consciousness of man as the supreme divinity."[34] Human consciousness, still the focus of fundamental thinking, was not to yield absolute dependence, but in sharp contrast its own absolute supremacy. Even as early as March of 1841, God was posed as the antithesis — not the support or engagement — of a free human life.

It is critically important to see that the destruction of belief in God became for Marx an ethical imperative — not simply a political or social strategy. Marx even employs Kant's vocabulary: this destruction is a "categorical imperative."[35] Religious thinkers can never understand the character of authentic Marxism unless they understand this profoundly moral commitment, as if to the stamping out of a virulent disease. Marx's is one of the earliest expressions of this hatred for the person of God, found in his dissertation with its apotheosis of the person of Prometheus.[36] What Christ is to Kant, Prometheus is to Marx: the embodiment of a morally developed humanity. With the Prometheus of

33. Marx, *Contribution,* p. 50; emphasis in the original. This project, the criticism of religion, contains the fundamental call to be radical: "To be radical is to grasp the root of the matter. But for man the root is man himself. The evident proof of the radicalism of German theory, and hence of its practical energy, is that it proceeds from a resolute positive abolition of religion."

34. Karl Marx, *The Difference between the Natural Philosophy of Democritus and the Natural Philosophy of Epicurus,* "Forward to Thesis," in *Marx and Engels on Religion,* p. 15. The full sentence in Aeschylus reads: "In one word, I hate all the gods that received good at my hand and with ill requite me wrongfully," as in the translation of Herbert Weir Smyth, *Aeschylus,* Loeb Classical Library (Cambridge: Harvard, 1973), p. 305.

35. Marx, *Contribution,* p. 42.

36. For an illuminating development of this theme, see Joseph C. McLelland, *Prometheus Rebound: The Irony of Atheism* (Waterloo: Wilfrid Laurier University Press, 1988).

Marx, humanity is now in competition with God. God, the relentless enemy of Prometheus, is the antihuman. To destroy this God constitutes a moral claim upon human beings, just as Prometheus knew and suffered for the death of Zeus that was to come if Prometheus remained faithful — a death devoutly to be wished.

Ethics and the death of God merged in Friedrich Nietzsche in two ways. The death of God is already a cultural, even an epistemological, phenomenon: belief in the Christian God has become unbelievable.[37] His death is not an event to come or to be worked, as with Marx, but an event which has already occurred; but, like the bursting of a great star billions of light-years away, its news has not yet reached human beings — though human beings have effected this death themselves. And how have human beings accomplished this? By their own cultural development, a development into the forms of knowledge and morality that Nietzsche's *Gay Science* traces through the first three books that build to the death of God. Human beings have developed from a growing set of perceptions and experiences, uncommon common sense about humanity (bk. 1), through advances in affectivity and art (bk. 2), to disciplined knowledge, logic, science, and morals — all of which lead inevitably to the death of God (bk. 3). Human development necessitates God's death. Moral courage demands that this death be acknowledged.

One should emphasize that Nietzsche is not arguing an ontological change, but an epistemological one, something very close to the sociology of knowledge: Christian belief has become unbelievable. He is asserting what is incapable of human faith any longer. Locke wished to establish which objects human understanding is capable of entertaining; Nietzsche determines which objects are capable of belief — and the Christian faith in God is not among them. One can no longer believe even in this belief. Unlike Marx, Nietzsche does not attempt to bring this death to pass, but to formulate a teaching to deal with its aftermath.

Thus Spoke Zarathustra celebrates Zarathustra as a moral teacher of a wisdom he is eager to give away. His teaching is to counter the nihilism that could issue out of the death of God. His premise is almost the exact opposite of Kant's conclusion: the ethical enterprise emerges in its shape and necessity from the cultural fact of the death of God: "I teach you the Overman."[38] The

---

37. Nietzsche's specification of the death of God is precise and nuanced and deserves to be cited as a corrective to its misunderstanding in popular usages: "Das größte neuere Ereigniss, — daß 'Gott todt ist,' das der Glaube an den christlichen Gott unglaubwürdig ist — beginnt bereits seine ersten Schatten über Europa zu werfen." See Friedrich Nietzsche, *Die Fröhliche Wissenshaft*, V, no. 343, in Giorgio Colli and Massino Montinari, *Nietzsche Werke, Kritische Gesamtausgabe* (Berlin: Walter de Gruyter, 1973), vol. 2, pt. 5, p. 255.

38. Friedrich Nietzsche, *Thus Spoke Zarathustra*, trans. Walter Kaufmann (New York: Viking Press, 1968), prologue, no. 3, p. 12 (punctuation slightly altered).

Overman becomes the new moral ideal. The position Prometheus held in the honor of Marx, the Overman holds in the moral aspirations of Nietzsche: the human must be overcome in the heroic progress to the Overman. The mission of Zarathustra takes its issue from this call of the heroic: "I shall show them the rainbow and all of the steps to the Overman."[39] His instructions stood in contrast to the lessons of the "teachers of virtue" and their securing of contagious sleep for humanity.[40]

If the Overman is the great challenge to human history, the will to power is its basic moral energy: "A new will I teach men: to *will* this way which man has walked blindly, and to affirm it, and no longer to sneak away from it like the sick and decaying."[41] The heroic will constituted the fundamental moral dynamism. "Alas, that you would understand my word: 'Do whatever you will, but first be such as are *able to will*.' "[42] And the entire "On Old and New Tablets" builds in hymn to the sovereign will: "O thou my will! Thou cessation of all need, my *own* necessity! Keep me from all small victories! Thou destination of my soul, which I call destiny! Thou in-me! Over-me! Keep me and save me for a great destiny!"[43]

But all of this is cast into ambiguity when the realization dawns that no victory or no achievement is final, that there is no final overcoming. The return of all things and of all states is sempiternal. All victories are provisional. With a finite amount of matter in the universe and an eternal quantity of time, everything must reoccur endlessly — indeed had already endlessly reoccurred.[44] All of the past, even the "last man," will return, and return endlessly.[45] The hope for something beyond the provisional only mirrors the efforts and the history of Sisyphus. This realization works a profound change in Zarathustra. He becomes the teacher of the eternal recurrence, and this intractable return of the same posed the fundamental challenge to the project to which he has given his life. The eternal return becomes the alternative to the creating God.

Thus Spoke Zarathustra must put the three together: the Overman, the will to power, and the eternal return. One becomes the Overman — realizes the possibilities of her or his humanity supremely — by willing absolutely the

39. Nietzsche, *Thus Spoke Zarathustra*, prologue, no. 9, p. 24; see no. 3, p. 12.

40. Nietzsche, *Thus Spoke Zarathustra*, pt. I, no. 2, "On the Teachers of Virtue," pp. 28-30.

41. Nietzsche, *Thus Spoke Zarathustra*, pt. I, no. 3, "On the Afterworldly," p. 32.

42. Nietzsche, *Thus Spoke Zarathustra*, pt. III, no. 5, "On Virtue That Makes Small," p. 172.

43. Nietzsche, *Thus Spoke Zarathustra*, pt. III, no. 12, "On Old and New Tablets," p. 214.

44. Nietzsche, *Thus Spoke Zarathustra*, pt. III, no. 2, "On the Vision and the Riddle," pp. 155-56.

45. Nietzsche, *Thus Spoke Zarathustra*, pt. III, no. 13, "The Convalescent," pp. 217-20. Zarathustra is taught by the animals to accept and to proclaim the eternal return.

eternal return, by loving and accepting the eternal return.[46] This radically re-
defines the heroic human being. He or she becomes a process of development,
of advance toward the Overman. The finality of human nature is to become a
bridge to the Overman, while the foundation of human nature is fundamentally
the will to power. Human activity must be recognized in its possibilities and in
its glory in these terms.

Nietzsche can then move atheistic consciousness to a deeper level than
Marx. What is God? The antihuman, the destruction of the entire heroic and
humanistic project of Zarathustra and the progression of humanity to the Overman. God is the limit, the finitude of humanity. All of Zarathustra's doctrine
pounds against God as against its absolute contradiction. "But let me reveal my
heart to you entirely, my friends: If there were gods, how could I endure not to be
a god! Hence there are no gods. Though I drew this conclusion, now it draws
me."[47] The human being and God: one is necessarily the refusal of the other.

Lastly, human development is furthered by Sigmund Freud in a manner
no less passionate than Friedrich Nietzsche's. Freud undertakes his treatment
of religion and religious ideas in order to call his readers to advance beyond
illusion into a world where affirmations are rationally grounded, through a
process that he terms "*'education to reality.'* Need I confess to you that the sole
purpose of my book is to point out the necessity for this forward step?"[48] The
removal of God, of this illusion, will throw human beings on their own resources, as both Marx and Nietzsche also argued. Only then will one learn to
make a proper use of human abilities. Atheism emerges in Freud's writings as
a necessary condition for the Enlightenment's project of self-realization and
self-reliance. The destruction of conviction about God is the beginning of
authentic human freedom, though Freud's resultant ethics emerges much more
stoic than that of his predecessors. For

> men are not entirely without assistance. Their scientific knowledge has taught
> them much since the days of the Deluge, and it will increase their power still
> further. And, as for the great necessities of Fate, against which there is no
> help, they will learn to endure them with resignation.[49]

Like Nietzsche, Freud found in the advance of science the extirpation of religion.

Through a consideration of the origins and path of development, thought
Freud, one can offer an assessment of the past and trace the emergence of God

46. Nietzsche, *Thus Spoke Zarathustra*, pt. III, no. 16, "The Seven Seals (Or: The Yes
and Amen Song)," pp. 228-31.

47. Nietzsche, *Thus Spoke Zarathustra*, pt. II, no. 2, "Upon the Blessed Isles," p. 86.

48. Sigmund Freud, *The Future of an Illusion*, trans. and ed. James Strachey (New York:
Norton, 1961), p. 49 (emphasis his).

49. Freud, *The Future of an Illusion*, p. 50.

and religion as a mental asset for the self-protection of civilization. The basic force or drive behind any human development, even that of religious ideas, is the same: "The libido there follows the paths of narcissistic needs and attaches itself to the objects which ensure the satisfaction of those needs."[50] To understand the needs out of which religion has come, it is essential to recognize that parallel to the components of the total human personality — the superego, the ego, and the id — stands the corresponding and massive cultural triad that is civilization, the human person, and nature. These are lodged in continual hostility and threat — and their intractable struggle provides the context or horizon of intelligibility for the emergence of religion. Each component is mortally hostile to the others and must maintain its own integrity, influence, and control through continual dominance.[51] Hostility, threat, struggle, and control — these characterize the context in which Freud examines religion.

Within this structure of endless conflict, one asks about the psychological significance of religious ideas. They are technically illusion; that is, beliefs not grounded in evidence but in wish fulfillment and formulated to handle the threats delivered by nature and by civilization.[52] Seemingly promising, these illusions are ultimately destructive of human growth. Religion apes, as well as supports, civilization. Civilization is constituted by knowledge and regulations; religion, by beliefs and practices. Religion mirrors, as well as suggests, psychopathologies: as beliefs or illusion, religion corresponds to Meynert's amentia, a "state of acute hallucinatory confusion"; and as practice, it can be seen as a universal obsessive neurosis — issuing out of the Oedipus complex.[53] Religion is ersatz civilization, substituting for the knowledge and rational conduct of culture irrational beliefs and obsessive practices. When civilization is inadequate or when it falters, religion subsumes the three tasks of civilization against nature: human "self-regard, seriously menaced, call for consolation; life and the universe must be robbed of their terrors; moreover, human curiosity, moved, it is true, by the strongest practical interest, demands an answer."[54] On the other hand, the beliefs and practices of religion can reconcile the human person to the instinctual renunciations demanded by civilization.

The lengthy genesis of the idea of God can be traced from pre-animistic or magical stages, animistic stages, through totemism and polytheism to monotheism. For Freud also, the "death of God" occurs, but not as the Marxist project for the future or Nietzsche's epistemological fact in the recent past. This death

50. Freud, *The Future of an Illusion*, p. 24.
51. Freud, *The Future of an Illusion*, chaps. 1-2, pp. 5-14.
52. Freud, *The Future of an Illusion*, pp. 30-33.
53. Freud, *The Future of an Illusion*, p. 43 and n. 3.
54. Freud, *The Future of an Illusion*, p. 16.

occurs rather at the origins of religion — as the historical event of the killing and eating of the primeval father by the sons, the regret and fear that followed this event and the rules of totemism that arose as an attempt to ease the guilt and to appease the father. God emerges out of human history, rather than out of ethics (as with Kant) or out of human religious experience (as with Schleiermacher). The death of God is not the terminus of belief, as with Nietzsche, but its origin. As he wrote in his study of Leonardo da Vinci: "Psycho-analysis has made us aware of the intimate connection between the father-complex and belief in God, and has taught us that the personal God is psychologically nothing other than a magnified father."[55]

God is not a neutral statement leveled at humanity. Religious ideas become destructive of the human, inhibiting responsibility and growth. "The whole thing is so patently infantile, so foreign to reality, that to anyone with a friendly attitude to humanity, it is painful to think that the great majority of mortals will never be able to rise above this view of life."[56] So profoundly does God inhibit human development that religion can be listed as the great enemy of science: "Of the three powers which may dispute the basic position of science, religion alone is to be taken seriously as an enemy."[57]

What is the future of religious ideas, of God? Marginalization and extinction. There will be an increasing turning away from religion as human beings develop in their rationality, and to inhibit this disengagement would be to inhibit that human development. Gradually, painfully, the human intellect is coming into its own and breaking the bonds around it, placed and tightened by religion: "The voice of the intellect is a soft one, but it does not rest till it has gained a hearing. Finally, after a countless succession of rebuffs, it succeeds. This is one of the few points on which one may be optimistic about the future of mankind, but it is in itself a point of no small importance. . . . The primacy of the intellect lies, it is true, in a distant, distant future, but probably not in an infinitely distant one."[58] The lines between the enlightened and the religious could not be more antagonistically drawn: rational and irrational, humane development and blind inhibitions, knowledge and belief, realistic and obsessive practice.

---

55. Sigmund Freud, *Leonard da Vinci and a Memory of His Childhood,* trans. James Strachey (New York: Norton, n.d.), p. 103. See Sigmund Freud, *Moses and Monotheism,* trans. Katherine Jones (New York: Vintage, 1939), pt. III, sec. 1, pp. 102-10.

56. Sigmund Freud, *Civilization and Its Discontents,* trans. and ed. James Strachey (New York: Norton, 1961), p. 21.

57. Sigmund Freud, *New Introductory Lectures on Psychoanalysis,* trans. and ed. James Strachey (New York: Norton, 1965), p. 160.

58. Freud, *The Future of an Illusion,* p. 53 (emphasis his).

V. A Reflection

The apologetics of the early nineteenth century argued to the reality of God from human nature and its entailments: God makes possible human life in the fullest sense. The rising atheism of the later decades of that century also took the human as the point of departure, as the arena within which the struggle was to be conducted, and argued exactly to the opposite conclusion: God alienates humanity from itself and from its promise.

This attack was conducted by a philosophical anthropology that moved through differing and at times overlapping levels in its analysis of the human being and of human development. Feuerbach saw the human being as sensuous self-consciousness, with this self-consciousness uniquely able to focus upon the human species; for Marx, this sensuous self-consciousness was both socially constituted in communal solidarity and called to engage in human life as revolutionary praxis; for Nietzsche, what lay beneath all praxis, however revolutionary, was the human being as the dynamism of the will to power, the bridge to the Overman and heroic human transcendence; for Freud, the human being was psychologically constituted even in the eros of its self-affirmation and life by its collective and personal history, and by the inner struggles of its psychic components and its development, identified with progress, toward scientific rationality.

For all of these, God loomed as the great enemy. For Feuerbach, belief in God fixed the human essence outside of itself; for Marx, it alienated the human person from the practical, revolutionary activity by which alone praxis could achieve freedom; for Nietzsche, God was the external finitude of the Overman as something which would always transcend and so limit in frustration the Overman; for Freud, belief in God was the permanent infantilization of the human being.

What actually happened to the understanding of God under this massive rise of atheism in the nineteenth century? Much more occurred than the conception of God as a projection of the human, a grammatical realization that theology was really anthropology. Something much darker and more destructive had been discovered in the divine. One can take a leaf from another book to address this question.

When Ignatius of Loyola in his *Spiritual Exercises* wanted to name the diabolical, to specify what Fyodor Dostoyevsky's Ivan called "the spirit of self-destruction and non-existence," he did not use the term "Satan," and only rarely the name "Lucifer."[59] He spoke repeatedly of "el enemigo de natura humana"

---

59. For "Lucifer," see the "Meditación de dos Banderas," in the *Spiritual Exercises, Monumenta Historica Societatis Iesu, Monumenta Ignatiana,* ser. II, vol. 1, *Exercitia Spiritualia,* ed. Josephus Calveras and Candidus de Dalmases (Rome: Institutum Historicum Societatis

— the enemy of human nature.[60] The profound insight into the diabolical carried by this designation resumes a great deal of scriptural tradition and bears very much upon the dialectics of the nineteenth century: the diabolical is the destructively antihuman. Nietzsche perceptively saw this conclusion implicit in the commitments of Continental atheism:

> Theologically speaking — listen closely, for I rarely speak as a theologian — it was God himself who at the end of his days' work lay down as a serpent under the tree of knowledge: thus he recuperated from being God. — He had made everything too beautiful. — The devil is merely the leisure of God on that seventh day.[61]

This emerges as the final and devastating judgment upon all religious reality: God is the alienation of humanity from its own essence, from its social freedom, from its dynamic possibilities, from its mature self-responsibility and growth. God is the enemy of humanity. This is the unique conclusion of the atheism whose rise one can trace in the nineteenth century. It can subsequently assume even the experiences that go with the "religious," with all of its sense of integrity and dedication, so long as with John Dewey one will separate "the religious" from the concept of God, dismissing the latter as fundamentally incredible to the cultivated.[62] This judgment — that underneath the mask of God one finds not so much the visage of the human as the face of Satan — is perhaps the most radical change in religious understanding in the history of religious belief. The divine has been turned into the diabolical. God has been transformed into Satan.

Iesu, 1969), nos. 136, 137, and 138. For Dostoyevsky, see "The Grand Inquisitor," pt. 2, bk. 5, chap. 5 of *The Brothers Karamazov,* trans. David Magarshack (Baltimore: Penguin, 1958), vol. I, p. 295.

60. Ignatius of Loyola, *Spiritual Exercises,* nos. 7, 10, 135, 325, 326, 327, 334; see also *enemigo,* nos. 8, 12, 217, 274, 314, 320, 325, 329, 347, 349, 350.

61. Friedrich Nietzsche, "Beyond Good and Evil," in *Ecce Homo,* trans. and ed. Walter Kaufmann (New York: Vintage, 1989), p. 311.

62. See the proposals of John Dewey in *A Common Faith* (New Haven: Yale University Press, 1934).

CHAPTER 7

Von Balthasar's Valorization and Critique of Heidegger's Genealogy of Modernity

CYRIL O'REGAN

If once very much an adiaphora in philosophical and theological discourse, genealogy increasingly has come to play a more and more central role, indeed, has become so "inscripted" that it itself has become in some places the script. However regrettable this inversion of priorities may be, genealogical production shows little sign of abating, and in philosophy, at least, it is responsible for much of the most interesting and vital work of the past decades. In any event, the genealogical scene is definitely lively and its landscape embattled. Four issues seem particularly divisive and thus taxonomically decisive: (1) Is the difference between the contemporary and the classically modern such that it in principle justifies marking off the contemporary by the epochal indicator "post"? (2) Assuming an affirmative answer, are the relations among the postmodern, modern, and premodern to be construed in an agonistic or nonagonistic way? (3) Is the attitude taken toward the postmodern or modern that of praise or blame and, relatedly, are the differences between them and the premodern to be celebrated or mourned? (4) Has history or being come to be regarded as so radically contingent that effectively all epochal language and normative judgment is undermined?

The post-Nietzschean current in contemporary philosophy and theology constructs its position around the following set of fundamental options. The real difference of the present is asserted, such that the primary agonistic moment is between this now and a past that includes the modern and the premodern. Though disdaining explicit evaluative discourse, definite, if often implicit, negative judgments are made with respect to both the modern and the premodern. And yet despite the normative thrust and implied epochalism, there is a fascination with the view of history or being as a pure play of contingency.

There are, of course, a multitude of other genealogical options, depending on the permutation and combination of responses regarding the fundamental questions outlined above. One option with which post-Nietzscheanism has negotiated, only finally to reject, is Heidegger's powerful genealogy. However much he has influenced the post-Nietzschean current, Heidegger's answers to the above four questions clearly mark off his position. He seems to deny that the now constitutes a real difference, conceives the relation between the modern and premodern as nonagonistic or agonistic depending on whether the premodern is epochally or normatively defined, has no compunction about decrying modernity and anything in the premodern tradition that made it possible, while at the same time pulling the rug out from underneath evaluative appraisal by stressing that history is the history of being without why.

It is not clear which of these two rival theories will ultimately carry the philosophical day; nor is it clear which will win out in theology, if either. Certainly, in both fields the post-Nietzschean is making headway. Yet whatever the final outcome, it cannot be gainsaid that Heidegger's genealogy has been hugely important in philosophy and has stirred, and continues to stir, engagement with theology. The work of Hans Urs von Balthasar constitutes at once one of the most searching and extensive theological engagements with Heidegger's genealogical thesis of the century and a paradigm for the kind of revision of genealogical schemes dictated by a specifically theological mode of construal.

Von Balthasar's texts show him to be in direct negotiation with Heidegger's genealogical position. Heidegger's work is thought to merit extended comment, and important tropes of Heidegger's analysis of modernity and its emergence are taken over wholesale. Moreover, Balthasarian engagement is consistent as well as being direct. It is present in the earliest phase of von Balthasar's career as he struggles to come to terms with nineteenth- and twentieth-century German philosophical and literary thought, as it is present in the later, more obviously theologically interested thought of the great triptych of *Herrlichkeit, Theodramatik,* and *Theologik.* Our focus here will be on the later work, *Herrlichkeit* in particular, though from time to time we will draw on texts from the earlier and later periods to illustrate a point.

Von Balthasar's most extended engagement with Heidegger's genealogical thesis occurs in the multivolume text *Herrlichkeit,* now available in English translation as *The Glory of the Lord (GL).*[1] This work shows a von Balthasar

---

1. I will use the abbreviation *GL* throughout for *The Glory of the Lord,* followed by volume number only or by volume and page numbers. Hans Urs von Balthasar, *The Glory of the Lord: A Theological Aesthetics,* vol. 1, *Seeing the Form,* trans. Erasmo Leiva-Merikakis, ed. Joseph Fessio, S.J., and John Riches (San Francisco and New York: Ignatius Press and Crossroad, 1982); *The Glory of the Lord: A Theological Aesthetics,* vol. 4, *The Realm of Metaphysics in Antiquity,* trans. Brian McNeil, C.R.V., Andrew Louth, John Saward, Rowan Willams, and Oliver Davies, ed. John Riches (San Francisco: Ignatius Press, 1989); *The Glory of the*

entering deeply into the assumptive world of Heideggerian genealogy. Yet a broad range of agreements on fundaments merely sets the stage for a vigorous contestation in which at different points he questions Heidegger's demonizing view of modernity, his understanding of the enabling role played by premodernity and the theological tradition in the modern debacle, his selection of the pre-Socratics and Hölderlin as normative sources, and finally the radically historicist note struck by Heidegger. Heidegger, it turns out, is as much philosophical enemy as friend, but then just the kind of enemy one needs to wake theology from its scholastic slumber, just the kind of enemy to reprove and prove theology in a world where theology and philosophy are marginalized discourses.

I. Valorization of Heideggerian Phainesthetics

The very first page of *The Glory of the Lord* (*GL* 1:17) hints at the two important philosophical interlocutors who have something to say about the status of aesthetics in modernity as well as its relation to other forms of discourse, that is, Hegel and Heidegger. The opening paragraph has at its center the question of "beginning." The phrasing seems to recall Hegel's famous opening question about the nature of science in *Science of Logic:* "With what do we begin?"[2] The evocation is important and suggests that Hegel is a presence to be dealt with in Balthasarian texts, a position confirmed when, in the important first volume of *Theodrama*, von Balthasar critically engages Hegel's famous thesis on the death of art.[3] The very first page also clearly betrays the presence of another interlocutor by maintaining that the question of beginning may be "untimely" *(unzeitlich),* a description that regularly attends Heidegger's account of the truly philosophical act of interrogation. That this other interlocutor is not simply another philosophical interlocutor in *The Glory of the Lord* gradually becomes clear as *GL* 1 begins to unfold a plea for beauty and its fully ontological character. The question of beginning shifts from Hegel's structural-formal question about whether we can have a transcendentally secured foundation or must always begin in *media res* to Heideg-

---

Lord: A Theological Aesthetics, vol. 5, *The Realm of Metaphysics in the Modern Age,* trans. Oliver Davies, Andrew Louth, Brian McNeil, C.R.V., John Saward, and Rowan Williams, ed. Brian McNeil, C.R.V., and John Riches (San Francisco: Ignatius Press, 1991).

2. Georg W. F. Hegel, *Science of Logic,* trans. A. V. Miller (London and New York: George Allen & Unwin, Humanities Press, 1969), pp. 69-78. This question opens Hegel's discussion on the category of Being.

3. Hans Urs von Balthasar, *Theo-drama: Theological Dramatic Theory 1: Prolegomena,* trans. Graham Harrison (San Francisco: Ignatius Press, 1988), pp. 54-70.

ger's material question about the relation between art and those discourses of modernity that have taken on the mantle of the scientific and methodological precision.

GL 1 then initiates a conversation with Heidegger that reverberates throughout the whole of *The Glory of the Lord* and has its highlight in *GL* 4-5, especially *GL* 5. Though it will eventually turn out that the conversation is far from being uncritical, *GL* 1 establishes a number of preliminary points of rapprochement. In line with Heidegger, von Balthasar makes note of the modern fragmentation of discourse (*GL* 1:78) and comments on the rise of philosophy considered as an exact science to a place of eminence and the attendant relativization of aesthetic or artistic forms of articulation (1:72). Von Balthasar highlights also, as does Heidegger, the subjectivization of reality and thus all discursive forms, one of the invidious effects of which is the deontologization of beauty (1:22), which means, of course, nothing less than its erasure. These are the diagnostic features that serve as the prod, on the one hand, for a constructive rehabilitation of the ontological nature of beauty that has both historical and systematic aspects and, on the other, for an argument that beauty, ontologically specified, may serve the role of bridge between the various discourses of philosophy, art, and religion. For von Balthasar this means that beauty and truth are fundamentally related, indeed that beauty is nothing other than ontological disclosure defining truth.

Without explicitly acknowledging Heidegger's revolution concerning the nature of truth, von Balthasar understands beauty in *GL* 1 to be the lighting of being or splendor.[4] Considered thus, beauty must necessarily be regarded as a form of truth, though truth considered under the aspect of *phainesthai*.[5] As such, truth is *aletheia* in the primordial Greek sense, a lighting whose privileged medium is certainly not that of propositional discourse.[6] In some sense, von Balthasar continues a line of argument developed in *Apocalypse of the German Soul* (1937) and *Truth* (1947) where he jettisons the primacy of the proposition. Truth as correspondence gives way to the metaphor of the lighting up or *apo-phainesthai*, itself conveying the encounter with truth as disclosure or

---

4. On a formal level at least, neither Heidegger nor von Balthasar would contest the view that beauty is normatively defined as *ekphanestan*, that is, what shines forth. For Heidegger, see *The Question concerning Technology and Other Essays*, trans. W. Lovitt (New York: Harper & Row, 1977), p. 34. See also p. 156 for the importance of the metaphors of splendor and light in the aesthetic context.

5. For Heidegger's reflection on *phainesthai*, see Martin Heidegger, *On the Way to Language*, trans. Peter D. Hertz (San Francisco: Harper & Row, 1971), p. 38.

6. Heidegger, *The Question concerning Technology*, p. 12. Propositional truth as the correctness of a statement (*Richtigkeit der Aussage*) also comes under attack in Martin Heidegger, *Grundfragen der Philosophie: Ausgewählte Problem der Logik*, ed. Friedrich-Wilhelm von Hermann (Frankfurt am Main: Klostermann, 1984).

aletheuein.[7] Though he has ready at hand other, more classical resources to legitimate his move beyond propositionalism and correspondence,[8] von Balthasar finds in Heidegger a proximate precedent for the semantically close relationship between beauty, "the holy," and glory. More importantly, it is Heidegger who persuades him that such a move is urgent in the face of beauty and/or the holy's erasure in the modern world.

GL 1 establishes a vocabulary for engagement that is subsequently enacted in other volumes of *GL*, especially 4 and 5. These volumes clearly show that von Balthasar is in essential agreement with some Heideggerian axioms. He agrees in principle that metaphysics risks ontological impoverishment when in the name of clarity and exactness it cuts itself off from the sources of disclosure in reality. Though his list of suspects is not nearly as long as Heidegger's, he finds some examples of this misstep in the classical period and considers the modern period to be characterized by it. Rationalism is, von Balthasar believes, modernity's systemic deformation (*GL* 1:661). Aristotle is canonized by neither genealogist, though von Balthasar treats Aristotle more by omission than by the kind of persistent rereading and critique characteristic of Heidegger;[9] for both, Scotus seems to instantiate the kind of formal-logical mania that characterizes all that can go wrong in metaphysics and did in fact go wrong in Scholasticism (*GL* 5:16-19).[10] Moreover, after Heidegger, von Balthasar not only thinks it possible for theology to enter a compromising alliance with a deficient meta-

---

7. See the French translation of von Balthasar's 1947 work on truth, Hans Urs von Balthasar, *Phénoménologie de la vérité*, trans. R. Givard (Paris: Beauchesne, 1952), p. 21, where in the context of a defense of the nonpropositional nature of truth he evokes Heidegger's notion on truth as *a-letheia*. Here, plausibly, von Balthasar is showing some familiarity with the later Heidegger, though such is not necessary, given a position already articulated in the famous introduction to Martin Heidegger, *Being and Time*, trans. Edward Robinson and John Macquarrie (New York: Harper & Row, 1962). There Heidegger argues that *apo-phainesthai* is a phenomenal lighting that is more primordial than propositional truth. Aristotle's separation of *logos apophantikos* and truth as *aletheuin* is subverted. A subversion announced in the introduction of *Being and Time* is further articulated in sects. 7 B, 33, 44.

8. Von Balthasar's main conceptual pair in *GL* of "form" and "splendor" calls to mind the aesthetic categories at work in the thought of Aquinas, Albert, and Bonaventure.

9. Aristotle gets less than a fifth of the pages devoted to Plato in *GL* 4 (see pp. 222-26). In Heidegger's collected works there are major studies of Aristotle's *Physics* and *Metaphysics*. See, for example, Martin Heidegger, "Vom Wesen und Begriff der Physis Aristotles, Physik B 1," in *Gesamtausgabe Abteilung 1. Veröffentlichte Schriften 1914-1970*, ed. Friedrich-Wilhelm von Hermann, vol. 9 (Frankfurt: Klostermann, 1976), pp. 235-301.

10. Von Balthasar's anxiety with the possibility of a decadent propositionalist Scholasticism is apparent from early on, and arguably provides a motive for the consistently resourcement orientation of his thought that issues in the great studies on Origen, Nyssa, and Maximus. For one of Heidegger's least recherché treatments of Scholasticism, see Martin Heidegger, *Basic Problems of Phenomenology*, trans. Albert Hofstadter (Bloomington: Indiana University Press, 1982), pp. 71-121.

physics in which the *doxa* is lost,[11] but also judges this historically to have been the case. Indeed, the critical purchase of theological aesthetics is to rescue theology from precisely such a misalliance, which, it seems, is a constant ingredient of history, but one taking different forms in different periods. If the tendencies of modernity hardly bode well for a theology that would be *doxological* in the strict sense, then neither the speculative grammar of Scotus, nor the Scholasticism of Suárez, nor the degenerate Thomism of the nineteenth century are calculated to preserve the irreducible moment of mystery and the emptying adorative response that defines the biblical and patristic attitude to God and the cosmos. In addition, von Balthasar agrees with Heidegger, though for different reasons,[12] that Platonism or Neoplatonism presents special difficulties for a mode of thought that structurally speaking considers itself to be postmetaphysical.

II. The Authority of Heidegger's Hölderlin

The significant role played by Hölderlin in *GL* 4 and 5, von Balthasar's two volumes on metaphysics, also betrays the authority of Heidegger. Von Balthasar's discussion of metaphysics is framed by epigraphs from Hölderlin, whose work, it is said later, constitutes the most significant literary recovery of the splendor of being in modernity (*GL* 5:298). And while *GL* 5 ends with von Balthasar's assessment of the possibility and necessity of a theology of Christian glory that is beyond metaphysics, he is manifestly in conversation with Heidegger, who is portrayed as accomplishing the most significant modern philosophical retrieval of glory (5:449). In *GL* 5 von Balthasar not only presents fairly sizable accounts of Heidegger (5:429-51) and Hölderlin (5:298-338), but also brings them into a revealing proximity with each other in B.5 of section 2 of the text. In B.6 von Balthasar renews his treatment of modern philosophical

11. One of Heidegger's most explicit statements about the loss of *doxa* is to be found in Martin Heidegger, *Vom Wesen der Wahrheit zu Platons Höhlengleichnis und Theätet* (Frankfurt am Main: Vittorio Klostermann, 1988), pp. 246-58, 262-322. Plato, of course, is made the culprit, by forcing the issue between truth and falsity and associating *doxa* with the latter.

12. Heidegger's hostility to Platonism derives from the judgment, shared with Nietzsche, that Platonism represents the overcoming of the ontological difference by bringing Being within the ordinance of episteme or the idea. Von Balthasar does not accept this view. Platonism is not characterized by this focal loss of transcendence. Nevertheless, as he indicates throughout *GL* 4, Platonism may incite an indirect loss of transcendence by depersonalizing what is beyond the order of beings and by thinking of the relation of beings to beyond under the aspect of necessity. While Christianity need not be allergic to contact with Platonism, it has to be on its guard. *GL* is consistent with von Balthasar's earlier work on Maximus the Confessor; where Maximus is praised for such resistance, Pseudo-Dionysius is condemned.

figures that favorably, if not obviously, respond to glory without including Heidegger explicitly in the trajectory. Heidegger obviously would be gratified to be found among the poets and outside a trajectory of modern metaphysics he abjures. Fulfilling Heidegger's wishes, however, is hardly von Balthasar's real intention in *GL* 5. The association of Heidegger and Hölderlin in B.5 also strategically permits a critical foothold. Hölderlin and Heidegger, as well as Goethe (5:339-408) and Rilke (5:409-28) (who in the text intercalate between them), are judged relatively successful in retrieving cosmic glory, while it remains open to question whether they succeed in retrieving a more transcendent glory that is more than beauty, and which consequently is Christianly redeemable — an issue raised explicitly in the third and concluding section of von Balthasar's reflection on metaphysics (5:613-56).

Though it might be argued that the association of Hölderlin and Heidegger could in part be explained by von Balthasar's Germanism, inasmuch as he earlier in *Apocalypse of the German Soul* saw Hölderlin and Heidegger as belonging essentially to the same cultural trend,[13] here the association is perspicuous in a qualitatively different way. Not only is the Heidegger under review the Heidegger who has left behind the existential analytic of *Dasein* (being-there), but Hölderlin is the Hölderlin refracted through Heidegger's concerns with nihilism and the erasure of holy as the shining of Being. Indeed, Hölderlin's status is determined in large part by the role he plays in Heidegger's metanarrative of the "forgetfulness of Being" *(Seinsvergessenheit)* and/or thesis of desacralization *(Entdivinisierung)*. This is indicated in two different ways in the volumes on metaphysics. It is indicated indirectly by the epigraphs and what amounts to their Heideggerian exegesis on the opening pages of *GL* 4, and more directly in the actual reading of Hölderlin carried out in *GL* 5. The epigraphs, which announce the flight of the gods and the loss of hope in genuine transcendence, provoke a systematic set of Heideggerian judgments. In the very first pages von Balthasar points to the harms of aesthetization subsequent to the demise of the sacred as glory (*GL* 5:13),[14] criticizes psychologism (5:19), and praises Rilke's poetry for its nontitanic posture of letting-be, a posture canonized by Heidegger and associated with both Hölderlin as precursor and Rilke as disciple. All of this seems to indicate von Balthasar's appropriation of Heidegger's view of modernity forged in large part by his reading of Hölderlin. Hölderlin in a sense, therefore, functions as a figure for a certain view of the transcendence of modernity, found worthy of both examination and contestation.

13. Hans Urs von Balthasar, *Apokalypse der deutschen Seele: Studien zu einer Lehre von letzen Haltungen,* vol. 1, *Der deutsche Idealismus* (Salzburg, Leibzig: Verlag Anton Pustet, 1937), pp. 293-346.

14. See the essay of Hans Urs von Balthasar, "Revelation and the Beautiful," in *Explorations in Theology,* vol. 1, *The Word Made Flesh,* trans. A. V. Littledale with Andrew Dru (San Francisco: Ignatius Press, 1989), pp. 95-126, esp. pp. 105-6.

In his actual reading of Hölderlin, von Balthasar recapitulates important aspects of the Heideggerian reading. This reading is nonliterary in the strict sense. The idiosyncratic features of Hölderlin's style, his syntactic regressions and innovations that would be grist for the mill for literary theorists, and which are now the means for opening up the "antiphilosophical" Hölderlin,[15] are eschewed by von Balthasar, as they were by Heidegger. Hölderlin is a poet of definite themes, and his enterprise is capable of synopsis in key words. Like Heidegger, von Balthasar thinks of Hölderlin as at once engaged in a critique of modernity and in an attempt to recover the traces of theophanous presence in a time that is unpropitious (*GL* 5:311). It is in the context of this attempt that von Balthasar, after Heidegger, valorizes the poetic enterprise. He does so by focusing on the sayings of Hölderlin made famous by Heidegger's commentaries;[16] namely, the paradox that poetry in the modern world at least is the most innocent — read nonutilitarian — yet also the most dangerous of occupations (5:311). Poetry is a self-denuding exposure to divine presence or suffering response to its absence (5:311).[17] As such poetry is a doxological enterprise, and as doxological its response is quintessentially a religious one. If Heidegger is convinced that in Hölderlin one finds a nonalienating response to what in religious language can be called divine immanence, or what in more nearly philosophical language can be called *physis*, von Balthasar is equally convinced that Hölderlin captures in an exemplary — though not necessarily unsurpassable — fashion the power and splendor of a theophanous cosmos (5:299). The extraordinarily real and deep philhellenic thrust of Hölderlin is recognized by both. There is nothing at all academic or secondhand about this retrieval (5:318), something that obviously cannot be said of all the major figures in the German and English romantic movement, where the retrieval of Greece in part plays the role of a culturally legitimating agent and source of authority for a mode of thought uniquely modern and post-Enlightenment in its basic orien-

15. See Theodor Adorno, "Parataxis: On Hölderlin's Later Poetry," in *Notes to Literature,* ed. Rolf Tiedermann, trans. Shierry Weber Nicholson (New York: Columbia University Press, 1992), vol. 2, pp. 109-49; Paul de Man, "Heidegger's Exegeses of Hölderlin," in *Blindness and Insight,* 2nd ed., Theory and History of Literature, vol. 22 (Minneapolis: University of Minnesota Press, 1983), pp. 246-66; and Warminski, *Readings in Interpretation: Hölderlin, Hegel, Heidegger,* Theory and History of Literature, vol. 26 (Minneapolis: University of Minnesota Press, 1987), pp. 45-71. All three readings challenge Heidegger's view of a vision in Hölderlin, at once total and ontological.

16. For reflections on Hölderlin's sayings on the innocence and danger of poetic occupation, see Martin Heidegger, "Hölderlin and the Essence of Poetry," trans. D. Scott, in *Existence and Being,* 3rd ed. (London: Vision Press, 1968), pp. 293-315.

17. Here von Balthasar seems to be in negotiation with such texts as Heidegger, "Essence of Poetry," p. 313, and Martin Heidegger, "What Are Poets For," in *Poetry, Language, Thought,* trans. Albert Hofstadter (San Francisco and New York: Harper & Row, 1971), pp. 89-142, esp. pp. 91-94.

tation. Hölderlin, both would agree, is unique in romanticism in the way that he lives and feels the classical world. In this sense, Hölderlin is indeed a supreme modern Greek, a Homer, or better, a Pindar *redivivus*.

Yet, for both, Hölderlin is not exhausted in his Greek retrieval. His modernity places him in a more complicated situation that he is forced to negotiate. Part of this complication is that as a poet Hölderlin is forced to mint a language of adorative response to the world that seems to deny its divine or sacred attribution (*GL* 5:312), indeed, that seems to convey more nearly the absence than the presence of the gods (5:308). Acknowledging the modernity extra in Hölderlin's situation, however, does not encourage von Balthasar to focus, as with Heidegger, on the night which has fallen on modernity and thus to privilege the poet as the one who espies the traces of the departed gods. Still, with Heidegger, von Balthasar shares a normative view of the poetic act and believes that the poetic praxis and reflection of Hölderlin serve as an illustration that poetry can neither evoke presence nor mourn its absence unless it drops its titanic posture, unless it becomes truly a culture of humility (5:310) running counter to the will to power that marks the modern period (5:312). For both, the poetic in modernity, as in the classical world, serves as a superb instantiation of *Gelassenheit* (releasement). More, the genuinely poetic act is a form of prayer in which the monological circuit of modernity is transcended (5:314-20). Though a major object of *GL* 4 and 5 is to argue that Christianity escapes Heideggerian strictures, von Balthasar agrees with Heidegger's reading that Christianity is implicated in the crisis that Hölderlin faces. Christianity has at least to take some historical responsibility for the effacement of the holy and the glory of the cosmos that is a major cause of Hölderlin's anxiety and the subject of his greatest poetry (5:652). Accordingly, von Balthasar shows no discomfort in validating, as Heidegger does, the attempt and partial success of Hölderlin's recovery of the theophanous nature of the cosmos. For von Balthasar the health of Christianity does not rest on the evacuation of divine presence from the world, the resort to a pure *kerygma*, a position Heidegger himself early in his career seemed to suggest.[18] Rather, the historical healing of Christianity and its possibility of being a sacramental sign to the world is precisely the recovery of the mythological dimension that in modernity has given way to either procedural or speculative forms of thought.

---

18. Around the time of *Being and Time* Heidegger had a much friendlier relation to Christianity than later. See Martin Heidegger, "Phenomenology and Theology," in *The Piety of Thinking: Essays by Martin Heidegger*, trans. James E. Mart and John C. Malado (Bloomington: Indiana University Press, 1976), pp. 5-21. The later Heidegger is by and large hostile to Christianity. Still, any positive reference to Christianity takes essentially the same tack of distinguishing after Bultmann between faith and theology and favoring the former. For one such asseveration, see Heidegger, "The Word of Nietzsche: 'God is Dead,'" in *The Question concerning Technology*, pp. 53-112, esp. p. 105.

The other side to von Balthasar's retrieval is his focusing on key words, a characteristic Heideggerian hermeneutical tactic. As it turns out, these key words reinforce the thematic emphasis. The key words for von Balthasar resemble those of Heidegger. "Holy," "divine," "light" belong to Heidegger's lexicon. "Glory," in one sense an insignificant addition, ultimately represents a critical supplement that will help relativize many of Heidegger's conclusions concerning the invidious role played by Christianity in the eclipse of the holy that characterizes modernity.

For it is clear that one essential thrust of *GL* as a whole, but especially *GL* 4 and 5, is apologetic. There are different levels to the vindication of Christianity. At the lowest level, Christianity is exonerated of the Heideggerian charges that in principle it discourages mystery and encourages the desacralization of the world. At a higher level, while von Balthasar openly confesses that Christianity consistently intersects with philosophy or metaphysics throughout the Western tradition, not every such intersection need be read as contributing to the nihilation of *physis* and the would-be theophanous universe. At this level, the effort is made to read the tradition against Heidegger and plea for its acquittal. At the highest level, Heidegger's own program is questioned as to whether it can guarantee one of its sometime stated aims: the recovery of the glory of the cosmos. Further, Heidegger's program is questioned as to whether it, and not Christianity, is more nearly nihilistic insofar as it, and not Christianity, transgresses the ontological difference between Being and beings. We will return to the apologetic side of *GL* later in section III.

If von Balthasar reads Hölderlin as refracted through Heidegger, he reads Heidegger as reflected through a reading of Hölderlin. For von Balthasar's discussion of Heidegger in *GL* 5 is situated in a section dealing with the trajectory of classical retrieval that transcends the modern subjectification of reality by the representational subject and views the world as a play of dynamic emergence. This prospectus, shared by Goethe and Hölderlin, and found in the twentieth century in Rilke and Trakl (*GL* 5:433), represents an attempt to transcend the fateful intersection in modernity of rationalism with will, ultimately an uncontrollable and totalizing *libido dominandi*. Heidegger shares with these figures the impulse to break with the principle of sufficient reason, to transcend the why (5:443) that is responsible for ridding reality of mystery and reducing it to the status of object (5:441-43).[19] But for Heidegger the liberation of the whylessness and gratuity of reality is accompanied by a particular disposition. This disposition is just the exact contrary of the titanic disposition so

---

19. For a good account of von Balthasar's commitment to truth as mystery, see von Balthasar, *Phénoménologie de la vérité*, pp. 117-214. For Heidegger's critique of the hegemony of logic, see especially Martin Heidegger, *The Metaphysical Foundations of Logic*, trans. Michael Heim (Bloomington and Indianapolis: Indiana University Press, 1992).

typical of modernity; it is one of radical self-abandonment or *Gelassenheit* (5:438). Von Balthasar recognizes the medieval precedents for Heidegger's depiction of this attitude of humility and openness, while at the same time assenting to the Heideggerian position that this attitude is the primordial Greek attitude and via Hölderlin a modern possibility. And it is *Gelassenheit* that points the way to a qualitatively different view of the nature of freedom than that held by modernity either in the mode of freedom of the will or the energetics of self-determination. Freedom is a form of ecstasy toward mystery, an openness toward reality not understood as a neutral fact to be epistemically grasped but a revelation that evokes the response of the whole person. Rendered in noninstrumental language, this ecstasy takes the form of praise and thanksgiving (5:433-34). Von Balthasar is aware that the disposition of ecstasy implies a notion of truth that is neither that of correspondence nor of the certitude of the Cartesian subject. Truth is disclosure, the lighting of Being that can never be so mastered that nondisclosure is not an ingredient in disclosure. Von Balthasar, in his review of Heidegger's contribution to a fundamentally aesthetic view of truth, has no problem on one level validating the alpha privative in Heidegger's view of truth as *a-letheia*.[20]

In *GL* 5 the Hölderlinian figuration of Heidegger reinforces the Heideggerian figuration of Hölderlin. This serves not only to confirm a liaison suggested by Heidegger himself, but to somewhat relativize Heidegger's relation with Nietzsche. While von Balthasar has obviously read Heidegger's commentaries on Nietzsche (*GL* 5:433), he yet makes no explicit attempt to spell out the relationship. The reasons for von Balthasar's relativization of this association can only be conjectured. One reason, of course, is sheer redundancy. The exegeses of Hölderlin and Nietzsche belong to the same period of Heideggerian reflection and prosecute essentially the same diagnosis and critique of modernity and the metaphysical tradition. Admittedly, however, when it comes to a decision as to which figure offers the more compelling recipe for breaking the power of the egological circuit and thus moving beyond nihilism, Hölderlin's Diotima is to be preferred to Nietzsche's Zarathustra. A second plausible reason is that von Balthasar is in general in *GL*, and especially in his exposition of Heidegger in *GL* 5, more focally interested in the somewhat more normative thrust displayed in Heidegger's Hölderlin commentaries. A third plausible reason is that von Balthasar has reason to think that as long as Heidegger is in concert with Hölderlin, prospects exist for something other than a Nietzschean-like dismissal of Christianity. Yet, as we shall see later in section III, von Balthasar remains to a degree engaged with a Heidegger more determined by Nietzsche, though this engagement proves to be largely negative.

---

20. See von Balthasar, *Phénoménologie de la vérité*, p. 21. For von Balthasar, however, the finite apperception of reality does not mean that truth as such is finite.

Von Balthasar's engagement with the "later" or post-*Kehre* Heidegger in *GL* is on the whole profoundly positive. Moreover, it is this engagement that sets the provisional terms for his own genealogical account, which like Heidegger's does not privilege the explicitly philosophical over the literary. The terms can only be provisional, since von Balthasar will unearth numerous instances of interpretive failure in Heidegger and expose a set of deeply questionable interpretive practices that not only vitiate Heidegger's reading of the metaphysical tradition but also undermine his summary dismissal of the Christian tradition.

III. Contestation of Heidegger's Genealogy

As we have seen, the terms in which von Balthasar sets his genealogical account are ineluctably Heideggerian. Though the erasure of the holy as divine presence is just one of the descriptions Heidegger uses to mark modernity, it serves a prominent role in Heidegger's ever-spiraling discourse about modernity's basic flaw. Heidegger demonizes the egological framework of modernity, traceable back to Descartes's search for a *fundamentum inconcussum veritatis*, that he cannot avoid suggesting a rift between modernity and premodernity that makes modernity a *novum*. It is his considered view that the modern is the working out of the premodern derailment of the forgetfulness of being or the erasure of glory. The bile in evidence with respect to the modern period and its technological essence, in which reality is totally demystified and reduced to the status of available resource *(Gestell)*,[21] cannot be read to connote a full or partial exoneration of the classical tradition. Rather, in the woeful trespass of modernity the true face of the classical is revealed.

Minor variations notwithstanding, there is remarkable consistency in Heidegger's narrative. Descartes is not the *fons et origo* of the eclipse of the holy and the erasure of the ontological difference that is the condition of the mysterious and enigmatic nature of reality. Moreover, the roots are not discoverable proximally in the late medieval or Renaissance tradition, though Heidegger shows himself unhappy with medieval metaphysics, particularly in the shape of the speculative grammar of Scotus,[22] begrudging with respect to the possibility of Thomistic *esse*, and harsh in his assessment of the close relation between

21. For a good account of *Gestell* as that which is set before a subject for its use, see Heidegger, *The Question concerning Technology*, p. 15.
22. See Heidegger, *Basic Problems of Phenomenology*, pp. 77-121, where Heidegger critiques the medieval essence-existence distinction in Aquinas and Scotus, determining that both are in the final analysis essentialist. In the 1930s the Scotist determination of Being as the most universal and empty of categories becomes a trope to be contested.

theology and philosophy which, in his view, invariably favors the dogmatism of belief over the openness of the question.[23] The origin of the obscuration can, he believes, be traced back to the very beginnings of classical philosophy in Plato. With hypnotic regularity Plato is denounced as forgetting the ontological difference by objectifying *physis* and turning *aletheia* into the correspondence of thought and reality, that is, reality as idea.[24] "Fall" *(Abfall)* in metaphysics is thus at its inception. Indeed, metaphysics is nothing but fall, its history the history of the forgetfulness of the lighting of Being glimpsed in a primal but not unsurpassable way in pre-Socratic Greek thought, in Anaximander and Heraclitus, but also in Sophocles and even Homer. Functionally, if not absolutely, pre-Socratic Greek thought serves the role of norm by which the deviation of metaphysics is judged. The whole metaphysical tradition with Plato as its alpha and Nietzsche as its omega constitutes a single line of deformation. Whatever merits Heidegger feels he can attribute to Aristotle and Kant in the context of a close reading of the *Metaphysics* and *Physics* and the first *Critique* are withdrawn. In Heidegger's history of metaphysics Aristotle, for instance, can justly be remembered as the philosopher who covered over the aboriginal senses of *energeia* and *aitia*.[25] Scotus and medieval metaphysics in general are dots on the line that extend into the modern period via the anthropological revolution of Descartes that in turn reaches via Leibniz, Kant, and Hegel to Nietzsche. One way of talking about the systemic flaw of metaphysics is to designate it as *ontotheological,* by which term Heidegger means to suggest that the ungroundedness of the gift of Being or, as he later suggests, Appropriation *(Ereignis),* is identified with a ground *(to theoin).*[26] In one way or another every major figure in the metaphysical tradition is implicated in fateful narrowing of Being into a being as the ground of being. Whether this ground is referred to as idea, actuality, reason, or will is a matter of indifference to Heidegger. Every and any identification levels Being by putting it on the level of the cognizing subject, reneging on the promise held out by philosophy in its rendering of its constitutive act as *thaumazein.* After his early Bultmann period, only rarely does

---

23. See Heidegger's harsh judgment of Christian theology in Martin Heidegger, *Introduction to Metaphysics,* trans. Ralph Mannheim (New Haven and London: Yale University Press, 1959), pp. 6-7.

24. The classic text is Martin Heidegger, "Platons Lehre von der Wahrheit," in *Wegmarken* (Frankfurt am Main: Vittorio Klostermann, 1976), pp. 203-38.

25. See Heidegger, *The Question concerning Technology,* pp. 6-8; also Heidegger, "Vom Wesen und Begriff der Physis Aristotles, Physik B 1," pp. 242-43.

26. For a particularly declarative assertion of this point, see Martin Heidegger, *Hegel's Phenomenology of Spirit,* trans. Parvis Emad and Kenneth Maly (Bloomington: Indiana University Press, 1988), pp. 98-100, 124-26. See also Martin Heidegger, "The Ontotheological Nature of Metaphysics," in *Essays in Metaphysics: Identity and Difference,* trans. Kurt F. Leidecker (New York: Philosophical Library, 1960), pp. 35-67.

Heidegger show himself disposed to believe that Christianity escapes the parameters of the ontotheological fallacy. For the most part, he asserts, Christianity uncritically accepts a metaphysical model that prioritizes cause and effect.[27] This in itself indicates for him that Christianity construes the relation between Being and beings after the manner of *techné* and not after the manner of *poiesis*, the event or happening of revelation or disclosure. Christianity, on Heidegger's considered view, is imbricated in a productionist metaphysics.[28]

Covering essentially the same metaphysical terrain, von Balthasar contests Heidegger's reading at every point. By omitting treatment of the pre-Socratic philosophers, von Balthasar severely limits the kind of criteriological significance they have in Heidegger's texts and the critical purchase they have over against Plato and the classical tradition. Moreover, *GL* in general, and *GL* 4 in particular, evinces something like a concerted attempt to deny that Platonism in general, and Plato in particular, represents the logocentric immanentization of Being (*GL* 4:166ff., 280ff.). Admitting that the medieval period is not without deformations, von Balthasar exonerates this epoch in both its more metaphysical and religious instantiations of the charge of ontotheology. He also contests Heidegger's reading of modernity in which the essentials of modern philosophy are inscribed in Descartes and simply await enucleation. Neither Leibniz nor Kant, for example, can without further ado be plotted on the Cartesian line. Both systems are rich enough to show more than traces of transcendence with regard to the representational horizon of modernity. And even Descartes has moments in which the egological framework of his thought is undone (*GL* 5:458, 460). This review constitutes but a sketch of a rich contestation. This essay will limit itself to outlining von Balthasar's acts of resistance to: first, Heidegger's reading of Plato as the site of metaphysical fall, and of Kant, who radicalizes a declension there from the beginning, as an exemplary instance of the tendency of modernity to subjectivity; and, second, to Heidegger's reading of Hölderlin as pivotal for his diagnostic of modernity and the imagining of a way out. These acts of resistance demand different critical moves, in the case of the former rehabilitation, in the case of the latter critical limitation.

III.1. Rehabilitation of Plato and Kant

Though the rejection of the Heideggerian reading of Plato is far from trenchant, it can be seen to inform von Balthasar's explicit discussion of Plato in *GL* 4 and

---

27. See, for example, Heidegger, *The Question concerning Technology,* p. 28.
28. One Heidegger commentator who has clearly grasped this point is Michael E. Zimmerman. See Zimmerman, *Heidegger's Confrontation with Modernity* (Bloomington: Indiana University Press, 1990).

also his defense of the *kalokagathon* in *GL* 1 and 5. In *GL* 4 a portrait emerges that is decidedly at odds with the logocentric profile of "Plato's Teaching on Truth" and a host of other Heidegger texts. On von Balthasar's reading, both the source and culminating point of Platonic philosophy is in excess of concept. Far from validating a correspondence theory of truth in his famous discussion of *to agathon* (the good) in the *Republic* (bk. 7), Plato's view could not be more excessive. Von Balthasar agrees with Friedländer's definitive riposte to the Heideggerian reading.[29] The good is not an objective correlative to an act of intellect, being insofar as it is assimilated by a noetic act, but rather that which exceeds knowing and the known (*GL* 4:179-80). As excessive, the good is the quintessentially aesthetic. Von Balthasar points to a passage in the *Republic* (bk. 6, 509a) where the good and the beautiful are brought into alignment without necessarily becoming identical. The good is something of extraordinary splendor *(amechanon kallos)* (*GL* 4:180). Here the good is the nonconceptualizable revelation that is at the base of concept and the promise of its interruption. No less than Plotinus is Plato aware that revelation has the property of suddenness *(exaiphnes)* beyond all method and intellectual cognition. Von Balthasar is convinced that a fair assessment of Plato's discursive practice is sufficient to expose as caricature the picture of an unrelenting rationalist, almost de rigueur since Nietzsche. Among other things, the rationalist reading willfully ignores the presence of myth in Plato's texts and their function (4:195-97).

In addition, the discussion of the *kalokagathon* (1:25, 59; 5:201-4) rhetorically functions to unite Heideggerian concerns about the eclipse of ontophany with a classical Platonic vocabulary, thereby subverting the distanciation between Heidegger and Plato. Moreover, to the degree to which the Heideggerian scheme seems to function dyadically, that is, only with the pair of truth and beauty and excluding the good,[30] to that extent von Balthasar believes it is implicated in the very process of immanentization that on one level at least Heidegger mourns (1:59). Here von Balthasar seems to be in essential agreement with the kind of critique of Heidegger offered by Emmanuel Levinas.[31]

By placing Kant (5:481-513) in the line that stretches from Descartes through Spinoza and Leibniz to German idealism, von Balthasar, at one level, is doing nothing more than reciting a fairly standard reading of the history of

---

29. Paul Friedländer, *Plato 1: An Introduction,* trans. Hans Meyerhoff, Bollingen Series, 54 (Princeton: Princeton University Press, 1969), pp. 221-29.

30. In Heidegger, "Platons Lehre von der Wahrheit," *to agathon* (the good) functions in a purely ontological fashion and excludes any moralizing interpretation (pp. 227-30). See also Heidegger, *Introduction to Metaphysics,* where he has little difficulty connecting *on* (being) and *kalon* (the beautiful) (p. 132), but where *on* is never brought into relation with *agathon* (the good) as that which might possibly define it.

31. See Emmanuel Levinas, *Totality and Infinity: An Essay in Exteriority,* trans. Alphonso Lingis (Pittsburgh: Duquesne University Press, 1969).

philosophy. But on another level, he is presenting a specifically Heideggerian genealogy, for it is clear that Heidegger's critical pair of the forgetfulness of Being and/or the effacement of epiphany is regulative for understanding the trajectory. Importantly, however, it is not assumed beforehand that forgetfulness or effacement is absolute in all cases, indeed, in any case, nor that the measure of forgetfulness or effacement is equal in all. If Leibniz fares well, von Balthasar thinking that Leibniz's project is not summed up, as Heidegger thought, by the principle of sufficient reason (5:472),[32] Kant fares even better. Without it ever being suggested that Kant escapes the tendency to anthropologize epiphany, von Balthasar offers a reading conspicuous in its generosity and its lack of attention to the first *Critique*. This defocusing is, of course, itself a major, if not the major, act of hermeneutic generosity, for it is on the basis of the first *Critique* as defining Kant that Heidegger can feel justified in plotting Kant in his line of modern degeneration.[33] Von Balthasar freewheels through Kant's work, picking out the epiphanic scraps from Kant's precritical writings (*GL* 5:481-89), construing the *Critique of Practical Reason* as a necessary complement to the first *Critique*, indeed, a complement that retrospectively situates the agenda of the first *Critique* as the attempt to move beyond thought's dominating power and control (5:489-96), and reading the third *Critique* (5:496-513) as a recovery of at least some of the revelation of reality surrendered by the first *Critique*.

In a certain, perhaps ultimately positive sense, von Balthasar's reading of Kant is superficial. That is, von Balthasar paints something like a portrait of Kant's evolution and traces some of his significant and enduring interests. The hermeneutic effect, however, is anything but shallow. By reading Kant in this way, von Balthasar sets up a block against Heidegger's deep but also profoundly ahistorical reading, in which Kant becomes a creature of the first *Critique*. Kant is recontextualized by an account of his own textual history. Each of the three areas of Kant's writing treated by von Balthasar reveals ways in which Kant escapes the anthropologization of epiphany. For von Balthasar, the precritical

32. It is clear that Heidegger regards the principle of sufficient reason as both summing up Leibniz's own program and contributing significantly to the demise of ontophany in the modern period. For Heidegger's specific critique of Leibniz, see *The Metaphysical Foundations of Logic*, pp. 54ff. For an example of his more general critique, see Martin Heidegger, *The Essence of Reasons*, trans. Terrence Malik (Evanston: Northwestern University Press, 1969), pp. 11-33.

33. There is some discrepancy between the revisionist-retrievalist reading the Kant of the first *Critique* receives in Martin Heidegger, *Kant und das Problem der Metaphysik*, 4th rev. ed. (Frankfurt: Klostermann, 1973), and the role Kant subsequently plays in Heidegger's genealogical scheme. This is plausibly explained by a change in Heidegger's view of Kant. At least as plausible, however, is the view that revisionist retrievals and genealogies play different roles in Kant. The former, the plunging of *Destruktion* to hear the unsaid in a great thinker's thought, concerns the possibilities of thought, not its actuality. Genealogy, by contrast, focuses on the said and thought in the actuality of its expression.

writings show a Kant so entranced by the sublimity of the cosmos that the self is effectively forgotten. The Kant of the second *Critique* is a Kant who responds to the moral law as sublime. In stressing the sublimity of the moral law, von Balthasar underscores the element of surrender involved in the response of the human subject or agent. Again in his analysis of the *Critique of Judgment* von Balthasar seeks points in Kant's enterprise that open it up ontolologically. The area of reflection in the third *Critique* that provides the best opportunity for such an opening is Kant's reflection on the Sublime, for the Sublime indicates a loss of cognitive control not evident in the same way in a response to the beautiful. The dissonance experienced by the subject seems to bring the self beyond the self, to point to an ecstatic existence open to a disclosure to which it corresponds neither conceptually nor aesthetically in the strict sense. Recognizing that in the main Kant's view of the Sublime is fairly formal, von Balthasar in a bold move associates the Sublime with the Good exposed in his analysis of Kant's ethics. By so doing, he effectively puts himself in conversation with some postmoderns, especially Lyotard,[34] who make this move in order to gain a vantage point from which to critique modernity.

III.2. Deconstructing Heidegger's Hölderlin

While there is a sense in which his treatment of Hölderlin recycles material from *Apocalypse of the German Soul*, von Balthasar's reading in *GL* 5 seems calculated not simply to recall Heidegger's reading but to contest it. The strategies for counterreading, as we shall see, closely follow those at work in von Balthasar's reading of Kant, with one major difference. Whereas in the case of Kant von Balthasar has to struggle against a reading that would place Kant in the line of perdition, in the case of Hölderlin he has to contend with a reading of superlative generosity that exempts Hölderlin from anything to do with modernity's systemic forgetfulness of Being. Thus von Balthasar's counterreading is here counterhagiographical, whereas it was counterdemonic in the case of Kant. In this counterreading it is suggested that the Hölderlin of pure Greek

---

34. Kant's distinction of the sublime is central to Lyotard's thought. With it Lyotard feels he has critical purchase over modern thought, for it is the sublime that functions like the good in that it relativizes certitudes and pieties. See Francois Lyotard, *The Postmodern Explained: Correspondence, 1982-1985*, trans. and ed. Julian Pefanis and Morgan Thomas (Minneapolis: University of Minnesota Press, 1993), pp. 1-16; also *Lessons on the Analytic of the Sublime*, trans. Elizabeth Rottenberg (Stanford: Stanford University Press, 1994), pp. 147-90. In *Heidegger and the Jews*, trans. Andreas Michel and Mark S. Roberts (Minneapolis: University of Minnesota Press, 1970), pp. 40-41, 79-80, Lyotard suggests that it is Heidegger's fundamental deafness to the sublime that is the condition of the possibility of the bombast of his Greco-Roman phainesthetic.

retrieval, the Hölderlin who escapes the tragic fate of modernity, is in an important sense an idealized fabrication. And precisely because the Heideggerian portrait of Hölderlin focuses overwhelmingly on the great hymns,[35] von Balthasar challenges the limited textual range of Heidegger's commentary, questioning the accuracy of the image projected. We begin with the image and its two dimensions.

By insisting on romanticism and idealism as the cultural-historical contexts for Hölderlin's work (GL 5:299, 315-20, 334), von Balthasar agrees with Adorno that Heidegger basically represses the question of the relation between Hölderlin and the philosophical tradition from which he emerged.[36] For von Balthasar, of course, idealism in particular does not simply serve the role of background scenery; rather, it is a powerful ingredient in Hölderlin's operative ideology and saturates his work as a whole. One symptom of this is the titanic strain in Hölderlin that is not fully transcended even in, or especially in, the announcement of self-renunciation. Von Balthasar presents an analysis considerably more inclusive than Heidegger's. Concretely this means that von Balthasar's own treatment does not exclude commentary on Hölderlin's two major nonpoetic works, Hyperion (GL 5:305) and Empedocles (5:327-31), texts vital for Hölderlin's literary reputation. Reinscribing these two texts assists von Balthasar to paint over Heidegger's pure but somewhat insubstantial portrait. Importantly, it lends support to the perception that the titanic posture lies deep in Hölderlin, albeit in a mutated form, and that the idealist ethos is anything but an idle wheel. The three hermeneutical necessities of recognizing Hölderlin's idealist ethos, the reality of his titanic gestures, and the textual actuality of Hyperion and Empedocles together serve to point to the difference between Hölderlin and the Greek piety he is supposed to have recovered in a crystalline pure form. Thus, even if Heidegger's picture of Greek piety were to be accepted — and not all the details are — Hölderlin can no more serve the role of pure Hellene than Germany and Greece can successfully be yoked together in sacred marriage.

35. Granted that Heidegger does occasionally refer to the fragmentary poems of Hölderlin's latter period that have so attracted the postmodernists, and even quotes a few times from Empedocles, his real concern seems to be a philosophical exegesis of the hymns. "Germanien" and "Der Rhein" have a volume devoted to them, as do "Der Ister" and "Andenken." "Brot und Wein" also comes in for considerable discussion, and many other hymns at least merit an essay. For book-length interpretations by Heidegger of individual hymns of Hölderlin, see Gesamtausgabe, vol. 39, Hölderlins Hymnen "Germanien" und "Der Rhein," ed. Susanne Ziegler (Frankfurt am Main: Klostermann, 1980); Gesamtausgabe, vol. 53, Hölderlins Hymn "Der Ister," ed. Walter Biemel (Frankfurt am Main: Klostermann, 1984); Gesamtausgabe, vol. 52, Hölderlins Hymn "Andenken," ed. Curd Ochwadt (Frankfurt am Main: Klostermann, 1982).

36. Adorno, "Parataxis," p. 120. See also Jacques Taminaux, Heidegger and the Project of Fundamental Ontology, trans. Michael Gendre (Albany: SUNY Press, 1991), pp. 201-3.

Von Balthasar also challenges another significant omission from Heidegger's depiction; that is, the absence of any recognition that Hölderlin's Greek retrieval is found in the context of relation, even tension, with Christianity.[37] Even if it is agreed that Hölderlin's works involve no allegiance to orthodox forms of Christianity (*GL* 5:316) — an assessment von Balthasar shares with Adorno[38] — this cannot be taken to imply that Hölderlin's relationship to Christianity is superficial. The aesthetic attraction exercised by the luminous figure of Christ is every bit as compelling as that of the Greek gods and heroes, suggesting that Hölderlin's aesthetic universe may be decidedly more stressed than Heidegger's somewhat Apollonian figuration. Hölderlin's poetic task, therefore, does not simply involve an archaic regression; nor is it defined by the attempt to respond to the epiphanic pull of Christ *and* the Greek pantheon. Rather Hölderlin's task calls for adjudication *between* the epiphanic claims of the Greek gods and heroes, *and* Christ.[39] The result, of course, is an oscillation in which Christ is neither uniquely valorized nor absolutely reduced to being a mediator of Greek-style cosmic epiphany. On the one hand, the figure of Christ remains an obsession that disturbs the would-be closed framework of the Greek gods (*GL* 5:319); on the other, Christ is domesticated by being put on the same level as Dionysius and mediator figures like Empedocles, Diotima, and Heracles, in whom epiphany or glory is either immanentized (5:302) or naturalized (5:319-20). By now it should be obvious that even a trace of Christian presence is sufficient to compromise seriously the Heideggerian case for Hölderlin as pure philhellene.

Heidegger, of course, does not so much argue as assume a case for Hölderlin's retrieval of the originary Greek response to reality as *epiphaneia.* Yet von Balthasar in his reading of Hölderlin avoids Heidegger's dogmatic self-destruction and instead addresses a position open to someone inclined to read Hölderlin in a Heideggerian way. This revised Heideggerian reading would acknowledge the Christian surface of Hölderlin's texts, but go on to argue that the Christian surface is denied by the non-Christian, even anti-Christian depth content. Christian symbols and terms continue to be used, but their meaning and existential import have been fundamentally altered (*GL* 5:318). Though this might be described as a form of demythologization, what is more nearly afoot is a process of remythologization in which Christian terms and Christian dispositions are translated into another idiom. Effectively, however, this suggests that Hölderlin can be linked to the strong subversionist-revisionist tendency

37. For this point, see John D. Caputo, *Demythologizing Heidegger* (Bloomington: Indiana University Press, 1993), p. 151.

38. See Adorno, "Parataxis," p. 137.

39. Gadamer understands this point well. See Hans Georg Gadamer, "Hölderlin and Antiquity," in *Literature and Philosophy in Dialogue: Essays in German Literary Theory,* trans. Robert H. Paslich (Albany: SUNY Press, 1994), pp. 67-86, esp. pp. 75-80.

that characterizes much of romanticism's relation to Christianity and that found its most obsessively consistent enactment in the poetic practice of Blake. From the point of view of discourse, this kind of reading of Christianity against itself in the name of another ideological frame of reference may be called *metalepsis*.[40]

Now, as von Balthasar knows well, *metalepsis* is original neither ideologically nor as a practice to romanticism; it is itself a Christianly hallowed operation (*GL* 5:409). It is standard Alexandrian hermeneutical practice, and in *On Christian Doctrine* it is canonized by Augustine. For Augustine, the expropriation of extrabiblical symbols for Christian purposes, the so-called *spoils of the Egyptians*, is not only a right but a duty. Von Balthasar is aware that in the modern world, especially in the case of romantics such as Schiller (5:513-46), the metaleptic process can be turned against Christianity. He does not think, however, that such a practice is systemic in Hölderlin. The Christ figure maintains some degree of integrity, even on occasion exercising a decided counterpull to the beautiful Greek cosmos. Still, traces of *metalepsis* there are, and any such traces are calculated to give von Balthasar pause. Indeed, this is one of the reasons for von Balthasar's ultimate preference for Goethe (5:339-408). Unlike Hölderlin, Goethe never confounds Greek with Christian sensibility. While he may prefer the Greek, each has its own integrity. His work, therefore, shows no evidence of *metalepsis*. By contrast, if Hölderlin's Christian orientation is genuine enough for him not to practice a consistent form of metaleptic subversion, it is not strong enough to prevent incidences of such subversion. Hölderlin, consequently, is Christianly dangerous in a way Goethe is not.

Resisting Heidegger's reading of Hölderlin and other figures in modernity involves von Balthasar in questioning certain endemic interpretive practices. Admittedly, such questioning remains for the most part implicit, von Balthasar, the narrativist, only rarely rising to the kind of reflective metalevel in which the rationale and justification of hermeneutical principles gets debated. Still, what von Balthasar has by implication identified as being hermeneutically problematic in Heidegger has in recent studies of postmodernity become thematized. It is Veronique Foti who best captures the postmodern sense of unease with Heidegger's interpretive practices and who brings to completion a significant trend of resistance.[41] At the center of Foti's inquiries is Heidegger's reading of Hölderlin, though Heidegger's reading of Rilke, Trakl, and Mörike also comes in for examination. Without overformalizing, it seems fair to say that her

---

40. The word *metalepsis* goes back to Aristotle's *Metaphysics* where it has the meaning of participation (1072b20). However, its deployment here is rhetorical rather than metaphysical, and as such it more nearly resembles the use to which it is put by literary critic Harold Bloom, who makes it one of his primary revisionary tropes whereby belated writers deal with earlier authoritative figures by outmaneuvering them.

41. Veronique Foti, *Heidegger and the Poets: Poesis/Sophia/Techné* (Atlantic Highlands, NJ, and London: Humanities Press, 1992). For Hölderlin, see pp. 44-77.

counterreading of Hölderlin has in view five interpretive practices, all but the last applicable in principle to nonpoetic texts. These are: (1) *hypostatization* of a text; that is, its abstraction from its cultural context (p. 45); (2) *dehistoricization* of a text; that is, its abstraction from its particular moment in history and the ideological ambiance in which it is inserted (p. 56); (3) *decontamination;* that is, the tendency to purify a text of elements that would make a text something less than a pure instance of Greek-German epiphany (pp. 64-66); (4) *totalization;* that is, the tendency to so link Greece and Germany that no other tradition, even within the classical West, contributes to an aesthetic, nonmetaphysical philosophy;[42] (5) *allegorization;* that is, making poetry a "cryptogram" for philosophy (pp. 53-54). The first four of these practices essentially form two pairs, with the fifth standing on its own. Hypostatization and dehistoricization are obviously related, as are Heidegger's tendencies toward decontamination and totalization in which the link between Greece and Germany gets absolutely privileged. For her reading of Heidegger's interpretation of Hölderlin and other German-speaking poets, Foti can appeal to such authoritative Heidegger critics as Adorno and Derrida. If the former seems to gesture to the first pair, the latter seems to point to the second.[43] In continuity with both of these critics, however, Foti seems to sustain Heideggerian criticisms of the classical tradition. She regards the tradition as ontotheological in the pejorative sense and dominated by a capturable presence, answered successfully, however, only in the Derridian notion of the trace. Materially, Foti's position is hardly hospitable to von Balthasar's professedly ontotheological commitment. Fortunately, material rapprochement is not a requirement for a hermeneutical alliance. And such an alliance is indeed forged, with Foti essentially naming the kinds of Heideggerian interpretive practices that need not be limited to poetic texts, and that von Balthasar shows do in fact extend beyond the poets.

By contrast with Heidegger, von Balthasar's account of metaphysics in *GL* 4 and 5, as in his earlier work on German idealism and his studies on the church fathers, has a cultural and historical orientation. Texts arise in specific cultures

---

42. Caputo has developed the decontamination and totalizing points in some detail in Caputo, *Demythologizing Heidegger*. As well as being dependent on Foti, Caputo also expresses a dependence on Derrida, especially Jacques Derrida, *Of Spirit: Heidegger and the Question,* trans. Geoffrey Bennington and Rachel Bowlby (Chicago and London: University of Chicago Press, 1989).

43. Adorno, "Parataxis," pp. 120-21; Derrida, *Of Spirit.* Though Derrida's text has Heidegger's Trakl interpretation front and center, his observations about Heidegger's practice of decontaminating his favorite authors from anything to do with the metaphysical tradition and Christianity and his insistence on making the connection between Greece and Germany at all costs are generalizable. He does point out, however, the subversion of symmetry in Heidegger's equation: Germany is ultimately much more equal than Greece. The points about decontextualization and dehistoricization are also touched on in Derrida's rich text.

with specific cultural drifts, and both change over time. An account of the history of metaphysics is, among other things, an account of the background configuration of the culture and ideology of particular varieties of thought and particular texts that are perceived to have something like classic status. As Ernst Behler suggests, one of the reasons Heidegger's history of metaphysics is so schematic is that it intends to be deep.[44] Heidegger's history of metaphysics is not simply the history of the thought of or response to Being; it is nothing less than the history of Being. For von Balthasar the history of metaphysics does not and cannot have this kind of status. The history of metaphysics is not vertical in the way Heidegger suggests it is; it is organic with something like horizontal spread. Here von Balthasar moves much more nearly in a Hegelian than in a Heideggerian orbit, though, like Hegel, he is persuaded that the history of discursive responses to Being bears some close relation to Being. An ingredient in von Balthasar's resistance to Heideggerian verticality and depth is the privileging of *Dasein* in Heidegger's thought (*GL* 5:621) that cuts across the break between "early" and "late" Heidegger (5:448). Von Balthasar seems to entertain as suspicion what for critics like Jonas and Adorno functioned as fact, that despite Heidegger's restriction of epistemic limits,[45] *Dasein*, at least in the form of the Heideggerian philosopher, *knows*. In an important respect, therefore, von Balthasar's history of metaphysics is superficial, precisely because it is horizontal. And thus, though Derrida and von Balthasar have obviously different material commitments, the issue between von Balthasar and Heidegger is isomorphic with the issue between Derrida and Heidegger. What is to be chosen: profound superficiality or superficial profundity?

   GL 4 and 5 also resist the totalizing of the Heideggerian metanarrative that is archaeoteleological in kind. The sequence of shapes of thought and response, both defined by and defining classic texts, figures a history that is essentially open at both ends. Von Balthasar, for instance, does not understand his account of Greek myth (*GL* 4:43-154) to be an account of an originary state with normative value, no more than he understands Heideggerian phainesthetics to bring Western thought to a close. While he hardly disqualifies and indeed confirms Greek beginnings, von Balthasar insists on the Greek mythic view as a permanent resource for the Western tradition, with the caveat, however, that it is not to be regarded as the only or even most important resource. His view, therefore, essentially rests on a neither-nor. Greek beginning neither has the unsurpassable and normative status Heidegger gives to it, nor does it have the status that would

---

44. See Ernst Behler, *Confrontations, Derrida/Heidegger/Nietzsche*, trans. Steven Taubeneck (Stanford: Stanford University Press, 1991), pp. 34-36.

45. See Hans Jonas's epilogue to *The Gnostic Religion: The Message of the Alien God and the Beginning of Christianity* (Boston: Beacon Press, 1963), entitled "Gnosticism, Existentialism, and Nihilism."

be accorded it in a more Hegelian-like progressivist scheme where it is reduced to an evolutionary redundant form of thought and experience.

Von Balthasar's resistance to Heidegger's totalization also covers his reading of the "break" between modernity and premodernity, a "break" on which Heidegger rhetorically insists and ultimately explains away. Heidegger is relentlessly consistent in giving the name Descartes to the site of the break that is not a break, a wound already healed before it is opened. As we observed earlier, von Balthasar at least in part agrees with this assessment of Descartes's fundamental philosophical gesture and its paradigmatic significance for modernity. For von Balthasar, the Cartesian hypothesis is just that; it does not have, and cannot have, categorical properties. Closely examined, Descartes is more than his turn to the cogito, just as many of the major figures of modernity influenced by subjectivity are not exhaustively defined by it. Elements of countersubjectivity can be diagnosed in Descartes and the tradition of subjectivity, such that Descartes's status as defining a radical break is undermined.

Descartes's status as pure point of origin is further put in doubt in von Balthasar's genealogical scheme when at certain points nominalism (*GL* 5:206, 482), the Reformation (5:285), and even the thought of Eckhart (5:50) are suggested as fundamental points of departure for modern thought. The pluralization of origin could easily be attributed to the theologian's lack of philosophical rigor, but then it might also be attributable to a cultural-historical mode of explanation in which origin is never pure and its assertion is predicated on particular interests in explanation. If the interest, for instance, is the orientation to subjectivity that is characteristic of modernity, modern reflection in particular, then Descartes can serve as the mark of difference. If the interest is the observed loss of purchasing power in language, then the so-called break can be pushed back to the nominalism of the fourteenth and fifteenth centuries. And if the interest is the modern tendency to blur the boundary between the divine and the human, then Eckhart marks a site of fundamental change. But here, to turn a Heideggerian adage against its author, possibility is indeed higher than actuality. The assertion of multiple ways of marking the break between the premodern and the modern points to the possibility of multiple origins and the impossibility of a single origin.[46] Denying the possibility of a categorical identification of origin of modernity, and more specifically undermining the originary role accorded by Heidegger to Descartes, does not rule out a less categorical, more taxonomic way of talking about the premodern and the modern, and their difference, and even identifying Descartes as the clearest point of inception for the anthropological regime that declares itself in metaphysics and

---

46. Von Balthasar here moves beyond the monogenism that deconstructionist-oriented thinkers take to be a serious fault in Heidegger's genealogical scheme. See Caputo, pp. 5-7, 96-97.

aesthetics. Consistently in *GL* 4 and 5, as well as elsewhere,[47] von Balthasar identifies the premodern with a fundamentally cosmological orientation and modernity with an orientation that is fundamentally anthropological in kind, as he holds out, like Heidegger, for a form of thought that represents a *pharmakon* for modernity's aesthetic and/or phainesthetic decline.

After such a rehearsal it is safe to conclude that von Balthasar's acceptance of the basic Heideggerian terms does not commit him to Heidegger's substantive proposal. Resistance is both widespread and deep. And even if von Balthasar's narrative style diffuses the agon somewhat by not marking off clearly the major points of genealogical difference, still von Balthasar's criticisms of Heidegger can be rendered in a more thematic and reflective mode, and so rendered, they resemble in the closest possible way criticisms leveled at Heidegger by a variety of postmodernists. At the same time, von Balthasar's critique of Heidegger unites him with Hans Blumenberg, a genealogist with whom otherwise he has little in common. *The Legitimacy of the Modern Age* refuses to speak of history in an ontological or evaluative mode, as it refuses to countenance a language of the holy or its erasure as setting the terms for a discussion of modernity.[48] Nevertheless, its critique of Heidegger bears a strong family resemblance to that excavated from von Balthasar's texts. Heidegger's "history of being," Blumenberg argues, functions without an accessible historical context, while at the same time succumbing to the mythology of an absolute beginning. Modernity, as conceived by Heidegger, at one level at least, is a pure irrational irruption immune to historical study and explanation. And Blumenberg is sufficiently out of sorts with Heidegger as to agree with his religious critics that the discourse of the holy that guides Heideggerian genealogical interpretation may very well be a secularization of Christian discourse.

Nevertheless, in the final analysis von Balthasar is less interested in burying Heidegger than correcting him. As the most aesthetic philosopher of modernity, Heidegger merits Christian rehabilitation. Part of this rehabilitation, however, involves a renunciation of the attack on the classical and modern traditions as sites of the obscuration of Being and the forgetfulness of the ontological difference. In short, required is an acknowledgment that the metaphysical tradition is not ontotheological in the pejorative sense; namely, that the thinking of Being

47. In *GL* 4 Dionysius and Eriugena are identified as two of the main exemplars of the cosmic tradition in Christianity (4:320, 348). With respect to Western thought in general, Neoplatonism is regarded as a major vehicle for a style of thought praised for its inclusiveness and its extrasubjectivity dimension. In *GL* 5, of course, Heidegger and Hölderlin are especially praised, as is Goethe for continuing the cosmic dispensation into modernity. In *GL* 6 von Balthasar admits, however, that the cosmological style of theology, which in one sense is an enduring possibility, may very well be passé (6:21).

48. Hans Blumenberg, *The Legitimacy of the Modern Age,* trans. Robert Wallace (Cambridge and London: MIT Press, 1983).

as the supreme instance necessarily transforms Being into a being. That it is possible to avoid ontotheology in the bad sense both agree. Both agree also that it is a matter of language. Heidegger thinks the privileged language is poetry. Von Balthasar agrees that poetic language is much more philosophically, but at the same time religiously and Christianly, significant than the propositionalists or evidentialists have granted. Yet he is convinced that biblical language is even more significant, indeed unsurpassable. He even holds out hope for theological language to the degree to which it allows itself to be normed by biblical language and does not go astray in its vocation for clarity and correctness. There may very well be forms of theological language that let Being be, that allow for and celebrate the gratuitousness and mystery of disclosure. There may also be forms of theological language that avoid tendencies in Heidegger's own account to immanentize, to transgress the ontological difference. It is to this theological response to Heidegger that we now turn.

IV. From Ontotheological to Theological Supplementation

Von Balthasar's weakly epochal scheme of succeeding cosmological, anthropological, and postanthropological regimes is intended focally as an account of different theological habits in the Western tradition,[49] but also perhaps peripherally of the different metaphysical habits, given the chronic interlacing of philosophy and theology. The postanthropological opening is both postmodern and postmetaphysical. If von Balthasar finds in the retrieval of a scriptural view of reality the definitive postmetaphysical posture, then this does not prevent him from issuing more nearly metaphysical challenges to the Heideggerian phainesthetics that presents itself as an alternative to the premodern and modern metaphysical tradition. One form the challenge takes is the more or less systematic preference for Thomistic *esse* over Heideggerian *physis*. This Thomistic preference recalls the position adopted by a neo-Thomist like Cornelio Fabro in both his defense of Thomas against general metaphysical charges and his concerted counterattack on behalf of the essence-existence distinction.[50] However, von Balthasar does not follow Fabro by linking the defense of *esse* to the model of efficient causality (that Fabro takes to be Thomas's greatest achievement but that Heidegger believes to be the quintessence of metaphysical defor-

49. Perhaps the most succinct account of these habits is found in von Balthasar's popular text, *Love Alone: The Way of Revelation* (London and Dublin: Sheed and Ward and Veritas Publications, 1968), p. 12.

50. Cornelio Fabro, *Participation et causalité selon Saint Thomas d'Aquin* (Louvain: Publications universitaires de Louvain; Paris: Editions Beatrice Nauwelaerts, 1961).

mation).[51] Rather, von Balthasar interprets Thomistic *esse* as phainesthetic, as the phenomenal lighting of a particular thing supported or subtended by the ontological difference. Von Balthasar disregards Heidegger's judgment that the essence-existence distinction, inchoately present at least in Aristotle's distinction of *hoti estin* and *ti estin,* not only fails to do significant conceptual work but also obscures the original sense of *physis* as presencing. Rather, von Balthasar suggests that the distinction (1) serves as a block against the essentialism that, critics have argued,[52] comes to the surface in Heidegger's musings about *physis* (*GL* 5:433) and, more positively, (2) allows transcendence, and not a modality of descendance, to be inscribed within reality.

At a minimum, then, Thomistic *esse* has the same phainesthetic quotient as Heideggerian *physis.* In wishing to go further and suggest the superiority of *esse,* von Balthasar follows an interesting argumentative tack. Support of Heidegger's critique of the principle of sufficient reason that is the epitome of the Western logocentric tradition is basic. Von Balthasar quotes with approval the quatrain from Angelus Silesius's *Cherubinic Wanderer* that is at the core of Heidegger's critique in *The Principle of Reason:*

> The rose has no why or wherefore:
> It blooms because it blooms.
> It has no regard for itself, and does not ask
> if it is being looked at. (*GL* 5:441)

Von Balthasar's ontotheological redemption of mystery proceeds by pointing to the roots of this view in Eckhart (*GL* 5:441) and the German mystical tradition in general (5:52-78). The whylessness *(ohne Warum)* announced in Silesius, and countenanced by Heidegger, he suggests, is conceptually supported by Thomas's essence-existence distinction and ontologically exemplified in *esse* (5:472). On the basis of the concluding section of *GL* 5, however, it is clear that Thomistic *esse* is devoid of certain problems intrinsic to Heideggerian *physis.* For Heidegger, *physis* is the dynamic play of emergence that constitutes history and articulates truth as the play of disclosure and concealing. Taxonomically, Heidegger's understanding is Heraclitus filtered through Angelus Silesius. As von Balthasar well recognizes, the Heraclitean aphorism of *physis kruptesthai philei* (nature loves to hide itself) (frag. 123) is crucial for Heidegger's view of the historicity of truth (*GL* 5:444).[53] But the Heraclitean fragment (frag. 52)

51. See Heidegger, *The Question concerning Technology,* pp. 8-10; *The End of Philosophy,* trans. Joan Stambaugh (New York: Harper & Row, 1973), pp. 14-16.

52. Foti and Caputo lead the essentialist charge in recent literature on Heidegger. See Foti, p. 51; Caputo, pp. 148-49.

53. For one example of the importance of this Heraclitean fragment, see Heidegger, *Introduction to Metaphysics,* p. 103.

concerning the sportful play of *aion* is equally important, as Heidegger's commentaries on Nietzsche attest.[54] And it is this *aion* that plays without why *(ohne Warum)*, the occurrence of truth being an occurrence of because *(Weil)*.[55] History, therefore, as Rorty recognizes, is pure contingency.[56] But in this case the being of truth and the truth of being, as Adorno suspected, justify the terrible.[57] Von Balthasar concedes as much when he in *GL* 1 worries about whether the matrix of *physis* is demonic (1:59). The suggestion that ontophany is *kakophany* also emerges in von Balthasar's commentary on the terribleness of beauty in Rilke's first *Duino Elegy* (*GL* 5:421-22). On the most general level von Balthasar is asking the question about the consequences that follow from disallowing an ontotheological or theological interpretation of *to on*. In his view both the failure to underwrite Being as event by specifying its transcendentally substantial character and the failure to provide a scripturally determined description of the *summum esse* (highest being) that secures Being outside nothingness have serious consequences. One consequence, von Balthasar seems to suggest, and a disastrous one at that, is that history is voided of ontological reliability. Gratuity becomes indistinguishable from chance, mysteriousness indistinguishable from the unanticipatable. The concept of *summum esse* can be understood, among other things, as Thomas's attempt to underwrite the reliability of Being. As such, it in principle engages Heidegger's Heraclitean insouciance by offering a justification of Being — an *ontodicy* — by way of a theodicy, for the really real is indeed *to theoin*. Beyond the ontological difference is the theological difference of *summum esse* and the existent being as a unity of existence and essence.

IV.1. Balthasarian Theodicy versus Heideggerian Ontodicy

Strictly speaking Heidegger cannot have a theodicy, since his postmetaphysical thought abrogates the claim of *to theoin*. This abrogation is radical. It does not simply consist in the erasure of the name "God," whereby the erasure leaves only a space to be filled by another term or name, such as reason, will, or spirit.

54. Martin Heidegger, *Nietzsche: Volume 4. Nihilism,* trans. Frank A. Capuzi, ed. David Farrell Krell (San Francisco: Harper, 1982), p. 238.

55. Heidegger, *The Essence of Reasons,* p. 113.

56. Richard Rorty, "Heidegger, Contingency, and Pragmatism," in *Essays on Heidegger and Others: Philosophical Papers* (Cambridge: Cambridge University Press, 1991), vol. 2, pp. 27-49. For the conflict between the nostalgic-normative and the pure historicist elements within Heidegger's genealogical scheme, see p. 39.

57. For this criticism of Heidegger, see Adorno, *The Jargon of Authenticity,* trans. Knut Tarnowski and Frederick Will (Evanston: Northwestern University Press, 1973). Derrida seems to harbor the same suspicion. See Derrida, pp. 102-3.

Rather, the space is erased with the name "God." It is not, then, simply "God" who is undone, but the God function whereby the meaning, truth, and value of reality are secured and, of course, paradoxically in this securing lost.[58] Thus at a fundamental level, the *Destruktion* of metaphysics is a destruction of the possibility of theodicy, the dismantling of the possibility of being able to ask and answer "why" as one negotiates the phainesthetic milieu. As a mediator of the ontotheological tradition, von Balthasar can correctly be read as opposing Heideggerian nontheodicy or atheodicy with theodicy. Certainly, at a surface level, at least, this specifies von Balthasar's and Heidegger's engagement of the issue of theodicy.

But the real situation is more complex. In *GL* 5 von Balthasar seems suspicious in the case of Hölderlin and Heidegger about the titanic fundament in both. In Hölderlin's case the "let it be" seems to require a self-exalting sacrifice of the poet on behalf of the whole, and in Heidegger the exaltation of *Dasein*, at least authentic *Dasein*, is funded by Heidegger's talk of *Sein*'s (being's) "need" of *Dasein* (*GL* 5:447). Heidegger's relation to Nietzsche does not come in for discussion in *GL*, but given von Balthasar's awareness of Heidegger's commentaries on Nietzsche, as well as his abiding sense from *Apocalypse of the German Soul* that German thought's most feminine gestures are contaminated with masculine urges, we are put on notice that the will to power can masquerade as *Gelassenheit* (releasement) or that *Gelassenheit* can be another name for the will to power. Von Balthasar does not directly address the issue of what might be called the criteriology of *Gelassenheit* in either his discussion of Heidegger or Hölderlin, but in his reflections on Eckhart and the German mystical tradition the issue is raised (5:49). Von Balthasar suggests that without attunement *Gelassenheit* is empty, and without attunement toward a reality that is reliable attunement is blind. Even within the metaphysical context, the archetypal form of *Gelassenheit*, for von Balthasar, then, is Marian. The Marian amen in the annunciation to the great mystery of incarnation specifies the form of attunement that is uninfected by will to power and which yet trusts in the reality whose mystery and grace it acknowledges. In some interesting pages on Heidegger (5:439-42), von Balthasar maintains that the advent and truth discourse of the later Heidegger bears a parasitic relation to biblical speech. One obvious effect of this parasitism is that Heidegger's own discourse gains a certain kind of authority by its resonance with the authoritative language of the Western tradition.[59] Another is that under the aegis of that authority Heidegger can

---

58. For this point, see Heidegger, *The Question concerning Technology,* p. 100.

59. Von Balthasar's point here is similar to that made by Adorno in *The Jargon of Authenticity.* In that text Adorno availed himself of Benjamin's construct of the "aura" to indicate the nonsemantic surplus in Heidegger's language that was responsible for its authority.

disguise a subversive intent. Von Balthasar points out that Heidegger is conscious of the suggestion of fidelity contained in *Wahrheit,* without necessarily having to commit himself fully to the view that there is something that makes the "grace" of reality reliable (5:442). Arguably, the cumulative set of criticisms of Heidegger ultimately connotes that the opposition of theodicy to an atheodicy of whylessness decomposes into the opposition of two different kinds of theodicy. On the one hand, there is a Heraclitean ontodicy or anthropodicy substitute, infected by Nietzsche, in which one surrenders heroically and tragically to the play of chance that promises nothing or is nothing's promise. On the other hand, there is a play of surprise whose face one cannot discern — in this sense *physis kruptesthai philei* is correct — but which one trusts wears a smile, not a grimace.

In the context of *GL,* the opposition between Balthasarian theodicy and what we have diagnosed as a peculiar Heraclitean form of ontodicy most often takes the form of contrast between a phainesthetics of glory and a phainesthetics of beauty. Heidegger (*GL* 5:449), but also Rilke, and in a certain mood, Hölderlin, articulate the phainesthetics of beauty. Within the latter regime the kakophanous is either not allowed to appear or, if it does so, it cannot be fully integrated into the phainesthetic order. In *GL* 4 von Balthasar is especially conscious of the lack of integration in the Greeks that Heidegger so admires, though he does point to Greek tragedy's self-transcending gestures (4:101-54). But as there are also ways in which kakophany is not sufficiently integrated, there are ways in which it is integrated all too well. Hölderlin's view of the necessary *kenosis* and suffering of the *hen kai pan* (one and all) provides a brilliant example of such an overintegration that unfortunately repeats the worst examples of the Christian aesthetic tradition of theodicy (5:302, 647). In any event, beauty is the terrible, as Rilke maintains, unless beyond all expectation the formless and the ugly are embraced, but not annihilated, by form (1:198, 216). From a Christian perspective the form which brings beauty beyond itself to glory is Christ. This is, of course, the argument of *GL* as a whole, finding its programmatic statement in *GL* 1 and reaching its crescendo in the two volumes on Scripture that complete the first part of von Balthasar's masterwork (*GL* 6-7). Christ is the form of glory; not the Byzantine Christ, however, but the Christ of Philippians (Phil. 2:5-11), the Christ corresponding to the Suffering Servant of Second Isaiah, the kenotic Christ, who has entered the outermost precincts of the ugly and the oblivion of shining. Ultimately, therefore, von Balthasar's answer to Heidegger is not simply an ontotheological answer, not simply Thomist *esse,* but the biblical God of history who does not play Heideggerian hide-and-seek, but rather a God who reveals himself, and in whose self-revealing forever remains the incomprehensible one (*GL* 6:54). The final biblical-kenotic view of glory bears the obvious suggestion that incarnation finds its ultimate meaning in the cross, just as creation finds its meaning in the incarnation.

For von Balthasar the christological answer is at the same time a trinitarian reply. Though the movement from Christ to the Trinity is more substantially treated outside *GL*, especially in *Theodrama* and *Mysterium Paschale*,[60] notice of it is provided in *GL* 1:436-37. Even that text reveals the fundamentally Johannine orientation of his thought. The incarnation and the cross reveal a God who is the God of love, who is nothing but love. It is the perichoretic love between self-dispossessing trinitarian persons that interprets the transcendentals and beyond the sufficient why of Heidegger changes his contingent because into a why that is no why, that is the ontological and axiological reliability of grace.[61] Trinitarian love is thus the Christian answer to Heidegger's phainesthetics. Von Balthasar thinks that the whylessness of Angelus Silesius, championed by Heidegger, becomes grace only in the ecstatic communication of the divine milieu, and beauty is rescued from the would-be fatal reply of the ugly when it is taken up into the divine. For von Balthasar the answer to a Heracliteanly and Nietzscheanly deformed Angelus Silesius is simple. It is Angelus Silesius. Von Balthasar is convinced that Silesian whylessness must be intratextually interpreted by the Silesian aesthetics summed up in the following couplet from *Cherubinic Wanderer:*

> Beauty comes from love, and even the countenance of God
> Takes from her its beauty, or it would not shine. (*GL* 5:647)

IV.2. Genealogy and the Meaning of Nihilism

Clearly, there exists a close relation between von Balthasar's and Heidegger's account of nihilism, with von Balthasar framing the issue in the quintessentially Heideggerian manner of the forgetfulness of Being. This, of course, only touches the surface of the relation. In the pages that follow, I will first separate out two different tendencies in Heidegger's proposal of nihilism, and then proceed to examine how von Balthasar engages each of these aspects, particularly with a view to their ontotheological or theological correction or supplementation.

---

60. Hans Urs von Balthasar, *Mysterium Paschale: The Mystery of Easter*, trans. Aidan Nichols, O.P. (Edinburgh: T. & T. Clark, 1990); *Theo-Drama: Theological Dramatic Theory*, vol. 3, *The Dramatis Personae: The Person of Christ*, trans. Graham Harrison (San Francisco: Ignatius Press, 1992), pp. 505-35.

61. In *GL* 1:158 von Balthasar writes: "And this dispels the philosopher's objection that with the rise of Christian theology there has been a regress of Being from Being back to the existent. Being itself here reveals its final countenance, which for us receives the name of trinitarian love; only with this final mystery does light fall at last on that other mystery: why is there Being at all and why it enters our horizon as light and truth and goodness and beauty."

It is possible to say that just as there are essentially two different tendencies in Heidegger's depiction of the history of metaphysics, there are two different tendencies in his view of nihilism, with Hölderlin and Nietzsche providing their approximate labels. In the first case metaphysics is regarded as nihilistic to the degree to which its inception in Plato and its apotheosis in modernity constitute an occlusion of an epiphany that was the property of a premetaphysical past and/or a possibility for a postmetaphysical future.[62] Whether in its strong or weak epochal form, this view has a normative dimension. In the second, more Nietzschean rendition the normative element in Heidegger's nihilism proposal is recanted. The event character of Being is so radicalized that the refusal of disclosure becomes a function of a Heraclitean-like play of Being, in which responsibility is first shifted beyond the realm of beings and then denied as an appropriate demand of Being as Becoming.[63] Tendencies are not positions, however, and consequently should not be expected to be present in pure form. This is certainly the case in Heidegger's texts. Moreover, the Hölderlinian and Nietzschean labels are somewhat pragmatic, since while it is true that the normative view is most clearly to the fore in Heidegger's Hölderlin commentaries and that the radical-event view is conspicuous in Heidegger's reflections on Nietzsche, neither view is hermetically sealed from the other. Both in fact infiltrate and contaminate the other's textual spaces that accordingly cannot retain their purity.[64]

Since sections I and II have already documented von Balthasar's general avowal of the Hölderlinian version of Heidegger's nihilism thesis and extensively covered some of the ways in which this version is contested, there is no need to go over this ground again. It suffices to recall two aspects of Balthasarian

---

62. Caputo is persuaded that in the Heidegger-Hölderlin liaison the Greeks are not regarded as owners of the right kind of glance into being. They are proleptic, or, as Caputo puts it, placeholders for a vision that is as eschatological as it is apocalyptic. See Caputo, p. 25.

63. Commentators and critics have variously stressed one or the other. Joan Stambaugh, for instance, favors the disteleological, nonnormative view. Led by Heidegger's interpretation of Trakl, Derrida thinks Heidegger's epochal scheme reveals a "teleology of a narrative order." See Joan Stambaugh, *Thoughts on Heidegger* (Washington, D.C.: Center for Advanced Research in Phenomenology and University Press of America, 1991), pp. 138-56, esp. pp. 138-39; Derrida, p. 12.

64. Two examples will suffice. As a philosophical exegesis, "Brot und Wein" (in Heidegger, "What Are Poets For") could not be more normatively Hölderlinian in orientation, yet at the very end (p. 142) Heidegger adds a pure historicist note that undermines any advantage the Greek-like posture would have vis-à-vis other postures. By contrast, in the historicist-oriented *Nietzsche,* where Heidegger seems to surrender the possibility of value judgments, he nevertheless continues to speak as if Plato introduced a deformation into an epiphanic field launching a metaphysical tradition that is less than that which went before and less than that which is possible.

emendation that bear on the history of metaphysics as the history of nihilism. Von Balthasar agrees formally with Heidegger's assessment that the erasure of epiphany constitutes the forgetfulness of Being, as the forgetfulness of Being betokens nihilism. Materially, however, he disagrees with Heidegger's judgment that all the classical tradition and all the modern tradition are guilty of epiphanic trespass. If to modernity one can justly ascribe the symbol of "night," this does not imply, von Balthasar thinks, that "night" is a completely adequate descriptor. Night is relative, not absolute. More appropriately the classical and modern traditions can be regarded as constituted by the play of light and shadow. Thus, as Heidegger's monolithic genealogy calls for pluralization, his apocalyptic rendering of the occlusion of epiphany calls for a thematic of chiaroscuro. History, for von Balthasar, is not only the play of light and shadow, revelation and occlusion, it is a dynamic play which consequently permits the possibility that some periods may be dominated more by one than the other. A static interpretation that would view light or shadow dividing history into different aeons is rejected. This apocalyptic posture that von Balthasar noted in his early work to be endemic to German romanticism and Heidegger is to be resisted. Modernity does not constitute the kind of intensification of darkness and occlusion that would provoke expectations and demands of a transmutation whose source is outside history. To the recommendation that when speaking of nihilism one speaks in the language of chiaroscuro is subjoined a plea for a certain kind of sensibility. The kind of sensibility appropriate to such an examination is that best unfolded in the Christian tradition by Newman, but has its foundation in Aristotle's distinction between practical and theoretical reason. Von Balthasar implies that Heidegger mistakenly treats the genealogical enterprise as if it were in the order of demonstration and thus offers a far stronger version of a proposal of nihilism than he is entitled to. But apodictic judgments do not belong to the order of history.

The second feature of Balthasarian emendation regarding Heidegger's Hölderlinian rendition of nihilism is that of theological supplementation. Conceding that throughout history, and especially in the post-Reformation period, theology can function nihilistically, von Balthasar believes that most of the classical, and a significant part of the modern, theological tradition not only does not erase epiphany but rather represents privileged sites. While obviously a phenomenon not fully outside the Christian and theological milieu, nihilism is fundamentally outside. It is to be found especially in the modern secular world with its technocratic and materialist mentality and inhabits certain modern philosophical currents of thought, those with some claims — though not necessarily fully supportable claims — to being *sui generis* (e.g., Descartes) and those which quite obviously represent secularizations of Christian modes of thought (e.g., Hegel). On von Balthasar's view, then, Christianity, Christian theology in particular, is a *pharmakon* in the double sense of poison and cure made so current by Derrida. It, too, is poisoned and poisonous to the degree to which it is tempted to overconceptualize Christian mystery, to fall in love with system, and to misidentify itself in scientific and/or psychological apologetics. Yet by and large Christian theology is medicine against occlusion, and perhaps even inoculation against epiphanic loss. Admitting that there are sufficient grounds for the assertion of a crisis in modernity and of modernity — though not of an apocalyptic sort — von Balthasar is, nevertheless, firm in his belief that Christianity can be the safe haven of the epiphanic and the bastion against nihilism in the modern world. The following represents a consummate expression of von Balthasar's view:

> The decision falls uniquely — and the history of the modern period has no clearer result — for or against the Glory of Being, and history has fashioned the Either-Or so simply that it has become a decision between Christianity and nihilism. The "gods," the "divine," hold sway still only where God's personal love is recognized and acknowledged, and the storming-ahead of metaphysical speculation is bridled only where thought — in the same epiphany — confronts the not-to-be-mastered majestic freedom of the God of love. (*GL* 5:249)

Von Balthasar's either-or of nihilism *or* Christianity has two elements. First, and most obviously, there is the praise of the Christian option; second, there is something like a relinking of nihilism with atheism, a connection Heidegger consistently abjures.[65] Praise of Christianity, of course, is *conditional*. Christianity must avoid the various ideological pitfalls of modernity, as it must protect itself against discursive deformation. Von Balthasar is in complete agreement with Heidegger about the danger of discourses functioning at a second-order, technical, and monosemic level. Such forms of discourse do not allow reality, whether impersonal or personal, to disclose itself. Theological practices that tend in this direction, therefore, ought to be revised in a direction where discourse is more first-order, more metaphorical, and, of course, ultimately more prayer-like. Moreover, poetic discourses of the sort found in Claudel, Hopkins, and Péguy should be considered either as necessary supplements to theological discourse or themselves forms of theological discourse. Indeed, poetry's doxological matrix may well serve theology better in the modern period of eclipse than theology in the more strict sense of the term. Here von Balthasar validates a general Heideggerian train of thought, as he develops de Lubac's insight concerning the importance of the poetic.

In relinking atheism and nihilism, however, von Balthasar associates himself with a number of influential Catholic accounts of this hypothesis. Two are

---

65. See, for example, Heidegger, *The Question concerning Technology*, pp. 57-58; and Heidegger, *Nietzsche: Volume 4*, pp. 4-8.

especially interesting to the degree to which they illuminate von Balthasar's non-assertoric version. The work of the neo-Thomist Cornelio Fabro, especially in his study *God in Exile*, illuminates to the degree to which it proposes a much stronger version of the nihilism-atheism connection predicated on a reversal of Heidegger and bearing a family resemblance to that enacted by von Balthasar.[66]

Fabro theologically corrects and supplements Heidegger in ways that define a glaring contrast between him and von Balthasar. From von Balthasar's perspective, Fabro would be a thinker who has not learned the truly important Heideggerian lessons, i.e., that Christianity, too, can be the place in which mystery is excised in the lust to have answers, and that there are non-Christian renditions of mystery to which Christians might refer as critical challenges to their own forgetfulness. What Fabro has learned from Heidegger is a dogmatism of construal in which again the thematics of chiaroscuro are ignored and the illusion entertained that one can locate a pure, uncontaminated zone that stands out as reminder and, perhaps, also avenging angel for a period totally corrupted.

Although Henri de Lubac's linking of nihilism and atheism is not derived from Heidegger, von Balthasar's relation to de Lubac on this issue is altogether more positive. De Lubac tends to link nihilism with atheism only indirectly by way of an anthropologization thesis, and does so without making secular culture a *massa perditionis* and Christianity a de facto city of God. *The Drama of Atheistic Humanism* and *La postérité spirituelle de Joachim de Fiore* offer rich accounts of the various ways in which the anthropological milieu can strangle the transcendent impulse.[67] De Lubac does not find it necessary, however, to assert an absolute cleavage between church and world, the one totally pure, the other equally impure. Yet even in a contaminated situation judgment is called for, and given the necessity of decision, Christians are justified in worrying about the systemic reductionistic torque in modernity. The kinds of concrete and nuanced judgments of specific features of modern thought rendered by de Lubac, particularly in de Lubac's text on modern Joachimism, serve as a model for the

---

66. Cornelio Fabro, *God in Exile: Modern Atheism: A Study of the Internal Dynamic of Modern Atheism, from Its Roots in the Cartesian Cogito to the Present Day* (Westminster: Newman Press, 1968). While Fabro openly acknowledges that his basic plotline is influenced by Heidegger, he does not have to be too grateful. As MacIntyre has recently brought to our attention, there exists a Catholic precedent. In his *Die Philosophie der Vorzeit Verteidigt* (1853-60), Joseph Kleutgen offered the view that Descartes represented the definitive break with the classical tradition that constituted *die Vorzeit*. And just as in the case of Fabro, the scholastic tradition stood as the criterion of its deformation. See Alasdair MacIntyre, *Three Rival Versions of Moral Enquiry: Encyclopedia, Genealogy, and Tradition* (Notre Dame: Notre Dame University Press, 1990), p. 59.

67. Henri de Lubac, *The Drama of Atheistic Humanism,* trans. Edith M. Rirely (London: Sheed and Ward, 1949); Henri de Lubac, *La postérité spirituelle de Joachim de Fiore. Tome 1: de Joachim à Schelling* (Paris: Lethielleux, 1979).

kind of assessment of the credits and debits of modern thought prosecuted in *GL* 5.[68]

The second, more Nietzschean view of nihilism is recalled and contested neither as overtly or pervasively as the Hölderlinian version. Nevertheless, it is recalled at the end of *GL* 5 where von Balthasar engages Heideggerian post-metaphysical thought in something like systematic reprise and correction. Of particular importance to von Balthasar, as we have already pointed out in this section, is the constraining of the pure event character of Heidegger's "phenomenology of Being" (5:621). Though Heidegger's view of Being as event or *Ereignis* is hardly confined to his commentaries on Nietzsche, it does find there a significant minting in which it effectively undermines the possibility that "atheism" can function as an appropriate descriptor of a historical process dominated by occlusion, and, even more basically, undermines the very possibility of assigning culpability for the deepest occlusion or forgetfulness by insisting that all of history is ateleological erring. This implies that what is truly nihilistic is the Christian and Platonic positing of value and their intersection, whose empty constructs will inevitably, if belatedly, come undone. Here, of course, Heidegger's Nietzschean and Hölderlinian tendencies overlap. The surplus in the Nietzschean reading is Heidegger's pulling the rug from beneath the evaluative appraisal of the metaphysical tradition, a judgment based on a possible past and a possible future in which epiphany has scope and there is something like a maximum of letting be. In what has to be regarded as a definitive reversal of Plato, anamnesis and amnesia are the same. The stress on the pure event character of the history of Being places forgetfulness on the same level as memory. Construing history, therefore, as a scene of degenerative occlusion, or its opposite, ceases to make sense. History is the history of Becoming answering no questions, indeed dismantling their very possibility. Via Nietzsche Heidegger becomes unaccommodatingly Heraclitean. There is no process in history; nothing sediments in the way Hegel suggests it did. Reality is riddle because it is ever being born, ever new, the pure Becoming that Hegel rushed to domesticate in his Logic.

As the Nietzschean tendency in Heidegger is recalled at the end of *GL* 5, it is also contested. Since some of the basic elements of von Balthasar's contestation have already been rehearsed, I can be brief. Von Balthasar worries that this philosophical move, obviously calculated to support and guarantee the mystery of Being, may in the end succeed only in hallowing the arbitrary. Without the support of the theological difference, the ontological difference may prove itself an insufficient safeguard against atavism and immanentization.

---

68. For von Balthasar's high estimate of de Lubac, *La postérité*, see Hans Urs von Balthasar, *The Theology of Henri de Lubac: An Overview* (San Francisco: Ignatius Press, 1992), pp. 123-24.

Here, albeit in a less exigent register, von Balthasar is essentially repeating the highly influential criticisms of Adorno and Levinas. As von Balthasar contests Heidegger's excessively teleological Hölderlinian view of nihilism in which eclipse seems to have the status of a fatum, here he critiques a radically dis-teleological view in which the very possibility of normative judgment is dissolved. Von Balthasar is here pointing beyond the apocalypse of sheer contingency, what might be called after the novelist Paul Auster the music of chance, as in other situations he points beyond necessity and its choreography. What he points toward is the grace that subtends being, the symphonic music of the loving surprise of the expropriating space of the trinitarian persons, the music that Barth suggests that Mozart eschatologically heard.[69] The challenge to the Nietzschean extra brings Heidegger's view back into the Hölderlinian orbit of judgment of the tradition, classical and modern alike. This is the orbit within which von Balthasar's own account of nihilism moves, even as it hollows out from within much of the substance of Heidegger's account of genealogy and nihilism. It is in this hollowing out that von Balthasar concludes that Heidegger's most fundamental concerns are met in Christianity. At its aesthetic best at least, Christianity is able to resist the rampant subjectification of reality that erases epiphany. An epiphanically neutralized world is not only a catastrophe for the romantics and Heidegger, it is a Christian catastrophe. Not only does it represent the metaphorical death of God, it represents the Christian death of God, for a God that does not appear is not a Christian God, and a subject that cannot empty itself and surrender in ecstasy is not a Christian subject.

---

69. Von Balthasar makes much of the relation between Barth's theology and Mozart's music in his great text on Barth. See Hans Urs von Balthasar, *The Theology of Karl Barth: Exposition and Interpretation*, trans. Edward T. Oakes, S.J. (San Francisco: Ignatius Press, 1992), pp. 26-29.

CHAPTER 8

Naming God: Analogical Negation

KENNETH SCHMITZ

The philosophical questions of whether, how, and with what names we might speak to and about the High God of biblical religion have implications for the life of prayer, as well as for theological speculation.[1] It is not uncommon to hear that philosophy has nothing whatever to say in this regard, and that, if we are to speak to and of God at all, we must do so exclusively in the language of revelation. Because this position is fundamental, we should not be surprised to recall that it is not new, and that it continually assumes new shapes and draws upon new sources. The earlier agnosticism regarding the divine names is not so prominent at present as is a form of religious positivism. This positivism holds that, because the true nature of "Western" philosophy has been finally comprehended, it is no longer possible to maintain that philosophy has the capacity to speak truly, if inadequately, about God.

What is characteristic of this attitude in its several forms is the denial of analogy. Now such a denial is much more than a denial of a specific notion associated with Thomas Aquinas, for it seems to me that, if one is to speak of God at all, one must somehow speak with a broken voice that is not without

1. See Louis Dupré, *The Common Life: The Origins of Trinitarian Mysticism and Its Development by Jan Ruusbroec* (New York: Crossroad, 1984).

An earlier version of this essay, here somewhat revised, has appeared in German as "Gott mit Namen nennen," in *Internationale katholische Zeitschrift: Communio* 1, no. 93: 3-22, and in Dutch as "Het noemen van Gods naam," in *Communio: Internationaal Katholiek Tijdschrift* 1, no. 93: 1-19. Its appearance here in English permits me to acknowledge the influence that Louis Dupré's conversations and publications have had upon my own thought, especially in regard to the negativity present in all knowledge about God and the inseparability of a spiritual ground for all such knowledge.

some truth but that yet falls infinitely short of the full truth. Now that broken-ness, however we understand it — whether it be an analogy of being or of spirit or of goodness or of some other intelligibility — is neither mere equivocity, nor is it univocity. With that caution in mind, it may yet prove useful to reexamine the capacity of human thought and speech to say a word, however fractured, to. and about God. In what follows I will assume that the philosopher knows about the High God of biblical discourse. To be sure, we know too that, qua philosopher, in order to complete our project we would need to meet the challenge of proving whether such a God does exist.[2] But that is not the perti-nent question here. The question concerns, rather, the very possibility of naming such a God, of speaking to and about God. This issue does not belong to faith alone, but implicates philosophical views of language and reality as well.

Even faith itself encounters a certain discontinuity in its speech to and about God. Moreover, it is conscious of that discontinuity, calling it mystery, transcendence, and revelation. The language of sacrament transforms the wor-shiper, taking him or her up into a higher mode of existence. The element of formal likeness, so important to the sign-element in the symbolism, is ancillary to such an existential transformation of the worshiper. The analogical discourse of philosophy, on the other hand, takes the element of a tenuous and fractured relation-to-source as its stepping-stone. For analogy is a *conceptual* effort to articulate not directly the meaning of some aspect of the relation between humanity and God, but *how* that meaning already present can be translated into concepts. That is, a theory of analogy is developed within the limits of conceptual judgment and in terms of the propositional speech that expresses abstract meaning in terms of conceptual judgments. Analogy is, then, a second-level modification of language that reflects upon the movement of concepts in the articulation of meaning. The very elements that, so to speak, "move" within analogical discourse are the abstract concepts themselves and the propositions and judgments formed of them.

If doctrine, *doctrina,* "objectifies" religious speech through the appropria-tion of concepts, then analogy serves as a distinctive strategy within the artic-ulation of religious meaning. It follows that analogy is not new speech, is not the invention of new words, but is rather a distinctive way in which ordinary speech is used. Of course, analogy is not restricted to speech about God, but is

---

2. While I do not in all respects share Dupré's valuation of philosophical reason, his perceptive strictures regarding the impact of Kant upon the possibility of a philosophical proof of God's existence, set forth in *A Dubious Heritage: Studies in the Philosophy of Religion after Kant* (New York: Paulist Press, 1977), have not left my own position on the issue untouched. I have expressed my own increased sense of the boldness and difficulty of such a proof in "Theological Clearances: Foreground to a Rational Recovery of God," in *Prospects for Natural Theology,* ed. E. T. Long (Washington, D.C.: Catholic University of America, 1992), pp. 28-48.

broadly rooted in ordinary speech. Indeed, analogy comes naturally to the tongue whenever a likeness is recognized that is embedded in two or more things in such a way that it cannot be disengaged from them as a common property or attribute. Such a likeness so recommends itself that the same word or phrase is used somewhat differently for two referents, or the word or phrase designates things which, taken in their several wholes, are diverse from one another yet not simply unlike. An explicit and elaborate theory of analogy is the refinement of such a strategy. It arises within a speech situation in which the emphasis upon likeness that characterizes the order of abstract concepts is situated within a radical unlikeness. We shall see how radical that diversity can be when terms are used to speak of God.

If the foregoing is correct, then analogy is meant to show how it is possible to entertain the preposterous notion that a creature can communicate with its Creator out of resources that are proper to the creature in its constitution, capacity, and environment. I am not concerned here to distinguish the various modes of analogy, but only the very possibility of analogy as a mode of communication to and about God. We speak, perhaps improperly, of the "wing" of an airplane and the wing of a bird, and of the "goodness" of a person and of a fine wine. The meaning is very different in each instance, and yet airplanes do have wings, some persons possess exceptional virtue, and a few have fine cellars. We find this likeness-in-diversity, this continuity-in-discontinuity brought forward dramatically in religious speech. And properly understood, analogy can be an aid in deepening our understanding of the relation to God that is encountered in the life of prayer and sacrament. For there is an interior movement within analogous speech to and about God. It is a movement that is driven by the necessities inherent in a speech that, while it remains rational and conceptual, wills to preserve the mystery of God. For an appropriate understanding of analogy is a strategy for nourishing the relation between humanity and God within a growing realization that God is not human, at once increasing the intimacy and the distance of the relation, the immanence and the transcendence of God.

Take as an example the locution "God is wise." This may be said by a philosopher seeking to express the divine attributes, or by a devout believer seeking to glorify the Lord. Such locutions are always situated within a context, perhaps religious, certainly cultural, so that the very meaning of "wisdom" may already be complex before it is taken up into predication to and about God. Thus, it has been noticed that in the biblical writings wisdom has not always had a purely positive meaning, and that its applications are astonishingly diverse. It is said of craftsmen, of the aged, and of royal counselors; it is sometimes a gift from God, at other times so remote from us that it must be denied of all but God. Moreover, God is not only wise, but also glorious and merciful and fearful, and ultimately incomprehensible.

It is usual to speak of a threefold gradation in analogous speech to and about God. The gradation has received the technical names: the way of affirmation, negation, and supereminence *(via affirmativa, negativa et eminentior).* It is too easy to think of the first way as simply affirmative, after the model "S is P": "God is wise." And then it is said that such an affirmation is corrected by its exact denial, "S is not P": for if creatures may be said to be wise, then it is truer to say that "God is not wise." Let me call this the first negation *(via negativa prima).* Finally, the third mode of analogy is said to incorporate the first negation, concluding that, though God is not wise in the way creatures are, still God is after all wise in a way proper to God: "God is supersubstantial Wisdom." What is most bothersome about the schema is not the strictures of propositional and predicational language, nor the ambiguity of the copula, but the too easy continuity by which the predications follow from one another.

At this point we are not dealing with the usual patterns of speech, for the third mode of predication *(via eminentior)* is at once more affirmative than the initial *via affirmativa* and more negative than the initial *via negativa.* It is just this "more" that needs exploration in order to bring out the character of supereminence. I propose that we start with the third (supereminent) mode. At this third level, as I have said, the adjectival predication ("wise") has failed to express the divine wisdom even deficiently because its adjectival predication distorts the truth about God. And so the *via eminentior* has had to use substantive predication: "God is Wisdom." God, then, is supersubstantial Wisdom.

Beginning with this supereminent predication, however, we can mount a *discursus* from what we may call the new and upgraded *via affirmativa,* the substantive predication of the *via eminentior:* "God can be truly said to be wise just because God is essential Wisdom." Now, this new affirmation does not simply say that God is a certain kind of substance, for that is already implied in the initial affirmation by the subject term: "*God* is wise." In that initial affirmative predication the term "God" is already designated as a subsistent and perfect subject. But more is now being said than that God is a substance, even a very special kind of supersubstance. Indeed, there is a powerful negation operative in the supereminent affirmation, for it says "God is *not* wise, God is Wisdom."[3]

---

3. In order that the reader not be lost in the forest of negations that follows, I here append the major signs along the path of negation that is to follow: (1) First negation *(via negativa simplex):* "God is not wise." The traditional *via eminentior* incorporates this first negation in its recourse to superaffirmation: "God is Wisdom." (2) Second negation *(via eminentior negativa secunda):* "God is not Wisdom." (3) Third negation *(via eminentior negativa tertia):* "If it is as true to say of God that God is not Wisdom as to say that God is Wisdom, then it is also as *false* to say that God is not Wisdom as to say that God is." (4) Fourth negation *(via eminentior negativa quarta):* "Our predications to and of God are false as a whole but not wholly false inasmuch as we deny the mode of expression *(modus significandi)* and affirm what is meant *(res significata).*" The remainder of the essay explores this unfolding pattern of analogous negation.

The first negation ("God is not wise") is already contained in the *via eminentior* and accomplishes the following modifications in our speech to and about God: (1) It distinguishes God from creatures. Creatures instantiate wisdom, but God is its incomparable embodiment, essence, exemplar, and source: "God is Wisdom." (2) The predication identifies God with wisdom in such a way that it secures God's sheer self-identity, and even implies the identity of all predicates in the divine simplicity. The negation within the supereminent mode of predication breaks through the usual distinction between subject and predicate so as to preclude the possibility of detaching the predicate from God. The supereminent mode of predication raises the predicate to equal and identical status with the subject.[4] God is Wisdom by the divine nature or essence itself. God is not wise occasionally, as even the wisest person is occasionally ignorant or foolish. There may be some kind of complexity in God but not separability, not even the separability (of particular and universal, or member and class) implied in instantiation. God is not a case of being wise: God is self-identical, self-subsistent Wisdom.

Still, we cannot rest here. For we must hasten to add: God is not wise, neither is God Wisdom, nor even God's own Wisdom. This is the new supereminent *via negativa: via eminentior negativa secunda*. It deepens the sense of the negative expressed in the first negation *(via negativa prima)*. John Macquarrie asks whether God is totally unlike us, and he suggests that God can't be or we wouldn't be able to talk about God. But the new *via negativa* intends to say just that: "God is wholly unlike us." Not only is God not Wisdom; neither is God Goodness nor Beauty nor any other substantive perfection. Is God wholly Other, then? Not if "other" is simply a correlative term to "same" or "self" or "creature." As Nicholas of Cusa has told us, God is more other than absolute Otherness.[5] Speech has reached its limits. All signs fail. We are resigned to silence. And yet the philosopher inquires further, and the worshiper cries out: Lord, I would speak. Where then shall I turn? how shall I speak?

In order to proceed further we must become aware of the crisis initiated by the second negation, for this negation is a very precise one. It does not exclude names directly, such as body (which is capable of disintegration), or nutrition (which is capable of exhaustion), or reasoning (which is capable of error). Those names have already been excluded prior to the initial *via affirmativa* in accordance with Saint Anselm's principle that God is whatever it is better *absolutely* to be than not. This second *via negativa eminentior*, however, rejects just those

---

4. It is striking that Hegel's development of the absolute judgment in the second part of the *Science of Logic* also elevates and identifies the predicate with the subject. But Hegel utilizes a dialectical mode of negation, not an analogical one.

5. At this point we leave behind us the correlation of Same and Other set forth in Plato's *Sophist;* but we also leave behind Hegel's dialectical negation.

things which it is better for God to be than not: it rejects essential Wisdom, Knowledge, Love, Goodness, and the like. Terms such as "body" were excluded from the very beginning of the formation of any concept of the High God. Indeed, the very earliest *via affirmativa* had already included a negative force within it, since it had already excluded all but what we might call spiritual names, such as knowledge and love, and all but transcendental names, such as being, true, good, and the like. What is more, the initial *via negativa* had, therefore, been doubly negative, since it went on to deny of God the creaturely mode of perfection, namely, that of being wise in virtue of possessing a property. It negated attributive predication in the form of adjectival properties. The second *via negativa*, in addition, now *wholly* excludes Wisdom as such from God; yes — even the attributive essence, pure Wisdom Itself. For the second *via negativa* does not simply say: "God is not wise as creatures are wise." It goes on to say that God is not wise at all. The careful shadings of human language fall into indifference before God: the difference between adjectival and substantive attribution falls away, along with that between essences and properties, and between affirmations and negations. The second *via negativa* says it is truer to say that God is not wise in any way or sense at all, if by saying *that* the failure of human speech before the transcendent God is recognized and expressed.

The way forward lies in the silence induced by the collapse of essential difference. Still, out of that undifferentiated silence emerges a new hope and a third negation. For if it is as true to say that God is not wise/not Wisdom as it is to say that God is wise/Wisdom, it is also *as false* to say that God is not wise/not Wisdom as to say that God is.

To recapitulate: at this point we must hold together a threefold negation: (1) The negation that denies of God all ordinary adjectival modes of expression (*via eminentior negativa prima*): God is not simply someone wise, God is All-Wisdom. (2) The negation that denies of God all complexity, even that of the multitude of essential names, such as Divine Wisdom, Goodness, Power, etc. (*via eminentior negativa secunda*), since their unresolved difference threatens to destroy the divine simplicity.[6] Such a negation secures the divine simplicity without necessarily rendering that simplicity incompatible with some as yet unspecified distinctive form of inner complexity. This second negation is not strictly speaking exclusionary, for it is not meant to deny complexity as such but only that sort of complexity that invites separation or the possibility of

---

6. Hegel rejected any attempt on the part of metaphysics to attribute names to God on the grounds that the many names attributed to God came into unresolved conflict with God's reputed simplicity. At best the names were mere religious representations proper to the Understanding, when what was needed was the translation of our experience of God into conceptual reason. What the attempt came into conflict with, in truth, was Hegel's dialectical notion of negation. The negation being proposed in this analysis is not the correlative negation of the dialectic but the analogical negation of the supereminent way.

disintegration, even if only in our mode of expression.[7] This second supereminent negation can be further broadened and made more radical. It will then deny of God, not only all adjectival and substantive predicates, but *all differentiations* appropriate to human speech. Without being able to claim a knowledge of the multitude of human languages, it intends to deny *all* differentiations in every human tongue. In effect, then, especially if *language* is a tissue of differences, it intends the denial of all speech.

And yet a further negation remains: (3) The negation that denies, not simply the differentiations of human speech, but also the *indifferentiation* of human speech taken as a totality. So that we must say: not only is it as *true* to deny wisdom of God as to affirm it, but it is also as *false* to deny these predications. At this point all human speech is broken on the rock who is God. Even the denial of speech is denied. But to deny that indifference releases the differentiations of speech to a new and humbler mode of expression, a new and heightened mode of affirmation.

The second negation denies that the differentiations within human speech (including the substantive predicates) are applicable to God. The third negation denies that denial. The point needs clarification. When I say that the second negation denies the differences intrinsic to human speech (the substantive as well as the adjectival predicates), I mean precisely that it denies the difference between what is and is not or what ought or ought not to be said of God. For it says: "It is as true to say not wise/not Wisdom of God as to say is wise/is Wisdom." The third negation now denies that second negation, the negation that negates the difference among the elements of speech, and ultimately between is and is not. For the third negation says that it is as *false* to say "not wise/not Wisdom" of God as to say "is wise/is Wisdom." Now the second negation had collapsed the distinction between "not wise/not Wisdom" and "is wise/is Wisdom," between negation and affirmation. The third negation collapses the collapse, denies the collapse between "not wise/not Wisdom" and "is wise/is Wisdom." In so doing, however, it does not simply return us to the second negation, it points rather toward further affirmation and further negation. It is what Hegel might have called a speculative negation in contrast to a dead-end negation; it is negation with a future. But that future is not grounded in a dialectical correlation between negation and affirmation. It is an analogous future.

Once again, the third negation takes the following form: "It is as *false* to

---

7. Hegel is very precise on this point. He finds the predication of substantive names to God (Unity, Goodness, etc.) to fail. He charges that an irreconcilable inconsistency emerges in such predication, so that God seems to oscillate between being the *many* attributes assigned to God and being an absolutely simple *unity* without attributes. The further negations of analogous speech in our own analysis are meant to free our language from this impasse and reproach.

say that God is not wise/not Wisdom as to say that God is wise/is Wisdom."
The negation does not bear directly and simply upon the predicate "not wise/not
Wisdom." It bears rather upon the whole assertion made by the second negation
when that second negation has been taken up into the third negation. With that
modification the negation is no longer the relatively simple assertion: "God is
not even substantive Wisdom." It now takes form as: "It is as *true* to say that
God is not wise/not Wisdom as to say that God is wise/is Wisdom." Language
is turned back upon itself. The third negation makes clear that the negation
bears not upon the *predicate* as such but upon the *predication:* "It is true to
say. . . ." Notice, too, that in saying that "It is true . . ." the second negation still
bears upon the predicates "is wise/is Wisdom" and "not wise/not Wisdom," but
indirectly. The third negation is meant to deny the second, and so when it asserts
"It is *as* false . . . ," the negation bears only indirectly upon the predicates and
bears directly upon the totality of the prior assertion made by the second
negation.

This formulation makes clear that the negation has now shifted to the
predicational forms and away from the predicates. Notice further that the third
negation does not say that the second is false, but that it is *"as false as. . . ."* It
does not claim a truth contrary to that asserted by the second negation; it
neutralizes both and dissolves the distinction between truth and falsity. It negates the ultimate distinction within assertive speech. But it negates it in such
a way that in removing this ultimate criterion of cognitive language, it removes
the difference between successful (truthful) speech and its failure (false speech).
The symbol of this third negation is not the word "not" but the quiescence of
all speech: the negation produces a second silence.

Out of this second silence there arises again . . . speech. It is, however, a
new mode of speech, not a new vocabulary, but a new way of speaking to and
about God. It is chastened speech. But how, precisely, does this new speech arise
out of the total destruction of speech which the third negation has brought
about? The new mode of speech arises out of the failure of speech insofar as
the failure has been brought about by that negation. And so it is a kind of
resurrected speech, a speech that has died to itself in silence. For the person of
Christian faith, it arises out of the total claim that God makes upon him or her.
For God claims from him or her everything, not only silence but also speech.
And so the worshiper dares to speak again. It is faith at this point that carries
him or her through this silent "dark night" of the tongue. It is the unconditional
demand that he or she talk to God and not merely about God that moves the
worshiper beyond the death of the word. "What will I do, oh my love, if I cannot
praise Thee?" Did not Augustine confess just such breaking of the silence of his
adoration? And before him, did not the psalmist sing a new song? This may
seem an inappropriate intrusion of the religious reality into conceptual analogy,
but the philosopher must follow the lead of this *discursus* in pursuit of the

question set out from the beginning, namely, to understand how one can speak to and of the High God. For I have been asking all along about conceptual analogy as an aid to clarifying religious speech. Moreover, in preserving the character of religious speech, I have used the double phrase "speech to and about God." For speech *about* God gets the power it has from speech *to* God. In turn, for the believer his speech gets its power from speech by God.

Admittedly, however, it is not enough to say that the religious person must speak to and about God. The problem I set was to show *how* that might be possible. Let us return, then, to the third negation. Taken along with the second, it comes to this: "If not wise/not Wisdom is as true as is wise/is Wisdom, yet it is also as false." Through this total denial of the denial of speech, the various forms of predication and the predicates themselves are left floating free in what seems to be a total linguistic drift.

Indeed, the obvious observation is that speech has been reduced to utter chaos. It is as though human speech has shattered upon the transcendence of God. It is the word "utter" in "utter chaos" that needs clarification. The objector might say: "You have described a state in which everything is permitted, so that any name will serve as well or as poorly as any other. Why isn't any term as inappropriate as any other in this state of linguistic anarchy?" Again, in a speech that has lost all of its differentiation as well as its unity, everything is permitted, so that this linguistic chaos is no longer speech, nor is it even silence: it is the babble of Babel. Nevertheless, there is no road back once this deepening negation of speech has begun. And so, if I will not be silent even though speech has failed, and if I must still speak to and of God, an objector might ask why will not a discredited word such as "body" or even one such as "evil" serve as well as "wise/Wisdom"? All utterances will have become equally meaningless.

The reply must be made as follows: In reducing speech to "utter" chaos the third negation reduced it as a totality. And so the reduction does not permit reentry into speech at an earlier or lower level prior to and oblivious of the negations that have intervened between the ordinary and straightforward use of language and the third negation. We must not forget, however, that the term "wise/Wisdom" has not been the subject of direct denial in the third negation. On the contrary, the term has (if I may so speak) regained an equilibrium with the term "not wise/not Wisdom," inasmuch as both have been put out of play insofar as they are in play within their prior contexts. What has been directly negated has been the whole context of differentiated and undifferentiated speech. For speech does not simply name a referent; it also expresses a language as a whole. It expresses the context, so that its negation does not foreclose the emergence of a new context. It is this latent power of affirmation presiding within negation that is the surprising resource from which speech comes to new life.

But to justify this surprising power of the affirmative-in-negative and negative-in-affirmative, we must first set aside inadequate understandings of negation. We might put the matter thus: Can there be any residue of meaning left after the threefold negation? Can we make any sense out of retaining the proposition "God is still in some sense wise/Wisdom"? It cannot be retained if negation is taken in one of the three following senses: if negation is thought of as removal, erasure, or exclusion.

1. *Negation understood as removal:* No residue of meaning can be left of our original propositions, "God is wise/Wisdom," if negation is thought of as a step-by-step removal, as though affirmative words first matched objects isomorphically by a one-to-one correspondence. The first negation would detach the name by introducing a semantic space between the name and its object or referent. A second negation would presumably introduce a further detachment, increasing the semantic distance. The process would weaken the original power of reference, until the name became more and more obscure in regard to its referent. This, it seems to me, is not the true meaning of the "way of remotion."

2. *Negation understood as erasure:* Nor would any meaning be left of the original assertions if negation were simply an erasure, an abolition or annihilation. That is, negation cannot be understood as a destruction of an affirmative token which stands for an object, as happens when we erase a word or number and write another in its place as though to remedy a mistake.

3. *Negation as exclusion:* Nor should we take the notion of exclusion too literally. For if we do, we introduce an external division between God and humanity, an exclusion that makes of God a transcendence that is impervious not only to human speech but to the human heart as well. That might suffice for Deism, but not for properly religious speech in the biblical manner. God would then be taken as a wholly Other who cannot be in intimate presence to and with the creature, not even to the creature's inner being. God then would be taken to be an object set over against or beyond creatures.[8] If God is transcendent only in that way, then God is excluded from intimacy with creatures and simply is not the biblical Lord. Hegel has shown that such an exclusive God is merely the false infinite, the crypto-finite. By denying names of God, religious speech certainly does not intend to reduce the otherness of God to an external relation.

What kind of negation is operative here, then, if the above senses of negation are not operative? And how are we to begin to recover the sense of

---

8. Louis Dupré has expressed a caution "about the universal applicability of the concept [of the sacred as simply Other]." The interaction between the transcendence of the biblical God and the modern secularization of the world has yielded such a concept, but see the full discussion in *Transcendent Selfhood: The Loss and Rediscovery of the Inner Life* (New York: Seabury Press, 1976), pp. 18-30.

our speech to and about God through negation? Suppose that we understand religious negation as follows: we retain the meaning and value of the original expression ("God is wise") in some sense, but let the thrust of the negations function eventually to put brackets around the whole locution in order to qualify it in such a way that we may continue to use the expression but only with that qualification. This is not unlike the symbols in which ordinary terms are used and continue to be used, even though the original context has been outstripped and the expression resituated in a new context. It is important to recognize, therefore, that the meaning of terms and propositions bears an intrinsic relation to the contexts in which they are expressed. It will follow, then, that the retention of the original term or expression does not leave the initial meaning unchanged when the original context is negated.

Ian Ramsey held that in religious language the empirical character of ordinary usage was transcended without being destroyed or excluded.[9] But he resisted the temptation to think of the empirical character as the basis upon which religious language finally rested, so that religious language would be construed as a sort of curious afterthought. Thus, for example, in talking about the first and second persons of the Trinity, the ordinary meaning of the father-son relationship provides the initial model. But the meaning is converted into its religious and specifically Christian sense by the accumulation of "qualifiers" ("unbegotten," "only-begotten," "eternally begotten," "one in being with the Father"). These so radically transform the ordinary sense of the relationship and alter its meaning that religious discourse is not to be understood as a sort of merely derivative secondary metalanguage, but as an original mode of speech that carries within it ordinary empirical elements of meaning (models) transformed by powerful qualifiers. Indeed, the qualifiers play a more definitive role in determining the properly religious sense than do the models which they qualify, since they invert the order and convert the empirical elements into a sublanguage or subtext.

My only reservation regarding this very helpful approach to religious language is that, despite Ramsey's intention, the empirical elements within religious language may easily carry an undue weight, so that we think of these elements as the primary base of religious language, rather than seeing religious language as drawing upon ordinary terms. More pertinent still, Ramsey's analysis bears more upon the terms than the context, though his stress upon nicknames and odd expressions points in the direction of a transformation of the linguistic-psychological atmosphere as a whole. The successive negations of the present analysis, on the other hand, bear unmistakably upon the context of the

9. Ian Ramsey, *Religious Language: An Empirical Placing of Theological Phrases* (New York: Macmillan [1957], 1963), and *Christian Discourse: Some Logical Explorations* (New York: Oxford, 1965).

whole locution and not directly upon the terms. For that reason, it seems to me, the transformations operate at a more fundamental level.

Indeed, without falling into the extravagances of de Maistre and the traditionalists, or the romantics, it is not too much to say that analogous negation indicates that religious language discloses itself as the original and ultimate mode of language. The negations determine the way in which the initial affirmations ("wise/Wisdom") are to be used, and so the negations show how the affirmations are to be continued in power. Or, if you will, the negation expresses by means of the negated finite affirmation a meaning that is true of the infinite. The third negation in speech to and of God, then, declares not simply a new context, but that God is not a human being inasmuch as human language collapses before the ineffable God. This declaration is not simply indeterminate or indiscriminate, however, for by sustaining the original affirmation within it the declaration spells out the determinate sense in which God is not a human being.

I have spoken more than once of the power of the negative. The phrase is, of course, Hegel's. But I do not use it here in the correlative sense of the Hegelian dialectic.[10] I use it, rather, in the analogical sense, for the negative has not been developed here within the conflictual dynamics of the dialectic, but rather along the path of analogical supereminence. Along that path the successive negations are obviously more negative than the initial *via negativa*. What is not so obvious is in what sense, if any, the affirmations are more affirmative than the initial *via affirmativa*. When negation operates not simply to remove, erase, or exclude, it is able to produce profoundly affirmative disclosures that contain the prior qualifying contexts within them.

An illustration or two may help us at this point. For example, I receive a disclosure when a friend rejects what I am convinced is a reasonable plea. The "No!" may be ambiguous, however, in its disclosure. For the "No!" may turn back upon my friend and reveal him in a new and sadder way as not being the friend I had hoped in. Or, conversely, it may redound upon me and disclose my request and complacent expectation as questionable, disclose an arrogance that strikes deeply into recesses of my self and that I find painful to uncover. Yet the result is not without gain. Let us consider another example: There may grow in my awareness a sense of frustration, a sense of limit to my capacities in some definite direction. To my passionate wish, there begins to sound a

---

10. It is possible to see in analogical negation the subordination of the moment of dialectical opposition, which for Hegel was absolute. However, it is a mistake to equate all opposition of affirmation and negation with Hegelian or post-Hegelian dialectics. And indeed, poststructuralists have sought to break loose from those strictures, though for the most part in the direction of a secular humanism. Analogical negation, on the other hand, retains a certain affinity with the speculative (as distinct from the dialectical) aspect of Hegel's *Logic*, but it moves beyond system in the direction of transcendence.

profound ontological "No!" so insistently that I am forced to acknowledge it or be broken by defying it. The result once again is not simply negative.

A final example: I may be beleaguered by assaults from without and self-doubts from within so that I become exhausted, and this at a time when the evil one moves to bring my whole being into danger of shipwreck. Now, if into such weakness there steps for a moment a friend who holds his hand over me to hide my weakness and let me recover so that I might myself stand again — who utters a "No!" to the tormentor, "No further!" — that "No!" is a revelation to me, and a disclosure of a most affirmative and affirming sort.

My theme, of course, is the power of negation in speech to and of God, and the examples are intended to point to the deep recesses of life from which that speech wells up. In saying, "God is not a human being," we are not only expressing a negation, we are also expressing an affirmation of great meaning, to which faith is fully alive. For the negation "God is not a human being" is also an affirmation, since the negation reveals a meaning that is not exhausted by the structure of the way in which we express it. In saying that God is not a human being, we are not simply withholding a predicate from a subject, or merely excluding one substance from another. We are affirming that God and *only God is* God. Now, to say that "God is God" is not for the religious speaker an empty tautology. It is a shout of adoration and an anchor of fidelity. It is a protest against false gods, and the affirmation of who God is.

Having reached such a negation-affirmation, in what sense does the name "wise/Wisdom" still possess any meaning? The second negation ("It is true to say of God that God is not Wisdom") was the denial of the assertion that "God is Wisdom." The second negation was then modified by the third negation, which expressed the limits of assertive language in a form that embraces the previous negations and the previous affirmations: "If it is as true to say of God that God is not Wisdom as to say that God is Wisdom, yet it is also as false to say that God is not Wisdom as to say that God is."

One might object that the "as" distorts the intent of the second negation, which wants to say that it is *"truer"* to say "God is not Wisdom," and not simply that one assertion is "as true as" the other. But, as previously mentioned, this would be an unacceptable sense of negation; that is, it would understand negation as removal, erasure, or exclusion. What is more, if the previous assertions are in some sense true and we are trying to determine in what sense they are true, then once true they remain always *in some sense* true. That sense of truth is what is at stake here. Moreover, the very thrust of the negations is energized by the sense that the assertions are also equally *in some sense* false, and we are trying to determine that sense. For that reason, this third negation was directed toward the totality that constitutes assertive speech in both its affirmative and negative modes.

In negating the previous denial ("God is not Wisdom"), the third negation has rendered both forms of assertion ("is Wisdom/is not Wisdom") inoperative in the previous contexts. But it has also rendered them equal, so that it permits the retrieval of "is wise/is Wisdom," since if it is no less false it is also no less true than "not wise/not Wisdom." The retrieval, however, may seem as desperate as fishing for dinner in a heap of scraps. One might munch on a piece here and there, but without being able to put a meal together. Still, this third negation invites the believer to meditate upon the profound mystery of divine ineffability; but it does not or should not lead him or her to be resigned to an absolutely indeterminate negation of speech to and about God. It must be borne in mind that the third negation bears not directly upon the predicates but upon the truth/falsity distinction at the base of assertive language. It is to that expressive root that a fourth negation addresses itself.

We have been led to one last negation. Whereas the third negation gathered up the normative differential (T/F) in language in order to deny assertive language as a whole, the fourth negation insinuates itself *between* the inseparable factors of our speech to and about God. For the fourth negation demands that we draw a distinction between what we intend *(res)* by our expression and how *(modus)* we express what we intend. We have been led to the classical distinction between the mode of signification *(modus significandi)* and the reality meant *(res significata)*. It is a very curious negation and a curious distinction. For it says: "What you mean to say is not what you say." At the same time it recognizes that such a disparity is in principle unable to be remedied or overcome. Such a distinction presupposes that the mind can detect differences that are not separable, distinctions that are not separations.[11]

We sometimes correct a friend, saying, "Surely you didn't mean to say that, did you?" And he or she may accept our correction by agreeing that the expression badly suited the intended meaning, so that our emendation is accepted as an improvement. But in speech to and about God, the fourth negation says there is in principle no better way, no possible emendation. This may be the very best way of saying what you mean to say, but still, if your expression is to possess truth no matter how inadequately, it must be denied that what you say is what you mean to say. The example brings out by contrast the unrevisable, unemendable character of the expressive situation in religious speech. It is the situation in which we find ourselves in naming God.[12]

We may appreciate this absolutely unrevisable character more by a con-

11. This is not easily accepted wherever nominalism with its conflation of distinctions into separations has gained a foothold, as it has in much of the philosophy of the past several centuries. Yet the very possibility of a metaphysics of analogy depends upon the efficacy of distinctions that are not separations.

12. A theory of linguistic closure would absorb what is meant into the meaning of what is said. Analogous speech enlarges the sense of the meaning of what is said by opening it out *toward* what is meant.

sideration of the disparity between a translation and its original. The absolute disparity recognized by the fourth negation and the distinction between *res* and *modus* is adumbrated by the relative disparity between a translation and its original. For translation from one language to another always leaves a certain residue; the greater the residue the richer the original is likely to be. For in the work of translation we meet the ineradicable and inseparable differences of structure, nuance, and connotation that belong to the character of each language, so that often no quite satisfactory match can be found. Still, a translation at its best manages to say fairly adequately what the original says. Not so with speech about God.

The grounds for the fourth negation are to be found in two necessities inherent in religious discourse: (1) the need to talk to and about God; and (2) the need to affirm that God is God and not human. The fourth negation releases a meaning by enclosing that meaning in the *modus significandi* and setting the enclosed meaning off from the full meaning intended *(res significata)*. More is intended than can be expressed. The negation, then, is brought to bear no longer upon the whole expression (as in the third negation) in order to reject it *in toto*, but upon our mode of expression in relation to the totality of expressed and inexpressible meaning. The totality of *modus* and *res* constitutes a *determinate mystery*. This mystery is guided by a discriminatory negation, a determinate negation bearing not upon predicates (the names as such), but upon the modes of human expression (the manner of naming).

Indeed, the mystery is doubly determinate. For the fourth negation bears both upon the naming and the name. It bears directly upon the naming: recognizing the semantic distance between our manner of naming and the God who is named. But it does also bear indirectly and through the medium of the distinction (between manner and intent, *modus* and *res*) upon the name (for example, "wise/Wisdom"). For it permits the name to specify the determinate direction of the whole expression and gives to the mystery a modest and open definitiveness. The scope of the fourth negation and its distinction is coextensive with religious speech, even in its nonassertive forms. For the fourth negation and its discriminatory distinction plays a role even in regard to speech that is only implicitly assertive, such as praise, appeal, and the like. This is because nonassertive modes contain a determinate intelligible meaning within them.

In sum, then, it is important to notice that the fourth negation does not bear indifferently upon the whole expression, as did the third negation. The fourth negation discriminates *within* the locution, but not simply among the parts of speech that make it up. It does not analyze the syntactical elements, but draws attention instead to the syntactical structure as a distinctive factor within the whole locution. It casts light upon the mode of expression in distinction from what is intended. And so the fourth denial with its distinction exposes the deficiency in the expression by conceptually isolating what in the saying is deficient and what is not. It is our mode of expression that is deficient. What we are saying is deficient as to its mode, its manner; but it is not *wholly* deficient. The fourth negation discloses a deficiency that is not total in all respects.

To be sure, there is a sense in which the expression as a whole is deficient without being wholly deficient. It is deficient in the way in which a feverish person is wholly ill, or a beautiful symphony is wretchedly performed. The expression is wholly deficient in this sense: we cannot express what is meant apart from the defective mode of expression, any more than we can hear that particular performance without the dreadful cacophony inextricably embedded in it. And yet we do hear that specific symphony. The example limps in one aspect, however. For we hope that wretched performances are avoidable, whereas this deficiency is not; it is inevitable, written into the difference between the creature and the creator. For that reason, then, it is forever impossible to winnow out the deficient mode in order to leave the meaning bare and pure. Can such a distinction actually be made? As surely as we might distinguish between *esse* and *essentia* without ever being able to separate the one from the other, as though we were to encounter *esse* without *essentia*.

Can such a distinction be effective in naming God and calling upon God by name? The fourth negation by its very nature does not separate out meaning and mode of expression as two positive entities, as one separates the hull from the pith, permitting us to throw away the shell-like modality and to directly confront the residue, the pithy meaning. The fourth negation does not divide, it distinguishes imperfectly. It encircles the meaning, defining and thereby limiting it. In so doing it lights up and brings into relief a certain limitation inescapable in our expression that allows the meaning to escape, to overflow the confining mode. But by drawing attention to the limiting factor, the meaning intended, which is present both in and beyond the mode of expression, is thereby also lighted up indirectly: this is the indirection of analogy. For the meaning that is both expressed and intended is transfinite yet determinate. The predicate "wise/Wisdom" survives as an open directive toward a fuller meaning. Provided we are ready to build in the negations traced out along the way of supereminence, we are entitled to say something determinate to and of God: "God is somehow, after all, wise; and though we do not know what it means for God to be wise, we do know that it is not wholly false but somehow true to speak to and of him as wise." The predicate no longer functions as an adjectival or even as a substantive predicate, but as an analogous directive open to the divine plenitude.

Can such an analogous meaning that lies beyond the structures of speech be expressed? Yes and no. It is ineffable in the sense that no form of speech can confine it and express it in an ordinary and adequate fashion. But it can be expressed indirectly, for that is just what the fourth negation accomplishes as it builds upon the prior negations leading up to it. In distinguishing the mode of speech from what is meant, the fourth negation discloses the meaning that lies beyond the limits of the syntactical form. The disclosure comes about through negation, which does not incorporate the meaning wholly and definitively within the forms of speech as comprehending it, any more than we comprehend the full meaning of *esse* in the limited composites in which we find it. The meaning that lies beyond the forms and modes of speech is expressed in the very denial of the adequacy of those modes and forms. Yet the negation is not total by way of absolute indeterminateness. In this way, the negation expresses an affirmation. The meaning is determinate yet inexhaustibly open. It is open not by a simple indeterminacy, a mere negative infinity. It remains open in a certain direction, along a certain path that points us toward an inexhaustible glory. The fourfold negation offers a way of understanding not what is meant *(res)* by the way *(modus)* in which we say it, but what is englobed in the total locution, comprising both *res* and *modus*.

An inference remains that has been only lightly touched upon. In distinguishing the mode of speech appropriate to us, we also disclose the ground for our mode of expression in the finitude of our being. Our way of speaking is proportionate to our way of being. And the discrimination of our mode of expression from our intention places our whole being within the restricted area designated by the modality. This discloses the being and the Being that escape us on every side. If our mode of expression is rooted in and appropriate to our own restricted mode of being, then the deficiency we have noted in our expression (without being able to discard it) will be acknowledged as the very condition, not simply for our speaking, but also for our being at all. To throw that away is not simply to throw away our voices but our lives as well.

In praise to God we try to reach out beyond ourselves by calling God's name (appeal) and telling God's name (praise). We do this, however, not by leaving ourselves behind, but by recognizing that what must finally be said is that God is God and not a human being, and then, once again, silence. But it is a silence in which the original humble attribution of wisdom still lives. And so when we dare speak again, we offer the predicate as a modest return from among those of our gifts that are best and most noble. The fourfold transformation by successive negations plays out its role as a conceptual performance that can carry the believer, who must speak to God and of God, beyond his or her creaturely horizons to magnify the Lord. That necessity, that "must," is the Word of God at work in the speaker. Beyond every negation lies affirmation, for what draws us out of silence and into religious speech is not the power of the negative but the inexhaustible power of the divine affirmation by which God has created us, and created us with tongues of flesh and spirit.

CHAPTER 9

Mystical Literature and Modern Unbelief

JAMES WISEMAN, O.S.B.

Of the many areas within religious studies to which Louis Dupré has directed his interest in the course of his scholarly career, mysticism has held his attention for a particularly long time. The importance of mystical literature for him during his own student days is a matter of public record, for he has written of the "impression of awe" that came over him when, at the age of nineteen, he began reading passages from the diary of the sixteenth-century Jesuit mystic Balthasar Alvarez. These passages, he says, "suddenly seemed to open up a wholly new, heretofore hidden perspective on life."[1] In the ensuing half-century, Dupré has continued reading mystics, offering courses and publishing scholarly articles about their works, and giving more popular lectures that in turn have become small books serving to introduce a wider public to the riches of the Christian mystical tradition.[2]

Not surprisingly, Dupré has at times dealt with the very subject of the present paper. Noting that the words of contemporary religious discourse often "merely serve as signposts in the search of a religious experience without faith," he has suggested that the practical atheism of much of our culture could nowhere find a clearer spiritual echo than in the negative moment of the Christian mystical tradition, often called the *via negativa* or "apophatic way." Modern seekers, imbued with the mentality of a largely secular environment, may find the "language" of silence so prominent in apophatic mystics like Pseudo-Dionysius or Meister Eckhart to be the only one they can readily un-

---

1. Louis Dupré, general introduction to *Light from Light: An Anthology of Christian Mysticism*, ed. Louis Dupré and James Wiseman (New York: Paulist, 1988), p. 3.

2. See, e.g., *The Deeper Life: An Introduction to Christian Mysticism* (New York: Crossroad, 1981) and *The Common Life: The Origins of Trinitarian Mysticism and Its Development by Jan Ruusbroec* (New York: Crossroad, 1984).

derstand.[3] The purpose of the present paper is to consider why and to what extent this might be so, and to do so in dialogue with some of Dupré's published works. I will first review some of the factors that have led to the current situation and will then discuss the potential significance of the apophatic mystical tradition for those seeking spiritual meaning in our day.

I. The Phenomenon of Modern Unbelief

Some scholars would no doubt question the accuracy of a phrase like "the practical 'atheism' of our culture," which Dupré has at times used and whose early modern roots he has traced in his most recent book, *Passage to Modernity*. After all, surveys indicate that the vast majority of Americans claim to believe in God, and a recent study of religious attitudes on college campuses emphasizes the deep and pervasive desire of many students to know and be nourished by God.[4] On the other hand, studies also indicate that the number of agnostics or atheists in the United States has grown from 2 percent of the population in the 1950s to about 8 percent today — the largest rate of growth of any belief system.[5] There is no sign that this rate is abating.

There are, of course, various (and often complementary) ways of tracing the roots of modern unbelief. Some would harken back to ancient Greek philosophy and Protagoras's dictum that the human person (and not the gods) is the measure of all things. Others, like Dupré himself, have called our attention to the early modern period, especially in Italy, as a locus for the first stirrings of "the assumption that the human mind alone conveyed meaning and purpose."[6] Michael Buckley has focused on the excessive rationalism of seventeenth-century theologians as a major source of modern unbelief.[7] Still others have emphasized the role of mechanist philosophers of the Enlightenment such as Diderot, or of the still more recent "masters of suspicion": Marx, Freud, and Nietzsche.

Especially challenging to many traditional formulations of Christian belief is contemporary cosmology, which can easily appear to leave no place for a God so intimately concerned with life on earth that not even a sparrow could fall to the ground "without your Father's knowledge" (Matt. 10:29), a God whose very

3. Dupré, general introduction to *Light from Light*, pp. 23-24.
4. Michael J. Hunt, *College Catholics: A New Counterculture* (New York: Paulist, 1993).
5. Larry Witham, "The Changing Church," *Washington Times*, April 1, 1994, p. A10.
6. Dupré, *Passage to Modernity: An Essay in the Hermeneutics of Nature and Culture* (New Haven: Yale University Press, 1993), p. 89.
7. Michael Buckley, *At the Origins of Modern Atheism* (New Haven and London: Yale University Press, 1987).

"location" could in some sense be mapped. As Karl Rahner noted several times in his voluminous writings, it was not all that long ago that a leading theologian like Francisco Suárez could seriously inquire whether the glorified Christ was enthroned *in* or *above* the empyrean, the outermost heavenly sphere of a compact, geocentric universe. Today a question like this sounds consummately quaint, for we recognize a cosmos of immeasurably greater extent than anything Suárez could have imagined (and one that has *no* center at all!). Within this universe, some scientists even speculate that, given sufficient time, conscious forms of life are likely to develop on any of hundreds of millions of habitable planets. While a realization of the vastness and complexity of the universe is by no means inherently inimical to a sense of religious awe — after all, such a realization regularly inspired outbursts of devout wonder in someone like Pierre Teilhard de Chardin — in fact it has proven religiously alienating for many. The physicist and Nobel laureate Richard Feynman, for example, once declared: "It doesn't seem to me that this fantastically marvelous universe, this tremendous range of time and space and different kinds of animals, . . . all this complicated thing can merely be a stage so that God can watch human beings struggle for good and evil — which is the view that religion has. The stage is too big for the drama."[8] One could certainly argue that Feynman's understanding of "the view that religion has" does not reflect the position of the most respected religious thinkers today, but there is no doubt that a sense that "the stage is too big for the drama" has led many scientists and other intellectuals to distance themselves from traditional religious beliefs and practices. Just as the discovery of new lands during the age of exploration posed great challenges to Christian thinkers as they encountered other world religions, so too are new discoveries about the universe as a whole challenging us today.

In an attempt to meet this challenge, some influential theologians are advocating concepts of God radically different from the personal being whose dealings with humanity are described in the scriptures of Judaism, Christianity, and Islam — and they are doing so primarily because they find those descriptions incompatible with their understandings of modern science. Thus Gordon Kaufman, whose decades-long reflection on the concept of God recently culminated in a book fittingly entitled *In Face of Mystery,* writes that "if theological claims are to be intelligible and relevant in today's world, they must be formulated in close interconnection with modern cosmological, evolutionary, and ecological ideas. Most contemporary theological reflection has almost completely ignored this task, and this has contributed substantially to the increasing implausibility of the symbol 'God' in the modern intellectual

---

8. Richard Feynman, interview with William Stout in 1959, transcript, California Institute of Technology Archives, quoted by James Gleick, *Genius: The Life and Science of Richard Feynman* (New York: Random House, Vintage Books, 1992), p. 372.

world."[9] In his quest to render the symbol plausible, Kaufman rejects the notion of a personal God that was cultivated and enjoyed in traditional piety, inasmuch as this was "the product of a rather literalistic reading of the metaphors that dominated the tradition."[10] Instead, he refers to God as "the ultimate mystery," which we daily confront but about which "we really do not know what we are saying."[11] About the most he will allow himself in specifying this mystery is to say it is "that cosmic serendipitous creativity which manifests itself in the evolutionary-historical trajectory that has brought humanity into being and continues to sustain it in being."[12]

Less sophisticated in exposition, but perhaps more influential on the popular level, is the English theologian Don Cupitt. He, too, rejects the notion of God as a really existing, infinite person. Rather, "God (and this is a definition) is the sum of our values, representing to us their ideal unity, their claims upon us and their creative power." For Cupitt, the basic reason why many resist this conclusion is "because it is coupled with the admission . . . that religion is entirely human, made by men for men. This admission is now inescapable."[13] There could scarcely be a clearer expression of what Louis Dupré has so often referred to as the modern assumption that the human mind alone conveys meaning and purpose. Joined to that assumption is another, whose roots are also discussed at length by Dupré in *Passage to Modernity:* that nature is altogether self-supporting and self-moving, having attained a transcendence of its own rather than receiving its being, meaning, and direction from a God.[14]

Many other thinkers in fields other than theology have adopted this understanding of nature and have expressed their willingness to live with the concomitant uncertainty and ambiguity. The nuclear physicist Steven Weinberg writes that there is indeed an almost irresistible temptation to believe there is something or Someone for us outside the confines of this world and that "the honor of resisting this temptation is only a thin substitute for the consolations

9. Gordon Kaufman, *In Face of Mystery: A Constructive Theology* (Cambridge: Harvard University Press, 1993), p. 12.

10. Kaufman, p. 333.

11. Kaufman, p. xii.

12. Kaufman, p. 375.

13. Don Cupitt, *The Sea of Faith* (Cambridge: Cambridge University Press, 1984), pp. 269 and 265.

14. On this same point, Joseph Bracken has written: "The world view of both theist and non-theist involves an explicit or implicit appeal to faith as well as to arguments based on reason. The non-theist, for example, accepts on faith that the world as a dynamic matrix of interconnected causes and effects is its own explanation. For him or her, therefore, it is an absolute, that which is simply given and which requires no further explanation beyond itself. . . . The world as a self-sufficient totality is the object of faith for the non-theist" ("The Issue of Panentheism in the Dialogue with the Non-believer," *Studies in Religion/Sciences Religieuses* 21 [1992]: 217).

of religion"; nevertheless, he has opted for this "honor" and found it "not entirely without satisfactions of its own."[15] His fellow physicist Feynman once expressed a similar willingness to live in a universe that seemed ultimately purposeless when he declared that "there are many things I don't know anything about, such as whether it means anything to ask why we're here. . . . I don't have to know an answer. I don't feel frightened by not knowing things, by being lost in a mysterious universe without any purpose, which is the way it really is as far as I can tell. It doesn't frighten me."[16]

A number of students I have taught would resonate with that statement. They feel no attraction to any traditional religion, not, it seems, because they might otherwise be obliged to modify their behavior but because they do not find any of them to ring true to their experience. One student of mine recently wrote:

I feel it would be impossible for me to choose a religion, to adopt a set of beliefs, in order to answer the questions that surely puzzle me. The truth is, I don't need religion, at least not a traditional or established religion. As for life's questions, I will deal with them in my own way. One does indeed want to understand everything, experience everything, and know everything. But if we spend all of our time worrying and trying to explain the experience of life, we will miss the joys of life and the elation of having the chance to affect the world and promote the human race.

Even students who consider themselves committed adherents of one or another of the great world religions will at times readily admit that there is much they do not even begin to understand. John Caputo speaks for many of them when he writes: "Faith makes its way in the dark, seeing through a glass darkly, and it is genuine only to the extent that it acknowledges the abyss in which we are all situated, the undecidability and ambiguity which engulfs us all. We do not know who we are, not if we are honest, or whether or not we believe in God: that is the point of departure for any genuine faith."[17] This, it seems to me, well expresses the state of mind which has been for many of our contemporaries a "point of departure" not for genuine religious faith but rather for agnosticism or atheism. What might the writings of the mystics have to say to persons facing Caputo's "undecidability and ambiguity," persons whom Dupré calls "modern seekers of spiritual meaning"?

---

15. Steven Weinberg, *Dreams of a Final Theory* (New York: Pantheon, 1992), p. 261.

16. Richard Feynman, interview with Christopher Sykes of BBC-TV, 1981, quoted by Gleick, p. 438.

17. John Caputo, *Radical Hermeneutics* (Bloomington: Indiana University Press, 1987), p. 281.

II. Apophatic Mysticism and Its Relevance Today

Many studies of mysticism begin by noting how notoriously difficult it is to define the term. Granted the difficulty, it is at least generally recognized today that the original meaning of "the mystical" in Christianity referred to the "hidden" (Gk. *mystikos*) presence of Christ in the Hebrew Scriptures and the ability of a person to grasp this "mystical" sense of the text if he or she read with what we are wont to call "the eyes of faith." One of the most frequently used texts in this regard was the Song of Songs, whose narrative sense (in the form of a dialogue between a bride and her beloved) could also be understood "spiritually" or "mystically" as referring to the relationship between the soul (or the church as a whole) and Christ the Bridegroom. Hippolytus of Rome and Origen of Alexandria were among the first Christian practitioners of this kind of mystical reading of Scripture. Shortly thereafter the same insight was applied to the sacraments, likewise now called "mystical" because one could perceive, in faith, the hidden presence of Christ in the elements of baptismal water or eucharistic bread and wine.[18] Many of the early Christian authors who wrote about Scripture or the sacraments in this way would at times also allude to the positive effect that this kind of encounter with the divine had upon themselves, while today this note of private (or even extraordinary) experience of divine presence actually predominates in popular understandings of mysticism. The experiential element is also crucial for the very determination that a particular text should be regarded as "mystical"; Dupré is surely correct in writing that this designation will normally be applied if, for most or all readers, a text is "conducive to that special religious perception of reality in which the various functions of the mind, the affective as well as the cognitive, become united in a uniquely harmonious and often intensively experienced manner."[19] Although a criterion of this sort does not allow for a hard-and-fast dividing line between the mystical and nonmystical, it does permit us to say that a list of preeminent mystical writers in the Christian tradition would include Origen, Gregory of Nyssa, Pseudo-Dionysius the Areopagite, Bernard of Clairvaux, Bonaventure, Meister Eckhart, Jan van Ruusbroec, Julian of Norwich, Catherine of Siena, Teresa of Avila, John of the Cross, and Thomas Merton — a far from exhaustive list.

Among the typological distinctions that can be made among these and other Christian mystics, the most important for the present study is that between the more apophatic authors — those emphasizing the incomprehensibility of God, "denying" (Gk. *apophanein*) the ability of our concepts and ideas

---

18. For details and specific texts, see Louis Bouyer, *The Christian Mystery* (Edinburgh: T. & T. Clark, 1990).

19. Dupré, general introduction to *Light from Light*, p. 6.

to comprehend God — and the more kataphatic, with their greater trust in the ability of human images and concepts to say something true, even if incomplete, about divine reality. The two approaches are not mutually exclusive; Harvey Egan in particular has emphasized that any genuine Christian mysticism will contain both kataphatic and apophatic elements.[20]

Moreover, even among Christian mystics of a predominantly apophatic stripe, there are significant differences: some, like Gregory of Nyssa, stress the ultimate unknowability of God without offering detailed methodological reflections on the matter; there is no science of negation in Gregory. As Raoul Mortley has observed, "to accumulate negative descriptions of God is to do no more than assert that God is nameless, and it is this general assertion which Gregory wants to make. How the negatives work, or even which negatives are used, is not a matter of great import to him."[21]

On the other hand, Dionysius — influenced not only by Gregory and other Christian authors but in a significant way by the Athenian Neoplatonism of Proclus — is methodologically astute. The foundation of the kataphatic aspect of his doctrine is found in the divine names, names that are not of our own making but "only what scripture has disclosed." Even though the Deity "is inaccessible to beings, since it actually surpasses being," still it is "not absolutely incommunicable," for in the divine names it "generously reveals a firm, transcendent beam, granting enlightenments proportionate to each being, and thereby draws sacred minds upward to its permitted contemplation."[22] When Dionysius turns to the apophatic pole of his thought, writing at the end of *The Divine Names* that even "Trinity" and "Unity" are only names that we use "for that which is in fact beyond every name," and listing in the last chapter of *The Mystical Theology* a multitude of negations that must be said of "the Cause of all" — that it is not substance, not wisdom, not equality or inequality, not sonship or fatherhood, beyond both assertion and denial — his move is akin to Proclus's claim that the One is exalted above all contrast and all negation. Dionysius's negations are in this sense simultaneously affirmations, for he is in fact ascribing a higher form of reality to "the Cause of all," in reference to which all words fail "in the brilliant darkness of a hidden silence."[23]

20. Harvey Egan, S.J., "Christian Apophatic and Kataphatic Mysticisms," *Theological Studies* 39 (1978): 399-426.

21. Raoul Mortley, *The Way of Negation, Christian and Greek*, vol. 2 of *From Word to Silence* (Bonn: Hanstein, 1986), p. 191.

22. *The Divine Names* 1, 2, in *Pseudo-Dionysius: The Complete Works*, trans. Colm Luibheid (New York: Paulist, 1987), p. 50.

23. *The Mystical Theology* 1, in *Pseudo-Dionysius: The Complete Works*, p. 135. This dialectical relationship between negation and affirmation in Dionysius indicates an important way in which he differs from a modern theologian like Gordon Kaufman. We have already seen that the latter forthrightly denies personality of God, on the grounds that this attribution

References to such silence are heard again and again in the literature of apophatic mysticism, for a certain pessimism about the efficacy of language regularly accompanies an interest in negative theology.[24] Meister Eckhart, himself strongly influenced by Dionysius, claims in one of his sermons that to say "God is a being" is not true, for God is "a transcending nothingness [about which] St. Augustine says: 'The best that one can say about God is for one to keep silent out of the wisdom of one's inward riches.' So be silent, and do not chatter about God; for when you do chatter about him, you are telling lies and sinning."[25] Two and a half centuries later, John of the Cross made much the same point in describing the experience of being touched by what he believed to be the substance of God: "I would desire not to speak of it so as to avoid giving the impression that it is no more than what I describe. There is no way to catch in words the sublime things of God that take place in these souls. The appropriate language for the persons receiving these favors is that they understand them, experience them within themselves, enjoy them, and be silent."[26] Much closer to our own time, Henri Le Saux was convinced that the great gift that his adopted country of India could make to the Christian world was its "aspiration to total silence," for "only when the soul has undergone the experience that the Name beyond all names can be pronounced only in the silence of the Spirit does one become capable of this total openness which permits one to perceive the Mystery in its sign."[27] In these and other markedly apophatic writers, one constantly finds the refrain that the reality of God, absolute Mystery, far transcends the capacity of human thought or speech to comprehend it. What Raoul Mortley writes at the very end of his lengthy study of negative theology in ancient Greek and early Christian thought — that "the contribution of the *via negativa* is to assert the hiddenness of the divine"[28] — is no less true of later Christian thought. But what might this apophatic tradition have to say to men

---

was just the product of "a rather literalistic reading of the metaphors that dominated the tradition." For Dionysius, on the other hand, the "nonbeing" of the transcendent Goodness "is really an excess of being," God's "nonlife" is really "superabundant life," etc. (see, e.g., *The Divine Names* 4, 3). For this reason, Dionysius can consistently begin his most apophatic treatise, *The Mystical Theology*, with a prayer addressed "O Trinity, higher than any being, any divinity, any goodness! Guide of Christians in the wisdom of heaven," whereas one could not expect Kaufman to address any such prayer to his "cosmic serendipitous creativity."

24. On this point, see Mortley, p. 41.

25. Meister Eckhart, "German Sermon 83," trans. Edmund Colledge, in *Meister Eckhart: The Essential Sermons, Commentaries, Treatises, and Defense* (New York: Paulist, 1981), p. 207.

26. *The Living Flame of Love* 2, 21, in *The Collected Works of St. John of the Cross*, trans. Kieran Kavanaugh and Otilio Rodriguez, rev. ed. (Washington, D.C.: Institute of Carmelite Studies, 1991), p. 665.

27. Henri Le Saux, *The Eyes of Light* (Denville: Dimension Books, 1983), pp. 41 and 43.

28. Mortley, p. 277.

and women of our own day, especially those who are unbelievers or who are in some way disillusioned with Christianity?

First of all, it should be acknowledged that it will have little or no meaning for persons like the late Richard Feynman who, as we have seen, simply accepted "being lost in a mysterious universe without any purpose" and focused his brilliantly imaginative mind almost exclusively on questions of natural science. There are others, however, whom Dupré calls "spiritual seekers," who have an abiding sense of the *mysterium tremendum et fascinans*. To such persons, perhaps for very diverse reasons, the doctrines of the church that are intended to enshrine the mystery may seem instead to entomb it. While it may be relatively easy for men and women raised in the Christian faith to feel at home with the more kataphatic trinitarian reflections of an Augustine or a Ruusbroec, for those who do not share this faith or who have become alienated from it because its proclaimers have seemed to "know" too much, the starker journey into the divine darkness to which a mystic like Eckhart calls his readers may well offer a more compelling invitation to take a closer look at the Christian way. As Dupré has written, "The 'language' of silence may in many cases be the only one the modern seeker understands at the start of his journey."[29]

Dupré's point does much to explain the continuing attraction which so many people have for the writings of Thomas Merton, whose apophatic leanings have been explored in several scholarly studies,[30] and who described in an oft-quoted letter his own manner of praying as "a kind of praise rising up out of the center of Nothing and Silence, . . . a direct seeking of the Face of the Invisible."[31] Out of the experience of this apophatic prayer, which he never allowed to be crowded out of a daily schedule filled with a plethora of diverse responsibilities, Merton was able to feel keenly what he once called "the attitude of those who are no longer satisfied by a mystery whose presentation is reduced to the level of *things*." So, too, he became ever more able to understand how "the temptation to atheism which is confronting many Christians at the present time" bears a certain resemblance to the "nights" spoken of by John of the Cross and other apophatic mystics, and therefore how this temptation might ultimately effect a salutary stripping away "of our imperfect images of God."[32]

---

29. Dupré, general introduction to *Light from Light*, p. 24.

30. William H. Shannon, *Thomas Merton's Dark Path: The Inner Experience of a Contemplative* (New York: Farrar, Straus, & Giroux, 1981), and John F. Teahan, "A Dark and Empty Way: Thomas Merton and the Apophatic Tradition," *Journal of Religion* 58 (1978): 263-87.

31. Merton to Abdul Aziz, January 2, 1966, in *The Hidden Ground of Love: The Letters of Thomas Merton on Religious Experience and Social Concerns*, ed. William H. Shannon (New York: Farrar, Straus, & Giroux, 1985), p. 64.

32. Thomas Merton, "Contemplatives and the Crisis of Faith," in his *The Monastic Journey*, ed. Patrick Hart (Garden City, N.Y.: Doubleday, Image Books, 1978), p. 226.

Merton's reference to the mystical "nights" leads to a related point. According to John of the Cross, the worst sufferings of the "passive nights" are those which make one feel utterly rejected by God. Persons undergoing this purification, he writes, "feel so unclean and wretched that it seems God is against · them and they are against God."[33] It may be asked, however, whether the modality of this suffering will not necessarily be quite different for many persons in our own day. Such at least is the conviction of the Sanjuanist scholar Steven Payne, who has found from his own experience as a spiritual director that many of those coming to him for counsel do indeed exhibit all the classic signs of John's nights and yet do not find themselves helped by reading his texts. The reason, Payne concludes,

> generally has to do with the fact that their own spiritual journey seems to have followed a different course than the ideal Sanjuanist pattern of ever-deepening commitment to the Church and the Christian faith. Many are disturbed, not by the impression that God has rejected them, but by the feeling that God, faith, and prayer may all be illusory. In the Christian kingdom of sixteenth century Spain it was hardly possible to doubt the reality of God, so the anguish of the "dark night" was experienced primarily as a threat to one's own self-esteem, sense of worth, etc. In the twentieth century, however, the same "impasse" or crisis point may be experienced primarily as a challenge to believe in a loving Lord; we discover, painfully, that the deity we believed in when we started out on the road of prayer quite literally does not exist, and that Divine reality (whatever it may be) transcends all we have imagined. When John's account of the sufferings of the "passive nights" is transposed into this modern key, it seems to accord more closely with the experience of many people today.[34]

These words might well lead us to think of another Carmelite saint, one who had indeed learned much from the works of John of the Cross but whose experience was much more in this "modern key." Toward the end of her autobiography, Thérèse of Lisieux recounts the events that followed the first clinical signs of her approaching death from tuberculosis. Her first reaction was one of great joy that she would soon be called to that eternal life for which she had staked her all in entering Carmel. At that time she enjoyed such a clear and firm faith that she was convinced that nonbelievers were actually speaking against their own inner convictions when they denied the existence of a transcendent realm, "that beautiful heaven where C·d Himself wanted to be their Eternal Reward." After a few days, however, that joy passed and she

---

33. John of the Cross, *The Dark Night* 2, 5, 5, in *The Collected Works*, p. 402.
34. Steven Payne, quoted in the report on the Seminar on Spirituality, *Proceedings of the Catholic Theological Society of America* 39 (1984): 178.

was left only with the terrible fear that heaven was a mirage and that death was not the gateway to eternal life but rather a grinning mockery which, personified, was saying to her: "You are dreaming about the light, about a fatherland embalmed in the sweetest perfumes; . . . Advance, advance; rejoice in death, which will give you not what you hope for but a night still more profound, the night of nothingness."[35]

How she dealt with this trial helps illustrate the nature of genuine mysticism in the original Christian sense of the term. Some have denied that Thérèse was a mystic on the grounds that her life was free of the presence of or even the longing for extraordinary mystical phenomena. Indeed it was, but we have already seen that such phenomena did not belong to the essence of the mystical as this was understood in the early Christian centuries. According to that understanding, with its emphasis on the "hidden" but real presence of Christ in the Scriptures, the sacraments, and the world around us, "the main thing is to be fully convinced that Christ is living in us, and especially *to act accordingly,* not to experience more or less directly the feeling that this is indeed so."[36] Such behavior did indeed characterize the lengthy period of the saint's trial of faith, which actually lasted up to the time of her death. No longer having the joy of faith, she did everything she could at least to carry out its works, above all those flowing from "the new commandment" of Jesus: that we not merely love others as ourselves but as Jesus loved us. Noting that we naturally seek out the company of those who are saintly and affable and tend to avoid the company of those less perfect and, humanly speaking, more disagreeable, she would seek out the latter, for she knew that a kind word or amiable smile would often suffice to make these "wounded souls" bloom and would in any case respond to the challenge of the gospel.

Such behavior is fully in accord with the emphasis on love of both God and neighbor that one regularly finds emphasized in the apophatic mystics. Dionysius argues that "yearning" *(eros)* and "love" *(agape)* are "used by the sacred writers in divine revelation with the exact same meaning," namely, to signify the power or capacity by which God "is enticed away from his transcendent dwelling place and comes to abide within all things," even as the same power stirs us to return to God.[37] The author of *The Cloud of Unknowing* insists that God "can be taken and held by love but not by thought,"[38] while Merton, in a well-known letter, writes that "it is the love of my lover, my brother or my child that sees God in me, makes God credible to myself in me," just as "it is

35. *Story of a Soul: The Autobiography of St. Thérèse of Lisieux,* trans. John Clarke, 2nd ed. (Washington, D.C.: Institute of Carmelite Studies, 1976), p. 213.

36. Louis Bouyer, *Mysterion: Du mystère à la mystique* (Paris: O.E.I.L., 1986), p. 348 (emphasis mine).

37. *The Divine Names* 4, 12-13, in *Pseudo-Dionysius: The Complete Works,* pp. 81-82.

38. *The Cloud of Unknowing,* ed. James Walsh (New York: Paulist, 1981), chap. 6, p. 130.

my love for my lover, my child, my brother, that enables me to show God to him or her in himself or herself."[39] For such authors, the God who cannot be comprehended and who might seem altogether absent can nevertheless be attained through love — and this emphatically includes the love of other human beings, especially ones like a certain ill-tempered nun in the Carmel at Lisieux in whom Thérèse, using no doubt unwittingly the original terminology of Christian mysticism, could still find "Jesus hidden in the depths of her soul."[40] This emphasis on love which one finds in the apophatic tradition and the way it was practiced by someone like Thérèse might well be a further reason why some spiritual seekers of our day would be attracted by this tradition. The kind of kinship likely to be felt was once hinted at in terms of simple eloquence by Walter Kaufmann when he wrote: "Even the difference between theism and atheism is not nearly so profound as that between those who feel and those who do not feel their brothers' torments."[41]

Nothing that has been said above should be construed as some kind of proof that contemporary unbelievers will ineluctably be drawn to the literature of Christian apophatic mysticism, but only as an indication that this could well be the case for some of them. Cyprian Smith, who notes in the opening chapter of his book on Eckhart that the writings of that medieval Dominican "have a fascination and attractiveness uniquely their own [for] . . . a wide variety of very different people,"[42] nevertheless feels that many unbelievers see Eckhart as someone who does not really belong to the Christian tradition and so tend to read their own ideas into him. Where Smith has found Eckhart really helpful is with people of his acquaintance "who were growing disillusioned with Christianity because they unconsciously needed the apophatic dimension which Eckhart supplies. He has, in other words, strengthened a faith which was languishing for lack of proper nourishment but which nevertheless still existed."[43]

With special reference to apophatic authors of an earlier era, a further reason to beware of expecting too much to come of their being read by anyone today, believer or unbeliever, has been noted by Dupré himself. He warns that

> the doctrines, life styles, and methods of a previous age were conceived within the reach of a direct experience of the sacred. This has for the most part ceased to exist. The language of past mystics, those of the eighteenth as well

39. Thomas Merton, "A Letter on the Contemplative Life," in *The Monastic Journey*, p. 222.

40. Thérèse of Lisieux, *Story of a Soul*, p. 223.

41. Walter Kaufmann, *The Faith of a Heretic* (Garden City, N.Y.: Doubleday, Anchor Books, 1963), p. 168.

42. Cyprian Smith, *The Way of Paradox: Spiritual Life as Taught by Meister Eckhart* (New York: Paulist, 1987), p. 1.

43. From a letter of Cyprian Smith to the present writer, March 13, 1995.

as those of the fourteenth century, strikes the modern reader as antiquated in a manner in which that of philosophic and literary classics does not, because the very experience that is being articulated is no longer present even in that minimal way in which virtually everyone in past ages shared it. A confrontation with the past may be necessary, but the shape of spiritual life in the future will be entirely our own.[44]

For this reason, it is likely that apophatic authors of our own time, ones who have themselves experienced what Karl Rahner often called "a wintry season" in the secularized world, will be more capable than past authors of building bridges across the divide between religious belief and unbelief. Merton and Le Saux have numerous avid readers spanning a wide spectrum of belief and unbelief. Rahner himself belongs in their company. He has rightly been included in some anthologies of mystical literature, not only because of some of his published prayers addressed to God as "holy Mystery" but also because he has honestly confronted the questions raised for Christianity by modern scientific, technological culture. He concluded an article that first appeared on Christmas Eve of 1965 with words that include some of the major themes found in the Christian apophatic tradition from its very inception: the incomprehensibility of God, the ultimate inefficacy of our words, and the centrality of love. They may fittingly conclude this article as well, for they convey something of the religious power that spiritual seekers of our time may find in that tradition: "We can master life with scientific formulae insofar as one has to make one's way among various events, and this may frequently be successful. But man himself is grounded in an abyss which no formula can measure. We must have sufficient courage to experience this abyss as the holy mystery of love — then it may be called God."[45]

---

44. Louis Dupré, "Spiritual Life in a Secular Age," in *Ignatian Spirituality in a Secular Age*, ed. George P. Schner (Waterloo: Wilfrid Laurier University Press, 1984), pp. 23-24.

45. Karl Rahner, "God Is No Scientific Formula," in *Grace in Freedom*, trans. Hilda Graef (New York: Herder and Herder, 1969), p. 195.

CHAPTER 10

Art and the Sacred:
Postscript to a Seminar

KARSTEN HARRIES

I

In the spring semester of 1975 Louis Dupré and I co-taught a seminar on the topic "Art and the Sacred." In discussions we had been having the preceding year certain disagreements concerning the relationship of art to the sacred had surfaced, disagreements that will be apparent to anyone who attempts to reconcile what is asserted in *The Meaning of Modern Art*[1] with Dupré's *The Other Dimension*.[2] Many years have passed since that seminar, and even more since I wrote my book on modern art, which in several ways now seems inadequate. Continuing work on Hegel and Heidegger has helped me to gain a clearer understanding of the "modern world," an expression that, like "modern art,"[3] names not so much the world we actually live in as an illuminating construct, and of the difficulties involved in any attempt to assign art a significant place in that world. If that "new realism" called for by the book's last chapter is to become a reality, and I continue to think it important that art and not just art move in this direction, it must be possible to take a step beyond this modern world and leave behind the project that supports it, a project Sartre then helped me to interpret.

But such a step becomes impossible if we agree with Sartre that the

---

1. Karsten Harries, *The Meaning of Modern Art: A Philosophical Interpretation* (Evanston: Northwestern University Press, 1968).

2. Louis Dupré, *The Other Dimension: A Search for the Meaning of Religious Attitudes* (New York: Doubleday, 1972).

3. Cf. Harries, *The Meaning of Modern Art*, p. xiii n. 4.

fundamental human project is to become like God, that "fundamentally man is the desire to be God," a claim that Sartre thought followed from "an a priori description" of human being.[4] Even if Sartre's understanding of the fundamental project helps us understand the "modern world" and the progress of modern art, the renunciation of that flawed project seems to me to be a precondition for a full self-affirmation and to hold the key to that new realism toward which the ending of the book gestured uncertainly. Now, however, I am more likely to speak with Nietzsche of the need to overcome the spirit of revenge, "the will's ill will against time and its it was."[5] It is this ill will that speaks to us in Sartre's description of the being of the for-itself as lack, vainly desiring to become God. The project to become like God is born of an exaggerated demand for security, which in turn presupposes an inability to accept all that makes human beings vulnerable and mortal, open to friendship and love.

Even more it was developments of the past thirty years, for example, the works of artists like Oldenburg and Smithson, Beuys and Kiefer, that called for a reassessment of *The Meaning of Modern Art*, especially of its concluding chapter, "Beyond Modern Art." At the time I had not heard of postmodernism, and yet there is a sense in which this book called for postmodern art, although too much of what has been labeled postmodern participates in what I criticized in that book as "The Search for the Interesting." The conclusion called for art that would no longer pursue the novel or interesting, that would so re-present fragments of the familiar world that we would once again attend to their silent "speech," return to the endless task of interpreting "the book of nature," and in such interpretation gain some understanding of our vocation. I refer here to "the book of nature" to suggest that what I had in mind sought to move art in the direction of what might be considered the sacred. Thus in my conversations with Louis Dupré, I insisted on continuity, indeed on a partial identity of art and the sacred, while he emphasized their essential difference. We decided to offer our joint seminar in the hope that such a public *Auseinandersetzung* would help us both to arrive at a clearer understanding of the issues and their significance. Traces of that course survive in much that I have written since, especially in my essays on architecture.

---

4. See Jean-Paul Sartre, *Being and Nothingness*, trans. Hazel E. Barnes (New York: Philosophical Library, 1956), pp. 557-75. See Harries, *The Meaning of Modern Art*, p. xiii n. 3. I reconsidered my agreement with Sartre in the preface to the Japanese translation by Takeo Narukara, *Gendai Geijutsu e no shisaku-Tetsugakuteki Kaishaku* (Tokyo: Tamagawa University Press, 1976).

5. Friedrich Nietzsche, *Thus Spoke Zarathustra*, trans. Walter Kaufmann, in *The Portable Nietzsche* (Harmondsworth: Penguin, 1976), p. 252.

II

Dupré's insistence on the essential difference between art and the sacred is supported by the realities of today's artistic and religious life. The history of Western art could be written as a history of the progressive emancipation of art from everything foreign to its essence. The first part of such a history might discuss the emancipation of art from religion; the second the emancipation of art from representation; the third the emancipation of art from the demand for all external meaning and content. A remark by Frank Stella made in a discussion broadcast in 1964 as "New Nihilism or New Art?" helps mark this last stage:

> All I want anyone to get out of my paintings, and all that I ever get out of them, is the fact that you can see the whole idea without confusion. . . . What you see is what you see. . . . I don't know what else there is. It's really something if you can get a visual sensation that is pleasurable, or worth looking at, or enjoyable, if you can make something worth looking at.[6]

Such a painting is not meant to point beyond itself, is not meant to be taken as either symbol or allegory. Its point is not to say something. It can therefore be neither true nor false. And yet it is precisely this, here explicitly renounced, quality of pointing beyond itself that would seem to be inseparable from all sacred art. As suggested by the broadcast's title, a conception of art such as that endorsed on this occasion by Stella entails the divorce of art from the sacred. What matters here is not that the work point us toward a higher reality, but that art objects provide an occasion for enjoyment.

Supported by the central strand of philosophical aesthetics and art history, by Baumgarten and Kant, Panofsky and Fried, we can call such an approach to works of art as first of all occasions for pleasure, albeit pleasure of a quite distinctive kind — aesthetic. Such an aesthetic understanding of art leaves no room for religious art. On this view the point of art is to provide us with experiences that bear their telos within themselves and are thus set off from the rest of life, which has been bracketed, distanced. The autotelic character of aesthetic experience thus understood is reflected in the understanding of the work of art, which is to be a self-sufficient aesthetic object, a whole possessing the necessary closure.[7]

Louis Dupré's understanding of art, especially of art today, tends toward the aesthetic. Thus he considers the aesthetic realm an autonomous province removed from what we usually mean by reality: "What artists dimly felt in the

---

6. Bruce Glaser, "Questions to Stella and Judd," in *Minimal Art: A Critical Anthololology,* ed. Gregory Battcock (New York: Dutton, 1968), p. 158.

7. See Karsten Harries, *The Broken Frame: Three Lectures* (Washington, D.C.: Catholic University Press, 1989).

past, they now bluntly assert, namely, that the work of art is not an imitation of nature, subject to an extrinsic code, but that it creates its own norms and reality."[8] Although I agree that the development of Western art can be understood as a movement tending toward the increasing autonomy of art, this tendency has never gone unchallenged. In the course of the past three decades such challenges have indeed come close to defining a new mainstream, a development that gives support to the distinction of postmodern from modern art. But this development cannot challenge the claim that *to the extent* that the aesthetic approach has governed the evolution of modern art, such art has to exclude the sacred.

Should we be troubled by the implied dissociation of art and the sacred? Should we not rather insist that, just as science has only in relatively recent times come into its own, so has art? Some, no doubt, will object that, contrary to what is claimed by the aesthetic approach, the development that I have sketched here must lead art away from its essence. But how are we to understand that essence? What do we ask for when we ask for the essence of something? To ask for the essence of art is to ask for what it is that makes something a work of art. But, as Heidegger has noted, the search for essence is by its very nature circular.[9] Where are we to look for the essence of art? In works of art, of course. But how do we know what to count as a work of art unless we already know what art is? The truth or falsity of the aesthetic conception of art cannot be decided by looking at art. Is it even meaningful to speak here of truth and falsity? When we say something like "A is the essence of art," we express what we take to matter about art. And what we take to matter about art, and indeed about anything, will inevitably be bound up with the concrete way in which we exist in the world, including what others take art to be. In this sense the aesthetic conception of art can be understood as a function of the modern world. My questioning of the aesthetic approach — and only given such questioning does my insistence, *pace* Dupré, on a more intimate tie between art and the sacred make sense — is bound up with critique of what could be called the shape of the modern world.

III

If Dupré and I agree pretty much in our understanding of modern art, we also agree that art's claim to autonomy and its separation from the sacred did not

---

8. Dupré, *The Other Dimension*, p. 21.

9. Martin Heidegger, "The Origin of the Work of Art," in *Poetry, Language, Thought*, trans. Albert Hofstadter (New York: Harper and Row, 1971), p. 18.

always characterize it. Thus Dupré remarks that it did not characterize the art of archaic societies. I am no longer quite as confident of this as I once was: we may be projecting into archaic society dreams of a more integrated form of life. But more important is another point: With his remark on archaic art and religion, Dupré grants that it is possible for the two to be inseparably linked:

> Nevertheless art and religion are intimately connected. At one time they were even indistinguishable. Primitive rites and archaic religious objects were also man's earliest artistic expressions. Art did not express an attitude independent of what we would now call religion. Indeed, it is not even correct to say that artistic achievements were for the purpose of expressing religious attitudes, for the terms art and religion had no separate meaning for man.[10]

This suggests that if there is a sense in which we can say that the modern period has witnessed the emancipation of art from what is extrinsic to it, so there is a sense in which the modern period has witnessed the emancipation of religion from what is extrinsic to it. Religion may thus be said to have purified itself of art. This is how Hegel understood the superiority of Christianity over Greek religion, and Dupré follows Hegel on this point:

> Thus religion became caught in its own aesthetic *images*. The Greek gods, at least as we know them through Homer and Hesiod, were conceived as human ideals. The more perfect they grew, the more they lost their meaning as religious symbols, that is, as finite appearances which reveal an infinite *transcendence*. Ultimately their perfect containment within finite forms, their aesthetic potential, killed the Greek gods. Their very conception demanded an aesthetic treatment, long before poets and sculptors made them into actual works of art. Once they received it, they turned into sculpture and literature, and died to religion altogether.[11]

Dupré grants that art loses a great deal of its former significance when it loses its connection with religion, although presumably not something that really belongs to it, and thus he also insists that once religion and art come to be differentiated, it is essential that the difference between the two be asserted and preserved. It is not a degeneration of art that lets it sever its ties to religion. The very dynamism of religious transcendence lets religion leave art behind. From the very beginning Christianity thus has struggled to keep its proper distance from art.

A number of points here invite questioning. I grant that religious experience is open to transcendence. But how should transcendence be understood? Just what is being transcended? Temporal reality? Reason? The dynamism of

---

10. Dupré, *The Other Dimension*, p. 229.
11. Dupré, *The Other Dimension*, pp. 169-70.

religious transcendence, especially when one adds the attribute "infinite," carries with it the danger of a radicalization of transcendence that threatens to so empty it and therefore also God of all meaning that mysticism and atheism come to coincide. But must transcendence be thought in opposition to temporal reality, to sensuousness? Just the link of transcendence to both eternity and disembodied spirit I find questionable. Is this link in fact essential to Christianity? For the time being, I shall leave this question open. What I do want to insist on is this: to the extent that spirit is privileged at the expense of sensuousness, it will be impossible to arrive at a full self-affirmation.

IV

On the very first page of *The Other Dimension,* Dupré writes that "Modern life has many facets which develop autonomously."[12] We have to understand claims to the autonomy of art in this context of the splintering of the modern world, a splintering that means inevitably also the disintegration of individuals. Phrases such as "war is war," "business is business," "art for art's sake" also belong to this context.[13] Thus when we go to a museum or concert we leave behind the concerns and burdens that are part of everyday life. The term *aesthetic distance* is telling. And is religious life today not marked by a similar distance? Religious life, too, seems to have separated itself from the whole of life, a separation that may well seem demanded by the separation of church and state on which this republic is founded.

And yet, Dupré also emphasizes on this first page, "it is equally obvious that religion cannot survive as a *particular* aspect of life." He thus links the importance of the sacred to its "unique power of integration."[14] But does this not suggest that to the extent that art sets itself up as an autonomous sphere, it has to be attacked by any genuinely religious person? This implies a more general claim: so understood, religion is incompatible with a way of life that scatters itself into autonomous provinces, even, or perhaps especially, when one of these claims the title "religion." Given a commitment to an integrated way of life, one may well want to call the modern insistence on the autonomy of art false — false in the sense of doing violence to what life should be. Art for art's sake seems linked to the individual's inability or unwillingness to affirm himself or herself in his or her entirety, a phenomenon of our self-alienation.

12. Dupré, *The Other Dimension,* p. 1.
13. See Hermann Broch, "Der Zerfall der Werte," in *Erkennen und Handeln,* vol. 2 of *Essays* (Zurich: Rhein, 1955), p. 42.
14. Dupré, *The Other Dimension,* p. 18.

Does this then argue for the kind of understanding of art and religion Dupré calls archaic? Must Christianity not distance itself from all such archaic views? From its very beginning biblical religion is shadowed by iconoclasm. Think of Moses smashing the golden calf. Israel's God is invisible. Such attitudes carried over into the early church. In this connection Arnold Hauser quotes Asterius of Amasia:

> Do not make a picture of Christ; the humiliation of the Incarnation to which He submitted of his own free will and for our sake was sufficient for Him to endure — rather let us carry around in our soul the incorporeal world.[15]

There is no need here to rehearse the history of Christian iconoclasm. That the marriage of art and Christian faith should have been an uneasy one from the very beginning is to be expected, given Christianity's emphasis on the spirit, on the one invisible God, who suffers no other gods.

And yet, this God incarnated himself and thus closed the gap between spirit and body. Must we understand the incarnation with Asterius of Amasia as a humiliation? Should we not understand it rather as a mysterious necessity, demanded by both body and soul, sensuousness and spirit? And if so, should we not join those who appealed to the incarnation to defend art, this human incarnation? But modernity has difficulty accepting the incarnation, which confronts us with the paradox that Mary should be God's mother, daughter, and bride, just as it has difficulty granting more than an aesthetic significance to art. Even Christians today tend to relegate the incarnation to a past that lies behind us. Christianity has become the religion of the no longer present, the dead God, the religion of a spiritual and increasingly empty transcendence.

We have inherited Christianity's suspicion of religious art. If we are no longer iconoclasts, this is because we have difficulty taking the religious function of art seriously. Hegel forcefully makes this point:

> . . . there is a profounder grasp of truth, in which the form is no longer on such easy and friendly terms with the sensuous material as to be adequately accepted and expressed by that medium. Of such a type is the Christian conception of truth; and above all it is the prevailing spirit of the modern world, or, more strictly, of our religion and our intellectual culture, which have passed beyond the point at which art is the highest mode under which the absolute is brought home to human consciousness. The type peculiar to art production and its products fails any longer to satisfy man's highest need. We are beyond the stage of reverence for works of art as divine and objects deserving our worship. The impressions they produce is one of a more re-

---

15. Arnold Hauser, *The Social History of Art*, trans. Stanley Godman (New York: Vintage, n.d.), vol. 1, p. 138.

flective kind, and the emotions which they arouse require a higher test and a further verification. Thought and reflection have taken their flight above fine art.[16]

Dupré, it would seem, would find little in this statement to disagree with. And is it not supported by the shape of our modern world?[17] Could today's concept and performance art not be cited as proof that art in what Hegel considers its "true sense" is coming to an end, whereby Hegel means such art that "has established itself in a sphere which it shares with religion and philosophy, becoming thereby merely one mode and form through which the divine, the profoundest interest of mankind, and spiritual truths of the widest range, are brought home to consciousness and expressed."[18] Thought and reflection have "indeed taken their flight above fine art." Given that flight, it is difficult to take seriously iconoclast controversies. Dupré's understanding of both art and religion accepts this conclusion: on his view, too, religion has left art behind. The question remains whether a religion that thus leaves art and sensuousness behind must not also leave the whole human being behind. And must it then not also leave religion behind?

V

In our joint seminar Dupré claimed that I was more pessimistic than he concerning the possibility today of a genuinely religious art. I replied that of the two of us he seemed to me the greater pessimist. In *Transcendent Selfhood* he was to repeat his claim, glossing the following passage from *The Meaning of Modern Art*:

> Modern art thus appears either as an attempt to restore to man lost immediacy or as a search for absolute freedom. In either case man has given up his attempts to discover meaning in the world of objects; if there is to be meaning it must have its foundation in something beyond that world. But it is no longer possible to give definite content to this transcendence,[19]

---

16. Georg Wilhelm Friedrich Hegel, *Vorlesungen über die Ästhetik, Jubiläumsausgabe*, ed. Herman Glockner, vol. 12, pp. 30-31. Translated by E. P. Osmaston in *Philosophies of Art and Beauty: Selected Readings from Plato to Heidegger*, ed. Albert Hofstadter and Richard Kuhns (Chicago: University of Chicago Press, 1976), pp. 390-91.

17. See Karsten Harries, "Hegel on the Future of Art," *Review of Metaphysics* 27 (1974): 677-96.

18. Hegel, *Jubiläumsausgabe*, vol. 12, p. 27; trans. p. 388.

19. Harries, *The Meaning of Modern Art*, pp. 153-54.

with this remark:

> Though I have reservations about the pessimistic conclusion, a great deal of evidence supports the basic premises.[20]

That disagreement concerning our respective pessimism — I think myself an incurable optimist — suggests that we are looking for something quite different. The passage Dupré cites does indeed claim that modern art has ceased to attempt "to discover meaning in the world of objects." But my book did not claim that modern art circumscribed what art might be and become in the future. Rather it called on art to discover — today I would say re-present — meanings that do not have their foundation in human freedom. Though God may no longer call us, this does not mean that human beings are not called at all. Listening to these meanings, I observed, "takes modesty and patience, modesty because first man must recognize that he depends for meaning on something transcending his freedom, patience because we capture meaning only in fragments."[21] In this sense I concluded with a call for an art "content to explore the meanings of the world."[22] I don't consider this a pessimistic conclusion. But Dupré's gloss on the cited passage passes over the possibility of "discovering meaning in the world of objects," seizing instead on the phrase, "if there is to be meaning it must have its foundation in something beyond that world." To such a world-transcendent meaning that could ground and integrate our little worldly meanings, I did and do claim, we today can no longer give a definite content, except in bad faith. I do not consider this at all a pessimistic conclusion, but rather a life-affirming one. I am deeply suspicious of the gap that is supposed to separate the many little meanings that are part of our usual dealings with persons and things from one great world-transcendent meaning supposed to be necessary to ground the former.[23] I am suspicious of appeals to transcendence thus understood. To be sure, I, too, insist that to live a full life human beings must recognize that they depend for meaning on something transcending their freedom. But this transcendence is not to be understood in opposition to the world and to time. It is very much a worldly or, perhaps better, an earthly transcendence.

20. Louis Dupré, "Images of Transcendence," in *Transcendent Selfhood: The Loss and Rediscovery of the Inner Life* (New York: Seabury Press, 1976), p. 60. An earlier version of this chapter was distributed in our seminar. It bore the title "The Enigma of Religious Art" and did not yet include what is now this chapter's last section, "The New Meaning of Religious Art," which the cited passages help to introduce. Just this section seems to me to preserve some hint of the spirit of our discussions.

21. Harries, *The Meaning of Modern Art*, p. 159.

22. Harries, *The Meaning of Modern Art*, p. 159.

23. See Karsten Harries, "Questioning the Question of the Worth of Life," *Journal of Philosophy* 88 (1991): 684-90.

At the core of our disagreement was thus a very different understanding of transcendence and of its relationship to language and to the senses. In one of our last sessions, Dupré suggested that he wanted to go further with his understanding of transcendence than I was willing to go. Dupré suggests how far he would have the individual go in his book *Transcendent Selfhood*. There he concludes with a discussion of mystical experience which opens the self to a transcendence that it bears within itself and must realize if it is not to become "*less* than itself."[24] But what really separated us was not so much that one wanted to go further than the other, but rather that we wanted to go in different directions. The word "transcendence" that we both liked to use, if in rather different senses, helped to blur what separated us. As Dupré reminds us, "The important thing to remember . . . is that the term transcendent, so essential for religion, develops dialectically and takes various meanings in different contexts. It is always transcendent in relation to what surrounds it."[25] I called transcendent "what eludes our concepts and words." But in that sense we transcend ourselves precisely as embodied, temporal beings, where, as Nietzsche recognized, the body should not be placed in opposition to soul. With Nietzsche's Zarathustra I would rather say that the self, which Zarathustra calls both "body" and "a great reason," transcends the spirit, "your little reason."[26]

Self-transcendence may of course and indeed must also be understood in a very different sense. Think of Petrarch, who, led by curiosity to climb Mount Ventoux, discovers the power of the human soul to transcend the here and now, the limits imposed on it by the body and the senses, which inevitably tie us to a particular point of view and thus to a particular perspective. But the mind, in what Petrarch calls its agility, is not so limited: vast as is the expanse that Petrarch could survey from his mountain, the soul leaps to what lies beyond the Alps, to Italy, to the Pyrenees, which are too far away to be seen; and the soul leaps further still, beyond the present to past and future, and finally to God. The soul cannot be assigned a place as readily as can the body.

That same sense of transcendence is presupposed by the mysticism of Meister Eckhart:

> Yesterday as I sat yonder I said something that sounds incredible: "Jerusalem is as near to my soul as my body is, and though I am as sure of this as I am of being human, it is something even learned priests seldom understand. My soul is as young as the day it was created; yes, and much younger. I tell you, I should be ashamed if it were not younger tomorrow than it is today.[27]

24. Dupré, *Transcendent Selfhood*, p. 104.
25. Dupré, *The Other Dimension*, p. 16.
26. *The Portable Nietzsche*, p. 146.
27. Raymond B. Blakney, *Meister Eckhart: A Modern Translation* (New York: Harper, 1957), p. 134.

While I admit the possibility and recognize the seductive power of such self-transcendence, I also fear its anarchic potential. Like Heinrich von Virneburg, the archbishop of Cologne who accused Eckhart of heresy, I am suspicious of words that claim a freedom that must leave behind the familiar world with its norms and rules:

> For if Life were questioned a thousand years and asked: "Why live?" and if there were an answer, it could be no more than this: "I live only to live!" And that is because Life is its own reason for being, springs from its own Source, and goes on and on, without ever asking why — just because it is Life. Thus if you ask a genuine person, that is one who acts [uncalculatingly] from his heart: "Why are you doing that?" — he will reply in the only possible way: "I do it because I do it!"[28]

To live well, Eckhart seems to be telling us, we should not have to ask for the point of life, for justifications, but simply open ourselves to and accept the mystery of life. And the same goes for the actions that make up life. They will be done spontaneously, from the heart. If we are such genuine persons, we will not act the way we do because there is some commandment or law; we will follow our hearts and for the sake of our hearts suspend the claims the world makes on us. Freedom here collapses into an immediate spontaneity.

That Eckhart himself was worried about the possibility that his mysticism might invite political and moral anarchism is suggested by the following passage:

> There are people, who say: "If I have God and God's love, I may do whatever I want to do." They are wrong. As long as you are capable of acting contrary to the will of God, the love of God is not in you, however you may deceive the world. The person who lives in God's love and by God's will takes his pleasure in whatever God prefers and refrains from any act contrary to his wishes, finding it impossible to omit what God wants, and impossible to go contrary to him.[29]

The good life is here understood as a life lived in such a way that we feel that we have no choice. We do God's will. In such a life there can be no tension between how we live and how we ought to live, between inclination and duty. But this is a very formal characterization of the good life. Eckhart's kind of mysticism makes it difficult to give sufficient content to the idea of God to allow it to function as the measure of our human being or to retain that unique power of integration that Dupré attributes to the sacred. The distance from Eckhart

---

28. Blakney, p. 127.
29. Blakney, p. 193.

to Sartre is not as great as it might seem, as is shown by this text from Norman Cohn's *Pursuit of the Millennium:* Suso

> describes how on a bright Sunday, as he was sitting lost in meditation, an incorporeal image appeared to his spirit. Suso addresses the image: "Whence have you come?" The image answers: "I come from nowhere," — "Tell me, what are you?" — "I am not." — "What do you wish?" — "I do not wish." — "This is a miracle! Tell me, what is your name?" — "I am called nameless Wildness." — "Where does your insight lead to?" — "Into untrammeled freedom," — "Tell me, what do you call untrammeled freedom?" — "When a man lives according to all his caprices without distinguishing between God and himself, and without looking to before or after. . . ."[30]

As all definite content is recognized to be profoundly incompatible with the divine transcendence, the divine comes to be thought of as a nameless wildness, and abyss within the self. But God, once he has become so indefinite, threatens to evaporate altogether. God becomes undistinguishable from an infinite, empty transcendence. Such an empty transcendence cannot provide human beings with a measure and thus leads to a new experience of freedom. This freedom again, acknowledging no measure, must degenerate into caprice.

This development is essentially also a movement of introversion. The individual is cast back into himself or herself. In medieval mysticism we have one root of very modern subjectivism. The text by Suso is thus strangely close to Sartre, notwithstanding the fact that the latter is a self-proclaimed atheist. Already in the fourteenth century we find a conception of freedom as radical as anything the existentialists would come up with much later, an understanding of transcendence that has to leave behind the sacred. Dupré's understanding of self-transcendence, which likes to appeal to the Rhenish mystics, tends in this direction.[31] Modern self-transcendence does indeed invite a teleological suspension of the ethical. But this is an invitation I think we should resist. Kierkegaard's Abraham is no knight of any faith I think worth having.

VI

I have suggested that we can distinguish a material from a formal self-transcendence. In the former case what is transcended is precisely that linguistic or conceptual space in which things must find their place if they are to be

---

30. Quoted in Norman Cohn, *Pursuit of the Millennium,* 2nd ed. (New York: Harper, 1961), p. 186.

31. See Dupré, *Transcendent Selfhood,* pp. 18-30.

understood and comprehended. Material transcendence points in the same direction as the Kantian thing-in-itself which is present to us only as appearance. What invites talk of a thing-in-itself is the fact that, even if appearance is constituted by our language or concepts as such appearance, what thus appears is not created by our understanding, but given. Inseparable from our experience of things is a sense of this gift, an awareness that our understanding is finite, and that, as well, the reach of our words is limited. Everything real is infinitely complex and thus can never be fully translated into words. Like Kant's "aesthetic idea," the "real" is "inexponible." The rift between thing and word, between reality and language cannot be closed. Speaking that refuses to recognize this rift must degenerate into idle talk.

Language opens human beings to reality. Yet, as Heidegger emphasized, language conceals even as it reveals. Where this essential concealment is forgotten, language cannot but replace reality with a false, merely linguistic reality — and that holds also for religious reality. This is why religion cannot dispense with art, especially with art that does not rely on words, such as architecture. To be sure, human being is essentially a dwelling in language. But the house of language is not a prison. Art may be understood as a way of opening the windows of that house, and so may poetry, which should not be understood as a speaking that is privileged in that it offers particularly effective descriptions of things, but rather as speaking that re-presents the essence of language in such a way that it becomes conspicuous, and that means a speaking that opens up the rift between language and reality that is essential to language.[32]

With my talk of a new realism I meant to suggest that art has the power to recall us to a sense of the gift of reality, where this means also that art discloses the rift between language and reality, a rift that is a presupposition of all meaning. What puts us in touch with material transcendence, a transcendence within the visible, within the sensible, is first of all the body. Here it is important to keep in mind that the embodied self is also a caring, desiring self. What it discloses is not just an assemblage of mute facts, but an inevitably meaningful configuration of objects of desire or things to be avoided. To be in the world is to be claimed in countless different ways by persons and things. What I call material transcendence may thus not be reduced to the mute presence of things. To be open to it is inevitably to be affected, moved, claimed. Material transcendence thus also refers to the affective base without which all our talk of values and divinities is ultimately groundless: idle talk.

In this sense material transcendence seems to me a necessary but not

32. Karsten Harries, "Poetry as Response: Heidegger's Step beyond Aestheticism," in *Philosophy in the Arts*, vol. 16 of *Midwest Studies in Philosophy* (Notre Dame: University of Notre Dame Press, 1991), pp. 73-88.

sufficient condition for what may be called "sacred transcendence."[33] What it lacks is precisely that "unique power of integration" Dupré takes to be a defining attribute of the sacred. Sacred transcendence is material transcendence experienced as possessing an integrating power.

Consider the story of Jacob's ladder, found in Genesis 28:11-17, which served to establish the traditional symbolism of the church as house of God and gate of heaven: Jacob came to "a certain place." Tired, he lay down to sleep, taking a simple stone for his pillow. And he dreamt

> that there was a ladder set up on the earth and the top of it reached the heaven: and behold, the angels of the Lord were ascending and descending on it! And behold, the Lord stood above it and said, "I am the Lord, the God of Abraham your father and the God of Isaac: the land on which you lie I will give to you and to your descendants; and your descendants shall be like the dust of the earth and you shall spread to the west and to the east and to the north and to the south; and by your descendants shall all the families of the earth bless themselves. Behold, I am with you, and will keep you wherever you go, and will bring you back to his land; for I will not leave you until I have done that of which I have spoken to you." Then Jacob awoke and said: "Surely the Lord is in this place. This is none other than the house of God, and this is the gate of heaven."

A particular place is experienced as filled with the presence of the divine. But this place, this Bethel, is not only God's dwelling place, but opens up to what is experienced as the integrating center of an ongoing, expanding human community. Jacob responds to this dream experience by rising and by raising the stone that had served him for a pillow from a horizontal into a vertical position. That this simple act speaks to us presupposes that the same stone speaks differently when in a horizontal position and when raised to become a vertical pillar. Jacob's pillar is the archetype of the church and a paradigm not just of sacred architecture but of sacred art, of art understood as a re-presentation of material that even before taken up by some artist "speaks," re-presentation that understands itself as response to divinity, to some higher integrating power.

This is how Heidegger understands the Greek temple as world establishing, where world does not mean a collection of mute facts but an order that assigns to persons and things their proper places:

> In setting up the work the holy is opened up as holy and god is invoked into the openness of his presence. Praise belongs to dedication as doing honor to the dignity and splendor of the god. Dignity and splendor are not properties

---

33. See Dupré, "The Sacred as a Particular Category of Transcendence," in *Transcendent Selfhood*, pp. 19-22.

beside and behind which the god, too, stands as something distinct, but it is rather in the dignity, in the splendor, that the god is present. In the reflected glory of this splendor there glows, i.e. there lightens itself what we called world.[34]

In his discussion Heidegger links the world establishing of what he calls great art to an openness to what I have called material transcendence: the work is said to set up a world and to set forth the earth. But like Hegel, Heidegger, too, suggests that ours is an age when "great art together with its natural has departed from among men,"[35] had to depart because the now-ruling sense of reality makes our finite understanding the measure of reality, and thus has to obscure what Heidegger calls the "earth" and what I have called "material transcendence." Much art today struggles to keep human beings open to this elusive dimension, without claiming the integrative power needed to establish a world in Heidegger's sense. But without such openness, without the experience of a positive transcendence, religious discourse has to degenerate into idle talk. To keep itself thus open religion must turn to art. Religion needs art to preserve a sense of the sacred and thus to preserve itself.

34. Heidegger, "Origin," p. 44.
35. Heidegger, epilogue to "Origin," p. 79.

CHAPTER 11

Public Reason and the Common Good

WILLIAM O'NEILL, S.J.

Kant's paean to the "unlimited freedom" of "public reason" in a new "age of enlightenment" was merely the denouement of a drama originating with the dissolution of the "ontotheological synthesis" of medieval Christendom.[1] Indeed, the stage was set with the exaltation of God's ineffable freedom in late medieval nominalism. Ockham's divinely "ordained order" was divested of its inner teleology:[2] moral precepts derive not from our natural finality but from the "absolute potency" of the divine will.[3] And yet the drama was not without its irony; for the very "godlike" freedom of Adam lauded by Pico della Mirandola was to render God a supernumerary in creation — in the human comedy, Adam's progeny would be "the molders and the makers" of themselves.[4]

Of these epochal developments we are, as Louis Dupré so persuasively argues, still heir. In part I of this essay, I consider the fateful consequences for the role of "public reason" of unmooring freedom from teleological (eudaimonistic) determinations of *libertas*.[5] (Post)modern interpretations of public morality, I argue in part II, are bedeviled by the demise of the classical ideal of

---

1. Immanuel Kant, "What Is Enlightenment?" trans. Peter Gay, in *The Enlightenment: A Comprehensive Anthology* (New York: Simon and Schuster, 1973), pp. 385-88; Louis Dupré, *Passage to Modernity: An Essay in the Hermeneutics of Nature and Culture* (New Haven: Yale University Press, 1993), p. 11.

2. Dupré, *Passage to Modernity*, p. 128.

3. William Ockham, *Opus nonaginta dierum* c. 95.

4. Dupré, *Passage to Modernity*, p. 124; Pico della Mirandola, *Oration on the Dignity of Man*, as quoted in P. O. Kristeller, "The Philosophy of Man in the Italian Renaissance," *Italica* 24 (1947): 100-101.

5. See Kant, "What Is Enlightenment?" p. 386. For Kant, "public reason" is principally that of the "scholar rationally addressing his public." For John Rawls, "public reason" represents our "shared and public political reason." See Rawls, *Political Liberalism* (New York: Columbia University Press, 1993), pp. 9-11, 212-54.

the common good. The neo-Kantian reconstruction of the "good will" in the theories of John Rawls and Jürgen Habermas falls prey to the "empty formalism" of Kantian *Moralität* decried by Hegel, while neo-Aristotelian eudaimonism succumbs to cultural *(sittlich)* relativism — in Auden's poignant words, we are finally "Children afraid of the night / Who have never been happy or good."[6] And yet, I conclude in part III, traces of the classical ideal, present in the critiques of Rawls and Habermas, offer the promise of a discursive retrieval of the common good for a postmodern, pluralist society.

I. The Eclipse of Practical Wisdom

In opposing the Sophists, Aristotle distinguishes the intellectual (dianoetic) virtue of *phronesis* from theoretical and technical reasoning. *Phronesis* is "practical wisdom," aiming at the perfection, not of an art, but of the *phronimos*. For the Aristotelian *phronimos,* virtuous activity *(arete)* is desired for its own sake, as a constitutive specification of happiness *(eudaimonia)*. Inclusive "of all intrinsic goods," *eudaimonia* is conceived architectonically, as an end "final without qualification."[7] And yet attaining virtue is not morally self-indulgent as some moderns charge, for *eudaimonia* is tempered by the moral ideal of "general justice."[8] Indeed, not only is the perfection of the *phronimos* determined by the virtue of "particular justice," it has as its natural harmonic the ideal fruition of the common good in the formation of the just *polis.*

It is thus that Aristotle speaks of general justice as "complete virtue in the fullest sense," for it "tends to produce or conserve the happiness (and the constituents of the happiness) of a political association."[9] In attaining "general justice," as Theognis (or Phocylides) says, "the whole of virtue is summed up."[10] The prudential agent, whose virtuous life is ordered to the good of the *polis,* thus differs from the merely clever *(deinos)* agent who is equally adept at pursuing "unscrupulous" ends. For prudence *(phronesis)* implies a common perception of "sublimity," a common "seeking what is right" *(sunesis),* even as the sublimity of the perfect community *(koinonia teleios)* is expressed in the

---

6. W. H. Auden, "September 1, 1939," in *The Collected Poetry of W. H. Auden* (New York: Random House, 1945), pp. 57-59.

7. Aristotle, *Nicomachean Ethics* 1097al5-b21. Cf. J. L. Ackrill, "Aristotle on Eudaimonia," in *Essays on Aristotle's Ethics,* ed. Amélie Oksenberg Rorty (Berkeley and Los Angeles: University of California Press, 1980), pp. 21-24.

8. See the discussion in Bernard Williams, *Moral Luck: Philosophical Papers, 1973-1980* (Cambridge: Cambridge University Press, 1981), pp. 40-53.

9. Aristotle, *Nicomachean Ethics* 1129b6-1130b8.

10. Aristotle, *Nicomachean Ethics* 1129b30.

blessedness *(eudaimonia)* of its members — in the sublimity of the perfect community, all share singly, not *en masse.*[11]

For Thomas Aquinas, too, moral perfection *(libertas)* presumes the *"communitas perfecta,"* for the "common good is the end of each individual member of the community."[12] Thomas cedes general justice or *"iustitia legalis"* primacy over all the moral virtues inasmuch as it directs them to the common good which "transcends the individual good of one person."[13] For "nothing stands firm with regard to the practical reason, unless it be directed to the last end which is the common good," that is, the "common final cause."[14] Yet far from implying the apotheosis of the state, the transcendence of the common good rests in the flourishing of the perfect community, for the common good "flows back" upon its constitutive members. In the words of Jacques Maritain, the perfect community is thus a "whole composed of wholes" — neither an artifice of interest occasioned by contract, nor the suprapersonal "total organism" of German romanticism.[15]

The elegant Aristotelian tapestry was, alas, fated to unravel with the rise of nominalistic legal theory. Even in Suárez's interpretation of Thomas, "the function of reason remains purely informative, not legislative."[16] As Suárez writes in his treatise *On the Laws,* "although the rational nature is the foundation of the objective goodness of the moral actions of human beings, it may not for that reason be termed law." For "the intellect is merely able to point out a necessity existing in the object itself, and if such a necessity does not exist therein, the intellect cannot impart it; whereas the will endows [the

---

11. Aristotle, *Politics,* trans. Ernest Barker (London: Oxford University Press, 1946), 1280b32-1281a10 (emphasis added). The Aristotelian conception of the "perfect community" reflects its finality and sufficiency for human flourishing. Cf. *Nicomachean Ethics* 1094b7-10, 1129b15, 1143a1ff., 1160a9; *Politics* 1252a1, 1253a38. For Hans-Georg Gadamer's interpretation of the relation of *phronesis* and *sunesis* in the *Nicomachean Ethics,* see *Truth and Method,* trans. Joel Weinsheimer and Donald G. Marshall, 2nd and rev. ed. (New York: Crossroad, 1991), pp. 322-24.

12. Aquinas, *Summa theologiae,* II-II, Q. 58, a. 6, 7, 8, 12.

13. Aquinas, *Summa theologiae,* II-II, Q. 58, a. 6, 12.

14. Aquinas, *Summa theologiae,* I-II, Q. 90, a. 2. Thomas understands the common good analogically; indeed, God is par excellence the *bonum commune* (*Summa contra gentiles* III, 17, 80). For assessments of the implications of an analogical interpretation for the good of the *civitas,* see Louis Dupré, "The Common Good and the Open Society," *Review of Politics* 55, no. 4 (1993): 689-92, and David Hollenbach, "The Common Good Revisited," *Theological Studies* 50 (1989): 85-87.

15. Jacques Maritain, "The Person and the Common Good," in *The Social and Political Philosophy of Jacques Maritain,* ed. Joseph W. Evans and Leo R. Ward (New York: Charles Scribner's Sons, 1955), p. 85.

16. Dupré, *Passage to Modernity,* p. 136. As Dupré remarks, nominalist philosophers "shifted the determinative moment of natural law from reason to the divine will, thereby changing its meaning" (p. 136).

object] with a necessity which did not formerly characterize it."[17] Increasingly, the law's obligatory quality derives not from its intrinsic, natural rationality (its common, final causality), but from the contingently "promulgated *placet* of the lawgiver."[18] Nominalist theology gave succor not only to the "champions of the divine right of kings," but to the nascent "new school" of natural law with its emphasis upon the natural rights of individuals.[19] Indeed, the modern natural lawyers of the seventeenth and eighteenth centuries looked less to the natural finality of the common good as a common end than to the natural convergence of rational (prudential) wills. In *The Rights of War and Peace,* Grotius argues against the skepticism of Montaigne and Charron that "the first impression of nature" is "that Instinct whereby every Animal seeks its own Preservation, and loves its Condition, and whatever tends to maintain it." To our natural sociability, "Profit is annexed," for it is by the felicitous design of "the Author of Nature" that, being weak of ourselves and "in Want of many Things necessary for living Commodiously," we should the "more eagerly affect Society."[20]

The sea change in modern natural law theory adumbrated in Grotius is fully apparent in the writings of Hobbes and Pufendorf. For Hobbes, "the felicity of this life" rests no longer "in the repose of a mind satisfied. For there is no such *finis ultimus,* (utmost aim), nor *summum bonum,* (greatest good)."[21] Augustine's "restless heart," deprived of its divine telos, becomes "a continual progress of the desire, from one object to another" — the natural common good of "the old moral philosophers" succumbing to the "the war of all against all" *(ius omnium in omnia).* Hobbes thus opposes liberty as the "Right of Nature" *(ius naturale)* to "use [one's] power, as he will himself, for the preservation of his own nature," to the "Law of Nature *(lex naturalis)"* which "determineth, and bindeth."[22] Yet it is "the foresight of their own preservation," stripped of Grotius's natural sociability, that leads "men who naturally love liberty, and dominion over others" to submit to "that restraint

17. Francisco Suárez, *De legibus ac Deo legislatore* (1612), trans. James B. Scott, in *Selections from Three Works,* in *The Classics of International Law* (Oxford: Oxford University Press, 1944), bk. 2, chap. 5, p. 181; bk. 1, chap. 5, p. 66. Cf. bk. 2, chap. 6.

18. Dupré, *Passage to Modernity,* p. 137.

19. Dupré, *Passage to Modernity,* pp. 137-44.

20. Hugo Grotius, *The Rights of War and Peace,* ed. Jean Barbeyac (London, 1738), p. xx. The "minimalist core of universal moral principles" of the modern school of natural law, writes Richard Tuck, rests not in the metaphysical telos of the common good, but in the empirically demonstrable "desire for self-preservation" ("The 'Modern' Theory of Natural Law," in *The Languages of Political Theory in Early-Modern Europe,* ed. Anthony Pagden [Cambridge: Cambridge University Press, 1987], p. 117).

21. Thomas Hobbes, *Leviathan,* in *British Moralists: 1650-1800,* ed. D. D. Raphael, vol. 1 (Oxford: Clarendon Press, 1969), chap. 11, p. 32.

22. Hobbes, chap. 14, pp. 38-39.

upon themselves, (in which we see them live in commonwealths)."[23] For society is itself a grand artifice, "an artificial man" created by our mundane "*fiat*." And therein lies the irony, for to attain our "final end," we must subordinate our natural right of liberty to the ordained order of Hobbes's "mortal god," Leviathan.[24]

In a similar vein, Rousseau denies that civil society rests in our social instinct or natural sympathy (thus differing from Grotius as well as Diderot and the Encyclopedists). Yet where Hobbes's "contract of submission" *(pactum subiectionis)* resolves the will of all into the will of one, Rousseau depicts the social bond *(lien social)* as the will's self-limitation; indeed, it is only "with civil society" that we acquire "moral freedom, which alone makes man the master of himself." For, *pace* Hobbes, freedom is found, not in slavery to the appetites, but in "obedience to a law one prescribes to oneself."[25] Sovereignty arises through a "reciprocal commitment," so that in contracting "as it were, with himself," each person "finds himself doubly committed, first as a member of the sovereign body in relation to individuals [*souverain*], and secondly as a member of the state [*état*] in relation to the sovereign."[26] So it is that the "extravagant shepherd" of the *Confessions* justifies the sovereignty of the general will *(volonté général),* at once harking back to the natural rights championed by Locke, yet anticipating the romantic historicization of law as the general will of the *Volk* (people).[27]

Kant, one might say, purifies Rousseau's doctrine of the general will of the dross of experience, since the formal generality, or "universal voice," of will is entirely *sui generis.* One's (empirical) will is not, as for Rousseau, merely "part of a much greater whole"; rather the will's transcendental freedom is itself the "basis for the existence" *(ratio essendi)* of the moral law. Freedom of the will *(die Willkür)* is internally delimited by practical reason itself, i.e., the autonomous "self-legislation" of one's rational will *(der Wille).*[28] Categorical imperatives, expressed in synthetic, a priori judgments (i.e., the corpus of the law of nature), prescind entirely from the realm of prudential experience (formulable

---

23. Hobbes, chap. 17, p. 52.

24. Hobbes, pt. 2, chap. 17, p. 54. For Pufendorf's interpretation in *De jure naturae et gentium,* see Richard Tuck's assessment in "'Modern' Theory of Natural Law," pp. 99-119.

25. Jean-Jacques Rousseau, *The Social Contract,* trans. Maurice Cranston (New York: Penguin Books, 1968), bk. 1, chap. 8, p. 65.

26. Rousseau, bk. 1, chap. 7, p. 62.

27. Ernest Barker, *Social Contract: Essays by Locke, Hume, Rousseau* (Oxford: Oxford University Press, 1947), p. xxx. Ultimately, writes Barker, "I must reflect that if I am the thousandth part of a tyrant, I am also the whole of a slave. Leviathan is still Leviathan, even when he is corporate" (p. xxxv).

28. Rousseau, bk. 2, chap. 7, p. 84. Immanuel Kant, *Critique of Practical Reason,* trans. Lewis White Beck (Indianapolis: Bobbs-Merrill, 1956), p. 5 (pagination is that of the Prussian Academy edition, vol. 5).

in hypothetical imperatives). Indeed, for Kant, the original contract, whereby "all *(omnes et singuli)* the people give up their external freedom in order to take it back again immediately as members of a commonwealth, that is, the people regarded as the state *(universi),*" is "a mere idea of reason."[29] Accordingly,

> we cannot say that a man has sacrificed in the state a part of his inborn external freedom for some particular purpose [i.e., prudential end]; rather, we must say that he has completely abandoned his wild, lawless freedom in order to find his whole freedom again undiminished in a lawful dependency, that is, in a juridical state of society, since this dependency comes from his own legislative Will [*Wille*].[30]

Spun of abstract reflection, civic virtue, for Kant, is thus no longer the natural fruition of prudence (Aristotelian *phronesis*), but rather a rein upon it as the "subjective principle of self-love."[31] The "boundaries between morality and [prudential] self-love" have become "distinct and sharp."[32] Yet in so severing us from the realm of ethical *(sittlich)* experience, Kant bequeaths us a dubious heritage.[33] For nature has ceased to tell a moral tale. The epistemic separation of the transcendental ego as knowledge-constitutive subject from the constituted realm of nature implies that the "good will" alone is good, final and "without qualification."[34] Divested of natural finality, freedom is perforce confined to the private realm or "the inward domain of consciousness."[35]

Such "moral self-consciousness . . . inwardly related to itself alone," falls prey to Hegel's censure, for "it has identity without content." Morality *(Moralität),* arising from the "pure unconditioned self-determination of the will," is finally reduced to "an empty formalism" from which "no immanent doctrine

29. Immanuel Kant, *The Metaphysical Elements of Justice: Part I of the Metaphysics of Morals,* trans. John Ladd (Indianapolis: Bobbs-Merrill, 1965), pp. 315-16 (pagination is that of the Prussian Academy edition, vol. 6).

30. Kant, *The Metaphysical Elements of Justice,* pp. 315-16.

31. Immanuel Kant, *Religion within the Limits of Reason Alone,* trans. Theodore M. Greene and Hoyt H. Hudson (New York: Harper and Row, 1960), p. 31.

32. Kant, *Critique of Practical Reason,* p. 36.

33. Cf. Louis Dupré, *A Dubious Heritage: Studies in the Philosophy of Religion after Kant* (New York: Paulist Press, 1977).

34. Immanuel Kant, *Groundwork of the Metaphysic of Morals,* trans. H. J. Paton (New York: Harper and Row, 1964), p. 393 (1) (pagination is that of the Prussian Academy edition, vol. 4, while the number in parentheses refers to the second edition of Kant's *Grundlegung zur Metaphysic der Sitten*).

35. John Stuart Mill, *On Liberty,* ed. Gertrude Himmelfarb (New York: Penguin Books, 1974), p. 71. Cf. Dupré, *Passage to Modernity,* p. 131; Hannah Arendt, "What Is Freedom," in *Between Past and Future: Eight Exercises in Political Thought* (New York: Viking Press, 1968), pp. 143-71.

of duties" may be derived.[36] Kant's romantic critics such as Herder thus bid us return to the concrete "ethical life."[37] For only in the "concretely personal," the historic myth of the *Volk* or state, could Kant's "organic" conception of a kingdom of ends be redeemed.[38]

II. The Kantian Legacy: Rawls and Habermas

Hegel's synthesis of these differing strands in the sublation of *Moralität* into the realm of ethics *(Sittlichkeit)* was, however, to prove no less ephemeral. No longer anchored in the dialectical unfolding of Objective Spirit, ethics becomes "something relatively 'local and ethnocentric.'"[39] Ethical substance is fragmented in our myriad traditions and (social) nature, in Weber's words, "disenchanted."[40] Some modern moralists thus concur with Nietzsche that "skepticism regarding morality is what is decisive."[41] For Richard Rorty, "there is no such thing as *inner* freedom, no such thing as an 'autonomous individual,'" for finally "there is nothing deep inside each of us, no common human nature, no built-in human solidarity."[42] Others such as Alasdair MacIntyre abjure the language of abstract, universal rights in a neo-Aristotelian retrieval of concrete, traditional mores.[43] Yet such a radically contextualist position, argues Habermas, finally succumbs to "ethnocentric self-centeredness."[44]

36. G. W. F. Hegel, *Philosophy of Right,* trans. T. M. Knox (Oxford: Oxford University Press, 1952), par. 135.

37. Hegel, par. 137.

38. Lewis White Beck, *A Commentary on Kant's "Critique of Practical Reason"* (Chicago: University of Chicago Press, 1960), p. 125.

39. Richard Rorty, "The Priority of Democracy to Philosophy," in *The Virginia Statute of Religious Freedom: Two Hundred Years After,* ed. Robert Vaughan (Madison: University of Wisconsin Press, 1988), p. 259.

40. Max Weber, "Science as a Vocation," in *From Max Weber: Essays in Sociology,* ed. H. H. Gerth and C. W. Mills (New York: Oxford University Press, 1946), p. 148.

41. Friedrich Nietzsche, *The Will to Power,* bk. 1, trans. W. Kaufmann in his *Existentialism from Dostoevsky to Sartre* (New York: Meridian Books, 1956), p. 110.

42. Richard Rorty, *Contingency, Irony, and Solidarity* (Cambridge: Cambridge University Press, 1989), p. 177.

43. See Alasdair MacIntyre, *After Virtue,* 2nd ed. (Notre Dame: University of Notre Dame Press, 1984), pp. 36-78; *Whose Justice? Which Rationality?* (Notre Dame: University of Notre Dame Press, 1988), pp. 88-145, 326-403.

44. Jürgen Habermas, *Justification and Application: Remarks on Discourse Ethics,* trans. Ciaran P. Cronin (Cambridge: MIT Press, 1993), p. 104.

II.1. Rawls's "Kantian Constructivism"

Still others take up the Kantian banner. John Rawls, no less than Rorty, rejects appeals to a common final causality, a "built-in human solidarity." Indeed, for Rawls, it is precisely the want of such teleological justification which character- izes "public reason." For Rawls "political liberalism supposes that there are many conflicting reasonable doctrines with their conceptions of the good, each com- patible with the full rationality of human persons." At best, we can attain an "overlapping consensus of reasonable comprehensive doctrines" which respects the distinction of persons and their multiple and incommensurable conceptions of the good.[45] And yet the pluralism of our personal and collective ends is not to be lamented. On the contrary, "the diversity of reasonable comprehensive religious, philosophical, and moral doctrines found in modern democratic societies" is no mere adventitious historical condition, but "a permanent feature of the public culture of democracy."[46]

Neither does Rawls assume that the "autonomous individual" must needs be moral. For Rawls, our "rational autonomy" is modeled upon Kantian hy- pothetical imperatives which require merely that our choices be prudent or rationally coherent. Moral maxims are represented as the construction of suit- ably delimited hypothetical choice, so that while rational choosers may will "under moral laws," their subjection is "problematical" rather than "apodictic." In Rawls's "Kantian constructivism," a political conception of justice is thus founded upon the very hypothetical imperatives Kant denounced as "vain illu- sion and splendid misery."[47] The form, if not the modality, of moral judgment is retained, as is Kant's conception of prudence (as rational self-interest) — the onus now is to unite what Kant so assiduously rent asunder.

To this end, Rawls recurs to the heuristic idea of a social contract. Yet while for Kant the social contract was a "mere idea of reason" presupposing the a priori principles of right, the Rawlsian contract depicts the "first principles of justice" as themselves the outcome of an "original agreement." A "conception of right" is "constructed" as the contracting parties select the appropriate prin- ciples of justice in a "suitably defined initial situation."[48] Subject to a "veil of ignorance," Rawls's rational choosers are denied knowledge of their respective social roles, status, or position; their natural and acquired advantages; the specific circumstances of their society; and even their values, aims, and partic-

---

45. Rawls, *Political Liberalism*, pp. 134-35.
46. Rawls, *Political Liberalism*, p. 36.
47. Immanuel Kant, *Werke*, vol. 4, p. 161, as quoted in Ernst Cassirer, *Rousseau, Kant, Goethe: Two Essays*, trans. James Gutman, Paul Oskar Kristeller, and John Herman Randall, Jr. (Princeton: Princeton University Press, 1945), p. 24.
48. John Rawls, *A Theory of Justice* (Cambridge: Harvard University Press, Belknap Press, 1971), p. 118.

ular conceptions of the good. In Rawls's words, we are to conceive of a perspective "not distorted by the particular features and circumstances of the all-encompassing background framework" so that "a fair agreement between persons regarded as free and equal can be reached."[49]

Rawls accordingly "brackets" our particular, idiosyncratic interests, so as to model the stratified volition of moral persons as characterized by two "moral powers" and two correlative "highest-order interests in realizing and exercising these powers." The first moral power is "a capacity for a sense of justice that enables them to understand, apply, and to act from the reasonable principles of justice that specify fair terms of social cooperation." The second moral power is "a capacity for a conception of the good"; that is, a prudential "conception of the ends and purposes worthy of our devoted pursuit, together with an ordering of those elements to guide us over a complete life."[50]

Rawls assumes that the mutually disinterested parties to the original position, subject to the foregoing constraints, aspire to a "pure procedural justice," for in their rational (prudential) deliberation they "do not view themselves as required to apply, or as bound by, any antecedently given principles of right and justice."[51] Motivational assumptions in the original position are fixed by an index of primary social goods which represent the conditions under which our highest-order interests in developing and exercising our moral powers may be realized.[52] So it is, Rawls argues, that the rationally autonomous, contracting parties, under the veil of ignorance, will select a lexically ordered set of principles, deemed fair or impartial once the veil is lifted:

> *First Principle.* Each person has an equal claim to a fully adequate scheme of equal basic rights and liberties, which scheme is compatible with the same scheme for all; and in this scheme the equal political liberties, and only those liberties, are to be guaranteed their fair value.

> *Second Principle.* Social and economic inequalities are to satisfy two conditions: first they are to be attached to positions and offices open to all under conditions of fair equality of opportunity; and second, they are to be to the greatest benefit of the least advantaged members of society.[53]

---

49. Rawls, *Political Liberalism*, p. 23.
50. Rawls, *Political Liberalism*, pp. 103-4.
51. Rawls, *Political Liberalism*, p. 73.
52. Rawls, *Political Liberalism*, pp. 106-7.
53. Rawls, *Political Liberalism*, pp. 5-6. Rawls's formulation in *Political Liberalism* differs from the earlier formulation in *A Theory of Justice*, p. 302.

II.2. Habermas's "Discourse Ethics"

One might imagine the citizens of the original position conversing in terms formally analogous to those of Habermas's neo-Kantian discourse ethics. For Habermas, like Rawls, rejects a neo-Aristotelian, teleological account of "public reason." If in his later writings Habermas repudiates his earlier epistemological criticism, he nonetheless upholds the primacy of a self-reflective, emancipatory critique of the ethical substance of traditions.[54] The employments of practical reason are distinguished in terms reminiscent of Kant. The pragmatic or "purposive" employment of practical reason is expressed in the "semantic form of conditional imperatives" devoted to discovering the "appropriate techniques, strategies, or programs."[55] If, however, our ends, or in Charles Taylor's terms, our "strong preferences," are themselves at issue, we appeal to practical reason *(phronesis)* to elucidate our understanding of "the good life."[56] We invoke moral discourse, conversely, to "regulate interpersonal conflicts of action resulting from opposed interests."[57] In a Kantian vein, Habermas sharply distinguishes our differing, prudential interpretations of *eudaimonia,* which remain ethnocentric if not egoistic, from the formal, impartial stipulations of morality.[58]

Yet in contrast to Kant, the formal, deontological constraints of moral discourse are not generated "independently of experience," but rather are imposed upon ethical (prudential) judgment, such that the *intersubjective* redemption of practical validity claims is assumed *ab ovo* — one no longer legislates from the monological perspective of the noumenal self.[59] Only a de facto consensus (unlike Rawls's idealized agreement) attained in argument approximating the conditions of an ideal "unlimited communication community (unlimited, that is, in social space and historical time)" will suffice for the generation of valid (objective) claims.[60]

---

54. Jürgen Habermas, "A Philosophico-Political Profile," in *Habermas: Autonomy and Solidarity,* ed. and trans. Peter Dews (London: New Left Books, 1986), pp. 152-53; cf. *The Theory of Communicative Action,* vol. 1, *Reason and the Rationalization of Society,* trans. Thomas McCarthy (Boston: Beacon Press, 1984), pp. 273-337.

55. Habermas, *Justification and Application,* p. 3.

56. Habermas, *Justification and Application,* p. 4; cf. Charles Taylor, "The Concept of a Person," in *Philosophical Papers* (Cambridge: Cambridge University Press, 1985), vol. 1, pp. 97-114; and *Sources of the Self: The Making of the Modern Identity* (Cambridge: Harvard University Press, 1989), pp. 14-19, 42.

57. Habermas, *Justification and Application,* p. 6.

58. Habermas, *Justification and Application,* pp. 6, 24; cf. Habermas's assertion that from "a deontological viewpoint, therefore, moral deliberations must be kept completely free from goal-directed reflections" (p. 63).

59. Habermas, *Justification and Application,* pp. 1-2; cf. Habermas, *The Philosophical Discourse of Modernity,* trans. Frederick Lawrence (Cambridge: MIT Press, 1987), pp. 294-335.

60. Cf. Habermas, *Justification and Application,* p. 163. For his earlier appeal to an

While Rawls's original, prudential choosers are "mutually disinterested," Habermas assumes that moral interlocutors express their "sense of justice" directly. For the formal, procedural principle of morality prescribes that a moral norm is valid if, and only if, "*[a]ll* affected can accept the consequences and the side effects its *general* observance can be anticipated to have for the satisfaction of *everyone's* interests (and these consequences are preferred to those of known alternative possibilities for regulation)."[61] And while Rawls concedes that the mere universalizability of moral judgments fails to impose rational constraints upon prudential choice, since one remains logically free to opt out of the moral language game, Habermas's principle of universalization ("U") rests upon a "transcendental-pragmatic" justification inasmuch as every agent tacitly acknowledges it on pain of performative or pragmatic contradiction.[62]

Habermas, moreover, criticizes Rawls for shifting the theoretical problem of justification "from characteristics of procedures" to a "substantive normative concept of the person" — a gambit which, in Habermas's words, presents "an unprotected flank to the familiar neo-Aristotelian objections."[63] And yet precisely here, I wish to argue, Habermas reveals the lacunae, not only of Rawls's but of his own conception of public reason. For neither Rawls nor Habermas succeeds in offering a purely formal, procedural justification; indeed, as I will argue, both finally rest their case not on the formal but on the material formulation of Kant's categorical imperative and the "ideal of the moral person" it tacitly presumes.

III. A Retrieval of the Common Good

One might, of course, respond to these variations on a Kantian theme by recalling traditional Aristotelian or Thomistic motifs, thereby, in Eliot's words, keeping "our metaphysics warm."[64] Yet as Dupré convincingly argues, a mere repristination of the *polis* or *civitas* will not suffice. For we are heirs of modernity

---

"ideal speech situation," cf. "Toward a Theory of Communicative Competence," *Inquiry* 13 (1970): 372.

61. Jürgen Habermas, *Moral Consciousness and Communicative Action*, trans. Christian Lenhardt and Shierry Weber Nicholsen (Cambridge: MIT Press, 1990), p. 65. Habermas further refines the principle of universalization (U) in the principle of discourse ethics (D): "Only those norms can claim to be valid that meet (or could meet) with the approval of all affected in their capacity *as* participants *in a practical discourse*" (p. 66).

62. Habermas, *Moral Consciousness and Communicative Action*, pp. 76-109; see J. L. Mackie, *Ethics: Inventing Right and Wrong* (New York: Penguin Books, 1977), pp. 99-100.

63. Habermas, *Justification and Application*, pp. 28-29 n. 12.

64. T. S. Eliot, "Whispers of Immortality," in *The Complete Poems and Plays: 1909-1950* (New York: Harcourt, Brace & World, 1962), p. 33.

and of the ontotheological fragmentation brought in its wake.[65] How then to proceed? In this final section, I will proceed "analytically" in Kant's terms, by showing how traces of the common good must finally be presumed if Rawls and Habermas are to redeem their notion of public reason. Specifically, I wish to argue that the *form* of a public (universal or common) morality cannot be separated from its *content* (a material specification of the common good). In so doing, I conclude, we may derive a conception of the "terrestrial" common good which, far from succumbing to what Rawls terms "the fact of oppression," fully recognizes the basic rights we cherish.[66]

Rawls's general disavowal of teleological interpretations of public reason is tempered by his admission that the consensual primacy of "negative" liberty (that is, as specifying immunities from interference) in the original position is itself contingent upon the prior satisfaction of basic welfare needs. In the final chapter of *A Theory of Justice* Rawls concedes:

> The supposition is that if the persons in the original position assume that their basic liberties can be effectively exercised, they will not exchange a lesser liberty for an improvement in their economic well-being, at least not once a certain level of wealth has been attained. It is only when social conditions do not allow the effective establishment of these rights that one can acknowledge their restriction. The denial of equal liberty can be accepted only if it is necessary to enhance the quality of civilization so that in due course the equal freedoms can be enjoyed by all.[67]

Finally, the lexical priority of liberty must be understood as representing "the long-run tendency" or telos of "the general conception of justice consistently pursued under reasonably favorable conditions." For until "the basic wants of individuals can be fulfilled, the relative urgency of their interest in liberty cannot be firmly decided in advance."[68]

In a similar vein, Rawls admits in *Political Liberalism* that

> the first principle covering the equal basic rights and liberties may easily be preceded by a lexically prior principle requiring that citizens' basic needs be met, at least insofar as their being met is necessary for citizens to understand

65. See Dupré, *Passage to Modernity*, pp. 6-12; "Common Good," pp. 705-12; and *Marx's Social Critique of Culture* (New Haven: Yale University Press, 1983), pp. 1-57. I have developed my critique in greater detail in *The Ethics of Our Climate: Hermeneutics and Ethical Theory* (Washington, D.C.: Georgetown University Press, 1994), pp. 62-78, 119-23.

66. Rawls, *Political Liberalism*, p. 37. Rawls argues that "a continuing shared understanding on one comprehensive religious, philosophical, or moral doctrine can be maintained only by the oppressive use of state power."

67. Rawls, *A Theory of Justice*, p. 542; cf. also pp. 125-27, 137, 247.

68. Rawls, *A Theory of Justice*, pp. 542-43.

and to be able fruitfully to exercise those rights and liberties. Certainly any such principle must be assumed in applying the first principle.[69]

Yet such a "lexically prior principle," one might assume, would itself justify a set of basic claim-rights (for example, to subsistence). For if one of the "characteristic marks of a natural rights theory" is that it "assigns rights to persons by principles of equal justice" in virtue of their "natural attributes," subsistence claims, no less than negative liberties, would enjoy priority.[70]

Were the satisfaction of basic subsistence claims "assumed in applying the first principle," we could, however, no longer consign social and economic rights to the "twilight" realm of "utopian aspiration."[71] Indeed, the "lexical priority" of a principle guaranteeing basic welfare rights might tempt one to defer the recognition of particular liberties (for example, private property rights) until a certain "end-state" (for example, the satisfaction of subsistence claims) is attained. Yet inasmuch as basic rights derive from the natural attributes or prerequisites of exercising rational agency (security, subsistence, and liberties of effective participation), one might better conceive of them as mutually implicatory. Public reason would accordingly recognize the lexical priority of basic claim-rights to liberty and welfare over nonbasic rights' claims (for example, to private property).[72]

Conceiving an integrated regime of such basic rights as the "long-term tendency" of a well-ordered society introduces a teleological dimension to public reason, yet one broadly consistent with Rawls's political conception of justice. For the ideal of the social or common good defining the end-state of a well-ordered society refers primarily to society's basic structure, and hence, is properly a "political" good.[73] (Indeed, it comprises the ethical substance discriminating "reasonable" from "unreasonable" conceptions of the virtues.) Rawls himself acknowledges that in "the well-ordered society of justice as fairness" citizens do have such "final ends in common." For while "they do not affirm the same comprehensive doctrine, they do affirm the same political conception of justice," and this implies that "they share one very basic political end, and one that has high priority: namely, the end of supporting just institutions and of giving one another justice accordingly."[74]

---

69. Rawls, *Political Liberalism*, p. 7. Rawls concludes, however, "[b]ut I do not pursue these . . . matters here."

70. For Rawls's discussion of "natural rights," see *A Theory of Justice*, pp. 505-6.

71. Maurice Cranston, *What Are Human Rights?* (New York: Basic Books, 1962), p. 41.

72. For interpretations of the nature and mutually implicatory character of basic rights, see Henry Shue, *Basic Rights: Subsistence, Affluence, and U.S. Foreign Policy* (Princeton: Princeton University Press, 1980), pp. 13-87; and Alan Gewirth, *Reason and Morality* (Chicago: University of Chicago Press, 1978), pp. 48-128, and *Human Rights: Essays on Justification and Applications* (Chicago: University of Chicago Press, 1982), pp. 1-78.

73. Rawls, *Political Liberalism*, p. 203.

74. Rawls, *Political Liberalism*, p. 202.

Rawls's allusion to our "final ends in common" — suitably amended to include agents' basic welfare claims — qualifies Habermas's separation of individual morality *(Moralität)* and public ethics *(Sittlichkeit)*, for the social ideal of a regime of basic rights is not reducible to ethnocentric or egoistic comprehensive doctrines of the good. Yet our criticisms raise a further question, for if citizens in the original position are fittingly characterized by inherent, "natural rights," one wonders why such rights are bracketed, as it were, in the depiction of the original contracting parties. For while citizens in a well-ordered society are characterized by "full autonomy," that is, they "not only comply with the principles of justice, but they also act from these principles as just," the representative, contracting parties exhibit only "rational autonomy" in their deliberation.[75] Indeed, as prudential, mutually disinterested interested agents, aspiring to "pure procedural justice," they are unencumbered by any "antecedently given principles of right and justice."[76]

Rawls, in effect, assumes that the perfectly prudential agents in the original position model our "common practical reason," yet that their "highest-order" interest in realizing and developing their moral capacity for fairness (their "sense of justice") is subordinate to their "higher-order" interest in realizing a determinate conception of the good.[77] In Rawls's words, "the parties cannot invoke reasons founded on regarding the development and exercise of this capacity as part of a person's determinate conception of the good." Accordingly, their hypothetical choice is "restricted to reasons founded on regarding it solely as a means to a person's good."[78] Our "sense of justice," that is, does not of itself generate determinate moral (or political) principles, so that the exercise of rational, prudential autonomy is conceived independently of the apperception of a common good (characterizing full autonomy), or what we might in an Aristotelian vein term *sunesis* (seeking what is right).

Yet this is hardly perspicuous. For if among the political goods recognized in the original position is the realization and development of both moral powers, one wonders why only the latter should be regarded as constitutive of the parties' determinate conception of the good.[79] If, indeed, we assume that Rawls's depiction of fully autonomous citizens in the original position is "reasonable," would

---

75. Rawls, *Political Liberalism*, pp. 77-78. Cf. also Rawls's elucidation: "The difference between full autonomy and rational autonomy is this: rational autonomy is acting solely from our capacity to be rational and from the determinate conception of the good we have at any given time. Full autonomy includes not only this capacity to be rational but also the capacity to advance our conception of the good in ways consistent with honoring the fair terms of social cooperation; that is, the principles of justice" (p. 306).

76. Rawls, *Political Liberalism*, p. 73.

77. Rawls, *Political Liberalism*, pp. 90, 315ff.

78. Rawls, *Political Liberalism*, p. 315.

79. Rawls, *Political Liberalism*, pp. 310-15.

not the very reasons which *justify* the ideal of the moral person suffice, *pari passu*, to *explain* the motives of the contracting parties? (Such was the gravamen of Habermas's critique that in appealing to a substantive, normative *ideal* of a moral person Rawls has departed from a purely procedural interpretation of justice.)

While Rawls ostensibly applies the formal constraints of universalizability (consistent with Kant's "formal" interpretation of the categorical imperative) to the parties' hypothetical, prudential choice, the design of the original position presupposes the force of Kant's "material" formulation, that is, what Rawls himself terms moral persons' "*right* to equal respect and consideration in the design of their common institutions."[80] If we assume, then, that Rawls's rational choosers model the "value of persons that Kant says is beyond all price," we can no longer describe their original choice as "mutually disinterested."[81] For agents' rationally autonomous choice already exhibits their "final ends in common"; that is, what Rawls describes as their "end of supporting just institutions" (a regime of basic rights) and "of giving one another justice accordingly."[82]

While Habermas rightly observes that Rawls's invocation of "a substantive normative concept of the person" belies his aspiration to pure procedural justice, he errs, I believe, in decrying this fact.[83] For Habermas's own discrimination of prudential from moral reason is formally analogous to Rawls's distinction of rational and full autonomy — indeed, for Habermas, a "sense of justice" characterizes the interpretation of the principle of universalization ("U"). For Habermas concedes not only that affected agents accept the consequences and the side effects the general observance of a maxim can be anticipated to have for the satisfaction of everyone's interests, but also that their acceptance is motivated by respect for what Rawls terms agents' "moral powers," that is, respect

---

80. John Rawls, "Kantian Constructivism in Moral Theory," *Journal of Philosophy* 77, no. 9 (1980): 533, 546; "Fairness to Goodness," *Philosophical Review* 84 (1975): 539 (emphasis added). In the *Groundwork*, pp. 436-37 (2nd ed., pp. 80-81), Kant distinguishes the "form of the moral imperative" which prescribes that "Maxims must be chosen as if they had to hold as universal laws of nature," from the "matter" which prescribes that "A rational being, as by his very nature an end and consequently an end in himself, must serve for every maxim as a condition limiting all merely relative and arbitrary ends." Matter and form are united in a "complete determination" such that "all maxims as proceeding from our own making of law ought to harmonize with a possible kingdom of ends as a kingdom of nature."

81. Rawls, *A Theory of Justice*, p. 586. Yet consistent with the supposition of pure, procedural justice, Rawls argues that the design of the original position "does not include" the recognition of persons' "inherent worth and dignity." For while the "theory of justice provides a rendering of these ideas . . . we cannot start out from them" (pp. 585-86). In these pages, I have argued that the original position not only represents but presupposes the ideal of respect for persons.

82. Rawls, *Political Liberalism*, p. 202.

83. Habermas, *Justification and Application*, p. 28.

for persons as comprising a "kingdom of ends." In Habermas's words, "[a]nyone who seriously engages in argumentation must *presuppose* that the context of discussion guarantees in principle freedom of access, equal rights to participate, truthfulness on the part of participants, absence of coercion in adopting positions, and so on."[84]

Attaining and sustaining an "ideal" consensus rests finally upon "the communicative presuppositions of an inclusive and noncoercive discourse among free and equal partners."[85] Just as for Rawls, impartial consensus finally presumes a normative concept of the person. For the effective telos of attaining an ideal consensus, that is, one "without repression," thus presumes the antecedent recognition *(sunesis)* of mutual respect of agents already citizens of a kingdom of ends.[86] The latter, ethical ideal may, of course, be interpreted and applied in as yet unforeseen circumstances, yet it cannot be radically problematized.[87] For the maxim of respect functions constitutively in determining our self-knowledge so that raising *it* into question is to outstrip the bounds of (moral) sense.[88] For Habermas, as for Rawls, the ideal of respect limns the boundaries of our reasonable, comprehensive understandings of the good.[89]

84. Habermas, *Justification and Application,* p. 31 (emphasis added); cf. p. 56.

85. Habermas, *Justification and Application,* p. 52.

86. Habermas, *Justification and Application,* pp. 6, 13, 53. Cf. Habermas, "The Hermeneutic Claim to Universality," trans. Joseph Bleicher, in Bleicher, *Contemporary Hermeneutics: Hermeneutics as Method, Philosophy, and Critique* (London: Routledge and Kegan Paul, 1980), p. 205. See Habermas's assertion in *Justification and Application* that "[g]iven the communicative presuppositions of an inclusive and noncoercive discourse among free and equal partners, the principle of universalization requires each participant to project himself into the perspectives of all others" (p. 52). Cf. William Rehg's fine analysis, *Insight and Solidarity: A Study in the Discourse Ethics of Jürgen Habermas* (Berkeley: University of California Press, 1994), pp. 106-11, 134-49.

87. Cf., in contrast, Habermas's assertion that "[w]ithin the horizon of the lifeworld, practical judgments derive both their concreteness and their power to motivate action from their inner connection to unquestioningly accepted ideas of the good life, in short, from their connection to ethical life and its institutions. Under these conditions, problematization can never be so profound as to risk all the assets of the existing ethical substance. But the abstractive achievements required by the moral point of view do precisely that" (*Moral Consciousness and Communicative Action,* pp. 108-9).

88. Jürgen Habermas, "A Review of Gadamer's *Truth and Method,*" in *Understanding and Social Inquiry,* ed. Fred R. Dallmayr and Thomas A. McCarthy (Notre Dame: University of Notre Dame Press, 1977), p. 358.

89. Rawls, *Political Liberalism,* pp. 48-66.

IV. Conclusions

I have argued in these pages that the moral ideal of respect for persons in a kingdom of ends governs the exercise of public reason. Prudential rationality, internally constrained by the *ideal* of such a kingdom (embodied in a regime of basic rights), recalls the Aristotelian understanding of *phronesis* as practical wisdom, exhibiting our moral self-knowledge as members of a moral community. So too, we may say practical judgments find expression in *sunesis*, our common "seeking what is right." For the telos of a common good as our common end is always already presumed in our contractual deliberation.

In this respect Habermas's criticism of Rawls is on the mark; for our contractual thought experiment does not so much construct our natural rights through the heuristic appeal to self-interested choice as exhibit them in the design and critique of our institutional arrangements. Our consensus, that is, must be achieved de facto and not merely de jure; even as the discursive constraints posed by our basic rights permit us to redress systematic distortions in our consensual deliberations. The ideal of the common good thus commends itself on terms "political rather than metaphysical."[90] Indeed, our reflections turn less on the discourse of nature and natural finality than on the nature of discourse and the consensual finality of redeeming practical validity claims — what Aristotle calls in his *Politics* our natural endowment of "reasoned speech."[91]

Modest though they may be, the foregoing remarks suggest, I believe, what is at stake in retrieving a conception of public reason which succumbs neither to the Hobbesian "war of all against all" nor to the subordination of the individual to the "total organism" of the state.[92] For reason, in our discursive interpretation, is *ab ovo* public; its aim is not the protection of the presocial, abstract rights of mutually disinterested individuals, but the "making true" of our common end as a common good, that is, a regime of basic rights in a

90. Although the ideal of the common good persists as a leitmotif in modern Roman Catholic social teaching, the tacit shift from a perfectionist (teleological) justification to a more deontological interpretation leaves its metaphysical status somewhat ambivalent. Cf. *Mater et magistra*, n. 65; *Pacem in terris*, nn. 55-61; *Dignitatis humanae*, n. 6; *Gaudium et spes*, n. 26. For a modern reconstruction of the Thomistic understanding, see Ignacio Ellacuría, "Human Rights in a Divided Society," in *Human Rights in the Americas: The Struggle for Consensus*, ed. Alfred Hennelly and John Langan (Washington, D.C.: Georgetown University Press, 1982), pp. 52-65.

91. Aristotle, *Politics* 1253a9ff.

92. As Dupré observes, the cultural precedence accorded autonomy is such that "even to weaken it would inflict major injury to that very dignity that we are seeking to preserve." Finally, "[w]e need a conception of the *good* that itself includes individual autonomy" ("Common Good," p. 706).

well-ordered society.[93] Conceived thus, our basic rights (which include social, cultural, and economic claims) are not so much properties of abstract individuals as rhetorical constraints upon our communicative practices; that is, intrinsically social goods whose universal communication is presupposed for civic discourse.[94]

Just as for Aquinas, the end of the state is the flourishing of its members, so in our postmodern interpretation the common good is conceived distributively, in the basic, structural provision of security, liberties of effective civic participation, and subsistence. Securing these agential goods is consonant with differing conceptions of flourishing, yet, *pace* Rawls, the common good, so conceived, is necessarily constitutive of the good envisaged by rationally autonomous agents. Finally, the material content of respect, elaborated in a theory of basic rights and discursive virtues, is inseparable from the form of public reason, so that one may say, with Aquinas, the "common good is the end of each individual member of the community."[95] Our conclusions, of course, are far from a panacea, yet in the midst of the "negation and despair" of modernity, they hold the promise that we may yet, in Auden's words, "show an affirming flame."[96]

93. Although beyond the scope of this essay, a retrieval of the teleological character of public reason would likewise support an understanding of civic virtues as the "discursive" habits or dispositions presumed in attaining and sustaining an uncoerced consensus of free and equal citizens. For intimations of such a notion, cf. Rawls, *Political Liberalism*, p. 54.

94. In Dupré's words, a theory of such rights "may be shorn from its individualist origins if we conceive of those rights as given *with and through* the concrete context of society, rather than rooted in a presocial state of nature" ("Common Good," p. 709).

95. Aquinas, *Summa theologiae*, II-II, Q. 58, a. 9.

96. Auden, pp. 57-59.

PART 3

RETROSPECTIVES

Louis Dupré's Philosophy of Religion: An Indispensable Discourse on Fragments of Meaning

GEORGE P. SCHNER, S.J.

This essay will concern itself with some seventy articles and six books which span nearly forty years of reflection from 1956 to the present. Some of this material has appeared in more than one language, and occasionally in more than one form, such that there are over one hundred items concerning the philosophy of religion, if a rough count were made. Moreover, the discussion in any number of these pieces opens into Dupré's theological, ethical, and spiritual writings. It is impossible to separate easily the philosophical work from the rest. This cohesive and comprehensive character of his work is not, in my judgment, a sign of a confusion of modes of discourse and thought but evidence of the very harmony and interconnectedness of the realities Dupré has spent his life exploring and of the manner in which they ought to be explored. His insistent efforts to make the philosophy of religion an essential part of academic discourse and cultural critique have shaped an extraordinarily active career.

I recommend an image as the preamble to my remarks. Consider a weaver beginning the task of amassing an assortment of richly dyed wools in preparation for weaving a grand tapestry. Or imagine a painter assembling the pots of paint needed for an immense mural. Essential to Dupré's work is a symposium of truly disparate but intensely intelligent persons gathered with good food and good wine for a conversation across centuries about just what that tapestry or mural should look like. As he has passed through nearly forty years of writing, Dupré has maintained certain conversations, initiated new ones, taken advice and insight here and there, and in the end has provided us with his own unique and subtle work of art. There is an amazing continuity of themes throughout accounting for both breadth and unity across the years.

I. Introduction

I suggest dividing the works into three phases of development with moments of completion and new turns, as well as into five themes of continuity present through certain concepts and questions. A sixth form of continuity exists because of the authors who remain constant partners in Dupré's conversation. My analysis will benefit, then, from both a diachronic and synchronic rendering. It will be accomplished in three stages. First, this introduction will offer an initial synchronic view, previewing in general what the second stage will offer in historical detail and development. The final stage will resume the synchronic with the purpose of a modest suggestion of both appreciation and critique.

There are a number of threads to be followed, with varying degrees of interest and importance, in this body of philosophical work. There is hardly a major philosopher of the Western tradition, from the ancients to contemporary authors, whom Dupré does not mention, and his ever expanding horizon of questions leads him continually to map out implications across the whole field of philosophical problems. These two tendencies are as much the result of his classical education and interests, his extraordinarily broad reading and inquiry, as they are of the demands of the subject of his questioning, the religious dimension of human life. Nonetheless, there is a striking consistency across *three periods* of work: the *first period,* from 1956 to the publication of *The Other Dimension* in 1972; the *second period,* what I will call the middle period, which lasts until the mid-1980s; and the *third period,* the subsequent development toward the publication of *Passage to Modernity* in 1993.

The unity of these three periods is the result of *six forms of continuity,* involving themes and authors: (1) the *crisis of culture* brought about by modernity's construal of the relation of self, God, and world, which in effect constitutes a transformation of these three; (2) the *religious dimension of the self* within the context of this crisis; (3) the complex of topics which properly belong to a philosophical study of the *forms of mediation in religion* (the religious use of language, symbol, and myth; the activities of creation, salvation, sanctification, mysticism); (4) the relationship of *philosophical reflection and faith* to the religious dimension and its symbols as manifested in faith, in religions; (5) the role of this philosophical reflection on religion within education and culture in general; and (6) the *engagement with the Western philosophical tradition* and its organic continuity. The consultation of authors ranges across the entire history of Western philosophy, though there is a singular importance of both Kierkegaard and Hegel throughout (Marx is obviously equally important, but I leave observations about his importance to the review essay by Philip Chmielewski in this collection). An interest in phenomenology, particularly the work of Husserl and Duméry, passes into the background but is surely not set aside, and an increasing interest in Neoplatonism comes to the fore along with explorations in late medieval nominalism and Renaissance humanism.

Such continuity is only possible, of course, because there is true development and change. Five books of philosophical reflection mark the stages. After the publication of his dissertation on Marx, there follows *Kierkegaard as Theologian* (in Dutch in 1958, in English in 1963), which stands at the head of a period of sixteen years during which the groundwork for the entire corpus is laid. As I will show in some detail, all the major authors and themes emerge in this period, which itself culminates in the publication of *The Other Dimension* (which first appeared in 1972). A second stage includes the publication of two collections of articles, *Transcendent Selfhood* (1976) and *A Dubious Heritage* (1977). Both recapitulations continue and augment the general study of religion in *The Other Dimension*. The former also is a presage of Dupré's growing interest in spirituality and contains the barest hints of the next stage of development. I have chosen to take the article entitled "The Spiritual Crisis of Our Culture" as the best articulation within the texts of the third period of the new gestalt of questions and authors which will culminate in the publication of *Passage to Modernity* (1993). Throughout the earlier works there are hints which already prepare the reader for this later analysis, which is obviously only the first part of a comprehensive study of the crisis of modernity and of the religious self within it.

The aforementioned diachronic exposition will easily unfold. Imagining there to be a truly synoptic vision is a more difficult task and has led me to search out what is constant throughout the philosophical texts. The following thesis gathers up the synchronic view: the self, at its truest, is grounded in (even coincident with) the transcendent, but is dependent upon the mediation of symbols and their interpretation; this mediation is the exercise of human freedom and rationality, yet ironically we ourselves have invented a culture in which interiority is not simply endangered but obviated. Thus religion, Christianity specifically, labors under extraordinary constraints in its efforts to be the mode of interiorization and integration for the self, alienated as we are from ourselves, the world, and the transcendent, and from the exercise of religiosity itself. This situation requires the most careful intellectual reflection and deconstruction, but equally so, the most persistent personal reorientation. For the study of this complex situation certain philosophical notions are judged inadequate, and basic principles are proposed which cannot be compromised.

II. Situating the Transcendent Dimension

II.1. Prologue to Diachronic Exposition: Grounding in Education and History, in Faith and Truth

Though a prolific writer, Dupré's work as a scholar and teacher has a basic intent discernible throughout the years: the formation of persons which "being a Christian teacher of the humanities"[1] attempts to achieve. The religious dimension of human life and its role as critic of culture and initiator of human transformation engender an engaged form of philosophical analysis which moves toward constructive proposals for intellectual development. The context for the themes of crisis, self, and mediation are the themes of faith, education, and history which constitute the environment in which the more technical details of Dupré's philosophy of religion unfold.

In an article in *Commonweal* in 1961, Dupré muses on "Philosophy's Uses and Abuses," giving advice to those who would be its students:

> Not experience but reflection, and this reflection not expressed in one unchangeable system but in an uninterrupted dialogue with man's historical growth: that is what philosophy offers its students.[2]

Such a definition means that philosophy cannot be studied without studying its history, a history which is not a mere succession of events but has its significance as the realization of human freedom. We build a world with distinctive characteristics in which we can realize ourselves and upon which we can reflect. However, if the contemporary world is marked by "the characteristically modern experience of anxiety,"[3] as well as by the lack of a sure belief in a rational ordering of the universe, ultimately grounded in the transcendent, it can be asked whether such a world is one in which humanity can realize itself and within which it can engage in life-giving reflection. An imperiled existential self, a world in crisis, the loss of the transcendent, a history of the reflection which is philosophy — already the essential elements which will preoccupy Dupré — are articulated in a brief article about teaching philosophy. And underlying these elements is a deep conviction that a study of the religious dimension of human existence is essential to a fully reflective life.

Thirty-one years later, this time in an article in the *Christian Century,* "On Being a Christian Teacher of Humanities," Dupré still sees the same crisis and

---

1. Taken from the title of Louis Dupré, "On Being a Christian Teacher of Humanities," *Christian Century,* April 29, 1992, pp. 452-55.

2. Louis Dupré, "Philosophy's Uses and Abuses," *Commonweal* 75 (1961): 36-38, here p. 38.

3. Dupré, "Philosophy's Uses and Abuses," p. 37.

still has confidence in the internal dynamics of a humanistic, liberal education with its attention to historical erudition, critical thinking, and moral education. When further shaped by Christian belief, this kind of education must treat God as more than an "object" of study and likewise the self, not as an object of scientific scrutiny alone, but as needful of a formation in interiority appropriate to the challenges of our culture. Such formation will aim at developing a contemplative self opened to otherness through the virtues of gratitude and respect. Dupré quotes a work of his own, *Transcendent Selfhood*, which was published midway between the 1961 article and that of 1992:

> Culture requires freedom, but freedom requires spiritual space to act, play, and dream in. The space for freedom is created by transcendence. What is needed most of all is an attitude in which transcendence *can be recognized again.*[4]

The concluding paragraphs of *Passage to Modernity* describe the same state of affairs:

> Once again we pass through a period of profound insecurity. Critical reflection calls for change. But we have not yet succeeded in grasping the meaning of that past, which constitutes our present self. While anxiously seeking a new wholeness we must nevertheless carefully protect those fragments of meaning that we possess, knowing that they may be the bricks of a future synthesis.[5]

I have begun with the role of philosophical reflection on religion within education and culture, because Dupré's "publishing" in the classroom and its self-conscious commitment to intellectual formation are essential to his *explication des textes* and the grand sweep of his systematic presentations. Dupré's interpretations are offered with the evidence of a careful reading, but also, importantly, with an invitation to thought. He considers the discourse which is the philosophy of religion to be indispensable to education and the culture it serves, however fragmentary that discourse may be.

Philosophical reflection has as an essential component the study (and construction) of the history of philosophy itself. Thus my sixth theme of continuity, the authors Dupré engages, is present because of a substantive and methodological conviction. Even if Dupré does not consider the history of Western thought to be, as it were, a single narrative which can be rendered once for all, as dogmatic rationalism or idealist history of ideas might propose, neither is it a haphazard collection of unrelated arguments which deserves an

---

4. Dupré, "Being a Christian Teacher," p. 455.
5. Louis Dupré, *Passage to Modernity: An Essay in the Hermeneutics of Nature and Culture* (New Haven: Yale University Press, 1993), p. 253.

equally piecemeal analysis. Articles both early, middle, and late express the notion that this history is a cumulative development, with discernible stages and effects which can be evaluated. Thus, for example, in 1964, in "The Philosophical Stages of Self-Discovery," the underlying theme is the adventures of the subject, its discovery, content, isolation, and modern predicament:

> Man's reflection on himself is a process in which he gradually becomes aware of himself as a subject, that is, an interiority distinct from the objective world of things as its meaning- and form-giving principle.[6]

This and other early renditions of the history of Western philosophy tend to be more straightforward than *Passage to Modernity* thirty years later, but elements of suspicion are already present, focused principally on the limitations of the self. However much the self may be "a dialectical movement of freedom which, in creating objective reality, creates itself,"[7] it is not *absolutely* free. Basic human freedom is exercised within the constraints of its paradoxical relation to both the material world and the spiritually transcendent. Both Marx and Kierkegaard, in rejecting Hegel's idealism, advance the understanding of human subjectivity as limited freedom but still risk lapsing into Kant's isolated and empty subject. Dupré credits existential phenomenology (e.g., Merleau-Ponty) with exploring the "situatedness" of the self, a subject always intending an object, a being whose essence is to posit itself in a world. Only within such a situatedness can freedom be exercised.

In these early discussions what receives particular attention is not the constituent character of the world itself or the means by which situatedness is actualized (culture and its symbols), but the solution to the paradox of subjectivity which is to be found in faith:

> To surrender oneself and one's immanent values to the transcendent, and, at the same time, to remain steadfast in one's conviction that one must and will regain the entire sphere of immanent freedom within the transcendent, that is the paradoxical achievement of faith.[8]

Faith does not remove the paradox but confirms it, drawing the human subject deeper within, resolving the problematic character of human freedom not through a renewed relation to the world, but in a "religious decision."[9]

Nearly twenty-five years later, two related articles appear which reassert the importance of the study of the history of philosophy itself, but now present

---

6. Louis Dupré, "The Philosophical Stages of Self-Discovery," *Thought* 39 (1964): 411-28, here p. 413.

7. Dupré, "Philosophical Stages of Self-Discovery," p. 415.

8. Dupré, "Philosophical Stages of Self-Discovery," p. 425.

9. Dupré, "Philosophical Stages of Self-Discovery," p. 426.

the difficulties of human self-constitution and the culture of modernity with a second paradox in mind. In 1987, in "Philosophy and Its History," the question of acquaintance with past philosophy is posed against the background of two options which emerged in the nineteenth century: the reduction of philosophy to an item of cultural history (with a pursuant relativization of all philosophic thought) or the limitation of philosophy to logical and linguistic analysis (as an ahistorical enterprise). Presuming that it is a demand internal to philosophy to make arguments and claims of lasting quality and definiteness without denying their cultural-historical conditions, Dupré asks whether philosophy can risk to admit its own historicity in face of such a paradox. In reply he argues that

> if temporality forms an essential dimension of being, the study of former reflection constitutes an essential task of humanity's ultimate self-understanding. Without it, the definite character of that understanding is not safeguarded but distortingly empoverished.[10]

In 1967 the question was whether and how the self can be said to be free; by the late 1980s the question is whether and how philosophy can claim to speak the truth. The link between the two questions is temporality, though not the idealist "absorption of the temporal into the eternal as forgetfulness of existence"[11] which Kierkegaard criticizes, but temporality under three aspects: (1) the human subject as essentially a being-in-time (the question of human freedom newly posed), to which are now added the following two issues, namely, (2) what is ultimately real as being itself historical, and (3) the changing symbols of culture which affect the manifestation of Being itself. We are asking once again the perennial questions of Western thought: How are being and becoming related? permanence and change? autonomy and freedom? What is paradoxical for the human subject is mirrored in human reflection and cultural construction.[12]

Metaphysical novelty is to be found in the new relationship between immanence and transcendence which characterizes the modern period of Western culture. Even though distinctly new, it did not come about without its preparation in medieval Christian thought, in the originality of Renaissance thinkers, in its particular development in the early modern period, all the while indebted to Platonic and Neoplatonic philosophy. The homogeneity of reality,

---

10. Louis Dupré, "Philosophy and Its History," in *At the Nexus of Philosophy and History,* ed. Bernard P. Dauenhauer (Athens: University of Georgia Press, 1987), pp. 20-41, here p. 23.

11. Louis Dupré, "Is the History of Philosophy Philosophy?" *Review of Metaphysics* 42 (1989): 463-82, here p. 478.

12. Though substantially the same text, the 1987 article, "Philosophy and Its History," attends more to the reality of metaphysical novelty, and the article in 1989, "Is the History of Philosophy Philosophy?" gives the matter of meaning as permanent fuller attention.

the relative independence of the cosmos, and the receding of the transcendent to a position of detachment from nature and the self — these are the results now taken for granted in the modern relation of transcendence and immanence. Dupré is clear, however, that the medieval notion of the relation is abolished. It remains both basic to and more profound than the modern, even if now inconceivable. The philosopher, rather than the historian of ideas, makes the judgment of both uniqueness and continuity in the process of evaluating the meaning and truth of any particular attempt to articulate "our self-understanding as meaning-giving being in the world."[13] Given the evident propensity to celebrate the relativity of truth in contemporary Western thought, it would be naive to think that appreciating the "novelty" of these new relations is a simple matter. The momentousness of the novelty is dialectically related to the conceptualization of the permanent: the paradox of speaking truth and enacting freedom remains fragile.

The permanence intrinsic to philosophy is not to be gained, however, by an effort "to separate an eternal content (the *truth* value) from the temporal form of its discovery."[14] The lasting quality of philosophical argument and the perdurance of philosophical conceptualization stand in contrast to the passing character of the historical experience upon which we reflect and the inevitably contingent and changing symbols of culture which we employ. Thus a study of the history of philosophy both discerns and integrates:

> The form which this particular pursuit of truth takes consists neither in comparing the adequacy of various theories, nor in introducing a kind of coherence among them, but rather in showing the specific disclosure of Being in an irreducible yet ever growing (both intensively and comprehensively) complexity of philosophical reflection.[15]

Dupré criticizes Hegel for a conception of totality which imposes closure in the search for permanent significance by assigning too rigid a location for successive novel disclosures. He prefers Heidegger's sense of the present possibility of novelty in the disclosure of Being which makes all philosophers, not predecessors or successors, but contemporaries in their search to speak the truth.[16]

But what of faith, the resolution of the paradox of human freedom in which the self surrenders its "immanent values to the transcendent"? If the relationship of immanence and transcendence has been decisively sundered, can faith still bring about a moment of union, of integration? Further, how is the paradox of faith joined to the paradox of novelty and permanence in

---

13. Dupré, "Philosophy and Its History," p. 39.
14. Dupré, "Is the History?" p. 469.
15. Dupré, "Philosophy and Its History," p. 33.
16. Dupré, "Is the History?" p. 480.

philosophy? This brings me to the question of the relation of faith to philosophy, the fourth theme discussed in materials ranging from 1958 to 1990.

Whether giving access to a "realm of experience" or the "other dimension," faith as a part of human existence is presumed legitimate, real, worthy of investigation, having its own inner dynamics and logic, not in opposition to or excluded from reason, and not subsumed either under or into it. This presupposition will not seem odd for anyone acquainted with the "philosophy of religion" as it has been passed on to us in the twentieth century. In his 1971 address as president of the American Catholic Philosophical Association, Dupré clarifies a fundamental principle for the study of religion:

> The thinker who has no firsthand acquaintance with the experience on which he reflects tends to invent what he does not know. This usually results in some brand of natural theology which religious man is seldom able to recognize as the object of his worship. It is the sterile habitat of arguments for or against the existence of God.[17]

Religion which is shorn of its foundation in both faith and revelation becomes an impossible concept.

In an article on the philosophy of Brand Blanshard, Dupré reiterates the a posteriori character of religion and faith for the hermeneutic task of the philosopher of religion. If fundamental to each religion is its claims for a self-revealing transcendent reality, then the study of a given religion must be

> in accordance with the rules of its (religion's) specific nature. Those rules are not spelled out in dogmas or theological theories. . . . They have to be discovered through a patient analysis of the religious phenomena *as the believer experiences them.*[18]

Faith and the believer constitute a realm of meaning which cannot be "produced" by the philosopher, any more than any other such realm. But a caution has been added which echoes a stronger remark from the 1971 address. Philosophy is rightfully jealous of its autonomy:

> No philosopher can allow to see his science reduced to the role of a handmaid of theology. If it is one thing to have philosophy reflect upon a preexisting experience such as the religious activity; it is another thing to make it dependent upon an established system of thought.[19]

17. Louis Dupré, "Philosophy and the Religious Perspective of Life," *Proceedings of the American Catholic Philosophical Association* (1971): 1-8, here p. 4.

18. Louis Dupré, "Faith and Reason," in *The Philosophy of Brand Blanshard,* ed. Paul Schilpp (La Salle, Ill.: Open Court, 1980), pp. 996-1014; see p. 997.

19. Dupré, "Philosophy and the Religious Perspective," p. 7.

Though the texts are clear enough, it is important to note that it is theology (not faith) which Dupré criticizes for attempting to exercise domination. Moreover, there is a presumption that dogma and theology have wandered far from that inner logic of the revealing transcendent and the believer's experience. This indirect critique of Christian theology is no doubt justified for forms of theology which either oppose (or absolve themselves from responsibility to) rational thought entirely or defer to other modes of discourse for the concepts and rules to be used by theological reflection.[20]

Thus, when Dupré proposes two rules by which religious assertions are subject to the laws of rational discourse, he sums up the delicate balance between philosophy and faith:

(1) The basic possibility of a positive affirmation of the transcendent must be rationally justified. (2) No assertions concerning the transcendent are allowed to conflict with the principles of purely rational knowledge.[21]

The claim of philosophy to independence is not a unilateral one, however. Since religion does not simply extend the realms of common sense, science, or art but actually proposes unique claims, in observing the first rule all that philosophy can do is investigate and establish the rational *possibility* of such claims. At the minimum one has Kant's ideal of pure reason, and at the maximum one has the preapprehension of Being proposed by transcendental Thomists. In abiding by the second rule, philosophy should require no more and no less than the logic of assertions about the transcendent requires. There are, as it were, two sets of rules, though neither are in conflict nor subordinated to one another: the inner rules of faith and revelation, the logic of the transcendent itself, and the rules of philosophy, of rational investigation. What is at stake is the possibility of an adequate philosophical pluralism, evidenced in both epistemology and ontology, such that the central role of symbols in religion can be adequately dealt with. If philosophy does not permit faith's (a particular religion's) use of symbols as essential to the "rules of its specific nature," then neither faith nor revelation as modes of disclosure for the transcendent *can* be the object of philosophical investiga-

---

20. In this matter I see a convergence of interests between Dupré and Hans Frei. From within theology, Frei was concerned to discover what had occurred to render theology so problematic in the contemporary world. I would suggest that, on the one hand, he was searching for what had become of revelation as a founding principle of theology, and on the other hand, why theology had developed a problematic relationship with philosophy (and other modes of discourse) and with what results. See Hans Frei, *The Eclipse of Biblical Narrative* (New Haven: Yale University Press, 1974); and *Types of Christian Theology,* ed. George Hunsinger and William C. Placher (New Haven: Yale University Press, 1992).

21. Dupré, "Faith and Reason," p. 1000.

tion.[22] A difficulty allied to the displacement of symbols in certain kinds of philosophy is a similar displacement of "existential involvement" as an appropriate characteristic of rational knowledge; namely, a suspicion of faith itself, and, needless to say, of revelation as well.[23]

I conclude this first section of the first part of my diachronic exposition with remarks on a particularly important essay of 1989 entitled "Reflections on the Truth of Religion." In this essay Dupré considers which theory of truth is most apt for the discussion of the religious dimension of human life and concludes:

> The correspondence and coherence models remain indispensable for understanding the truth of religion. But the more they came to reflect the subjective turn of modern thought, the more they became removed from what religion itself has traditionally understood to be the essence of its truth.[24]

Religion claims to speak about the real, with language "corresponding" to it, though never being able to do so exhaustively. Caution about relying entirely on a correspondence theory of truth has a twofold aim based on two defining principles. The aim is to ensure that the philosophical investigation of religion collapses neither into an objectivizing nor a subjectivizing attitude, thereby simplistically reducing the transcendent into either an object of knowledge or a subjective construction. The defining principles are concerned with the nature of truth and divine disclosure. First, "truth refers to *being*, rather than to knowledge,"[25] and thus the primary human relation to truth is not correspondence of an intellectual or empirical sort, but a "correspondence" of devotion and fidelity, of enactment in the form of response. Second, the transcendent as divine disclosure or revelation is not what human beings produce and preserve, but what disrupts a closed world and by its very nature as transcendent does not simply originate in or submit to a "coherent" or established system of human meaning. In sum:

> Truth then consists in the right relation to the ultimately real and only that transcendent reality can enlighten us concerning the nature and even the

22. For an essay which deals with the necessary reciprocal interaction of philosophy and regions of meaning, consult Kenneth Schmitz, "Philosophy of Religion and the Redefinition of Philosophy," *Man and World* 3 (1970): 54-82.

23. For a brief and not entirely complete discussion of the history of the relation of philosophy and faith, see Louis Dupré and Jacqueline Mariña, "The Concept of Faith in Philosophy," in *Handbook of Faith*, ed. James M. Lee (Birmingham: Religious Education Press, 1990), pp. 47-70.

24. Louis Dupré, "Reflections on the Truth of Religion," *Faith and Philosophy* 6 (1989): 260-74, here p. 266.

25. Dupré, "Reflections," p. 260.

existence of that relation. This principle summarizes the fundamental belief about truth not only in the Judaeo-Christian tradition but, if I am not mistaken, in all others as well. It marks the constant factor in religious truth. Our own tradition stands out by its increasing emphasis on the second aspect — the need for a divine disclosure, a revelation.[26]

To speak adequately about the truth of religion is to be aware that both the relation itself and the awareness of it are given by the transcendent. However, Dupré concedes that

> Revelation itself cannot be rendered intelligible unless it still proves capable of being assumed within the modern pattern of speaking and thinking. However sublime and unique, a message confronts the elementary fact that, in order to be expressed, it must adopt an *existing* language and thereby integrate itself within a *praxis* of discourse.[27]

There is an ambiguity lurking in these remarks which should be brought forward for reflection. It concerns the term "intelligible." Dupré's remarks in this essay concerning Hegel express the problem in an analogous way. He credits Hegel with the insight that the Christian religion, as possessing an ontological richness surpassing all other modes of being and knowing, rightly has priority over philosophy as critical reflection: "The absoluteness of religious truth lies in the fact that its disclosure includes all reality without having to refer to any reality outside itself, and that it implies its own necessity."[28] Nonetheless, Hegel requires religious faith to lose its representational form and to be completed, as it were, by conceptual thought, to become itself more fully. Consistent with his reading of Hegel elsewhere, Dupré hesitates to accept this requirement.

But what of his own requirements, first, that revelation be "rendered intelligible" within modern thought, and second, that revelation inevitably adopt already existing discursive practices? I would suggest that the whole of Dupré's work in philosophy of religion rests on a careful answer to these two questions. He labors within a field of study delicately balanced between two worlds, worlds which, though claiming internal coherence, are presently very much worlds of fragmentation with a disturbed and disturbing interaction. As to the internal coherence of revelation, it is clear that

> For the religious believer, the ontological disclosure occurs entirely *within* the language of revelation. In the Christian revelation God's living Word provides, with its own disclosure, the conditions for the internal *justification* of its truth.

26. Dupré, "Reflections," p. 261.
27. Dupré, "Reflections," p. 262.
28. Dupré, "Reflections," p. 268.

The Spirit given with, and in, the Word testifies to the veracity of the message and enables the believer to see its evidence. But a justification of this nature is neither available nor sufficient to modern philosophy.[29]

Drawing upon Heidegger and the Neoplatonic traditions, Dupré suggests that the concept of "illumination" is apt for understanding the advent of the transcendent into the human sphere of existence. In symbolic form ultimate reality, the transcendent, approaches human being with an ontological richness which surpasses speech but does not negate or prohibit interpretation. In fact, it precisely requires it. The self-manifestation of the transcendent, the sole basis on which any religion can speak of the transcendent, bears with it its own logic, its own evidence. Yet this is still not a direct or uninvolving presence. Dupré again defers to Kierkegaard's notion of religious truth:

> It remains . . . a "pathetic-dialectical" message that is, one which after having been passively received, must still be dialectically interiorized. This translation into existence, essential to the religious disclosure, consists in a never-ending process of mediation.[30]

The second requirement, then, depends upon the first for its fulfillment. Adopting the discursive practices into which it makes its own self-disclosure, the transcendent of necessity transforms what it inhabits as symbol and initiates the transformation of human being through the work of interpretation and response, which the manifestation sets in motion. "The self-manifestation of the transcendent is, in the end, neither self-understanding nor understanding of Being. Though contributing to both, it also surpasses them in referring to the inexpressible."[31] It is not surprising that this summary remark is followed by an appeal to mystical writings as the most apt articulation of this paradox. Discerning the symbolic forms the transcendent itself adopts from those we ourselves invest with religious meaning remains an altogether unique problem, one in which all the elements of the discussion thus far — education, history, faith, and truth — have a role to play.

In conclusion, I have claimed that the two requirements for an adequate presentation of the truth of religion, the ontological nature of truth and the transcendent origin of the divine disclosure, are the key to Dupré's work. It is a warranted claim, I think, on at least three grounds. First, some form of definition, however complex, of the nature of the transcendent and of the necessity of interpretation is obviously foundation to the work of any philosopher of religion. Second, unlike either reductionist or essentialist efforts to

29. Dupré, "Reflections," p. 269.
30. Dupré, "Reflections," p. 270.
31. Dupré, "Reflections," p. 271.

define the religious dimension of human life and the cosmos, and its interpretation, Dupré acknowledges a complex of relations as the necessary starting point for a study of the transcendent and any form of relation to it. Third, it is not surprising, I think, that a more self-conscious articulation of this nest of concepts and relations which constitutes a definition comes only late in Dupré's work. To paraphrase T. S. Eliot, it is in our ending that we know our beginning.

Education, history, faith, truth — these are the topics which undergird the broad and detailed work of the philosophy of religion for Dupré. Let me turn now to the details of the first period's movement toward *The Other Dimension.*

II.2. First Period: Searching the Sources
from Kierkegaard to Duméry (1956-71)

Along with the publication of his first two books, some twenty-five articles inaugurate the first period. Not surprisingly, the first major work after his dissertation is *Kierkegaard as Theologian.*[32] Despite its broad scope, the focus is clear: the self — its freedom, its limitations both extrinsic and intrinsic, its temporality and finitude, its grounding in the transcendent. The book presents, first, Kierkegaard's life and its significance for his own philosophical and religious discoveries, followed by discussions of sin, grace, faith, Christ, and the church. Contrary to interpretations which read Kierkegaard's early personal traumas and subsequent authorship as evidence of a severely disturbed mind incapable of human or divine love, Dupré argues that "his difficult life is not the closed circle of a neurotic person, but the ascent of a man to religion."[33] Thus the category "individual" which first marks Kierkegaard's experience of his own isolation, his inability to communicate, and the need for one adequate reader for his reflections, becomes a religious category which marks the activity of authentic selfhood. The category likewise entails a refusal of mass culture's devaluation of the transcendent value of Christianity, and of the moment of access to the transcendent to be found in authentic selfhood.

Leaving aside the chapters on theological topics, let me comment on the chapter and related articles on faith and subjectivity. Three points remain constant: (1) the self as freedom is a self-constituting though not self-creating being;

---

32. Louis Dupré, *Kierkegaard as Theologian: The Dialectic of Christian Existence* (New York: Sheed & Ward, 1963). For brevity's sake, I will not attempt to place his interpretation in the context of the wealth of contemporary scholarship, but I will give at least some indication of recent like-minded works. In the case of Kierkegaard, a convenient reference is the following: Steven M. Emmanuel, "Recent Literature on Kierkegaard," *Religious Studies Review* 20, no. 4 (1994): 286-91.

33. Dupré, *Kierkegaard as Theologian,* p. 30.

(2) true subjectivity requires a return of subjective freedom to itself from its attempt at self-realization in objectivity; (3) this inward movement is deepest and truest when it is a relation to the transcendent object of faith, a paradoxical and repulsive object never to be attained. In Christianity faith's passion of inwardness which is faith is realized in the relation to Christ as God in time, the absurd coincidence of immanence and transcendence in the human person. Dupré summarizes as follows:

> The act of faith is precisely the attempt to integrate these two contradictory elements within one self not by reconciling them (for they are irreconcilable) but by accepting the opposition itself as a manifestation of man's fundamental insufficiency, receiving thereby the entire immanence from the transcendent, in virtue of the absurd.[34]

Whether this self and God are equally inextricable from the self-description of a particular religion is a further question which Dupré, at this point, treats as a problem of the symbolic but nonetheless given, historical character of revelation. In a review article on, among other works, Karl Jaspers's *Philosophical Faith and Revelation,* Dupré considers Jaspers's theory of "ciphers" for the transcendent as an example of an inadequate solution: it reduces ontological statements to merely historically determined or simply illusory claims, unsatisfactory for both metaphysician and antimetaphysician alike; and it renders religious symbols unambiguous, opaque, and hence unsatisfactory to the religious believer. Under both aspects faith collapses into the self and its Promethean efforts at the making of meaning, even transcendent meaning, this latter effort being self-contradictory. At this point Dupré presents Kierkegaard on the nature of authority and revelation as the appropriate response to Jaspers's proposal:

> Kierkegaard's answer to Jaspers' question, how an inward relation to the transcendent could ever accept a *given* revelation, is that no meaningful relation to the transcendent can be established except to the extent that it is *given.* Only in and through a given revelation can the dialectical tension between immanent freedom and transcendent be maintained.[35]

Does Kierkegaard achieve a reunion of them or does he only diagnose their severance, instantiate the unease with which his contemporaries (and

34. Louis Dupré, "The Constitution of the Self in Kierkegaard's Philosophy," *International Philosophical Quarterly* 3 (1963): 506-26, here p. 526.

35. Louis Dupré, "Themes in Contemporary Philosophy of Religion," *New Scholasticism* 48 (1969): 577-601, here p. 595. The second paragraph of this article, which begins a review of Hans Urs von Balthasar's *The God Question and Modern Man,* offers an intriguing preview of *Passage to Modernity.* Similar glimpses can be found throughout the other early works of Dupré.

perhaps all modern women and men) attempt to hold them together? In a commentary on *Sickness unto Death* published in 1987, Dupré offers an evaluation of Kierkegaard's efforts, now measured by the large context of that passage to modernity. The "heart of the problem," Dupré notes, results from the albeit appropriate effort

> to force the person to confront his strictly individual responsibility before God. This may well have been a correct practical maneuver for eliminating the ready temptation of escaping into the mass. Yet elevated into a theoretical principle it leads to a distorted vision both of the person and of his relation to the transcendent. If it is severed from its social context that relation turns into an abstraction without any content of its own.[36]

An emphasis on the concrete ethical obligations resulting from a person's relation to God cannot be without "the dense social texture," "concrete determination," or "horizontal dimension." This is so especially in contradistinction to "the mystic's impatience in attempting to achieve a more 'direct' approach to God."[37] A remark in another commentary, this time on *The Concept of Anxiety*, offers the following precision, that here we are considering the dangers of "religious infinity," not of the "eternal": "For it [religious infinity] may carry the religious person away from himself and his earthly task into an attitude of mystical indifference toward the finite."[38]

The same basic dynamic relating the three essential elements of religion, the self, the transcendent, and the mediation between them, is explored in somewhat different conceptual terms in Dupré's publications on phenomenology. I will consider five articles and the introduction to a selection of material translated from the works of Henry Duméry, beginning with a relatively late article which gives us helpful clues to reading the earlier materials. In 1992 the problems for investigation are stated as follows:

> (1) the relation between the psycho-empirical religious experience and its transcendent object; (2) the relation between the transcendental and egological reduction, on the one hand, and the *giveness* [*sic*] of a transcendent revelation, on the other; (3) the relation between the phenomenological conception(s) of truth and what religion considers to be its own truth.[39]

36. Louis Dupré, "*The Sickness unto Death*: A Critique of the Modern Age," in *International Kierkegaard Commentary: The Sickness unto Death*, ed. Robert L. Perkins (Macon: Mercer University Press, 1987), pp. 85-106, here p. 102.

37. Dupré, "*Sickness unto Death*," p. 103.

38. Louis Dupré, "Of Time and Eternity in Kierkegaard's *Concept of Anxiety*," *Faith and Philosophy* 1 (1984): 160-76, here p. 165.

39. Louis Dupré, "Phenomenology of Religion: Limits and Possibilities," *American Catholic Philosophical Quarterly* 66 (1992): 175-88, here p. 176.

Not surprisingly, these problems are consistent with the investigations in the early articles. However, just as temporality has come to the fore in the conversation with Kierkegaard, so here in the conversation with phenomenologists it is the role of symbols, the means of mediation, which has a particular prominence in the exploration of each problem. Though experience and object are related in religion on the basis of an uncompromisable givenness of the transcendent and an originating passivity of experience, the relation is a mediated one. Equally important is the truth that however much it is through symbolic expressions that the presence of one to the other is realized, interpreted, and preserved,

> unless he keeps in mind that the religious believer regards his symbols as in some way "revealed," the phenomenologist will miss what the religious believer considers to be essential in faith.[40]

The nature of the transcendent, precisely as transcendent, will always require that it be given priority both as to content and method of study, a priority which is expressed in the concept "revelation."

Thus, the active role of the believer in projecting symbols, and especially in the religious use of language, can be reduced to purely transcendental activity only at the risk of falsifying the very act and content of such intentionality. As well, Dupré hints at the determining social context of religious tradition from which the believer receives an already established field of symbols and interpretation as the basis of any further representations of the transcendent. Perhaps one of the greatest confusions in current appreciations of this priority of external over internal context in religion is the confusion of the givenness of the transcendent with the givenness of the community of belief and its symbolic forms. That confusion is just as troublesome as a former reduction of the transcendent into the subjective activity of meaning-giving. The first and second problems noted above come together in the most difficult case for phenomenological investigation: the founding symbol of an historic religion. What accounts for the absoluteness of a given symbol as a revealed symbol? The question is obviously only evaded by assuming either that the Absolute is intrinsically inexpressible or that all religious symbols are merely projections. Both presumptions are unsatisfactory to the believer. Though Dupré still finds much clarity in Henri Duméry's phenomenology of religion, he does not find there an adequate answer to this question. The paradox of religious faith, we have noted before, still remains to be investigated:

40. Dupré, "Phenomenology of Religion," p. 179.

To the believer, the ability to "see" is itself transcendently granted as part of a manifestation that appears entirely given. And yet that revealed interpretation itself presupposes a human act of conveying meaning.[41]

How does this assertion of receptivity affect the final problem, the question of the truth which religion claims for itself? Alluding only briefly to what we have seen him develop elsewhere, Dupré considers how phenomenology has proposed a theory of truth as disclosure, revisiting the theory of illumination familiar to ancient and medieval Western thought. Neither a correspondence theory which might render the transcendent another "fact" among others nor a coherence theory which might reduce the transcendent to a system of symbols and their interpretation is adequate to the surplus of reality which appears, with its own evidence, surpassing both the intending subject and the revealing symbol.

With this most recent article on phenomenology's usefulness in the study of religion as our guide, let me return to Dupré's early articles, with special attention to his introduction to the writings of Henri Duméry. Dupré's discussion of Husserl's *Logical Investigations* and *Ideas*[42] includes much helpful clarification concerning intentionality, truth, and how both relate to a notion of objectivity. A contemporaneous article on revelation poses the problems succinctly:

> There seem to be at least two requirements for an understanding of the religious act which phenomenology, insofar as it remains pure phenomenology, is hard put to fulfill: one is the maintenance of the transcendence of the religious object; the other, the insistence on its real existence (over and above its intentional being).[43]

Consciousness as intentional experience must not be reduced to either a correspondence or a psychological theory. In the former the object is never really "of" the mind, and in the latter it is too much "of" the mind. The object and the experience of the object cannot be distinct nor simply coincident. Husserl employs the expression "immanent objectivity" to deny a division into experienced object and experiencing intentional subjectivity. Dupré summarizes:

41. Dupré, "Phenomenology of Religion," p. 183.

42. Louis Dupré, "Husserl's Notion of Truth — Via Media between Idealism and Realism? Four Lectures on the *Logical Investigations* and *Ideas*," in *Teaching Thomism Today*, ed. George F. Mclean (Washington, D.C.: Catholic University Press, 1963), pp. 150-82.

43. Louis Dupré, "Philosophy of Religion and Revelation: Autonomous Reflection vs. Theophany," *International Philosophical Quarterly* 4 (1964): 499-513, here p. 501. Parts of this article also appear in Louis Dupré, *A Dubious Heritage: Studies in the Philosophy of Religion after Kant* (New York: Paulist Press, 1977). For this quotation see p. 76.

The object *belongs* to consciousness itself; it is not outside. It is not even an independent reality within consciousness itself. Rather, it is a moment of consciousness which is constituted as soon as consciousness itself is constituted. It is obvious that if one defines epistemological realism by the *independence* of the object from the act, Husserl can no longer be called a realist. But his immanentism of the object by no means weakens his notion of intentionality.[44]

Next, Dupré unfolds Husserl's notion of double truth, which he finds to be a return to Leibniz's distinction between *"vérités de raison"* and *"vérités de fait"*:

> All truth, therefore, is ultimately based on an intuition of *"die Sachen selbst"* — the "things" themselves. But in one case the intuition itself constitutes the evidence whose ideal correlate is truth — in the other the fulfilled meaning is only the starting point for an ideating abstraction which will give us the truth *in itself*. In the first case we have a factual, contingent knowledge — in the second "Erkenntnis vom Grunde," necessary and universal knowledge.[45]

The understanding of both intentionality and truth, then, leads to the problem of objectivity, not as to whether there is an object — that has already been dealt with by intentionality and the two kinds of truth — but rather its transcendence.

In another article Dupré considers more specifically Husserl's notion of God and faith. Though Husserl understood the question of God to be the fundamental question of philosophy, he did not treat it systematically. As a problem of teleology, the question of God arises from the radical contingency of consciousness. As beyond empirical beings, the self (and the collectivity of selves) is absolute in one sense, but as self-constituting ego it is in need of an infinite telos grounding its forward-moving, universal intentionality. But the problem remains, for Husserl as for any "argument" for God from teleology, whether this telos is an immanent part of the teleological movement itself; that is, whether the self is, finally, radically contingent. This question would require an investigation of causality, which Husserl declines to engage in.

Whether the infinite telos is truly transcendent to consciousness remains a question to be answered only by faith. As belief in teleology, religious faith offers salvation which, to quote Dupré,

> consists in the bestowal of meaning upon those purely contingent and unnecessary events which are the warp and woof of life and the despair of

44. Dupré, "Husserl's Notion of Truth," p. 157.
45. Dupré, "Husserl's Notion of Truth," pp. 160-61.

speculative reason. But the redeeming insight of faith is given to man only as he turns into himself.[46]

Dupré does not pursue these aspects of faith here, but does note what little Husserl does offer by way of a definition of faith:

> Rather than a blind instinct it would seem to be an intuition passively acquired like the passive synthesis of sense perception. Faith, then, turns out to be some insight, neither rationally structured nor rationally justified, that life, despite irrationality, suffering and death, has been arranged in an orderly fashion by a transcendent principle.[47]

Less than ten years later, Dupré unites the two strands of conversation we have considered so far, with Kierkegaard and Husserl, drawing together insights on temporality and symbolism in order to specify more clearly the nature of the religious self and its relation to God both transcendent and revealed:

> The experience of radical historicity together with an insistent perception of lasting selfhood evoke the expectation of an atemporal present at the origin of existence. Thus to know oneself is to remember oneself, and to remember oneself entirely is to remember one's origin. At this point immanence turns into transcendence, and autobiography into confession.[48]

Moreover, there is a harmonious relation in Christianity between this mystical piety and historical faith. Historical events and determinate symbols become the occasion for the turn inward, for the recollection neither merely remembers an historical past event of salvation nor wishfully anticipates a future consummation. Rather, the self enters through memory into the eternal, the still and silent center, in which it can "hear" the revelation of God and thereby become the contemporary of Christ. Obviously, more complex reflection on this unity of the mystical and historical is left for theological reflection proper, but what is clear is Dupré's confidence that such a unity can be achieved and that it will occur by means and because of the achievement of authentic interiority.

During this period of writing, Dupré has begun to amass the wealth of material necessary for the systematic treatment of philosophy of religion to be found in *The Other Dimension*. In fact, the introductory remarks to the collec-

---

46. Louis Dupré, "Husserl's Thought on God and Faith," *Philosophy and Phenomenological Research* 29 (1968): 201-15, here p. 213. See also Dupré, *A Dubious Heritage*, p. 90.

47. Dupré, "Husserl's Thought," p. 214.

48. Louis Dupré, *Transcendent Selfhood: The Loss and Rediscovery of the Inner Life* (New York: Seabury Press, 1976), p. 73. See also Louis Dupré, "Alienation and Redemption through Time and Memory: An Essay on Religious Time Consciousness," *Journal of the American Academy of Religion* 43 (1975): 671-79, here pp. 675f.

tion of writings of Henry Duméry give us an inchoate statement of the method and plan of *The Other Dimension*. Though brief, the preface contains four remarks about the underlying principles of *The Other Dimension*. First, in naming Duméry's main significance as a philosopher of religion, Dupré carefully lays out the believer's distrust of philosophy's reductionist attempts at "explaining" the religious attitude, particularly

> when philosophers first constructed arguments to prove God's existence and invented names to describe his essence *independently of the religious experience* within which the very thought of God originated.[49]

The second point explores why this is so; namely, because religious experience itself never fully reveals its own foundation even though it generates its own religiously authoritative and intrinsic interpretation. We have seen these two points stated elsewhere as, on the one hand, the tendency of philosophy to construct its own coherent and self-supporting system, turning philosophy of religion into religion, and on the other hand the tendency of religion toward gnosticism, toward attempting to become a philosophical system.[50] While philosophy must maintain a certain distance from the claims of the believer, it cannot engage in philosophy of religion except by attending to the believer's experience and interpretation, thus ensuring an appropriately grounded philosophy of religion rather than an autonomous philosophical construction. Third, as in the case of Duméry, attention to one religion and one tradition within that religion, namely, the Catholic experience of Christian faith, does not narrow excessively the philosopher's study, but

> [i]n probing the Catholic's response to a transcendent call Duméry reaches the universal depth where every man's being is related to the transcendent. The fact that this relationship is expressed in the specific terms of one tradition rather than in generalities makes Duméry's work more concrete and therefore also more catholic in the original sense of the term.[51]

Fourth and finally in this preface, Dupré in very brief form alerts us to the need to know the history of (1) the critics of religion (such as Hume, Kant, and Freud — to whom other names will be added); (2) the philosophers attempting to reorient the study of religion by exploring the origins of religion (Schleiermacher, Kierkegaard, Newman, Blondel); (3) both the importance and limitations of phenomenology as a method of discovering the meaning of the religious

---

49. Henri Duméry, *Faith and Reflection*, ed. Louis Dupré (New York: Herder and Herder, 1968), p. x.

50. Dupré, "Philosophy of Religion and Revelation," p. 508.

51. Duméry, p. xiii.

act (as in the work of Scheler, van der Leeuw, Eliade); and finally (4) the contribution of the American pragmatists James, Royce, and Hocking (though Dupré will not explore these authors at length).

Following the preface, the introduction to the Duméry collection develops at greater length what will become more thoroughly thematic in the third period of Dupré's writing. Neither the human person, as essentially freedom, nor God, as beyond all determinations, can be objectified. The believer, though unable to possess God as absolute truth, is not thereby exempt from the search for value and truth. Even as a way of salvation religion remains an encounter of human freedom with divine freedom. Revelation, however, is not excluded but rather is appreciated in its complexity by this refusal of objectivism. God can speak and act toward us, but not without entering into our realm of freedom and hence of interpretation, a point particularly pertinent to the problems associated with the most recent version of the search for the historical Jesus. In summary:

> To *understand* the religious meaning of Christ, it is not sufficient to register the historical facts of his existence. . . . The most essential characteristic of the religious object is that it must be received in a religious way, that is, that it must be *given* a religious meaning.[52]

A short piece entitled "The God of History" is useful for its clear articulation of the seeming dilemma in a theory of revelation which holds together the symbolic, human, and thus historical character of revelation with the authoritative character of the symbolic precisely as what *reveals* the transcendent. Any attempt to detach meaning from symbolic embodiment will result in either a trivialization of the symbol (as merely transient or subjectively occasioned) or of that which it reveals, the transcendent. We have already noted that the possibility of true ontological novelty may indeed be the result of encounter with the transcendent, with the disclosure of Being. In this early work Dupré already hints at such a possibility, albeit in distinctly Christian terms, as the Holy Spirit at work.

In the collection to appear in 1977, *A Dubious Heritage,* six articles on authors and matters of method from this early period are brought together, somewhat revised from their original appearance. In addition to those on Kierkegaard, Husserl, and Duméry already discussed, there are three on Hegel, Schleiermacher, and Blondel. These essays are the occasion to continue exploring the problems he posed in the introduction to the Duméry collection concerning the hesitation of the believer in face of philosophy, the particular character of religious experience, and the sometimes overextended pretensions of

---

52. Duméry, pp. xxx-xxxi.

philosophy. I follow these problems from Schleiermacher, through Hegel, to Blondel.

Schleiermacher is studied because of both the similarity of his description of religious experience to the work of phenomenology and also his definition of the self and its religious dimension as the coincidence of subject and object:

> In a sense, then, religion is nothing but a constant inward movement of consciousness, a continuous search for interiority. This interiority, however, should not be confused with immanence, as we will see further, for it is precisely in the interiority of consciousness that we become aware of the transcendent.[53]

After analyzing his definition of religion in *On Religion,* Dupré poses three questions about Schleiermacher's notion of an immediate consciousness of absolute dependence as the transcendent ground of all human consciousness: (1) Is religion compatible with reflective consciousness? (2) Is there an object to this feeling? and (3) Can the feeling have symbolic expression? The answer to all three is yes, but with a necessary metaphysical presumption, not merely a psychological or even phenomenological one:

> What made him (Schleiermacher) consider feeling to be the essence of the religious experience? The answer lies in the fact that the feeling of dependence reveals the transcendent ground of self-consciousness, the point where consciousness is no longer opposed to, but coincides with, reality.[54]

Dupré faults Schleiermacher with not seeing that the intrinsic dynamism of the religious act itself, as it attempts to break through the symbolic sensuous form it adopts, requires reflection:

> The religious act is thus both an *ekstasis* and an interiorization process. It is both immediate and reflective: Although it continually tends to split up into a subject-object opposition, it never does so.[55]

It is in Hegel that one finds an appreciation of this inextricable move from symbol to thought, from representation to reflection. Though the article "Hegel's Religion as Representation"[56] was first published in 1973 and therefore

---

53. Louis Dupré, "Toward a Revaluation of Schleiermacher's *Philosophy of Religion,*" *Journal of Religion* 44 (1964): 97-112, here p. 103. See also Dupré, *A Dubious Heritage,* p. 15.

54. Dupré, "Toward a Revaluation," p. 107. See also Dupré, *A Dubious Heritage,* p. 21.

55. Dupré, "Toward a Revaluation," p. 111. See also Dupré, *A Dubious Heritage,* p. 27.

56. Louis Dupré, "Religion as Representation," in *The Legacy of Hegel, Proceedings of the Marquette Hegel Symposium, 1970,* ed. J. O'Malley, K. Algozin, H. Kainz, and L. Rice (The Hague: Martinus Nijhoff, 1973), pp. 137-43. See also Dupré, *A Dubious Heritage,* pp. 53-72.

falls outside the preparation for *The Other Dimension*, properly speaking, I mention it here since there seems little doubt that Dupré had already thought the matter through. The article begins with a presentation of the historical development of reflection on the work of the imagination from Kant, through Fichte, to Schelling. Dupré sees this movement as a preparation for a nuanced understanding of the role of images, symbols, and narratives as the necessary means of mediation which, for Hegel, remain always insufficient to bear the fullness of Spirit itself in its own self-manifestation. The inwardization of these symbols is essential to their proper role in religion, as well as to their availability to philosophical reflection. Hegel thus provides a step beyond Schleiermacher, confirming the use of symbols and their inwardization.

Finally, the article on Blondel might stand as one last reiteration of the cautions and deep presuppositions which Dupré holds before his own mind as he moves toward his systematic presentation of the entire field of philosophy of religion. However comprehensive and detailed his exposition will be, he agrees with Blondel that philosophy is on the one hand limited in its reflection on the transcendent, yet on the other hand is impelled toward an investigation of its self-manifestation. That limitation, Dupré recognizes, includes Blondel's own effort to "bridge the natural order with the supernatural by means of action, (which) will strike the religious man as a voluntaristic immanentism, and the philosopher as an abdication of reason."[57] Leaving aside whether this criticism of Blondel overlooks the way in which the person of faith precisely *enacts* faith as the most rudimentary interpretation of it, one can appreciate its emphasis once again on the profound inadequacy of any attempt on the part of philosophy to make purely immanent the transcendent, much less to claim to explicate it exhaustively. One final summary remark:

> According to Blondel, this possibility (of the supernatural) is one which the philosopher *must* consider. Yet no amount of reflection can ever transform it into an actuality. Faith alone can gain entrance to a supernatural reality, but faith itself is ultimately supernatural and, in that respect, beyond experience. The paradox of faith is precisely that it affirms more than it can experience and that the affirmation itself, insofar as it is supernatural, lies beyond experience.[58]

However much Dupré has engaged in the careful task of sorting out the nature of the religious dimension of human life in this first period, there arises an all-encompassing question which may indeed have had a very particular

---

57. Louis Dupré, "Reflections on Blondel's Religious Philosophy," *New Scholasticism* 40 (1966): 3-22, here p. 18. See also Dupré, *A Dubious Heritage*, p. 106.

58. Dupré, "Reflections on Blondel's Religious Philosophy," p. 14. Ses also Dupré, *A Dubious Heritage*, pp. 102-3.

origin for him, but which expresses a deep uncertainty shared by believers and unbelievers alike. In his own words:

> Is modern man's world view still reconcilable with a religious attitude? If so, does such an attitude have anything in common with religion as it has been traditionally conceived?[59]

This is not simply a question of fact, but a philosophical question about the nature of religion itself and how believers themselves, in living out the religious attitude in modern culture, have both preserved yet transformed religion itself. Four notions are required to unfold an answer to the basic question: the sacred, estrangement and alienation, faith and human inventiveness, and religious symbols. Though he will have cautions about its use in later writings, here Dupré employs the term "sacred" to name the transcendent as it is experienced in contradistinction from the profane, and seemingly entirely lost as any form of direct experience in contemporary life. Thus the term "secular" names the world as we experience it, no longer in dialectical relation to the transcendent, no longer the place where the sacred is revealed and the profane relativized. Thus to say that we are "estranged from the sacred" because we are "*alienated* from (our) own ultimate reality"[60] is to say both more and less than traditional religiosity, Christianity in particular, means by saying that individual human beings are fallen, are sinners. What is being asserted here is that an entire culture has obviated the need for the transcendent, such that the question of alienation, put positively, is: "Can religion survive in a cultural environment which no longer needs it as an integrating factor?"[61]

Nor is this consciousness of alienation yet another phase of traditional negative theology, a hesitancy to speak about the transcendent based in reverence and awe.[62] It is a sense of alienation which is only potentially religious since it is rooted primarily in an assertion of human autonomy and inventiveness, in an increasing conviction that human being is the source and end of all meaning-giving activity. It takes the form of a Promethean hope, an ironic transformation of the Judeo-Christian hope in "an eschatological intervention of the transcendent."[63] Though Dupré does not explore the notion at length, it

59. Louis Dupré, "Secular Man and His Religion," *Proceedings of the American Catholic Philosophical Association* (1968): 78-96, here p. 78.

60. Louis Dupré, "Religion in a Secular World," in *Human Values in a Secular World,* ed. Robert Z. Apostol (New York: Humanities Press, 1970), pp. 11-20; see p. 13.

61. Dupré, "Religion in a Secular World," p. 11.

62. See Louis Dupré, "The Problem of Divine Transcendence in Secular Theology," in *The Spirit and Power of Christian Secularity,* ed. Albert Schlitzer (Notre Dame: University of Notre Dame Press, 1970), pp. 100-112.

63. Louis Dupré, "Hope and Transcendence," in *The God Experience,* ed. Joseph Whelan (New York: Newman Press, 1971), pp. 217-25, here p. 219.

is intriguing to consider whether all forms of inventiveness, of symbolic and interpretive activity as well as the invention of cultural artifacts of all kinds, are efforts to overcome alienation of all sorts. In naming and symbolizing that alienation as an estrangement from the transcendent, the religious person engages that paradox which we have already seen in our discussion of Kierkegaard and of phenomenology's efforts to describe the religious dimension. If human efforts to overcome alienation, the works of culture, are to succeed, they must be grounded not in a merely ideal future, in an ideal solution, in ideologically impassioned human inventiveness, but in response to the self-manifestation of the transcendent. It is the paradox of giving up human freedom in order to be in relation with the power of integration, of reconciliation of opposites, which is grounded in the nature of the transcendent itself, yet in doing so of being invited precisely into the activity of religion itself, its symbolizing, interpreting, enacting activities which Dupré identifies by the term "faith." For contemporary believers in Western society (and perhaps increasingly elsewhere), it is also the dilemma of being within a culture which disallows precisely this form of human inventiveness.

Efforts have been made to greet both paradox and dilemma. Dupré's historical works have already alerted us to many forms of accommodation to the situation on the part of apologists for the religious dimension. He himself will not follow either extremes of reductionist theories or simplistic reassertions of traditional religiosity. Throughout these articles on the crisis of contemporary religion, it is both a crisis of the culture and of the believer which he envisages. It is no surprise, then, that he eschews both the search for a fixed essence of religion and an a priori subjective ground for it. Religion is inherently dialectical, its terms flexible and relative to each other, no fixed denotative activity of language being possible precisely because of the nature of religion as a relation to the transcendent.[64]

Let me conclude this section with a summary statement which prefigures the contents of *The Other Dimension*. Religion interprets alienation as estrangement from the sacred which is equally an awareness of being drawn beyond experience, not to an object but to an intimate presence. This presence is realized in a unity between subjective disposition and object more intimate than any other act, being an act of faith, which names God in and through symbols, myth, and ritual. Thus, this "other dimension" of human existence remains both paradoxical and inherently dialectical.

64. Dupré, "Secular Man and His Religion," p. 83.

II.3. Threshold to the Second Period:
"A Search for the Meaning of Religious Attitudes" *(1972)*

The Other Dimension itself is a far too complex and complete text to study here in depth. Therefore, I have been selective in the following discussion of it, choosing to concentrate on the first half of the text.[65]

The introduction provides some important clues to the contents and method of the book. As we have already seen, Dupré studies religion as the attitude of faith, which does not simply passively receive the transcendent as the sacred made manifest but actively accepts, interprets, and lives a human relationship with the transcendent. Thus he distances himself from the then current radical or predictive studies of religion, from efforts at either constructive or destructive analysis, and proposes rather a sympathetic investigation which nevertheless maintains a critical philosophical distance, being the work not of a believer per se but of the philosopher. He notes the authors upon whom he is dependent and the singular importance of Hegel. He reasserts the origin of the concept of God from within the religious experience and proposes the dialectical movement of religion from dependence upon yet estrangement from transcendent reality, and the self as well, to the efforts to gain a new integration with the transcendent.

Chapter 1 locates an understanding of faith within the contemporary experience of uncertainty — of questioning, ambiguity, unease, anxiety — which marks not only the state of the self but the character of the presence, and absence, of the transcendent within Western civilization. Using the categories of symbol, dialectic relation, and the notions of sacred and profane, Dupré contrasts the basic form of the undivided life experience, in which religion is not separated from social and cultural structures, with the contemporary situation which does not possess such a harmony, and may or may not elicit a religious attitude. If religion exists for contemporary men and women, it does so as faith, exhibiting an element of decision which sets it off from premodern experience.

The following three sections explore the character of such religious faith. The first summarizes faith as passive, located in feeling yet not lacking inten-

---

65. This limitation is not just pragmatic. With Dupré I wanted to focus on the question of proper criteria and procedures for the study of religion rather than specific religious doctrines. Second, although the chapters of the second half (on God, creation, sin, and salvation) bridge philosophical and theological worlds, they would seem to lead to theological rather than philosophical study. It is important to note that Dupré's work on spirituality and mysticism belies the distinction between philosophy and theology, for the appeal of spirituality consists, Dupré asserts, in offering a realm of experience closer at hand to our secular culture and to the philosopher who keeps a distance from the theological (and moral) discourse of believer.

tionality, and differing from the metaphysical intuition of ultimate meaning, a notion satisfying intellectual curiosity rather than a symbol offering salvation. The second section explores faith as an active, though not theoretical, insight into the presence of an "object." It is not esoteric knowledge nor simple "belief," but rather "total existence" which involves volitional, emotional, and cognitive elements as an acknowledgment of the presence of the transcendent. Thus the third and final section recaptures the same characteristic of totality which the start of this chapter found to be structurally identical with so-called primitive religion. It asserts that faith, for the religious person, is a gift, something received and not invented, a situation difficult for the modern person to accept. Likewise, the very inwardness of contemporary faith as a more self-preoccupied and aware faithfulness can become a limitation of faith if it sets aside its necessary external, social manifestations and enactments. An integration of both the internal and external aspects of faith is what must be sought.

Thus the next chapter considers at some length the typical contemporary misunderstandings of religious faith. They are to be found, Dupré suggests, in scientific, anthropological, psychological, and phenomenological approaches to the question of the nature and content of religion. The objective and the genetic fallacy both receive attention, as does the reduction of religion to its subjective activities. Phenomenology is appreciated as a method which avoids these reductions, but a caution is registered as to the limitations of even phenomenology. The critique of this chapter reduces to a single rule: whatever method is used, the philosopher must respect the self-presentation of the religious experience by the person of faith. No simplistic reduction to origins or subjective states, no rejection because of lack of an empirical object, and, once again, no substitution of the self-articulation of religion itself by any method with pretensions to "correct," let alone invent, the religious attitude and its intended object will be acceptable for a philosophy of religion.

Chapter 3 asserts the more positive relations between faith and philosophy. On the one hand, philosophy itself can be shown to have mythico-religious origins and a long history of symbiosis with Christian theology. This history, however, neither authorizes religion to dominate philosophy nor emancipates philosophy in the form of metaphysics to generate a positive content for the transcendent, namely, a distinct god. Dupré also cautions against a too easy linking of the movement of the human self toward the transcendent to a purely philosophical affirmation of the personal or benevolent character of God. What little he has to say about arguments for the existence of God is to be found here and is fundamentally negative as to their ability to prove anything. Philosophy may well articulate the rudimentary awareness of the transcendent present in humanity, but it must accept the actual determinations of the forms of participatory knowledge which only the experience of the religious person can provide. He ends the chapter with a view from the other direction; namely, faith's need for reflection. Philosophical reflection can aid faith's own inherent dynamism to greater clarity and vision, though such a cooperation holds dangers for both. Philosophy must not too easily accept a "religious" solution to its metaphysical search, and faith must not substitute speculation for living experience. Hegel is once again a prime example of the delicate balance and the inherent problems of a philosophy of religion and of a religious philosophy.

Chapters 1-3 on methodology thus form the first portion of the introductory half of the text, passing from issues of verification to the primacy of participatory knowledge in the study of religion. Such knowledge nevertheless remains essentially mediate knowledge, and chapters 4-6 can be read together as one extended essay on the matter of symbolism, of mediation in religion. Symbols and myths in language and art: these are the everyday stuff of the life of religious faith, and as such are the proper immanent objects of a philosophical study of religion which bases itself on an investigation of the religious dimension of human experience. Once again, Hegel plays an important role in unfolding the character of symbols, their work of making present that which is symbolized. Equally important is the negativity of such symbols, concealing more than they represent and reveal. Language is considered briefly here, as the symbol par excellence, though full discussion is left to the next chapter. Functioning specifically as interpretation, language can never be entirely divorced from other symbols or able to conceptualize fully their overabundance of meaning. However, even if symbolic deeds are temporally, if not logically, first in religious symbolism, religious language, as verbal symbols which interpret, is ultimately the more adequate form of symbolism in religion. A discussion of sacraments and sacrifice, then, completes the fourth chapter, though the second half of *The Other Dimension* might have profited from a full chapter on rite and sacrament, on the social and institutional embodiments of religion, before passing from the discussion of salvation to mysticism. The omission is a significant one.

Chapter 5 on the symbolism of words reiterates the fundamental importance of philosophical language for religion, in its work of conceptualizing what nondiscursive symbols (and language) represent, thereby not only referring to the real, but explicitly and directly being able to conceptualize the transcendent. Before such explication can occur, however, we must revisit those philosophical options which are not compatible with the actual functioning of religious language, this time in the form of theories of language use, principally of the present century, which unduly delimit the possibilities of language and offer a reductive interpretation of it. In considering the characteristics of religious language, Dupré cautions against too simple a limitation of its nature to the apparent oddity of such usage or its doubly paradoxical assertions, speaking of the eternal in time and the objective as essentially subjective. Both oddity and paradox can function effectively only because of the dependence of the religious use of language on ordinary language, a dialectical relation through negation and transcendence. Moreover, the supposed oddity is not the result of actually referring to some separate reality in a cryptic fashion. Not surprisingly, it is in its activity as symbol that religious language shows its basic resistance to the entire range of misunderstandings that recent philosophy has proposed as theories of religious language.

Thus the final section of this chapter, "The Symbolic Nature of Religious Language," brings forward the discussion of the previous chapter. It does so, however, with an all too brief discussion of the typological interpretation of the Christian Scriptures. The section is a valuable insight into what might have been developed if Dupré had been in conversation at this point with those attempting to retrieve the great tradition's forms of exegesis and interpretation of the Christian Bible, forms which had flourished before the modern preoccupation with scientific exegesis and the loss of credibility and the consequent inattention to varying forms of interpretation. However, the section quickly passes from a consideration of "symbolic" as "typological" to wonderment whether the symbolic function is sufficient for religious affirmations in the present age. Though a critique of Hegel is not mentioned, one can read it beneath Dupré's limitation of the effectiveness of discursive language, and a preference for negative theology's rendering of discursive language as symbolic. He states clearly that the priority of the symbolic is based upon two essential principles: the subjective involvement of the religious speaker in the religious use of language, and the transcendent nature of its referent. Again, it is intriguing to consider whether this section, along with the appendix on religious art which follows, might have profitably been put in conjunction with the previous chapter's discussion of sacraments into a fuller discussion between the later chapters' consideration of salvation and mysticism. Both proclamation and interpretation of the Scriptures, as well as sacramental actions, occupy the realm of liturgy or worship, the realm par excellence of the symbolic as effective. Such a placement would also allow for a fuller philosophical reflection on the nature of association in communities by religious believers.

Chapter 6 completes the first half of the book and its laying of the groundwork for the chapters which follow. It concerns the language of myth as originating language coincident with symbols and ritual, its survival in the progress of human society, and its continuing role in contemporary religion. It defends myth against reductionist theories and explores its perdurance in purely secular forms. The question of the survival of myth in contemporary religion occasions a lengthy engagement with Bultmann in particular, in which Dupré proposes the maintenance of myth but the demythologization of faith. Once again, the importance of the relation of time to every aspect of religion is specified in the role of myth as reaching beyond history alone as the arena of religious reality.

The groundwork has been laid, and now the particularized content of a philosophy of religion can be considered. The chapters which follow, 7 through

12, parallel what Christian systematic theology would discuss in its traditional doctrines: revelation, God, creation, sin and salvation, union with God. What is missing is a discussion of the church, though the conclusion of chapter 11 on salvation offers a few paragraphs on the subject of the community, making a possible transition to a fuller discussion.

Of primary and central importance is the seventh chapter, on revelation. What is defined and clarified here depends upon the distinctions already made in the previous six chapters and gives a foundation to what follows in the next five chapters. This chapter also shows the abiding importance for the entire argument of Hegel on the one hand and Kierkegaard on the other. Perhaps illustrative of an entire book's argument is the following quotation:

> By themselves symbols, ideas, or events, however unusual, cannot point beyond the immanent universe to which they belong. Christians believe that Jesus was God. Yet any attempt to prove this on the basis of his deeds and words is doomed to failure. For the transcendent as such does not appear. What makes words and deeds surpass their intramundane appearance is the constitutive act of faith. Faith alone transforms events into religious events and words into revelations. Only the eyes of the believer perceive the revealed as revealed.[66]

Given the central importance thus far in the text of the symbolic, participatory character of religious experience, it is not surprising that revelation is not the communication of information in propositional form; rather, it is the self-manifestation of the transcendent in events, deeds, words. The problem for the philosopher of religion is to resist forms of reductionism on the one hand and to go beyond a merely negative theology of revelation which asserts the utter incomprehensibility of the transcendent. This requires assertion of four principles: (1) if God reveals, then God is necessarily a revealing God; (2) if what is revealed is truly "received," then the revelation acquires a genuinely contingent character in its "otherness"; (3) revelation as from and about God cannot be, as revelation, less than a presence of God, a communication of God's own self (i.e., not a mere message); and (4) the dialectic between *(2)* and *(3)* poses the question whether revelation, then, is a total manifestation of God, whether there remains anything of the transcendent still hidden. In the first three Hegel offers the best conceptualization of the matter, but in the fourth Dupré takes distance from Hegel's assertion of a full and complete manifestation of God, a complete intelligibility of both the total emptying of God into the finite and the transformation of the finite into the infinite in the activity of philosophical thought. Dupré maintains in the end the hiddenness of God.

66. Louis Dupré, *The Other Dimension: A Search for the Meaning of Religious Attitudes* (New York: Doubleday, 1972), p. 294.

In the next section on faith as the indispensable correlate to revelation, Dupré uses Kierkegaard to contradict Hegel's notion of a full manifestation chiefly through Kierkegaard's use of the notion of paradox. Hence the passage quoted above marks the transition from the first part of the text which clears the ground for a philosophy of religion to the second part which constitutes the unfolding of the concrete interpretation which is given to the revelatory events through the interpretive acts and words of the person of faith. Thus the final sections of this chapter discuss the relation of revelation to history (it consists of historical events, but not without interpretation), and the concomitant problems of relativity and permanence (the symbol itself, indispensable to revelation and its interpretation, transcends the present and requires continuity in interpretation). Both sections renew the importance of a discussion of time in relation to revelation and salvation, and, more particularly for Christianity, the relation of Scripture, tradition, and magisterial interpretation.

In each of the remaining five chapters, Dupré discusses a notion essential to religion, moving from its availability to philosophical explication, through the limitation of that explication by the actual dynamics of the religious dimension of life, to the details of the requirements and history of the religious interpretation of each notion or aspect. The reader passes through the necessary movement from God and God's nature to creation, religious alienation, salvation, and union with God. In each case, Dupré weaves together philosophical and Christian theological argument and interpretation, though analysis of examples from other religions is always in conversation with Christianity. Suffice it to say that Dupré ranges across the available classic and contemporary sources, no doubt selectively and in service of his basic argument and principles, but nonetheless in a manner which makes *The Other Dimension* a summit and watershed in contemporary philosophy of religion. Nearly twenty-five years of scholarship has passed since its publication, and Dupré himself has not sought to reconsider the major lines of his argument or the details of its exposition. As the next part of this essay will show, one path of development, i.e., the explicitly theological one, is not followed, and certain matters presently left unattended to are given voice during the next decade.

Let me conclude with two summary remarks. Is this a definitive work, or as Dupré himself wonders at the end of his introduction, is it just an interim work needing the further labor of "filling the gaps and correcting possible errors"?[67] He continues to write, no doubt, and both supplements and modifies several points. However, *The Other Dimension* clearly sets certain requirements for the philosophy of religion which Dupré has not set aside. What qualifications he does offer remain within the parameters he has now prescribed. A second remark concerns inventiveness rather than consistency. From the texts so far

---

67. Dupré, *The Other Dimension*, p. 12.

considered, where might one have expected his investigations now to take him? I would hazard the guess that it is both the strength of and the inherent difficulties involved in his recognition of the centrality of symbols in religious experience, language, and practice that lead through the next decade into his present investigation of the origins and effects of modernity. On the one hand, were we to have explored the latter half of *The Other Dimension,* the conversation would have become increasingly involved with Christian theology, its sources and contemporary problems. Such an investigation would have to focus, I think, on the rules internal to faith (Christianity in this case) and their practical embodiment in contemporary culture. On the other hand, he does not remain within the arid regions of merely methodological considerations either. His continuing investigation is neither a narrow preoccupation with criticism of insufficient methods and their results nor a limitation of his questions to the problems of the self and its religious dimension. Dupré now begins an investigation of religion and its symbols which takes him deep into the roots of contemporary culture.

III. Naming the Loss of Transcendence (1973-83)

The passage from the first to the second period of writing has its most obvious manifestation in the publication of *The Other Dimension.* That actual changes in one's thinking and writing hardly correspond with such arbitrary dates as those of publication is obvious, and I have already taken the privilege of violating such rigidity by being somewhat synchronic in my presentation despite its promised diachronic structure. The fluidity of a writer's life may indeed be compromised by periodization, and in Dupré's case this transition period is an excellent example. Two books appear which gather together materials from both before and after 1972, and toward the end of the decade it becomes difficult for the reader to be sure just where a moment of significant change takes place. As will become clear, I consider the contents of the *Fourth Annual Moreau Lecture,* "The Spiritual Crisis of Our Culture," to mark the transition, though that content is found in fragments elsewhere as well.

III.1. Acknowledging Kant's Limits

For philosophers of religion approaching Dupré's work, whether they are sympathetic to his basic principles or not, a notable omission in the vast range of topics and authors he considers is concentrated attention on the work of Immanuel Kant. There certainly is by no means complete neglect, and *The Other*

Dimension makes sufficient and pertinent reference to Kant throughout, as do Dupré's articles evaluating arguments for the existence of God. Moreover, a few vital paragraphs introducing *A Dubious Heritage* give essential, if brief, comments. Whatever problems Kant may have engendered for the subsequent discussion of religion, his project of transcendental critique succeeded in naming the new situation of religion within Western culture:

> After the spiritual revolution of the Renaissance, religion had become severed from the rest of man's spiritual life. Faith was no longer everything, as it was in the Middle Ages, but *something* and no one seemed to know exactly what. Kant's critical philosophy clearly circumscribed its limits.[68]

Kant's locating of religion's truth in and through subjectivity and the exercise of human freedom was substantially correct. Kant bequeathed us the problems of how to provide theoretical support for religious faith, how to analyze religious experience appropriately, and how to develop an appropriate critique of Enlightenment claims to absolute human autonomy. As we have seen, Dupré reads the subsequent history of philosophy of religion, when it is not attempting illegitimate reductions of religion to other realms of meaning and truth, as progressively discovering ways to deal with these issues.

Kant's notions of subjectivity and freedom are by no means simple repetitions of Christian notions of spiritual interiority, and his effort to relocate religion within morality was ultimately reductionistic. What Kant gained by recognizing the subjective involvement of the believer was offset by his strict refusal to admit of the self-revealing character of the transcendent referent of religion.

However, Dupré's principal focus will be not the difficulties with the use of specific, traditional symbols which embody revelation in Christianity, but with the history and dynamics of the category "transcendence."[69] Dupré does not allow the intrinsic demands of the religious experience itself to be compromised. This experience requires that in the religious event "idea and experience are given simultaneously, since the idea is no other than the experience recognized."[70] Thus it is fundamentally erroneous to separate the idea of God from the experience, and then proceed to attempt to "prove" that idea, or develop its logic independently. Second, the transcendent is precisely that which cannot be "proven" or established by rational thought, even by the believer:

---

68. Dupré, *A Dubious Heritage*, p. 1.

69. See Louis Dupré, "Transcendence and Immanence as Theological Categories," *Catholic Theological Society of America Proceedings* 31 (1976): 1-10.

70. Louis Dupré, "The Moral Argument, the Religious Experience, and the Basic Meaning of the Ontological Argument," *Idealistic Studies* 3 (1973): 266-72, here p. 275.

The religious act unquestionably intends its objects as really existing, but the transition from the existence of the intentional terminus *in the act* to its reality *beyond the act* cannot be made outside the religious consciousness.[71]

We are returned to Kierkegaard's paradox, to a hesitation about Hegel's philosophical articulation of the Absolute, to the unsatisfactory understanding of the immanent presence of the transcendent when categories of causality are used for explanation.

We have already seen how Dupré uses and evaluates the historical responses to Kant (by Kierkegaard, Schleiermacher, Blondel, Husserl, and Duméry), and I will presently consider his reading of Hegel as it develops during this and the subsequent period. In the essays on arguments for the existence of God, Dupré offers a reading of Kant's difficulties with ontological claims about the transcendent and indirectly continues a reflection on the nature of revelation. It is remarkably easy to summarize his discussion of such arguments: Simply put, they don't work, and for two essential reasons. First, what they must investigate is the actual experience of the transcendent in religious experience, and thus the ontological argument, as essentially religious in nature and origin, is the most rudimentary of all the arguments. Thus arguments cannot be "purely philosophical" either in being entirely constructive of a notion of God or in being absolutely distanced from any involvement with religious experience. Even if they do attempt to be such reflections, they fail for a second reason internal to their own argumentation: the demand for intelligibility in metaphysics or epistemology cannot establish and does not ultimately need a transcendent ground. On the one hand, neither order within the cosmos nor an ordered movement of the cosmos pointing beyond itself admits of a causal explanation culminating in the transcendent; and on the other hand, neither the dynamism of the mind nor the moral striving of humanity requires a transcendent foundation or goal. Both causality and intentionality are asked to do more than they can.[72]

Though published in 1990, an article on theodicy belongs conceptually with Dupré's work on the arguments, as it uses the same basic principles, theodicy being, in a sense, the arguments in reverse. To shape a better theodicy Dupré advocates a "concrete-religious versus the rationalist-abstract"[73] consideration of the problem of evil, recalling the necessity for logical expositions of the idea of God to be based upon religious experience. Similarly, he eschews

71. Dupré, "Transcendence and Immanence," p. 271.

72. For details on the various arguments for the existence of God, in addition to the article in n. 70 above, see Louis Dupré, "The Cosmological Argument after Kant," *International Journal for Philosophy of Religion* 3 (1972): 131-45; "The Argument of Design Today," *Journal of Religion* 54 (1974): 1-12; and *A Dubious Heritage*, chaps. 7, 8, and 9.

73. Louis Dupré, "Evil — a Religious Mystery: A Plea for a More Inclusive Model of Theodicy," *Faith and Philosophy* 7 (1990): 261-80, here p. 261.

argumentation based upon "a narrowly conceived, purely causal relation" rather than "a more inclusive relationship between God and creation."[74] Thus he attempts to avoid the unnecessary dilemma of human versus divine freedom, based on a confusion of levels of causality; likewise he avoids an abstract existence of values independent of human action; and thirdly, he opens the possibility for conceiving God not as rigidly impassible but vulnerable. Much as with the existence of God newly understood in his articles on the arguments, so here with the question of evil, Dupré suggests that philosophical reflection does not (and cannot) reduce to either rational clarity or intellectual illusion what must remain religious mystery.

III.2. Resisting Hegel's Solution

It is appropriate in this context also to consider the several articles on Hegel, even though they come only at the end of, and beyond, the decade of work I am presently considering. Dupré has already noted in the introduction to *The Other Dimension*, and gives evidence throughout, of the importance of Hegel's *philosophical* rendering of Christian faith, its dynamics and its content. If Kant had constructed in stark terms the boundaries for those remnants of Christian belief which could be salvaged within the Enlightenment world, Kierkegaard and Hegel question those boundaries and construct two quite different replies. We have already seen that it is chiefly Kierkegaard's notion of the self, its freedom, temporality, and relation to the transcendent that serve a defining role in Dupré's philosophy of religion. Consonant with Hegel, though primarily as a consequence of his phenomenological study of religion, Dupré accepts as essential to the study of religion its dialectical nature, as critique of culture and as movement between thought and representation, with the resultant impor-tance of imagination and of symbols. Further, ontological claims about the transcendent yet self-manifesting nature of God remain rudimentary, as in Hegel. In all three ways, as dialectical, as representational, and as revelatory, religion for Dupré, as for Hegel, is opposed to Kant's decontextualized and rationalist, nonsymbolic, and mute "religion within the limits of reason alone."

The articles on Hegel, which range from the mid-seventies to the early nineties, are themselves difficult to read, full of many careful distinctions, sketches which could only be fully realized in a book-length treatment.[75]

---

74. Dupré, "Evil — a Religious Mystery," p. 263.

75. Given Dupré's introductory remarks in the foreword to Cyril O'Regan, *The Un-orthodox Hegel* (Albany: State University of New York Press, 1994), pp. ix-xi, one might consider in part this dissertation by one of his students as a good indication of the direction a book-length study of his own might pursue.

Moreover, the recent publication of a new edition of the *Lectures on the Philosophy of Religion* has initiated a reconsideration of Hegel's development and mature thought on religion.[76] I wish to note only one development among several because it gives a clue to a shift of emphasis occurring in Dupré's move toward *Passage to Modernity*. It concerns Hegel's attempt "to provide a new religious justification of the modern age."[77] Such a legitimation of modernity must preserve the autonomy and necessary contingency of secularity; the religious believer, the Christian, may in fact deny ultimacy to this autonomy and necessity but cannot deny that secularity is the reality within which religion must make its claims. As well, such an interpretation as a religious interpretation cannot compromise the grounding in the transcendent, and that transcendent's autonomy and necessity. At its most daring, then, Hegel's project was to return religion to its role as the integrating force of culture, of history. Let me quote Dupré at length:

> Indeed his philosophy of Spirit constitutes, above all a critique of an age that has abandoned content for self-consciousness. The Church betrayed whatever spiritual authority it retained, when it entrusted itself to the self-conscious theology of reason. Religious justification requires a *continued transcendence*. But the justification of the modern culture of self-consciousness demands an Absolute that *integrates* as much as it *transcends*, and this the idea of God alone cannot provide. To define the Absolute as the process of the *Spirit* is to integrate self-consciousness as an essential part in it, without, however, collapsing one into the other. The adoption of a category more comprehensive than God is not entirely unprecedented, even though before Hegel it never was called to provide a religious legitimation.[78]

Hegel thus attempts to engage the chief characteristics of modernity: the turn to the subject, the loss of transcendence, the relativization of truth, the absolutization of human freedom, and the secularization of the sacred. To do so he transforms the Christian doctrine of the Holy Spirit into the Absolute as Spirit, while preserving God as "the transcendent factor of the creative process

---

76. For two contributions to this reconsideration, see Louis Dupré, "Transitions and Tensions in Hegel's Treatment of Determinate Religion," *American Catholic Philosophical Quarterly* 64 (1990): 429-40; and "Review of *Lectures on the Philosophy of Religion*, 3 vols., by Georg Wilhelm Friedrich Hegel. New translation by R. Brown, P. Hodgson, J. Stewart," *Religious Studies Review* 13 (1987): 193-97.

77. Louis Dupré, "Hegel's Absolute Spirit: A Religious Justification of Secular Culture," *Revue de l'Université d'Ottawa/University of Ottawa Quarterly* 52 (1982): 554-65, here p. 554.

78. Louis Dupré, "The Absolute Spirit and the Religious Legitimation of Modernity," in *Hegels Logik der Philosophie: Religion und Philosophie in der Theorie des absoluten Geistes*, ed. Dieter Henrich and Rolf-Peter Horstmann (Stuttgart: Klett-Cotta, 1984), pp. 224-33; see p. 231.

without ever coinciding with it."[79] A merely infinite God is a pure abstraction, and a merely immanent force within the dynamic unfolding of reality is no God either. The all-encompassing philosophy which results, despite its efforts to hold the transcendent in a paradoxical relation with both the finite and the infinite, seems inevitably to fail in two important ways: on the one hand, its transformation of the Holy Spirit into the Absolute Spirit redounds back upon Christian thought and practice in a fashion which results in the very seculari-zation of belief Hegel wished to challenge; and on the other hand, that same transformation only functions as a legitimation of modernity to the extent that it can be "practiced" in an irreligious manner.

Three other studies from this period are obliquely in conversation with Hegel and confirm the growing importance of assessing what has happened to the religious attitude specifically in relation to the shape of modern culture. Dupré moves from expositing the dynamics necessary to religion itself to ana-lyzing how these dynamics are fundamentally challenged by modernity. This means that both the categories of investigation are seen to be historically con-ditioned, as are the judgments for practical implementation. The most striking change of categories is the relinquishing of the notion of the sacred as useful to the analysis of religion, and the exploration of the actualizing role of myth, ritual, and symbol (religious art in particular) as limited within modern culture.

The category of the sacred obscures rather than illuminates what religion is for modern men and women. In Dupré's analysis:

> We seldom encounter the sacred in an objectively given, universally attainable reality, as the miraculous statue or the rustling of leaves in an oak forest were to our ancestors. Our way leads through private reflection and personal decision. Almost nothing appears directly sacred to us. In this respect we find ourselves at the opposite extreme of archaic man for whom at least in some sense everything is sacred. We no longer share a coherent, sacred universe with all other members of our society or our culture, as religions in the past did.[80]

We encounter a dilemma. The sacred is no longer available from outer sources of piety. Modern women and men cannot take seriously the traditional expres-sions of the transcendent, do not hold as true or efficacious the narratives and actions of historical religions. Thus, the rediscovery of the transcendent rests interiorly, in the inner self. Yet where and how is that inner self to mediate the transcendent?

The problem for contemporary religious art is a good index of this dilemma. More so now than ever, the use of symbols to convey transcendence

---

79. Dupré, "Hegel's Absolute Spirit," p. 555.
80. Dupré, Transcendent Selfhood, p. 29.

is dependent upon "a specific cultural context with particular religious doctrines."[81] Recognition is no longer spontaneous or effective, a situation exacerbated by the condition of modern art. Language (we might say education) is indispensable to the functioning of religious art, especially in modern art whose ambiguity and abstractness does little more than "create the vacuum in which man is able to perceive transcendence."[82] If the contemporary symbols used to portray the actual self-manifestation of God have become themselves excessively abstract, how can such abstract symbols teach the uninitiated what is inevitably concrete and determinate?

My final example of transition is Dupré's exploration of two interrelated facets of the "rediscovery of the inner life," the dynamics of ritual and the experience of alienation. Contemporary culture, Dupré often notes, shares with traditional mysticism both an experience of silence and absence, and a mistrust of objectifying the transcendent. Modern alienation is by no means simply religious, but it does point to the insufficiency of the objectivism of pure rationality, scientism, or social activism as the means to satisfy the need for a transcendent dimension in human life. Once again it is a self-contradictory situation which emerges when we consider so important a vehicle of religion as ritual, not simply in itself but in its present cultural context. Ritual is the symbolic action and word through which human beings overcome the very fleetingness of time, recapture the privileged moments of the past, and thus transform the ordinary gestures of the present into moments which assert their transcendence not only over time within time, but of the immanent within the transcendent.

However, it is one of the distinguishing characteristics of modern culture, its sense of the historical, which obviates these functions of ritual:

> The epoch that discovered history was also the first to grant priority to the future over the past. Belief in progress and effective action to realize it replaced the search for meaning in the past through remembrance and ritual repetition.[83]

Past events, seen as *merely* historical, can no longer be ritually invoked as vehicles for making present the salvific inbreaking of the transcendent in human history. Dupré returns us to insights gained from Kierkegaard:

> Total unsituatedness traps the self within a closed world of mere possibilities. But since freedom must be grounded in, and limited by, consistent actuality, *mere* possibility allows no genuine freedom. Kierkegaard who defined despair

81. Dupré, *Transcendent Selfhood*, p. 56.
82. Dupré, *Transcendent Selfhood*, p. 64.
83. Louis Dupré, "Ritual, the Sacralization of Time," *Man and World* 19 (1986): 143-53, here p. 150.

as lack of possibility, was right in diagnosing a self that is *mere* possibility as a self in despair.[84]

Does a culture whose situatedness is conceived precisely as total unsituatedness actually make possible the rediscovery of transcendence, a transcendence it not only denies but actively obscures? How will the self, turned inward in search, be able to realize in ritual and symbol that to which it has no access?

III.3. Toward Understanding the Culture of our Spiritual Exile

The name for this section of part III plays upon the title of an article published in 1976, "The Religious Crisis of Our Culture," in which Dupré lays out for the first time a differently focused answer to the same complex question about the nature and role of religion in human life which led to *The Other Dimension* and the essays of the middle period. The article highlights two changes that take place gradually through eight articles. The first change is from a priority on the religious crisis to an increasing preoccupation with the present shape and remote origins of the *culture* in which it occurs; and a movement from concern with the "crisis" as religious to an investigation of a more pervasive, fundamental *spiritual exile*. It will lead him to name that form of inwardness which contemporary humanity seeks as a "religion of silence,"[85] an experience of the inadequacy of religious symbols as derived from traditional religion and its claim to mediate the transcendent, and a rediscovery of contemplative inwardness which may come to acknowledge the presence of the transcendent once again. Let me quote a summarizing conclusion:

> Symbols are always needed. But even after he has received them from his religious tradition or personally discovered them, contemporary Western man continues to maintain a distance between his faith and what he knows to be tokens rather than images. Reluctant to view them as "analogous" to the inner presence, to give them a religious significance he has no choice but to invert the analogy from God to the creature and to abandon the analogy of similitude for the analogy of presence. By a strange paradox the secularization of the world has driven him to a higher degree of spiritualization in which he confronts God himself rather than his image.[86]

---

84. Dupré, *Transcendent Selfhood*, p. 62.

85. Louis Dupré, "The Closed World of the Modern Mind," *Religion and Intellectual Life* 1 (1984): 19-29, here p. 22.

86. Louis Dupré, "Negative Theology and the Affirmation of the Finite," in *Experience, Reason, and God: Studies in Philosophy and the History of Philosophy,* ed. Eugene Thomas Long, vol. 8 (Washington, D.C.: Catholic University of America Press, 1980), pp. 149-57, here p. 157.

The second change will be a move from the characterization of modernity and the contemporary secularized culture to the language of isolation and fragmentation, terms which continue but transform the importance of the notions of alienation and lack of integration from the previous period. To offer both an analysis of the situation and a tentative proposal for its redress requires Dupré to present an adequate description of the situation, an analysis of its causes and its critics, and an evaluation of its resources. I will offer brief summaries of these three vectors in his developing investigations, noting over all that the full exposition will take place only in *Passage to Modernity*.

As to the description of the situation, as early as 1976 he had adopted Husserl's conclusion that "the objectivist, naturalist attitude was probably Western man's original sin for which he was driven into cultural exile."[87] Moreover, this attitude of objectivism "consists more in an improper view of subjectivity than in an absence thereof."[88] Thus he will take exception to a too quick repudiation of isolated subjectivity in favor of receptive relationality (variously using Richard Rorty, Francis Jacques, and Alasdair MacIntyre as examples) but equally is hesitant about identifying Being with immanent appearance (using Michel Henry as the example). The end result may well be a secularized or desacralized society, but its primary characteristics are "the twin errors of a purely transcendent subject (objectivism) or a self-enclosed, purely immanent one (subjectivism)."[89] And the chief mechanism by which these errors work out their transformation of culture is an

> uninhibited pursuit of a drive, long present in the European mind, to separate, analyze, to take apart and, in a second stage, to reassemble into new syntheses over which the mind exercises full control. Clearly in such an attitude the unity of existing complexes can no longer be held sacrosanct.[90]

To fully understand these activities of autocratic constitution and technical control, Dupré attempts several "histories" of the causes as he sees them now, and as others have seen and criticized them from within modernity, which *Passage to Modernity* will delineate at length and in detail.

I recommend the clarity and succinctness of one essay, the *Fourth Annual Moreau Lecture*, "The Spiritual Crisis of Our Culture."[91] It divides the search

87. Louis Dupré, "The Religious Crisis of Our Culture," *Yale Review* 65 (1976): 203-17, here p. 203.

88. Louis Dupré, "Secularism and the Crisis of Our Culture: A Hermeneutic Perspective," *Thought* 51 (1976): 271-81, here p. 272.

89. Louis Dupré, "Alternatives to the Cogito," *Review of Metaphysics* 40 (1987): 687-716, here p. 716.

90. Dupré, "Religious Crisis," p. 205.

91. For the text upon which the following summary is based, see Louis Dupré, "The Spiritual Crisis of Our Culture," *Fourth Annual Moreau Lecture* (Wilkes-Barre: King's College, 1983).

for causes into three parts: the loss of nature, the loss of self, the loss of God. Late medieval nominalism and Renaissance humanism are the remote sources for the first, as culture becomes the business of transforming, not of cultivating, nature. Coincident with this rise of controlling objectivity was the loss of the self, as subjectivity's sole activity became the constituting of that objectivity. This modern self, which has lost its openness to transcendence through participation in its presence, comes to deal with God through the category of causality, eventually constituting God as an object as well.

This excellently clear and concise presentation can be supplemented by the several articles in which the critics of this development are considered.[92] Though he devoted a book-length study to only one of these critics, i.e., Marx, the articles of this period give evidence of Dupré's careful consideration of Freud and Nietzsche as well. I could not do better than to quote the summary of *Passage to Modernity*:

> Without unduly oversimplifying, we can, I think, conclude that each of the three great critics focused on one of the components of the onto-theological synthesis. Marx denounced the distorted relation of the person to the natural world, which has resulted in alienation from both the natural and social environment. Freud focused on the predicament of the modern self. Nietzsche both denounced the Platonic-Christian idea of transcendence and feared its departure. All three described our condition as having now become problematic, yet none identified the problem with modern culture as such.[93]

Finally, these same articles also evaluate the resources still present within modernity for addressing its own problems. The human choices which have shaped the culture have ironically produced the "crisis" which has eclipsed the essential avenues of escape. The remedy is equally ironic:

> Nevertheless, being born and raised in this particular culture we share its assumptions as well as its axiological fragmentation. And we have no choice in doing so. Hence I perceive no other road toward moral revalorization and cultural reconstruction but the one opened by modernity itself: the inward road. Subjectivity after having damned our age may still turn out to hold its redemption.[94]

Rediscovering inwardness is the precondition for recognizing true transcendence, and that moment is prior to rediscovering authentic religion. What will that discovery be like? It will be, for believers, a retrieval, and for the

92. See Dupré, "Religious Crisis," pp. 206-17; "Secularism and the Crisis," pp. 276-80; and "Closed World," pp. 22-27.

93. Dupré, *Passage to Modernity*, pp. 4-5.

94. Dupré, "Alternatives to the Cogito," p. 712.

thoroughly modern woman or man a new discovery, in which "the practice of spiritual life consists not in seeing God in a pre-existing image but in becoming an image through greater unity."[95] This occurs within the negative experience of absence, but not in a manner entirely antithetical to historical religion and its claims to mediate revelation. In two important texts from this period, we can gain clues to a difficult but necessary connection between interiority and historical religion.

Never absent, but also never thematically prominent, is the role of language in Dupré's consideration of religion. He is justly critical of the specialization of Christian theological language due to its capitulation to modern rationality, leaving it to contribute to rather than address the fragmentation of language that modernity has brought about.[96] Elsewhere he gives evidence of a certain confidence in the fundaments of Christian language, however much he asserts that existential significance must precede dogmatic concepts. That precedence, of course, is hardly foreign to Christian practice or theology. Moreover, however much he decries a pragmatist or reductionist appeal to social, relational determinates of a new retrieval of meaning, he can admit the following:

> It would be incorrect to assume that the community loses its role in the highly personal spiritual religion of the present. The contrary is the case. As soon as the believer adopts a model such as Christ (and the entire culture that has been shaped by it induces him to prefer this model over others), he joins a community, that is, he becomes a member of a group of like-minded individuals in the present. In this link, however loose, with a mystical body the believer becomes *actually* united with his model. It ceases to be a mere ideal; the community makes it into a *present* reality. By providing him with sacraments, scriptures, and a whole system of representations, the religious community enables the individual to incorporate his attitude into a living union with his model.[97]

95. Dupré, "Negative Theology," p. 154.

96. Dupré, "Closed World," pp. 27-29.

97. Louis Dupré, "Spiritual Life in a Secular Age," in *Ignatian Spirituality in a Secular Age*, ed. George P. Schner (Waterloo: Wilfrid Laurier Press, 1983), pp. 14-25; see p. 22. See also Dupré, "The Glory of the Lord: Hans Urs von Balthasar's Theological Aesthetic," *Communio* 16 (1989): 384-412.

IV. "An Essay in the Hermeneutics
of Nature and Culture" (1984-94)

The part of my essay on *Passage to Modernity* is remarkably brief for several reasons. Most happily, this volume of essays contains not only a distinguished essay by David Tracy on that text, but in some sense all the essays are, as the subtitle has suggested, "in conversation with" the questions raised by the text. Second, in *Passage to Modernity* Dupré has surpassed the limits of philosophy of religion, properly speaking, and of its modern existence since the Enlightenment. The dynamism of his quest for understanding the nature and present situation of religion, Christianity in particular, has led him to search outside the bounds prescribed by a philosophical reflection on religion. An adequate engagement and assessment of this work requires a conversation with a considerable group of experts, who themselves must not be narrowly engaged in merely specialized study.

The argument begins with a description of the classical and medieval antecedents to modern culture. They prepare for, though do not necessitate, the emergence of modern subjectivity, with its independent use of words and forms as symbols of its own self-expression on the one hand, and the emergence of modern objectivity, with its restructuring and controlling of reality as developed by science and technology, on the other. The search for deeper insight into the resulting disintegration of an integrated view of the cosmic, anthropic, and transcendent elements of Western culture requires a cautious unfolding of Renaissance humanism and the earliest emergence of what will become modern science. In this process the Neoplatonist notions of participation and illumination give way to Aristotelian causality and voluntarist, instrumentalist, and ultimately constructivist views of rationality. Dupré first explores the objectification of nature and its disconnection from the self and from any transcendent ground, the principle metaphor for the world becoming that of a machine. The second part of the argument retraces the same steps, this time to discover the fate of the human subject in the emergence of modernity. Once again, in order to understand this change it is insufficient to lay the blame, as it were, on Descartes's strategy for countering skepticism with the disembodied self. He must rather be understood as the inheritor of the progressive isolation of self, cosmos, and transcendent from one another, such that his ontologically ungrounded, disembodied, absolutized self can emerge with its mechanical world and objectified God. What follows is the absolutization of the subject's freedom and the blindness which ignores temporality in favor of the atemporal now, the "modo" which marks modernity.

The third part of the argument is thus prepared. However much it might be expected, Dupré does not now unfold in any direct way the fate of the notion of transcendence, let alone the notion of God in Western Christianity and secular culture. Rather his focus is the relation of "nature and grace" and their separation by the end of the Middle Ages into two realms, permitting on the one hand the development of a rationalist and objectifying study of God, and on the other a progressive loss of transcendence at the heart of the self, or at best a marginalization of spirituality at odds with both theology and science. As in the previous, highly nuanced, parts of *Passage to Modernity,* even more so here Dupré describes the tentative efforts to overcome the theological dualism of nature and grace and the religious crisis of the loss of transcendence. In the two final chapters we see the philosopher of religion at work, guided not by abstract considerations of the nature of religion but by a hermeneutic quest to discover the shape, causes, and future of the transcendent dimension of reality.

Three aspects of this "essay in hermeneutics" are of singular importance, two of retrieval and one of proposal. The first is the retrieval of a somewhat "lost" period of the development of Western culture, lost not least of all to Catholic intellectual thought. Between prizing the medieval synthesis of Aquinas and engaging the challenge of post-Kantian philosophy of religion, much of recent Catholic thought too quickly attempted a new synthesis based chiefly upon a marriage of Aquinas, Kant, Hegel, and Heidegger. If historical work was done, it tended to skip over the Renaissance and early modern period to the justifiably rich resources of patristic thought. It is not appropriate here to venture any judgments about Dupré's choice of exact origins or his appreciation of certain attempts at a renewed synthesis. In part at least it will be in the rereading of the developments from the Enlightenment to the present in the light of his sketch of its prehistory that his interpretation will prove itself. Hesitations from many quarters with premature grand religious solutions (or capitulations) to the excessively clear statement of "modern" principles by the Enlightenment may now well be confirmed by a more nuanced reading of the sources of the present, and perhaps by a rediscovery of patristic and medieval thought for other than revisionist purposes.

A second aspect of importance is the retrieval of Platonic and Neoplatonic themes and authors, linked particularly, though not uniquely, with Augustine. This retrieval is at the service, no doubt, of Dupré's conviction that the relationship of participation and not of causality is an essential ingredient in the synthesis that was lost and is now an ironically appropriate avenue within the contemporary situation. Previously Dupré has detailed the mystical element of religious life and the strange affinity of the modern experience of the absence of God with the negative theology of premodern times. I find it helpful that he broadens this aspect of his analysis with the phrase "the devout life," which functions as a more encompassing category than mysticism or spirituality. Of the three provisional syntheses (devout humanism, the religion of the heart, and the baroque vision), the discussion of Ignatius of Loyola is the one on which I am best qualified to comment. While Ignatius was indeed a mystic in the classic sense of the word, his spiritual exercises were precisely intended to form individuals for "contemplation in action," for a religious life not abstracted from the world but immersed in it, for an inwardness that was, however much founded in the unnameable mystery of God, centrifugal in its energy to return the self to the world, graced and transformed. Dupré himself notes that the language of Loyola, and that of Teresa of Avila and John of the Cross, is substantially different from the Neoplatonic tradition of Eckhart and Ruusbroec. And more so is it the case with the Reformers and the baroque vision. Were one to pursue further the Ignatian model, one would need to ask about its viability for women and men today as well as the role of symbols, language, and particularly of the Christian Scriptures in the perdurance of that synthesis.

The final aspect of *Passage to Modernity* to which I wish to give attention is not one of retrieval but one of proposal. In both the introduction and conclusion, Dupré identifies a basic principle underlying his study. Early in the text he states:

> Unless we assume that the cultural revolution of the modern age was an event of ontological significance that changed the nature of Being itself, much of what is discussed in the following chapters would bear little meaning to the present.[98]

And by way of summary very near the end of his text, he names that change:

> When modern thought distinguished the real as it is in itself from the real as it exists for itself, it initiated a new epoch in being as much as a new stage of reflection. Indeed, it opened a gap in the very nature of the real that will never be closed again. Despite the erroneous assumption that the meaning of the former depends entirely upon the latter, implied by the modern distinction between object and subject, the more fundamental view that mind stands in a creative relation to that physical reality on which it in other respects depends, is definitive.[99]

The question remains whether one can rewrite this summary to speak of a definitive change of relation based on a "fundamental view that mind stands in a creative relation to that *transcendent reality* on which it in other respects depends." How far does the fundamental ontological change which modernity has brought about change, first, the nature of the human relation to the transcendent, and second, the nature of the transcendent itself?

Though published after *Passage to Modernity,* the Aquinas Lecture, 1994,

---

98. Dupré, *Passage to Modernity,* p. 7.
99. Dupré, *Passage to Modernity,* p. 252.

entitled *Metaphysics and Culture*,[100] actually offers a splendid introduction to the former and hints at an answer to the question I have just posed. Its first section, "Symbols and Metaphysical Ultimacy," provides a brief miniature of the development from the ancients to the moderns, tracing the origins of the essay's main question: Can modern subjectivity reconceive itself as dependent on a transcendent givenness which conditions its meaning-giving activity? Such a reference to the transcendent itself will necessarily require intrinsically symbolic language, whose systematic and revelatory character philosophy must investigate. These many modes of symbolic activity which constitute the complexes we call cultures may well invite philosophy to reflection, but Dupré questions whether philosophy can fulfill its task of articulating the unity and transcendence of reality, given three great problems: the role of the human subject as the ultimate source of value and meaning; the contingency of humanly created cultural symbols; and the discovery of the historical, temporal character of reality itself. The next three sections of the essay consider how metaphysics must contend with these matters.

In "Culture, the Embodiment of Mind" Dupré sketches the gradually emerging recognition by philosophy that culture is an entity in its own right. This insight required discovering culture as a unique, spiritual organism, history as organic, and the idolatrous and fetishistic alienation which cultures engender when their products take on a life of their own. This new appreciation of the inventive and social character of meaning poses a seemingly insurmountable challenge to metaphysics and its reflection on ultimate principles: How can such an infinite variety of cultural patterns yield continuity, ultimacy, the transcendent itself? To answer this question, Dupré next considers two philosophical reflections which have moved beyond the neo-Kantian theory of symbols: the study of the ontological significance of time as developed by Husserl and Heidegger and hermeneutical philosophy as developed by Gadamer and Ricoeur. A contemporary search in metaphysics for unity and necessity (for the relation of beings to Being itself) must now pass through a study of human existence and its cultural expressions. Section 4, "The Hermeneutics of Culture," proposes a solution to the impasse of a search for metaphysical unity amid irreducibly diverse cultural expression. With a very brief caution (lest we misconstrue a kind of ontologism or metaphysical intuitionism), Dupré argues for an "ontological preapprehension," a "prelinguistic implicit apprehension" which constitutes the self-transcending dynamism impelling language and culture toward expressing the transcendent presence of being. We are faced with a paradox: no actual meaning is constituted without language, without contingent symbol, yet the entire activity of culture making, of symbol and meaning

---

100. Louis Dupré, *Metaphysics and Culture*, the Aquinas Lecture, 1994 (Milwaukee: Marquette University Press, 1994).

making, is grounded in and aims for the transcendent, the unspeakable. At this point Dupré introduces the notion that this dynamism is a *response* to a transcendent *call*. This sense of the disclosive and dynamic character of being, of the transcendent, is not developed, though it does recall Dupré's remarks in the first section on the Christian sense of revelation.

In the final two sections, Dupré faces the third obstacle to his proposal of how metaphysics can be generated from a consideration of culture: our present culture presents the extreme case of a culture which lacks any coherent synthesis of its own which could be the basis of a metaphysical reflection. The cosmic, the anthropic, and the transcendent dimensions of reality no longer form a synthetic whole for us, and the human subject has been emptied of content and reduced to a mere function. Dupré's solution is admittedly circular. If our present culture is to find its coherence and the person to retrieve a full humanity so as to defend and pass on the present cultural heritage, metaphysical reflection will be required. And in turn, metaphysics requires such a subject and synthesis to do its own proper work.

The circle is not a vicious one, though we might properly ask, how will the cycle of decline be broken? Surely both by the perceptive philosopher like Dupré who brings wisdom to the culture in response to a call, and by the transcendent itself initiating that call. I would willingly hear much more from Dupré on both these matters. We are not far here from the place where I began this entire exposition; namely, with the work of philosophical reflection as an essential part of education and with the grounding of all philosophy of religion in the living witness of the believing encounter with the transcendent. Likewise we still are in search of the meaning of the religious attitude, its symbolic embodiment and its cultural home.

V. Abiding the Return of Meaning

Concluding remarks are somewhat inappropriate in a review of the work of a still very active author. It is obviously not the time to make definitive evaluations. My brief remarks will be in keeping with my present purpose: to sketch an overview of Dupré's work in philosophy of religion and its development.

In the preface I suggested we imagine Dupré as an artist whose oeuvre has been slowly constructed in conversation with others, but decidedly in his own style. Commentary on scholarly endeavor, like art criticism, must respect the integrity of the work itself in its social location as well as in its disclosive power and skillful rendering. Dupré's work is not analytic philosophy of religion or primarily historical study, and it cannot be dissociated from his more theological, spiritual, and ethical writings. Since some would evaluate it by simply not reading it, a first comprehensive remark is to affirm the distinct value and importance of the *kind* of philosophy of religion Dupré engages in.

This leads directly to a second remark based upon a recognition of the move from description to interpretation which is constantly at play in the materials we have considered. It is not simply the descriptive presentation of particular authors (and the omission of others) and its accuracy and clarity which deserve comment, but the interpretation of both religion and culture which is constructed with the help of these authors. Oddly enough for a speculative thinker, Dupré's work is highly successful (dare one say accurate and truthful) when considered in its ultimate applicability. One cannot read his work without being challenged to rethink rudimentary conceptions of contemporary culture and religion.

Beyond these general comments, let me name the values I see in Dupré's style of philosophy of religion. In my judgment, philosophy of religion could valuably emulate the following in Dupré's work: (1) the conscientious placement of philosophical reflection as an activity within education, particularly as formation of persons and society, as an effort to rediscover the role of philosophy within contemporary society; (2) as with other authors such as Charles Taylor and Alisdair MacIntyre, the vigorous rereading of the history of Western thought in ways which extend the range of history to be considered; (3) the insistence that the reflection be upon the particular and living faith of believers, always alert to the tendency in philosophy to reductive or inventive strategies; (4) without neglect of the human subject, the move toward the investigation of the social embodiment and construction of both culture and religions, broadly understood as the mediated or symbolic metier of the transcendent dimension; (5) the close attention to critics of both religion and contemporary culture and to the art, literature, music, architecture — to all the forms of human invention which are the context and expression of religion. These words of appreciation may seem self-evident to many, but the recent philosophy of religion and the state of the contemporary study of religion suggest that these lessons still need to be learned in some cases, invigorated in others.

The lacuna I wish to note results in part from the conviction Dupré has about the constellation of elements in the present crisis of culture and religion, the sources from which that crisis comes and the resources with which it can be addressed. At root is his conviction that interiority, however meager its present manifestation in culture, is the necessary and apt, though not solely sufficient, means for a regeneration of both culture and the religious dimension of human life. Hence his preference for negative theology, for the Christian mystical tradition, for its Platonic and Neoplatonic affiliations. I am uncertain whether these resources will be able to achieve the regrounding in attentive abiding for the return of meaning from and through the transcendent itself without a movement beyond the language of transcendence which is silence. I thus take seriously the five points of appreciation I have already mentioned and look toward asking questions about the relation of the religion of silence and inward attentiveness to the actual language and practice of religion. In the particular case of Christianity the person-forming, world-forming, history-grounding, and highly reduction-resisting use of the Scriptures is the key activity of symbolic embodiment which in any age has moved believer and nonbeliever alike from receptive inwardness to living faith. As an indispensable discourse on fragments of meaning, contemporary philosophy of religion must search out, and interpret, precisely that pattern of meaning which joins fragments into a whole despite the necessarily elusive and diverse texture of any such discourse. Without inwardness as its companion the text is no doubt barren, but there is sufficient evidence that without the text the inwardness wanders and grows inattentive. Perhaps what I suggest would take philosophy of religion too far into the region of theology.[101] Nonetheless, Dupré's own principles of philosophical discourse lead me to hope for a trustworthy hermeneutic not only of person and of culture, but also of text.

101. Two essays already offer a glimpse of how this might be developed. See Louis Dupré, "Some Recent Philosophical Discussions of Religion," *Journal of the History of Ideas* 43 (1982): 505-18; "Experience and Interpretation: A Philosophical Reflection on Schillebeeckx' *Jesus* and *Christ*," *Theological Studies* 43 (1982): 30-51.

CHAPTER 13

"Modern Forms Filled with Traditional Spiritual Content": On Louis Dupré's Contribution to Christian Theology

PETER CASARELLA

With the exception of an early work on Kierkegaard and a few articles on contemporary theologians, Louis Dupré's literary output has not been devoted to systematic theology. In fact, even his writings on religion and spirituality studiously avoid adopting such a standpoint.[1] Major works such as *Transcendent Selfhood, The Other Dimension, A Dubious Heritage, The Deeper Life,* and *The Common Life* opt instead for a philosophical analysis of contemporary religious experience or a studied reflection on mystical selfhood unencumbered by technical theological distinctions. Yet if Louis Dupré has made a noteworthy contribution to Christian theology — and indeed he has — his contribution is not that of a complete outsider to the discipline.[2] The philosophical works as well

---

1. For example, he states in *The Deeper Life: An Introduction to Christian Mysticism* (New York: Crossroad, 1981), p. 15, "Our contemporaries turn to the mystics rather than to the moralists or theologians." Likewise, in *Passage to Modernity: An Essay in the Hermeneutics of Nature and Culture* (New Haven: Yale University Press, 1993), pp. 244-48, he argues how Catholic theology became homogenized in the age of the baroque and withdrew from the problems of contemporary culture, a development which in some fundamental way, he will contend, remains with us even today.

2. Because of restrictions of space, I have not treated Louis Dupré's research into non-Christian traditions in this essay. This is intended to limit the scope of the essay and not to diminish the significance of this part of his corpus. Cf. "Mysticism," in *The Encyclopedia of Religion,* ed. Mircea Eliade, vol. 10 (New York: Macmillan, 1987), pp. 245-61, and "Unio Mystica: The State and the Experience," in *Mystical Union and Monotheistic Faith,* ed. Moshe Idel and Bernard McGinn (New York: Macmillan, 1989), pp. 3-23. See also the essay by James Wiseman, O.S.B., in this volume.

as the commentaries on spiritual writers betray more than a mere acquaintance with the problems and methods of classical and contemporary theologians.

Dupré has consistently maintained that religious belief today is inextricably bound to the culture of modernity. In his view, a believer today is willy-nilly obliged to consider herself a modern believer. To adopt the spiritual outlook of the premodern world is neither desirable nor realistic, for that world is no longer ours to claim. Yet Dupré also recognizes that few theologians today would bind belief to modern culture uncritically. Modernity's promise to emancipate the devout from the shackles of traditional authorities has yielded mixed results, making the supposition of a modern framework more questionable now than ever before. The ambiguity of the current situation is often addressed by questions such as these: How do we name the present situation: modern, late modern, or postmodern? Where does modernity begin and when did it end? Does modernity have a future or has it been surpassed by so-called postmodernism? No less vexing are the questions about the place of Christian theology in this cultural matrix. Do the hermeneutical bases of the modern worldview represent a newly discovered self-assertion of the human subject (Blumenberg), or are they thinly veiled permutations of a secularized theology (Löwith)? Does revealed religion become void of its specific self-revealing content if interpreted in terms of its correlation to the ever changing notion of general human experience defined by the current cultural milieu (Barth, postliberal theology)? These are just some of the questions one might raise about the project of examining the experience of Christian faith in the context of modern culture.

These are also questions which have been addressed in the writings of Louis Dupré. Especially since the mid-1980s, his works have seen modern culture as a problem. For instance, in 1987 he claimed that the simultaneous appearance of the idea of the individual in Kierkegaard, Hamann, and Max Stirner reflects that "first inventory of the gains and losses of modernity made around the turn of the nineteenth century."[3] A similar point could be made about his own work. When surveying the notion of transcendent selfhood in the mystics and in contemporary religious thinkers, he assays the modern project and seeks to understand whether it still has a future.

Given that the future of modernity is far less certain in this late modern epoch than it was in the nineteenth century, Dupré's appraisal of its genuine gains is marked by realism. In fact, Dupré's most important contribution to Christian theology today rests upon his realistic vision of the complexity of modern belief. He offers no panacea to restore the damage incurred by modernity's fragmentation of spiritual life. Formulating methodological abstractions and promulgating spir-

---

3. Louis Dupré, "*The Sickness unto Death:* A Critique of the Modern Age," in *International Kierkegaard Commentary: The Sickness unto Death*, ed. Robert L. Perkins (Macon: Mercer University Press, 1987), p. 90.

itual techniques are not his aim. His contribution is both more concrete and more challenging. With great care not to oversimplify the diversity of the past, he names the present situation in three ways. First, he offers a genealogy of the spiritual crisis of the religious believer in the contemporary situation. Second, he presents a path of spiritual interiority in which the traditional *via negativa* converges with the modern experience of emptiness. Third, drawing upon a trinitarian theology of the image, he suggests that the spiritual content of the Christian tradition can survive in a genuinely modern form of expression. The relation of form to content is a peculiarly modern question, one which would not have been posed by Thomas Aquinas or Dionysius the Areopagite. Modern forms with traditional spiritual content recognize both modernity's turn to the subject of experience and the concrete expression of transcendent form in traditional Christian belief.[4]

This essay will examine the relation of the form and content of belief in three parts. The first part outlines Dupré's account of modern atheism and contemporary Christian faith. Here I distinguish his position from that of "secular theologians" and draw out the specifically Christian content of his spiritual theology. In the second part of the essay, I analyze his view of the genesis of modern Christian spirituality and the theological strengths and weaknesses that accompany it. This section explains the project outlined by Dupré and suggested in the title; that is, that some modern forms of thought have succeeded in transforming the content of traditional Christian belief without yoking these beliefs to the atheistic presuppositions of a secular age. Whereas the first part outlines the modern form of belief and the second the appearance of traditional content in this form, the third addresses the relationship between form and content. It focuses on Dupré's metaphysics of the symbol, an Ariadne's thread running from *The Other Dimension* (1st ed. 1972) to the Aquinas Lecture (1994). I conclude with some suggestions about how this theory of the symbol may serve contemporary Christian theology.

I. Holding Hard to This Poverty: Modern Culture and Modern Atheism

According to Louis Dupré, the most characteristic feature of modern atheism is not unbelief. Even more fundamental is the decline of the significance of the very question of belief and the rise of an attitude of indifference to questions of metaphysical ultimacy. Practical "a-theism" for him comprises an attitude common to believers and unbelievers alike:

4. The phrase "modern forms with traditional content" is taken from his discussion of Ignatius of Loyola in *Passage to Modernity,* p. 226.

We may call the prevailing climate a-theistic, not because faith has disappeared in our time, but because the question whether we believe in God or
not, retains little or no practical bearing upon our lives. Braving this hostile
climate the believer carefully nurtures the secret flame of faith — secret not
because he has to hide it, but because it has become hidden by its total
incongruity with a radically secular environment. Even to the believer himself
the flame of his faith has become secret, since it no longer enlightens his
whole life.[5]

Practical atheism is a more potent threat to the future of traditional belief in a
context in which the militant skepticism waged against religious truth claims
in the Enlightenment and among early twentieth-century humanists is on the
wane.[6] Practical atheism, too, derives from the crisis of our culture. Religion,
Dupré contends, no longer provides a vision of the world that integrates human
existence into a meaningful whole.[7] Once we can speak about the religious crisis
of our culture as part of our current predicament rather than its originating
cause, then religion has been compartmentalized into a private sphere of little
consequence to the culture. No simple return to biblical faith or mere assertion
of authoritative traditions can restore the spiritual fragmentation that modernity has produced.[8] Like Martin Heidegger, Dupré interprets Nietzsche's disturbing recourse to the Lutheran hymn and Hegelian epithet "God is dead" as a
description of the decay of a culture that has lost the whole realm of transcendent ideals undergirding its life and thought.[9]

The modern religious consciousness is no less profoundly aware of God's

5. Dupré, *The Deeper Life*, p. 14.

6. Louis Dupré, "Spiritual Life in a Secular Age," in *Ignatian Spirituality in a Secular
Age*, ed. George P. Schner (Waterloo: Wilfrid Laurier University Press, 1984), p. 14. My claim
is not that atheism of this sort has disappeared from late modern Western culture, only that
an outright refusal to take religious truth claims seriously seems no longer to be a defining
attitude of our nonetheless still secular milieu.

7. Nowhere is Dupré's unequivocal rejection of the current secularization clearer than
in the following: "For the idea of God is at the very basis of our value system itself. The
nihilism of our time, that is, the conscious abandonment of traditional values, is the final
stage of a disintegration of that basis. Until recently the process of decomposition was hidden
by the unmoving mask of a traditional god to whom we continued to pay lip service. Now
at last the mask has been torn off and behind it stares the emptiness of an abyss" ("The
Religious Crisis of Our Culture," in *The Crisis of Culture: Steps to Reopen the Phenomenological
Investigation of Man, Analecta Husserliana* 5 [1976]: 207. This essay was republished in the
Yale Review 65 [1976]: 203-17). In later essays Dupré will also call into question the attempt
to restore a disintegrated culture with a philosophy of values.

8. Dupré, "Religious Crisis," p. 205.

9. Dupré, "Religious Crisis," pp. 211-13. Cf. Martin Heidegger, "The Word of Nietzsche:
'God is Dead,'" in *The Question concerning Technology and Other Essays*, trans. William Lovitt
(New York: Harper & Row, 1977), pp. 53-112, esp. p. 61.

absence. However bleak the situation may be for the believer, Dupré insists that the cultural crisis of the West may still yield unexpected spiritual fruits. The memorable words of Emerson with which he concludes *Passage to Modernity* are characteristic of his almost prophetic attitude of expectation:

> We must hold hard to this poverty, however scandalous, and by more vigorous self-recoveries, after the sallies of action, possess our axis more fully.[10]

How is the believer to hold hard to the poverty of modern atheism? Far from embracing secularization as a positive development within Christianity, Dupré sees the crisis provoked by modernity as an impoverishment which the believer must nonetheless accept even though acceptance for him does not mean re-interpreting belief solely in the terms set by the modern agenda.

Dupré's dialectical response to modern atheism contrasts with secular theology. The secular theologian Paul van Buren argued that the gospel can contain only a secular meaning because empiricist linguistic philosophy had purportedly demonstrated that all theological talk about God was meaningless. Dupré retorted in a 1968 article in the *Christian Century* that naming the transcendent is justified by an intrinsic necessity of the religious act even though such naming cannot be demonstrated on purely empiricist grounds.

The reasons for his rejection of van Buren's position are fairly straight-forward. By its very nature the religious act requires a commitment to the transcendent.[11] Secular theologians are correct to see our age as one in which we judge reality empirically, viz., as objects, but they are incorrect to believe that the God to whom Christians remain committed can be understood on the same terms. Quoting Kierkegaard, Dupré maintains that Christianity paradoxi-cally places personality above the doctrine and is therefore not worth being saved as a religion without a personal relation to the transcendent.[12] Van Buren and other linguistic analysts rightly contend, according to Dupré, that the believer's commitment to the transcendent cannot be judged by the same stan-dards as empirically verifiable objects of knowledge; nevertheless, a constituting cognitive activity cannot be eliminated from the act of faith, as these analysts would have it. Without knowledge Christian faith would become nothing but a human commitment, the grounds of which are indistinguishable from any other worthwhile secular endeavor.[13] If religious language in general and the Christian gospel in particular are transformed into the humanistic, moral cate-

10. Dupré, *Passage to Modernity,* p. 253. On the spiritual importance of expectation, see Dupré, *The Deeper Life,* p. 14.

11. Louis Dupré, "Meditations on Secular Theology," *Christian Century,* November 20, 1968, p. 1470.

12. Dupré, "Meditations on Secular Theology," p. 1471.

13. Dupré, "Meditations on Secular Theology," p. 1472.

gories conceived by van Buren, the personal relation of the believer to the transcendent loses its distinctively religious character.

While distinct from secular theology, holding hard to the poverty of modern atheism means finding a language or symbolic structure to articulate the traditional content of Christian faith. Dupré has advocated a return to the *via negativa* of the Christian theological tradition as a way out of this impasse. Traditional Christian negative theology involves neither a flat denial of God's existence (as a terminal position) nor the experience that absolutely nothing at all is at the ground of our existence. Dupré's thesis would also be essentially misunderstood if one did not recognize that traditional negative theology challenges the very spiritual conditions of our age.

Dupré repudiates the easily digestible but nonetheless esoteric popular teachings that prevail in Western consumer culture today. The negative experience of God is not the exclusive privilege of what our Western contemporaries ordinarily conceive of as "the mystic."[14] The common depiction of a highly introverted individual obsessed with sublime thoughts and lacking roots in civil society and the church is often at odds with the Christian mystical tradition.[15] Christian mysticism in Dupré's view is an active response to approach "the common life" shared by contemplatives through the ages.[16] Far from legitimating the real fragmentation of social bonds in modern society, Christian mysticism dares to challenge the cultural and religious presuppositions of our age. For example, those who accept the risks of this task must also confront the asacramental and aliturgical character of modern spiritual life.[17]

In defending contemplative Christian action, Dupré advocates a dual commitment to the private interiority of the individual developed by modern thinkers and the authoritative communitarian aspirations of existing religious traditions.[18] The singularity of this twofold allegiance emerges in relief in his nuanced analysis of Alasdair MacIntyre's *After Virtue*.[19] He credits MacIntyre's

---

14. Dupré, *The Deeper Life*, p. 77.

15. Dupré, *The Deeper Life*, p. 88; *The Common Life: The Origins of Trinitarian Mysticism and Its Development by Jan Ruusbroec* (New York: Crossroad, 1984), passim, esp. p. 77.

16. Dupré, *The Common Life*, p. 31. For Dupré's analysis of the varieties of mystical experience, see the article "Mysticism" in *The Encyclopedia of Religion* and his introduction to *Light from Light: An Anthology of Christian Mysticism*, ed. Louis Dupré and James Wiseman, O.S.B. (New York: Paulist Press, 1988).

17. Cf. Dupré, *The Deeper Life*, p. 88; "Ritual: The Divine Play of Time," in *Play. Literature. Religion: Essays in Intertextuality*, ed. Virgil Nemoianu and Robert Royal (Albany: State University of New York Press, 1991), p. 205.

18. On the latter, see Louis Dupré, "Transcendent Selfhood and Religious Community," *Listening* 13 (1978): 38-47, and "Openness and Closedness in the Religious Community," in *Miscellanea Albert Dondeyne* (Louvain: Leuven University Press, 1974), pp. 67-74.

19. Louis Dupré, "Alternatives to the Cogito," *Review of Metaphysics* 40, no. 4 (1987): 707-14.

groundbreaking work with having found a precarious balance between a critique of the past and an inevitable acceptance of it. MacIntyre is correct to decry the disintegration of the concrete, universal norms that were mediated in the ancient *polis* by an individual's narrative continuity within the social fabric of a community not of his own making. The breakdown of this historical cohesiveness with modernity's primacy of the subject offered only the most abstract account of our moral obligations. Even the attempts by Pascal, Kierkegaard, and Schleiermacher to rescue a sense of transcendence within the subjective framework failed, for in taking the primacy of the individual subject as an axiomatic principle of modern thought, "[t]hey did not realize how much they spoke out of a condition of ethical poverty, rather than one of moral purity."[20] On the other hand, even though Kant's concept of an isolated, socially unconnected autonomy has been proven inadequate, writes Dupré, his insight concerning the self's irreducible responsibility for its actions remains convincing.[21] In the end modernity's problematic principle of subjectivity "cannot be de-invented."[22] Dupré seeks rather to retain both a principle of subjectivity and the concrete social institutions discovered by the modern era.

> We continue to have viable social institutions . . . but our particular problem lies in the individual's moral detachment with respect to these social structures. *They no longer convey meaning* to our lives, for meaning and value, by modern standards, must come entirely *from the individual subject.*[23]

Dupré therefore differs from MacIntyre in insisting that neither the Aristotelian theory of virtue nor a Benedictine withdrawal from a society will recover the transcendent relation at the heart of Christian belief. According to Dupré, we must first succeed in finding content for the new interiority of the modern epoch if we are to overcome the moral crisis of our society.

The religious content of modern belief appears in forms unknown to our spiritual predecessors. One can no longer presume a personal divine being as its object. Cardinal Newman, Dupré reports, foresaw the shock with which the experience of God's absence confronts the modern believer:

> What strikes the mind so forcibly is His absence (if I may so speak) from his own world. It is a silence that speaks. It is as if others had got possession of His work. Why does not He, our Maker and Ruler, give us some immediate knowledge of Himself?[24]

---

20. Dupré, "Alternatives to the Cogito," p. 713.
21. Dupré, "Alternatives to the Cogito," p. 707.
22. Dupré, "Alternatives to the Cogito," p. 714.
23. Dupré, "Alternatives to the Cogito," p. 712.
24. John Henry Cardinal Newman, *A Grammar of Assent* (Garden City, N.Y.: Dou-

God's absence is felt more acutely than ever before because modern believers feel that faith, even if accepted in an atheistic culture, is seldom the result of an inner necessity. The more open-ended and accessible to multiple interpretation our belief, the more we cling fiercely to the act of the will which seems to make it real. In the midst of this ambiguity, we face an inward emptiness that is only confirmed by the spiritual ambivalence of the world around us.

"The religious consciousness of absence," Dupré admonishes, "is not without precedent in the spiritual tradition."[25] The emptiness can therefore be given a spiritual meaning:

> The desert of modern atheism provides the only space in which we live and in which we must also first encounter the transcendent. The task of the modern God-seeker is to transform that desert into a solitude of contemplation. In some way all spiritual beginning requires solitude and detachment from the creature.[26]

A passive affirmation of modern secularism will not bring about *ipso facto* a conversion to the one in whom negative theologians such as Dionysius the Areopagite and Meister Eckhart professed their belief. Though the modern experience of a spiritually arid world does not conform to the mystic's contemplation of the dark night, secular emptiness can be the first step in following the mystic's way of purgation.[27]

The mystics speak of an inward path into the secret dwelling where God resides. Many metaphors have been used to describe this sacred space of interiority: "the ground of the soul" (Tauler), "the little castle" (Eckhart), "the interior home of the heart" (Catherine of Siena), "the inner castle" (Teresa of Avila), and "the house at rest . . . in darkness and concealment" (John of the Cross).[28] This "place" within is at once more interior to us than we are to ourselves *and* something ecstatic, beyond ourselves. Here in this hidden sanctuary we recognize not just who we are as defined by individual accomplishments but who we are *essentially*. In Dupré's own words, it is the place in which the person is recognized as self-transcending.[29]

Even though the christological element in the purgative way is easily overlooked in our current situation, its recovery is essential to joining traditional

---

bleday, 1955), p. 39, as cited in Louis Dupré, "Christian Spirituality Confronts the Modern World," *Communio: International Catholic Review* 12 (1985): 334. What follows in this paragraph is also taken from this article.

25. Dupré, "Spiritual Life," p. 17.

26. Dupré, "Christian Spirituality," p. 335.

27. Dupré, "Christian Spirituality," p. 339; "Religion in a Secular World," *Christianity and Crisis* 28 (1968): 74.

28. Dupré, *The Deeper Life*, p. 24.

29. Dupré, *The Deeper Life*, p. 25.

spiritual content with modern forms of thought.[30] Christ plays a prominent role among the Christian mystics, according to Louis Dupré, because through him one can take into account the essential role of creature as creature.[31] Christ is not just a teacher of wisdom to the enlightened but also the object of mystical love. His particular identity unites divinity and humanity in his very person: "[T]hrough the incarnation Christ includes *all* creation within himself (also in its finitude) and reunites it with its divine source."[32] Christ is the exemplar of creaturehood not just because he became like us but because his humanity is a dramatic symbol of God's outpouring love for us. The practical import of these assertions for the Christian life should not be underestimated. Searching for likenesses of Christ in those of our neighbors whom we are called to love, we are often disappointed. But if we learn through Christ the more perilous and less intuitive lesson of loving creaturehood for its own sake (as God himself does), then we can begin to grasp the meaning of the incarnation for the Christian mystics.

Moreover, the mystics' frequent admonition for abnegation and mortification must be understood as part of an interior battle for detachment from all creaturely desires.[33] Christian mysticism renounces not pleasure but the desire for pleasure. The mystic seeks not physical torment but the desire to reveal within the unity of body and soul an image of unadulterated, Christlike poverty. To describe this state of resignation Meister Eckhart coined the term *Gelassenheit,* releasement, a word which connotes waiting in expectation, openness without demands, and a willingness to be drawn into God's own vacuum.[34]

Significantly, Meister Eckhart never developed a trinitarian theology as rich as that of Jan van Ruusbroec.[35] In Eckhart's theology of the image, the creature is a dynamic reality constantly moving from difference from God to identity and back. The condemnation of some propositions of Eckhart by Pope John XXII made the theological ambiguity of this position well known. Dupré poses the question as follows: "[D]oes [Eckhart] mean that the created mind in its spiritual ascent moves into a divine reality where the distinctions between Father, Son and Holy Spirit no longer exist?"[36] According to Dupré, Eckhart seems to be inventing

---

30. On the compatibility of traditional negative theology and the positive claims of Christology, see Peter Casarella, "'His Name Was Called Jesus': Negative Theology and Christology in Nicholas of Cusa," in *Nicholas of Cusa on Christ and the Church: Essays in Memory of Chandler McCuskey Brooks,* ed. Gerald Christianson and Thomas M. Izbicki (Leiden: E. J. Brill, 1996), pp. 281-311.

31. Dupré, "Christian Spirituality," p. 338.

32. Dupré, "Christian Spirituality," p. 338.

33. Dupré, "Christian Spirituality," p. 339; *The Deeper Life,* chap. 4, "The Poverty of God."

34. Dupré, *The Deeper Life,* p. 44.

35. Cf. Dupré, *The Common Life,* chap. 2, "From Silence to Speech," for this and what follows.

36. Dupré, *The Common Life,* p. 25.

a new theologoumenon when he suggests that the Absolute is beyond the Trinity and the Godhead beyond the Father, at least one unknown to Scripture and the Fathers. For Ruusbroec and Louis Dupré, on the other hand,

> The Father is, indeed, the principle of darkness and silence, but a darkness that is to break out into Light, a silence that is to speak the Word. The theology of the image leads to what lies beyond images. Negative theology is an essential part of it. But it is not the final way station on the soul's pilgrimage.[37]

In contrast to Eckhart, Ruusbroec granted that there is a moment of identity with the unity of God without distinctions, but he rejected the thesis that God's being is total darkness into which everything comes to a definitive rest.[38] Eschewing all unitarian mysticism, Ruusbroec contends that we move out of divine rest *with* (not beyond) the divine persons. Grace actually moves the contemplative out of a passive resignation into an active involvement with the world, a spiritual rhythm which mirrors the uncreated, triune movement of the divine life.[39]

Eckhartian negative theology thus needs to be supplemented by a trinitarian spirituality of the common life. Dupré repeatedly reminds us that alongside the dramatic path of contemplative abandonment, there is also a Christian mysticism of the everyday.[40] The two ways are not mutually exclusive but stand in a complementary relation.[41] In *The Common Life* Dupré sketches out a mystical theology based upon trinitarian and social communion. Ruusbroec conceives of "the common life" *(dat ghemeyne leven)* in three phases, which are not temporally distinct: the virtuous life of longing for God in union with his created grace, the interior life in which we become aware of and are drawn into God's uncreated presence in the soul, and the contemplative life in which the soul withdraws into the pure unity within (not beyond) the communion of the three divine persons.[42] At the end of the second and in preparation for the third

---

37. Dupré, *The Common Life,* p. 27.

38. Dupré, *The Common Life,* p. 30. Jean Gerson, chancellor of the University of Paris, criticized Ruusbroec's autotheistic sayings in spite of this qualification, but recent scholarship by André Combes has shown that Gerson himself moves close to this kind of expression in his later years. Cf. James Wiseman, O.S.B., " 'To Be God with God': The Autotheistic Sayings of the Mystics," *Theological Studies* 51 (1990): 247.

39. Cf. Wiseman, " 'To Be God with God,' " p. 250.

40. Dupré, *The Common Life,* p. 53.

41. Cf. Dupré, *The Common Life,* pp. 49ff.

42. The three phases are articulated in *The Spiritual Marriage.* In *The Sparkling Stone,* his next treatise, the movement toward an active spirituality engaged in the world is even more pronounced since the opening line of that treatise speaks of a person "who is lifted up to the contemplation of God, and who goes forth to all in common." Cf. Wiseman, " 'To Be God with God,' " p. 244.

phase, the virtuous soul recognizes that "here God alone works."[43] In contrast to Eckhart, the complete self-surrender to the activity of God's grace in the soul moves out into an active life in union with the distinct persons of the Trinity.[44]

The specifically trinitarian character of Ruusbroec's vision of the common life comes out in the exegesis of the following passage from *The Spiritual Marriage*, II, 65: "And from out of the Divine Unity, there shines into [the contemplative soul] a simple light; and this light shows him Darkness and Nakedness and Nothingness." According to Dupré, this seemingly paradoxical juxtaposition of darkness and light incorporates the central themes of Ruusbroec's trinitarian theology. The passage occurs as the soul rests within the eternal silence of the Father and prepares to enter into communion with his relation to the Son through the Holy Spirit. "Darkness, nakedness, and nothingness" represent the unoriginate Father, the source of the entire Trinity.[45] The light which paradoxically shows darkness is the Son whose saving light is generally understood to be an outward expression of the Father's goodness. Since the "moment" represented by this image occurs "at the beginning of the contemplative life in the realm of the Father," the Son's light is still a hidden one, which reveals the unoriginate, fertile darkness within whom he himself is generated.[46] The birth of the Son is at once the movement of the incarnate Word into the world and in him the birth of all created things. The rhythmic eternal movement from Father to Son and from Father to all of creation cannot be separated for the contemplative because all things have their life and their being in him, the eternal Word spoken by the Father.[47] Light shines from out of the divine unity into the contemplative soul. The divine unity is the unity of the Spirit. The Spirit joins the Father and the Son, and in this supreme activity of unification represents the supreme love of the entire Trinity pouring out from the Father and Son. The unification that takes place supremely in the Spirit is the highest, undifferentiated, and unmediated unity of God but is not beyond or above the divine persons.

The contemplative soul follows the triune rhythm of God's own common life. In letting this supratemporal movement become the rhythm of our own

43. *The Spiritual Marriage*, II, 51. The translations from *The Spiritual Marriage* are taken from John of Ruysbroeck, *The Adornment of the Spiritual Marriage, the Sparkling Stone, and the Book of Supreme Truth*, trans. Dom C. A. Wijnschenck (London, 1916), the relevant sections of which are appended to Dupré's *The Common Life*.

44. The distinction between Ruusbroec and Eckhart on this point cannot be absolutized, as if there were no traces of a trinitarian spirituality in Eckhart's thought. Since writing *The Common Life*, Louis Dupré has publicly qualified the sharp distinction he draws in that work between the two approaches.

45. Dupré, *The Common Life*, p. 50.

46. Dupré, *The Common Life*, p. 50.

47. See also Dupré, *The Common Life*, pp. 60-61: "Nowhere does Ruusbroec claim that the creation and the birth of the Son coincide."

life, our normal preconceptions of the contemplative life are shattered. Life lived in the unity of the Spirit images the alternation from being to work and from essence to manifestation of the divine life. The unity of God's "common life" and ours is described most pregnantly in the following passage from *The Spiritual Marriage*, II, 45:

> He was sent down to earth to the common *(ghemeyne)* benefit of all men who would turn to Him. . . . Now mark how Christ gave Himself to all *(ghemeyne)* in perfect loyalty. His inward and sublime prayer flowed forth towards his Father, and it was a prayer for all in common *(ghemeyne)* who desired to be saved. Christ was common to all *(ghemeyne)* in love, in teaching, in tender consolation, in generous gifts, in merciful forgiveness. His soul and His body, His life and His death and His ministry were and are common to all *(ghemeyne)*.

Without Christ there is no way to grasp that which remains beyond our grasp and our achievement, namely, how the soul attains its own "superessence" in the divine life. In his incarnate life, Christ symbolizes the saving significance of God's own common life. His prayers and loving embrace to and from the Father represent the ebb and flow of the divine persons in Christ. Trinitarian mysticism therefore incorporates our whole life, a life whose beginning, middle, and end is the *imitatio Christi*.

To summarize this section, both Christian negative theology and trinitarian spirituality in their classical formulations are viable responses to the atheistic climate of modernity. These responses are not techniques, recipes, or antidotes. A return to the mystical approach to the transcendent will not "solve" the problem of modern atheism. By recovering these paths from the depths of the Christian tradition, the modern believer, however, can seek transcendence beyond his or her own self-fabrications. The task of seeking transcendent selfhood can still find a foothold in the spiritual impoverishment and isolated individualism of the cultural situation in which we find ourselves. This, I take it, is the meaning of holding hard to the poverty of modern culture.

II. Traditional Spiritual Content in Modern Forms of Thought

As an essentially spiritual stance, holding hard to the poverty of modern culture requires an understanding of the religious traditions that inspired and contributed to the modern discovery of the subject. Dupré's defense of negative theology and trinitarian mysticism are not isolated instances of his hermeneutics of recovery. Throughout his works he aims to restore the spiritual wisdom of the past that will speak to the modern age's crisis of faith.

What follows is a synopsis of Dupré's genealogy of the modern spiritual predicament. It should be underscored that Dupré explores the history of modernity's cultural crisis for other than historical reasons. This is not another version of the familiar story of what happens when traditional faith meets modern atheism. The genealogy is itself an essential part of the solution. Without a proper understanding of how modernity disintegrates, changes, and critically informs traditional belief, an intelligent response to our current crisis is simply impossible. By identifying faith with the known contents of a religious consciousness, modernity creates the illusion that the religious experience is familiar and close to hand. Nothing could be further from the truth. Holding hard to the poverty of our situation, we must also question our ready-made explanations of how we arrived at our present spiritual crisis.

Throughout this narrative, Dupré is negotiating the terms of a precariously balanced synthesis. Modernity requires a form of belief that affirms and accepts a subjective definition of truth, yet the traditional content of Christian belief also demands that the subject seek what is far beyond its own self-expression. Placing traditional spiritual content in modern forms of thought can change the meaning of the original message. That is the ineluctable, hermeneutical challenge of interpreting the tradition in modern terms.

In a recent work Dupré described Petrarch's famed ascent of Mount Ventoux as a paradigm of modernity's spiritual and intellectual struggle. Petrarch still required "the penetrating eyes of Augustine" in order to convey an objective quality and transcendent perspective to his introspection.[48] Although Dupré holds pre-Christian Hellenism in high esteem, he looks to Saint Augustine as a starting point for the genealogy of modern culture.[49] In fact, he seems inclined to portray the history of modern spirituality, to paraphrase Whitehead, as a series of footnotes to Augustine. Both the early Augustine's Neoplatonically inspired notion of interiority and the later Augustine's dialectics of sin and grace figure prominently in the passage to the modern predicament. Dupré sometimes seems torn between these two very different approaches advocated by this one seminal theologian. His treatments of modern figures display a similar ambivalence. For example, Dupré praises Hegel's spiritual theology but favors Kierkegaard's inquiry into the subjective situation of sin and despair even more. Likewise, Schillebeeckx is applauded for emphasizing modern religious experience, but von Balthasar receives an even more affirmative nod for plainly acknowledging that faith alone forms true

48. Dupré, *Passage to Modernity*, p. 98.
49. Cf. Etienne Gilson, *Études sur le rôle de la pensée médiévale dans la formation du système cartésien*, 5th ed. (Paris: Vrin, 1984); Charles Taylor, *Sources of the Self* (Cambridge: Harvard University Press, 1989), pp. 127-42.

Christian knowledge. In sum, inward growth into God's own image and the existential leap of faith go hand in hand in Dupré's account of the modern spiritual predicament.

Dupré's estimation of Augustine's value to the contemporary believer is almost as highly varied as the bishop's own intellectual changes of heart. In an early magazine article on the birth control controversy, Dupré castigates Augustine for his "strange, sexual pessimism."[50] Yet a far more positive evaluation of the bishop of Hippo serves as the dramatic conclusion to Dupré's later confrontation with MacIntyre:

> In the past the transcendence within immanence, the openness within the self-enclosure was secured by a religious view of reality. In the absence of such a view, I do not know what could serve as a viable substitute. . . . [I]s there in the end no substitute, and must we wait, with Alasdair MacIntyre, for a new Benedict? If we must, I think that we shall first need a new Augustine.[51]

Augustine's theology, in spite of its sometimes questionable denigration of the human body, is a key building block in the spiritual reconstruction of modern culture. For Louis Dupré no constructive proposal can afford to ignore the positive aspects of the Augustinian heritage.

What are these positive aspects? Augustine held the conception of the soul "the richest of all concepts."[52] By reading Neoplatonic writings, Augustine became converted to the life within.[53] From Neoplatonists and the Greek Fathers, he learned of a theory of participation by which the human soul is an image of God by nature rather than by any external analogy.[54] The spiritual life consists of " 'living toward the Image,' that is, in an increasing awareness of, and growing toward, that divine Image which holds the center of my very self."[55] In contrast to the Greek approach, which emphasized the spiritual indwelling of the three divine persons, Augustine added a psychological dimension that is absent in the Greek spiritual theology.[56] Augustine writes:

> I have poured forth my soul above myself. No longer is there any being for me to touch save my God.[57]

---

50. Louis Dupré, "From Augustine to Janssens," *Commonweal* 180 (1964): 338.
51. Dupré, "Alternatives to the Cogito," p. 716.
52. Dupré, *Passage to Modernity*, p. 118.
53. Dupré, *Passage to Modernity*, p. 94.
54. Dupré, *The Common Life*, p. 13.
55. Dupré, *The Common Life*, p. 13.
56. Dupré, *The Common Life*, p. 18.
57. Augustine, *Enarrat. in Psalm.* 41, 8 (*Patrologia Latina* 36:469; hereafter cited as *PL):* "Effudi super me animam meam; et non iam restat quem tangam, nisi Deum meum."

This statement exemplifies Augustine's theology of the soul's interior journey to the divine Archetype. "The practice of spiritual life consists not in seeing God in a pre-existing image but in becoming an image through greater unity."[58] Augustine uncovers the primacy of the subject that was to become a building block in the revolution brought about in modern thought.

Dupré emphasizes both psychological introspection and mystical theology as the roots of Augustine's "discovery," refusing to play one off against the other. This leads him to reject Charles Taylor's claim that "it was Augustine who introduced the inwardness of radical reflexivity and bequeathed it to the Western tradition of thought."[59] Taylor ignores the debt which Augustine owes to the intrinsically spiritual notion of the Neoplatonist writers that only the inward turn leads the soul to the spirit *(nous)*, which constitutes its inner essence. Moreover, Augustine's new psychological theory of the spiritual life, what Taylor calls "the inwardness of radical reflexivity," is predicated upon the transformation of the external images of the Trinity in the soul (memory, understanding, and love) into "a real, intrinsic image."[60] Psychology is superseded by mystical theology: "When the mind loves God and by consequence . . . remembers and understands him, then with respect to its neighbor it is rightly commanded to love him as it loves itself. For it no longer loves itself perversely but rightly when it loves God, by partaking of him in whom that image not only exists but is also renewed. . . ."[61] Augustine's delicate synthesis of spiritual introspection with real transcendence can also be distorted by the modern revolution. The Augustinian insight into the participable ground of the self in eternal truth is eclipsed by the modern turn to the subject as the sole source of meaning and value.

Augustine's prioritizing of divine presence over extrinsic analogies reflects a theological position which Dupré defends in a number of different contexts. Augustine held that the vestiges of the Trinity in the outer world are only similitudes compared to the images of the Trinity in the mind. Dupré radicalizes this conception considerably when he asserts that Augustine's claim that God dwells directly in the soul allows us to conclude that presence and identity are the decisive categories for the spiritual life today.[62] In Dupré's opinion, contemporary spiritual movements have stressed identity over analogy; that is, the ever greater likeness of God's presence in the soul to the divine archetype which it images, to any external resemblance between the infinite Creator and the finite creature.[63] Dupré contends that Augustine's theology of the image as-

---

58. Louis Dupré, "Negative Theology and the Affirmation of the Finite," in *Esistenza, Mito, Ermeneutica,* ed. E. Castelli (Padua: CEDAM, 1980), p. 378.

59. Taylor, pp. 123, 131, as cited in Dupré, *Passage to Modernity,* p. 93.

60. Dupré, *The Common Life,* p. 18.

61. Augustine, *De Trin.* 14, 14, 18 (*PL* 42:1050).

62. Dupré, "Christian Spirituality," pp. 336-37.

63. Dupré, "Christian Spirituality," pp. 336-37. Augustine continues to stress both

sumes a real union of the divine core of the finite creature with the Trinity, a single point where God and the creature fully touch. With this recognition, contemporary spiritual life can begin to recover the lost sacred quality of the finite as such. As Eckhart also stated, all are equally far from God in resemblance, but all are also equally near in identity. This holds not only with respect to their divine core but even to their imperfect finitude.[64] The spiritual shift inward initiated by the fourth-century bishop finds its completion in the modern notion that the presence of the divine is identifiable in all things finite, even in their ungodly finitude. Seeing the entire created cosmos as God's gift, however, is not the view of nature that has dominated modern thought.

In fact, Augustine's synthesis does not even survive the Latin Middle Ages. The most characteristic and damaging theological innovation of the modern age, namely, its separation of nature and grace, begins to take shape long before the advent of modernity.[65] For the Greeks, form resides within the appearing objects of which it constitutes the intelligible essence. Neither the ancient philosophers nor the Eastern Fathers know of a pure nature to which grace is added as a kind of superstructure. Dupré therefore follows de Lubac, von Balthasar, and Karl Rahner in decrying the late scholastic notion of pure nature as anything but a purely hypothetical construct.[66]

Thomas Aquinas is free of this sort of dualism because he never conceived of nature as an independent reality with a self-sufficient natural end. Dupré nonetheless finds fault with Aquinas's theology. He points to the same issue that followers of Scotus would eventually attack; that is, the Thomistic thesis that without the fall the incarnation would not have occurred. "Viewed from this perspective," Dupré argues, "redemption might be interpreted as a supernatural cure for a natural disease and, as such, as initiating a wholly different order of grace."[67] This position, if attributable to Saint Thomas in this form, would in fact endanger the delicate balance that holds Aquinas's synthesis together.[68]

For Dupré Aquinas provided the most organic union of Christian faith with the Aristotelianism of his day. The real dissolution of the medieval synthesis begins with the nominalist theologies of the fourteenth and fifteenth centuries.

---

elements, as when he states that even the outer man offers "a kind of resemblance to the Trinity" (quandam trinitatis effigiem) (De trin. 11, 1, 1 [PL 42:984]).

64. Dupré, "Christian Spirituality," p. 337.

65. See Dupré's Passage to Modernity, part III, and his "The Dissolution of the Union of Nature and Grace at the Dawn of the Modern Age," in The Theology of Wolfhart Pannenberg, ed. Carl E. Braaten and Philip Clayton (Minneapolis: Augsburg, 1988), pp. 95-121.

66. Cf. Louis Dupré, "Hans Urs von Balthasar's Theology of Aesthetic Form," Theological Studies 49 (1988): 306.

67. Dupré, Passage to Modernity, p. 172.

68. Cf. Peter Casarella, "On Dupré's Passage to Modernity," Communio: International Catholic Review 21 (1994): 557.

While John Duns Scotus makes a quasi-independent abstraction of pure nature, some nominalists take the distinction between absolute and ordained power to refer to successive moments in God. These theological developments will eventually lead to the idea of an independent order of secondary causes. Once the distinction between nature and grace becomes an actual separation, then theology can no longer rely on the analogy of nature in the fullest sense. Once the full force of the modern presuppositions becomes accepted, the only logical options are either an antiphilosophical fideism or a materialistic, noncreationist pantheism. The subsequent history of Christian theology is rife with examples of both.

In *Passage to Modernity,* Dupré outlines the attempted reunions and provisional syntheses of the fifteenth and sixteenth centuries. He surveys the contributions of Nicholas of Cusa ("the last thinker to reunite the . . . forces that had begun to pull the medieval synthesis apart"), humanist religion, Luther and Calvin, the spiritual theologies of Ignatius of Loyola and Francis de Sales, early modern Protestant mysticism and speculative thought, and the last comprehensive synthesis — the baroque. The legacy of the spiritual theologians of this initial period of transition represents important achievements, for they not only faced the crisis presented by the new definition of subjectivity but offered a still very traditional account of a Christian faith that could no longer be meaningfully expressed in scholastic categories.

This defense of early modern spiritual theology poses a sharp challenge to Hans Blumenberg's modification of the secularization thesis.[69] For Blumenberg the characteristically modern stance, human self-assertion, "re-occupies" the position left vacant by the conceptual failure of nominalist conceptions of divine omnipotence. *Pace* Karl Löwith, the modern view of unlimited human freedom is not so much a secularization of Christian eschatological hopes as a resolution of a traditional problem with a thoroughly modern solution. *Passage to Modernity,* however, considers figures who reverse the process of self-assertion by reoccupying modern forms of thought with traditional spiritual content. The *Spiritual Exercises* of Ignatius of Loyola, Dupré claims, is an exemplary expression of a modern spiritual method informed by traditional spiritual content:

> In presenting human creativity as descended from above, Ignatius inverted the naturalist view of the person, but that inversion would not have been

---

69. Hans Blumenberg, *The Legitimacy of the Modern Age,* trans. Robert M. Wallace (Cambridge: MIT Press, 1983). What follows is based upon Dupré's *Passage to Modernity.* Dupré's treatment of Blumenberg's thesis on p. 2 of *Transcendent Selfhood: The Loss and Rediscovery of the Inner Life* (New York: Seabury Press, 1976) is far less critical. Even in *Passage to Modernity,* the differences between Dupré's modern forms with traditional spiritual content and Blumenberg's emphasis on modernity's total discontinuity with the past are largely implicit. See, however, p. 226.

possible without the modern tension between a divine and human order conceived as separate centers of power.[70]

Accepting the modern norm of a subjective starting point, Ignatius nonetheless "transforms the anthropocentric ideal of creative self-development by placing it within a radically theocentric perspective."[71]

Many will be surprised with Dupré's contention that another modern form of thought with traditional spiritual content can be found in the legacy of Jansenius.[72] Nowhere is Dupré's dissatisfaction with the naturalist tendency in modern theology more evident than in his efforts to restore the tarnished reputation of this fellow Fleming and Louvain graduate:

> History has judged Jansenius severely, partly, I think because of his and his followers' devious way of carrying on a theological dispute. This has earned "Jansenism" the unprecedented number of five condemnations. Yet the polemical bishop was right on at least one crucial issue, namely, that the concept of *natura pura* — an order of nature independent of a "supernatural" order of grace — is an untenable concept within Christian doctrine.[73]

Jansenius recovered the substance of late Augustinian anti-Pelagianism in a form of thought that later influenced Pascal, Racine, and the spiritual movement known as "devout humanism."[74] In his intricate theology of nature and grace ("what may well be the most complicated system in modern theology"), he granted Augustine the same unique reverence and authority with which Calvin approached Scripture.[75]

Whereas late scholastic theology divided nature and grace into two separate orders of being, Jansenius replaced their juxtaposition in space with a temporal opposition before and after the fall. Adam's original state of justice was itself grace. In this state Adam did not need God's assistance to will to act rightly, only to be able to do so. After the fall, grace virtually eradicates nature's capacity to act naturally, for it is required for both the disposition and the ability to act. "Instead of a dualism of complementarity of a pure nature and a super-

---

70. Dupré, *Passage to Modernity*, p. 226.

71. Dupré, *Passage to Modernity*, p. 226. Cf. Louis Dupré, "Ignatian Humanism and Its Mystical Origins," *Communio: International Catholic Review* 18 (1991): 164-82.

72. Louis Dupré, "Jansenius, an Intellectual Biography," *Journal of Religion* 73 (1993): 75-82; *Passage to Modernity*, pp. 216-20.

73. Dupré, "Jansenius," p. 79.

74. Cf. Louis Dupré, "Jansenism and Quietism," in *Christian Spirituality III: Post-Reformation and Modern*, ed. Louis Dupré and Don Saliers, World Spirituality: An Encyclopedic History of the Religious Quest, vol. 18 (New York: Crossroad, 1989, 1991; London: SCM, 1990); *Passage to Modernity*, pp. 223-30.

75. Dupré, "Jansenism and Quietism," pp. 78, 82; *Passage to Modernity*, p. 217.

natural order, Jansenius' position ends up with a full-dressed battle between nature and grace."[76] Despite his strong protestations to the contrary, the result of Jansenius's revival of the Augustinian primacy of grace was not unlike Calvin's: God redeems only a select group whom he has predestined.

Jansenius's theology of grace may derive verbatim from Augustine, but at least one premise was fundamentally modern. In exalting grace, Jansenius separated a conscious intention, what he called an acting principle of love *(motivum caritatis)*, from the nature it was meant to heal and redeem. Jansenius's aim was just the opposite of the modern assumption hidden within his thought. His system was designed to ward off a separation of actual moral choices from their ontological substrate. Instead he implicitly validated "the modern primacy of the conscious self as the sole and ever-active source of meaning."[77]

Passage to Modernity ends with the provisional syntheses of the seventeenth century. Dupré's readers can expect a future synthesis of the trajectory of modern thought in the wake of the Enlightenment.[78] Without attempting to anticipate the scope or content of that volume, I will now trace some of the developments in the religious thought of these later centuries discussed in his publications prior to 1995.

Kant looms large on the horizon of all of Dupré's treatments of the modern age.[79] *A Dubious Heritage* deserves to be more widely read by theologians, for the essays gathered in this volume offer a penetrating analysis of the Kantian heritage bequeathed to modern religious thought.[80] According to Dupré, Kant further developed the Cartesian principle. For Kant subjectivity is not just parallel to the objective world but constitutive of objectivity. As Kant himself claimed, his critique of metaphysics discredited the traditional proofs for the existence of God in order to make room for a faith based upon the purely human experience of the moral law.

The consequences of Kant's thought for the subsequent philosophy of religion were threefold. First, since reliable theoretical knowledge is restricted to the objective, phenomenal sphere, the religious consciousness can expect no direct support of its beliefs from theoretical reason. Second, since the transcendent is no longer directly perceptible in the cosmic order, the religious consciousness must be redirected from the subject's knowledge of the world to its awareness of itself. Third, no transcendent reality can interfere with exercise of human freedom once the subject is conceived as essentially autonomous. The

---

76. Dupré, "Jansenius," p. 81.

77. Dupré, *Passage to Modernity,* p. 220.

78. There is at least a hint of a companion volume in *Passage to Modernity,* p. 253.

79. Below I discuss the influence of Kantian thought on his theory of the symbol.

80. Louis Dupré, *A Dubious Heritage: Studies in the Philosophy of Religion after Kant* (New York: Paulist Press, 1977). See especially the introduction, upon which the following is based. *A Dubious Heritage* is also reviewed in this volume in the essay by George Schner, S.J.

highly varied philosophical heritage of Kant which Dupré surveys — ranging from Hegel and Schleiermacher in the nineteenth century to Maurice Blondel and Henry Duméry in the twentieth — is therefore bound to justify religious faith on the basis of experience and to legitimate that experience within the context of human autonomy.

Kant's appeal to the experience of the moral law within is further refined by Schleiermacher and Hegel. According to Dupré, Schleiermacher set the agenda for all subsequent theories of religious experience (even after the nineteenth century), but Hegel was the more astute commentator on the spiritual predicament of the modern era. Dupré corrects the view that Schleiermacher's notion of religion as feeling is based upon a purely subjective determination of religious experience. From the beginning, feeling for Schleiermacher belongs to a stage of consciousness in which subject and object are basically identical.[81] Feeling precedes the more specific dynamisms of cognition or desire and therefore remains immune to attacks from either side.[82] Feeling is not something created by our subjective state but a condition in which the Absolute can reveal itself. In his more mature work, *The Christian Faith,* Schleiermacher clarifies the subject's mode of receptivity by claiming that only as feeling of *absolute* dependence does feeling reveal the Absolute.[83]

Despite Dupré's defense of the relative objectivity of the religious experience, he does not deny that Schleiermacher accepts and even radicalizes the principle of autonomy advocated by traditional Christianity's nineteenth-century trenchant critics (i.e., the "cultured despisers" of *The Speeches on Religion*):

> Schleiermacher felt that religion had nothing to fear from ethical humanism. His philosophy attempted to escape the Kantian dilemma of either religion or autonomy.[84]

In the end, Dupré criticizes Schleiermacher's marriage of religious experience with romanticist notions of autonomy. Schleiermacher failed to distinguish between a feeling of religiosity which is fully indistinguishable from the aesthetic experience and religion itself. As Hegel rightly points out, Schleiermacher posits a nonarbitrary symbolic expression as part of the intrinsic rationality of faith. By reflecting on its symbols, the religious mind "goes beyond the harmonious but self-complacent equilibrium of aesthetic consciousness."[85] Feeling is indeed

---

81. Dupré, *A Dubious Heritage,* p. 11.
82. Dupré, *A Dubious Heritage,* p. 10.
83. Dupré, *A Dubious Heritage,* p. 23.
84. Dupré, *A Dubious Heritage,* p. 9.
85. Dupré, *A Dubious Heritage,* p. 26. For a less sympathetic view of Dupré's recourse to Hegelian arguments in treating the distinction between religion and aesthetics, see the article by Karsten Harries in this volume.

a way station on the mind's journey to God, but it is not the final destination. Schleiermacher maintained that the direct experience of the idea of God is either purely arbitrary or a "corruption" of the immediate self-consciousness of the Absolute.[86] Dupré demonstrates convincingly, however, that reflection on concrete symbols is not subordinate to the felt experience of faith but integral to both its inception and survival.

More so than Schleiermacher, Hegel is the nineteenth-century figure who has contributed the most to a possible synthesis of traditional religious content with a fully modern form of thought. From the beginning both Hegel's atheist admirers and his critics from within orthodox Christianity denounced the presumption that the content of Christian faith could be joined speculatively to modern philosophical principles. By contrast, Dupré affirms that Hegel is virtually *sui generis* in modern religious thought, for he heralds neither "an atheist secularism masked by Christian terminology" nor "orthodox Christian doctrine."[87] Even though Hegel concedes a great deal to the modern project, the particular form of his justification of a secular culture still places him in line with modern thinkers who set out to preserve traditional religious content.[88]

With his theory of the Absolute Spirit, Hegel directs his avowedly secular contemporaries to a transcendent dimension that arises in the very process of reflection on thought itself.[89] The secular representation of the Absolute for Hegel does not stand higher than the religious one. "Nothing would be more foreign to Hegel's thought than the idea of an Absolute Spirit which stands above God and produces him."[90] Even when the religious representation has been surpassed by the necessary movement of thought toward philosophy, "faith continues to provide the content of philosophical thought." For Hegel only Christian theology — by that he means the Protestant Reformers' interpretation of the Christian faith — has introduced the pivotal philosophical notion of the unfolding of the self-revelatory Absolute Spirit in history.[91]

According to Dupré, Hegel's theory that the Absolute Spirit mediates itself in history is not completely unlike traditional Christianity's mystical theology of participation. Hegel's appeal to Meister Eckhart in his *Lectures on the Philosophy of Religion* expresses precisely what Dupré values most in the Dominican's

---

86. Dupré, *A Dubious Heritage*, p. 21.

87. Dupré, *A Dubious Heritage*, p. 351.

88. Dupré, *A Dubious Heritage*, pp. 53-72. What follows is drawn from Dupré, "Hegel's Absolute Spirit: A Religious Justification of Secular Culture," in *University of Ottawa Quarterly* 52 (1983): 554-74 (reprinted in *Neoplatonismo e religione, Archivio di Filosofia* 51 [1983]: 351-63).

89. Dupré, *A Dubious Heritage*, pp. 351-52.

90. Dupré, *A Dubious Heritage*, p. 362.

91. Dupré, *A Dubious Heritage*, p. 352.

theory of divine presence: "The eye through which I see God is the selfsame one through which God sees me."[92]

Yet Hegel is not a Christian mystic. His theory that the Absolute Spirit *must* mediate itself in history in order to know itself departs from all but the outermost fringes of orthodox mysticism. Though rooted in a traditional trinitarian theology for both its content and its initial form, Hegel's philosophy of Spirit develops into a distinctly secular mode of thinking. This occurs, according to Dupré, in two ways. First, the Spirit begins to be thought in its traditional representation as a distinct hypostasis of the triune God. Yet philosophical reflection on this theologoumenon reveals that Spirit is the all-consuming totality of revelation — the divine, its finite manifestation, *and* the process by which manifestation returns to its aboriginal unity. Second, Spirit, which must inhabit the community in order to develop, dwells not only in the community conscious of itself as religious. Spirit overcomes the opposition between a sacred and a secular sphere of life to the point where traditional ecclesiastical structures dissolve into the ethics of the world. Yet the social product of this sublation, "a philosophical kind of civil religion," offers a critique of the rationalist mores of the Enlightenment even as it deviates radically from the social structures of premodern Christendom.[93]

Even though Hegel's belief in the progressive secularization of the revealed form of religion is more optimistic than Dupré's, Hegel serves as an exemplary instance of a modern form of thought which preserves traditional religious content. He advances the idea of religious experience within the post-Kantian paradigm beyond Schleiermacher's pietistic notion of the feeling of absolute dependence. Against Schleiermacher, Hegel does not maintain that religious faith terminates in feeling. "All feeling," in Hegel's view, "remains ultimately self-feeling; faith is knowledge."[94]

He also develops a notion of the immanence of the divine in the world which conforms neither to typically modern nor premodern standards. The product of the unfolding of Absolute Spirit in Hegel's secular religion does not legitimate the Enlightenment, for Hegel's is an intrinsic synthesis which sees the ethical content of the revealed religion as a nonsubstitutable living presence in the practical affairs of civil society. Since the morality of the Enlightenment "united a purely abstract divine law with an exclusively human practical order," he deems the Age of Reason just as dark as that of the medieval church. From our vantage point, Hegel's secular religion seems paradoxical. Even though he believes that secularization is a necessary development from within Christianity, there is little room for a truly philosophical but originally

---

92. Hegel, *Vorlesungen I*, p. 257, as cited in *A Dubious Heritage*, p. 354.
93. Dupré, "Hegel's Absolute Spirit," p. 360.
94. Dupré, "Hegel's Absolute Spirit," p. 355.

non-Christian culture in Hegel's system. Above all, Dupré concludes, Hegel's thought is intrinsically related to the content but not the form of traditional Christianity. The connection lies less in his nominally Lutheran vocabulary and more in his attempt to justify modernity's discovery of the relative autonomy of the secular order on the basis of precepts drawn from Christian faith.[95]

Whereas Hegel tries to justify the modern form in religious terms, Kierkegaard draws upon traditional religious categories in order to challenge the overall shape of modern thought. In Kierkegaard, Dupré finds the late nineteenth century's counterpart to Augustine. Dupré's interest in Kierkegaard's thought spans the course of his career. His book and articles have dealt with Kierkegaard's dialectics of faith (1956), recent German literature on Kierkegaard (1957), *Kierkegaard as Theologian* (original Dutch 1958, English translation 1963), the constitution of the self in Kierkegaard's philosophy (1963), and Kierkegaard's critique of the modern age (1987). The hiatus of twenty-four years between the fourth and fifth publication is noteworthy, for Dupré developed his thinking on the philosophical origins of modern culture in the intervening period.[96] The article from 1987 therefore might be read as a comparison of Dupré's own analysis of the spiritual predicament of modern culture with that of the "Socrates for Christians," the one whose dialectical and existential experience of the transcendent first provoked him to write about religious themes in a systematic way.[97]

This last article, which analyzes Kierkegaard's mature anthropology in *The Sickness unto Death*, reveals the anguished Lutheran's attempt to mount a direct challenge to modern culture. Even while continuing to use traditional categories of sin and grace, Kierkegaard still accepts a fundamentally modern premise, the primacy of the individual. *The Sickness unto Death* contains a trenchant critique of the decline of individual responsibility in modern culture and thereby of the passionless, noncommittal attitude of mass society.[98] Authentic individuality, according to Kierkegaard, involves recognizing that modernity's emancipation of private subjectivity has resulted in its very demise.

> The person is forced to live his existence on various, separate levels. On each one he expresses himself differently according to the particular demands of

---

95. Dupré, "Hegel's Absolute Spirit," p. 351.

96. Some preliminary thoughts on Kierkegaard's place in the development of modern culture occur at the end of the chapter on "Kierkegaard's Religion as Freedom," in *The Dubious Heritage*, pp. 30-52. Kierkegaard also figures prominently in *Transcendent Selfhood*, esp. chap. 4, "The Diseased Self."

97. Louis Dupré, *Kierkegaard as Theologian: The Dialectic of Christian Existence* (New York: Sheed & Ward, 1963), pp. xii-xiii.

98. Dupré, *"The Sickness unto Death,"* p. 87.

his function; in none does he engage himself unconditionally. Existence withdraws behind a variety of social masks.[99]

The untruth which the crowd represents for Kierkegaard needs to be unmasked through a passionate search for religious inwardness. Kierkegaard's famous maxim that truth is subjectivity is not so much a license to exalt the modern discovery of human freedom as it is an awareness that an individual's true freedom is dialectical.[100] Faith — defined as a personal longing of the individual for eternity — is the only way of escape from the tyranny placed on true human freedom by ideals of political and social equality.[101] Only in the confrontation with God can man become an individual.[102] To exist for Kierkegaard means being in time yet acknowledging responsibility for eternity.[103]

One of the most innovative contributions of Kierkegaard to modern religious thought is his evaluation of the Augustinian-Lutheran doctrine of sin. Recognizing that one is a sinner before God is the only way to become an authentic individual.[104] Mid-nineteenth-century Danish Lutheranism had trivialized the existential dimension of the traditional doctrine. Kierkegaard tries to recover the original meaning of sin through a rather untraditional interpretation, namely, the identification of sin with "despair qualitatively intensified."[105] He thereby bestows a more religious meaning upon sin, conceiving of it as disobedience to the divine will. Sin is opposed to faith and its deontological relationship to God rather than to moral perfection. Kierkegaard comes very close at times to advocating despair as an inward path to God, for at least in the recognition of one's own despair those inclined to ape the splendid vices of the crowd will acquire the experience of radical finitude that is lacking in his spiritless society.

The Sickness unto Death does not repeat the largely Pelagian interpretation of original sin that Kierkegaard advocated in *The Concept of Anxiety*.[106] In the final redaction of *The Sickness unto Death*, Kierkegaard rejected the traditional notion that an original sin *(peccatum originale originatum)* is inherited by all of Adam's descendants; however, he also steers clear of the Pelagian notion that each person commits his own "original sin." Sin in its most primordial sense is

99. Dupré, *"The Sickness unto Death,"* p. 87.

100. Cf. Louis Dupré, "The Constitution of Self in Kierkegaard's Philosophy," *International Philosophical Quarterly* 3 (1963): 506-26, reprinted in slightly revised form in *A Dubious Heritage*, pp. 30-52.

101. Dupré, *"The Sickness unto Death,"* p. 89.

102. Dupré, *"The Sickness unto Death,"* p. 88.

103. Dupré, *"The Sickness unto Death,"* p. 98.

104. Dupré, *"The Sickness unto Death,"* p. 91.

105. Dupré, *"The Sickness unto Death,"* p. 92.

106. Dupré, *"The Sickness unto Death,"* p. 94.

an awareness that a real discontinuity between the individual and the eternal has been revealed in one's own existence. Unless discontinuity enters into consciousness, the individual will never see beyond individual acts of good or sinful deeds. With the awareness of discontinuity, however, comes the possibility of grasping an essential relationship of continuity with the eternal. Without sin man remains spiritless. Sin is therefore a central category in Kierkegaard's dialectical understanding of faith and existence.

Kierkegaard remains limited by the modern project even as he exhorts his contemporaries to break out of it. Kierkegaardian subjectivity conceives of the authentic self as determined by free, limited, passionate, and paradoxical choice. Real social communion is ruled out. Faith as knowledge is subordinated to an existential relationship to a wholly other, eternal Thou. Sin is resuscitated but ultimately reinterpreted in purely subjective terms. Kierkegaard advances the modern evaluation of subjectivity from a theoretical plane of dispassionate speculation to the real realm of personal relation. In spite of the ironic insight and intellectual courage which enabled him to break with idealism, Kierkegaard never questioned the principle of subjectivity itself. Yet more than any other theologian, he actually identified through his struggles the quintessentially modern form of Christian faith.

In his written corpus Louis Dupré has not devoted as much attention to twentieth-century Christian theologians as he has to their nineteenth-century predecessors. Perhaps his scholarly interests lie more in the historical and systematic foundations of twentieth-century theology than in its purveyors' programs for restoration or reform. On the other hand, his interpretation of two twentieth-century theologians sheds additional light on his interest in the modern form of religious experience. Even though they are seldom treated together, it is useful to consider his interpretation of Edward Schillebeeckx, O.P., and Hans Urs von Balthasar side by side since both make substantive contributions to Dupré's vision of faith and culture in the modern world.

Like Hegel, Schillebeeckx meets modernity on its own terms. According to Schillebeeckx,

> At a time when hardly any direct experience still corresponds to the traditional idea of God, the believer has no choice but to turn to those ambiguous intimations of transcendence inherent in the very heart of his worldly experience.[107]

In response to the loss of faith's cultural support in our secular age, Schillebeeckx binds anthropological and theological discourse. He embraces the inner refer-

---

107. Louis Dupré, "Experience and Interpretation: A Philosophical Reflection on Schillebeeckx' *Jesus* and *Christ*," *Theological Studies* 43 (1982): 31; see also p. 49.

ences toward an absolute mystery within our secularized experience of existence.[108] Dupré cautions against Schillebeeckx's "largely unenlightened" view of our radically secular situation, yet he praises the Dutch Dominican's insistence that the revelation of the Christian message can be received only in and through human experience.[109] He carefully distinguishes Schillebeeckx's account of the subjective element in revelation from the romantic notion that God's self-revelation is made manifest on the basis of our experiences.[110] Schillebeeckx is aware that we do not constitute the revealed Word and that the original experience of revelation is transmitted to us *in, not through,* our experiences.

This assertion raises hermeneutical questions regarding the relation of the original experience of revelation to its interpreted expression. Dupré detects an ambiguity here in Schillebeeckx's position. On the one hand, Schillebeeckx makes a necessary distinction between the original experience and the layers of interpretation that accompany it even before the formation of the canonical Scriptures. Schillebeeckx's well-known forays into historical criticism of the Bible in *Jesus* and *Christ* testify to his commitment to this distinction. Belief in the resurrection and the original experience of the event, for example, are not the same thing. Schillebeeckx argues that the apostles' postresurrection conversion experience need not be interpreted on the basis of visual sighting and an empty tomb if one stresses the cognitive element in the apostles' process of interpreting the event. Dupré raises no objections to bracketing the factual data reported in the New Testament, but he questions Schillebeeckx's failure to establish a unique connection of the Easter experience with its culture-bound expression.[111] According to Dupré, Schillebeeckx's frequent contention that the original experience "became" a message can be interpreted in two ways. In its more modest formulation, the distinction between original experience and interpreted expression protects against biblical literalism while affirming that every element in the New Testament is fully authoritative in structuring the contemporary experience of Christ. Yet Schillebeeckx seems also to support a more dubious hermeneutical principle when he emphasizes the priority of the original experience to its expression. For Dupré, by contrast, "revelation is intrinsically, not secondarily, a universe of discourse, divine expression, and hence message."[112] The form and content of revelation cannot be separated as easily as Schillebeeckx would have it. As a Word in human flesh, the layers of human understanding can never be completely peeled away. There is no original experience of God prior to the concrete appearance of the revealed message.

108. E. Schillebeeckx, O.P., *God the Future of Man* (New York: Sheed & Ward, 1968), p. 71, as cited in Dupré, "Experience and Interpretation," p. 31.

109. Dupré, "Experience and Interpretation," p. 37.

110. Dupré, "Experience and Interpretation," p. 37.

111. Dupré, "Experience and Interpretation," p. 43.

112. Dupré, "Experience and Interpretation," p. 44.

If Schillebeeckx's starting point in human experience bears a family resemblance to Hegel's secular religion, von Balthasar's theology stands closer to Kierkegaard's prophetic critique of the modern age.[113] Dupré focuses on the Swiss theologian's monumental effort to recover a theology of aesthetic form modeled on a premodern understanding of the epiphany of beauty. Whether interpreting the classics of the Christian theological tradition or such unofficial theologians of the modern era as Charles Péguy, Gerard Manley Hopkins, and John of the Cross, von Balthasar shows that Christ transforms the very meaning of culture by assuming an incarnate form. The concrete form of revelation is both tangibly present to human modes of perception and capable of infinitely greater interpretation. "Whatever divine form expresses does not cease to be 'mysterious' to the human mind."[114] Von Balthasar believes that Christ is the perfect expression of divine form. The expression belongs to the form itself. "God is able to express himself in Jesus because he is expressive in his divine nature."[115] The content of revelation appears in, not behind, the form.

Dupré upholds von Balthasar's claim that "form is 'the apparition of the divine mystery,'" yet he notes the problem of translation. The English word "form" means something more ephemeral than a self-disclosing mode of total concreteness (rendered in German as *Gestalt* rather than *Bild*).[116] Here Dupré also assays a critique of von Balthasar's claim for the absolute uniqueness of the form of Jesus Christ.[117] Von Balthasar, a far more critical exponent of negative theology than Dupré, contends that "an infinitely determined superform" is present in a fully visible concrete form.[118] Dupré asks whether a clearer distinction between the form actually perceived "with the eyes of faith" and the invisible form believed to be present on the basis of that perception is necessary.[119] Although von Balthasar is correct to emphasize the perceptibility of form (what he terms "the presence of a gnosis of faith"), Dupré also

113. Cf. Peter Henrici, S.J., "Zur Philosophie Hans Urs von Balthasar," in *Hans Urs von Balthasar: Gestalt und Werk,* ed. K. Lehmann and W. Kasper (Cologne: Communio, 1989), pp. 289ff.

114. Dupré, "Hans Urs von Balthasar's Theology," p. 311; "The Glory of the Lord: Hans Urs von Balthasar's Theological Aesthetics," in *Hans Urs von Balthasar: His Life and Work,* ed. David Schindler (San Francisco: Ignatius, 1991), p. 185.

115. Dupré, "Hans Urs von Balthasar's Theology," p. 311; "The Glory of the Lord," p. 199.

116. Dupré, "Hans Urs von Balthasar's Theology," p. 317; "The Glory of the Lord," p. 204.

117. Dupré, "Hans Urs von Balthasar's Theology," p. 317; "The Glory of the Lord," p. 204.

118. Hans Urs von Balthasar, *The Glory of the Lord: A Theological Aesthetics,* I (San Francisco: Ignatius, 1982), p. 432.

119. Dupré, "Hans Urs von Balthasar's Theology," p. 317; "The Glory of the Lord," p. 204.

believes that the vision of faith can move beyond the spiritual senses to the dark knowledge of learned ignorance. For Dupré von Balthasar's theological aesthetics unnecessarily downplays the way of negation and makes exaggerated and unsubstantiated claims for the absolute and immeasurable difference between Christian contemplative theology and every form of non-Christian mysticism.[120]

Dupré's tempered criticism of von Balthasar is outweighed by his deep appreciation for his sound insight. Theological aesthetics does require a clear delineation of the specific form of the Christian message.[121] In his treatment of non-Christian forms of religious expression, Dupré concludes, von Balthasar should have been more faithful to his own humanist conviction that Christ mediates all other forms.

From this brief survey of Dupré's treatment of two of the twentieth century's most influential Catholic theologians, one sees the importance of the relation of form and content to Dupré's overall project. He criticizes Schille-beeckx for positing an amorphous experience of revelation before its expression in a concrete historical form. Von Balthasar's thought seems to err in the opposite direction, for von Balthasar, in Dupré's estimation, tends to identify the historical manifestations of a revealed Word too closely with the inner dynamism of God's own form. Dupré himself supports the real difference and inseparable relation between the form and content of revelation. A distinction of some sort between absolute "formless form" and historically evolving appearances is both inevitable and necessary.[122] Yet Christian faith knows no approach to God's inexhaustible speech without recourse to finite, visible appearances. On these two points both Schillebeeckx and von Balthasar have made seminal contributions.

To summarize this section, Dupré's treatment of the evolution of modern Christian thought highlights new forms of thought which incorporate traditional spiritual themes. His interest clearly goes deeper than simply setting the historical record straight. He would like to see Christian theology today return to its sources in the mystical traditions. Above all else, this means that a spiritual life centered on contemplation in action is both a starting point and attainable goal of theological reflection.

Moreover, he also states that the traditional analogies of similitudes from Creator to creature need to give way to a new analogy of inner presence by which the creature inverting the relation encounters God in his or her own

120. Dupré, "Hans Urs von Balthasar's Theology," pp. 316-17; "The Glory of the Lord," p. 203.

121. Dupré, "Hans Urs von Balthasar's Theology," pp. 315-16; "The Glory of the Lord," p. 203.

122. The notion of "formless form" (forma nulliformis) is taken from Saint Bonaventure's Collationes in Hexaemeron II, 28, Opera Omnia, Quaracchi ed., vol. 5, p. 340b.

image.[123] In the face of modernity's fateful separation of the orders of nature and grace, he contends that a more harmonious conception of God's real and active relation to the world needs to be recovered. Dupré has published even bolder comments on the need to revise traditional theological notions of transcendence and immanence, which were not developed above.[124] In general, he favors a process understanding of divine engagement with history to the view that the immutable Creator is only causally joined to a relatively autonomous creation.[125] He has urged Christian theologians to consider the panentheistic proposals of modern thinkers like Hegel and Whitehead but has not yet spelled out his position on this complex issue in great detail. More central to his writing is the conviction that even though modern culture has propagated a questionable notion of subjectivity, the religious experience of transcendence still remains the proper starting point for theological reflection.

III. Theology and the Worlds of the Symbol

In this third and final section I will examine the development of Dupré's philosophy of symbolic forms and conclude with remarks about its significance for Christian theology and faith today. The analysis of modern culture's spiritual predicament and the survey of modern religious thought just examined are embedded within the notion of symbolic form. For Louis Dupré culture and history do not merely set the stage for but are constitutive of symbolic forms.

The breakdown of a natural form of analogical language forces the contemporary believer to seek signs of divine presence in a world that has become so secularized that the ancient dichotomy between the sacred and the profane is no longer meaningful.[126] The breakdown of the ancient cosmos forces the

123. The clearest formulation of this teaching is found in Dupré, "Negative Theology," p. 381.

124. Louis Dupré, "Transcendence and Immanence as Theological Categories," *Proceedings of the Catholic Theological Society of America* 31 (1976): 1-10.

125. Dupré, "Transcendence and Immanence," pp. 9-10. Cf. Dupré, *Passage to Modernity*, pp. 252-53; "The God of History," in *God, Jesus, Spirit*, ed. Daniel Callahan (New York: Herder and Herder, 1969), pp. 48-60; "Hegel's Absolute Spirit," pp. 362-63; "Experience and Interpretation," p. 48.

126. A subtle shift of emphasis takes place in Dupré's thought on this topic. That Eliade's distinction between the sacred and the profane no longer carries any weight in modern culture is emphasized only after he wrote his major work of the philosophy of religion. Compare *The Other Dimension: A Search for the Meaning of Religious Attitudes* (New York: Doubleday, 1972), pp. 15ff., 122ff., and 207ff., with "Idées sur la formation du sacré et sa dégéneration," in *Il Sacro: Studi e Richerche*, ed. E. Castelli (Paris: Aubier, 1974), p. 375. In the earlier work, he maintains that believers in the modern West divide the world into the

believer to turn inward for a new justification of human existence. Like Kierke-gaard, Dupré contends that human existence in the modern world cannot be understood apart from a genuinely religious consciousness. Although the book of nature is no longer legible to the modern mind, the quest to symbolize the inexpressible participable ground or the transcendent, effective cause of all reality must continue if we are to make sense of our existence. Turning to symbolic disclosure is not so much a substitute for traditional metaphysics as an attempt to recover the wisdom of the ancient cosmos in a form that still speaks from within the modern predicament.

Reality for Louis Dupré is fundamentally symbolic.[127] Subtle shifts can be noticed in the development of his thought on this issue. When the abridged edition of *The Other Dimension* was published in 1979, Dupré conceived of symbols as projective systems of the human mind. In *The Other Dimension* Dupré developed a theory of religious symbolization largely based upon the post-Kantian approach developed by Ernst Cassirer and Susanne Langer.[128] Dupré's early theory of symbolization consequently emphasizes the mind's process of shaping the content of sensuous perceptions into an independent representation: "In its own dualism between appearance and content the symbol manifests the internal opposition of the mind which it expresses."[129]

Several aspects of the theory of the symbol advocated in this early work, however, argue against a merely subjective determination of the symbolization process. First, he contends that when a symbol expresses meaningfully, it con-tains a surplus of meaning beyond what it directly discloses.[130] Symbolization transcends a merely aesthetic perception (in the Kantian sense) inasmuch as the symbolic expression can never be completely disjoined from the material form of the symbol itself. "The term 'expression,' then, as it is used here," he writes, "implies no separation between form and content."[131] In other words,

secular and the religious even though in other cultures, as in primitive societies, the sacred appears in the profane (p. 122). In the later works, the distinction between sacred and profane is seldom discussed, indicating the growing awareness of the profound crisis initiated by secularization.

127. Cf. Dupré, "The God of History," p. 51.

128. Dupré, *The Other Dimension*, p. 105: "To write about symbols today is to invite controversy. I fully realize that in adopting for the general discussion of symbolism the basic principles of Kant, Cassirer, and Susanne K. Langer, I have taken a particular position which is at least in part rejected by other schools."

129. Dupré, *The Other Dimension*, p. 108. According to Hegel, the Kantian imagination could only produce "a purely subjective succession of images," a kind of "picture thinking in which the pictures are recognized as such." For Hegel symbolic representation must prepare for the objectivity of thought rather than remain tied to the subjective realm of fantasy (pp. 112-13).

130. Dupré, *The Other Dimension*, p. 108.

131. Dupré, *The Other Dimension*, p. 108.

even if symbols are primarily representations of subjective activity, their meaning is by no means limited to the formal capacity of the subject to express private states, a major revision of nineteenth-century romantic theories of symbolic self-expression. The expression is not just the mode of communication of an inner state. That which symbols enable us to perceive is present in, not behind or beyond, the symbol's outward form.

Dupré also avoids a subjective determination of the symbol in *The Other Dimension* by pointing to the negativity of religious symbols. Religious consciousness is marked by a negative form of expressiveness that is present in a less potent way in all symbols. Religious symbols represent a transcendent, intentional object "primarily by showing what it is not and by concealing more than they reveal."[132] The religious consciousness always recognizes what Feuerbach and Freud take to be the Achilles' heel of precritical religious belief, namely, their anthropomorphic quality. If symbolic expressions are primarily subjective, then what is being represented symbolically in their view is not truly transcendent but an ideal projection of the human species or psyche. The objectivity of the symbol, Dupré argues, requires that we not limit religious symbolization to mere products of the imagination. The imagination contributes a polysemy of symbolic forms to the religious mind, but the mind's images convey a reality not reducible to the imagination's capacity to yield images of the divine. As Hegel noted, iconoclasm is as essential to the religious imagination as symbol-making itself.[133] If the religious consciousness is to be taken as an experience of a transcendent mystery, then the negative capacity of the symbol to defy a finite grasp is as essential to its mode of expressiveness as the positive contribution of the subject.

In spite of these nonsubjective elements, the theory of the symbol developed in *The Other Dimension* was still largely that of the post-Kantian tradition.[134] Dupré tempered the claim for the contribution of subjective expressivity by appealing to Hegel's critique of Schleiermacher and by insisting on the inexhaustible transcendent reality signified in sacraments. When his Aquinas lecture appeared in 1994, the post-Kantian tradition was still the starting point; however, sharper criticisms of it were introduced.[135] In *Metaphysics and Culture,* he concedes that even though Cassirer and Paul Natorp had begun to work out a philosophy of culture to supplement the epistemological critique of the Neo-Kantian school, in the end the post-Kantian tradition "failed to account for the expressiveness itself of symbolic expression."[136] Moreover, philosophers in this

132. Dupré, *The Other Dimension,* p. 121.
133. Dupré, *The Other Dimension,* pp. 122-27.
134. This aspect of the work met the judicious criticism of M. John Farrelly, O.S.B., in his review article in *American Ecclesiastical Review* 167 (April 1973): 284-87.
135. Louis Dupré, *Metaphysics and Culture,* the Aquinas Lecture, 1994 (Milwaukee: Marquette University Press, 1994), pp. 1-21.
136. Dupré, *Metaphysics and Culture,* p. 31.

tradition failed to account for the distinct yet inseparable domains of symbolic expressions:

> Philosophy alone recognizes that symbolic systems modulate in various ways the expressiveness of an ultimate presence. In order to succeed in its task, however, it must do more than incorporate the various symbolic systems within a single field of meaning, as Neokantian philosophies do when they declare symbols projective systems of the human mind.[137]

Metaphysics and Culture praises the traditional task of metaphysics to seek the unifying ground of all symbolic expressions of the real. Whereas many modern thinkers thought that Kant's Copernican revolution inaugurated a new, subjective platform for a critical philosophy of symbolic self-expression, Dupré seeks to understand how the concrete expressions of metaphysical ultimacy in the modern symbolizations of art, religion, and science can be grounded in a new philosophy of culture.

Metaphysics and Culture is written in the wake of Dupré's engagement with Marx's social theory of culture and his continued appreciation of Cassirer's attempt to overcome the subject-object opposition in interpreting cultural forms. In this lecture he defends the objective expression in concrete, finite forms of Hegel's Absolute Spirit.[138] A genuine philosophy of culture, he maintains, has no choice but to interpret the presence of the absolute in distinct, historically developing manifestations. "To capture the existential meaning of this symbolic march through time is the task of cultural hermeneutics."[139] Dupré does not contend — as some philosophers in the nineteenth century claimed for Hegel — that such a philosophy of symbolic forms has access to an unmediated unity beyond the pluriformity of distinct, linguistically bound expressions.[140] His claim is more appreciative of the still valid insights of the post-Kantian school. In other words, we can never hope to integrate the few fragments of culture which remain without the hermeneutical task of interpreting symbolic forms as we encounter them in history and culture. What Alasdair MacIntyre once claimed for the modern language of morality, namely, that we now possess only "the fragments of a conceptual scheme, parts of which now lack those contexts from which their significance derived," may actually be true of all of culture's symbolic forms.[141] Dupré's cultural hermeneutics names the

---

137. Dupré, *Metaphysics and Culture*, p. 10.

138. Cf. Louis Dupré, *Marx's Social Critique of Culture* (New Haven: Yale University Press, 1983).

139. Dupré, *Marx's Social Critique of Culture*, p. 34.

140. Dupré, *Marx's Social Critique of Culture*, p. 33.

141. Alasdair MacIntyre, *After Virtue*, 2nd ed. (Notre Dame: University of Notre Dame Press, 1984), p. 2.

symbolic fragmentation of the modern age as a broken heap of images even while poetically averring that "the promised land of the absolute lies indeed beyond language."[142]

Cultural hermeneutics incorporates a turn to language. How does Dupré relate language to experience in *Metaphysics and Culture*? Heidegger, he claims, was wrong to suppose that there is a preapprehension of being that goes beyond language, but transcendental Thomists were not misguided in affirming an implicit apprehension of the real prior to language. "Before the 'I' that speaks there must be expressiveness itself, an attribute of the absolute, that enables language to speak."[143] Thought and speech co-affirm the implicit intuition of being that is present in every act of judgment. Dupré points to the capacity of embodied persons to express thought in language as something distinct from the state of immediate intuition which Schleiermacher identified with feeling. Expressiveness is not just an individual possession but "an attribute of the absolute." It is the concrete, given horizon of all understanding which cannot be exercised independently of verbal acts. Nor can its abundance ever be exhausted by them.

What of the transcendent reality disclosed in the severed members of modern culture's body of symbolic forms? The novel (and questionable) contribution of modern culture is to carve out a distinct domain for the form of life which is religious. The rights and obligations of a sacred piety are protected so long as they do not attempt to adjudicate the claims made independently by politics, art, or science. Dupré wants to grant the distinctiveness of the religious domain even while questioning both its self-sufficiency and its separability. Religion is indeed an aspect of culture. No expression of religious belief evinces an immutable form that will remain untempered by the passage of time. "Because of the flexible nature of religious symbols, evolution *can* take place without any abandonment of traditional symbolism."[144] Religious symbols are formed in human ways by communities of believers. If these communities begin to worship the finite expressions rather than the divine realities revealed in them, then the living spirit of the tradition will be sacrificed at the altar of traditionalism.[145]

On the other hand, there is no genuine worship apart from the linguistic forms that are handed over by religious traditions. Just as there is no grasp of the ineffable absolute beyond the expressibility of language, so too the religious individual cannot begin truly to experience the absolute apart from the com-

---

142. Dupré, *Metaphysics and Culture*, p. 38. Cf. Louis Dupré, "The Broken Mirror: The Fragmentation of the Symbolic World," *Stanford Literature Review* 5 (1988): 24.
143. Dupré, *Metaphysics and Culture*, p. 39.
144. Dupré, "The God of History," p. 58.
145. Dupré, "The God of History," p. 56.

munally mediated forms of concrete traditions. "If a church is to be a community at all, it will always need a particular structure and a concrete authority."[146]
As individuals we simply cannot create religious traditions.[147] Dupré accordingly rejects Leslie Dewart's identification of belief in the modern world with
an undifferentiated "religious experience."[148]

> To the believer faith is always considerably more than a religious *experience*.
> An objective experience is experience only to the extent that it grasps its
> object, whereas the object of the religious act remains mostly transcendent
> to the experience. . . . The symbolization of Christianity and its evolution
> cannot be determined by the experience alone because it expresses more than
> a mere experience. Any renewal, then, in the symbolic expression of the
> religious intentionality must be made in close continuity with its original,
> determining expression in scripture and early tradition.[149]

If the modern trend to understand symbolization as a variable outward sign of
an indeterminate inward state continues, then Dupré's portentous prediction
that spiritual life in the future will be "all attitude and little representational
content" will come true.[150]

Even if religious experience is not a private experience, religious experience lives in a constant tension with its forms of expression.[151] This phenomenon is not simply a by-product of modern secularism issuing from the desire
of individuals to re-create forms of worship in accordance with the latest liturgical fashions. It is a permanent feature of any living tradition. The intentional
object of divine worship itself demands that forms of belief be subject to organic
development. At its highest moments the religious believer finds the outward
forms of belief to be insufficient. An experience of divine presence eludes the
precision of language, a discovery that Augustine made when he claimed to
"touch the eternal Wisdom" at Ostia.[152] Likewise, Odo Casel defended the ritual
re-presentation (beyond mere commemoration) of Christ's eternal birth, death,
and resurrection in the Eucharist.[153] The liturgical forms celebrate these sacred
mysteries even as the believer recognizes that the realities disclosed by the verbal
formulas transcend the here and now of the present historical moment. The
religious ritual symbolizes the eternal presence of the divine in history. Linguistic forms are neither dispensable nor terminal expressions of the divine nature.

146. Dupré, "Openness and Closedness," p. 74.
147. Cf. Dupré, "Religion in a Secular World," p. 76; "Spiritual Life," p. 22.
148. Dupré, "The God of History," p. 55.
149. Dupré, "The God of History," p. 56.
150. Dupré, "Spiritual Life," p. 24.
151. Dupré, "The God of History," p. 57.
152. Augustine, *Confessions* 9, 10.
153. Dupré defends Casel against his critics in "Ritual," p. 204.

The integration of symbolic form with the content of traditional Christian faith is *the* starting point of Christian theology. In my own opinion, to adopt this task of reinterpretation entails taking a much more aggressively confrontational stance to our current cultural milieu than Louis Dupré advocated in *The Other Dimension*. Instead of starting with the mind's capacity to create a symbolic world (even in the qualified form adopted in that text), one can begin with the fact that human existence itself is given as a symbolic expression of an inexpressible reality. The Christian theology of the creation of man and woman in God's image always relied on some such form of symbolic representation. John Scotus Eriugena and other Christian Neoplatonists formalized it into a theory of the world as God's theophanous speech and the human person as a microcosmos of all creation.[154] In this view, created human existence is a word spoken by God marked by its paradoxical capacity to rise above the rest of creation even as it remains constantly receptive to and dependent upon its divine source.[155] Men and women symbolize primarily by receiving an exemplary word rather than by creating a new representation. The turn to the symbolic self-expressiveness in human, created being need not be at odds with modern culture's insistence upon dynamic living forms in history.

The principal advantages for the believer of offering a more integrated understanding of symbolic form and religious content would be in the areas of liturgical and moral life. It is difficult if not impossible to separate the concrete symbolic forms which Christian communities follow from the meaning which they impart to our lives. Left unchecked, the unabated drive to conceive of the symbolic content of Christian worship as malleable expressions of our communal self-consciousness will only lead to greater spiritual fragmentation. At the same time, to freeze current symbolic and liturgical forms into a timeless essence is not only ahistorical but approaches a fundamentalist attitude that can only kill the spirit.

Similarly, a theory of Christian morality that accepts the separation of symbolic form from objective, religious content will quickly degenerate into ethical formalism or some version of moral relativism. In the modern context, separating form and content means either an abstract categorical imperative or an irreducible plurality of distinct forms of life with no normative vision of the truth. Kierkegaard mocked the Kantian moral presuppositions of his age by advocating a return to the simple but earnest task of imitating Christ.[156] What

154. Cf. Werner Beierwaltes, "Negati Affirmatio or the World as Metaphor: A Foundation for Medieval Aesthetics from the Writings of John Scotus Eriugena," *Dionysius* 1 (December 1977): 127-59.

155. Cf. Hans Urs von Balthasar, *Das Ganze im Fragment* (Einsiedeln: Benziger, 1963), pp. 264-68: "Der Mensch als Sprache Gottes."

156. Cf. Dupré, *Kierkegaard as Theologian*, pp. 147-81.

may be needed in our late modern situation is a theory of symbolic expression based upon the logic of following.[157] Louis Dupré's latest work offers resources for articulating such a theory when he draws out a phenomenology of the body's symbolic expressiveness.[158] Dupré's recovery of the aesthetic quality of form can also lead to a more explicit consideration of the desirability of the good disclosed in symbolic forms. Modern morality has normally separated the visibility of the good in concrete situations from the "ought" of personal responsibility. A comprehensive recovery of symbolic form with traditional religious content would have to acknowledge the modern distinction between personal morality and social communal obligation even while striving to restore the inner attractiveness of traditional forms of pursuing the good as both public and private expressions of faith.

Dupré frequently admonishes that together the cultural forms which he has assembled still only represent the bricks of a future synthesis. Modern culture fragments the unity which formerly held together the distinct symbolic worlds of politics, religion, art, and the study of nature. But it also enjoins us no less to seek its reintegration. Contemporary theologians will no doubt be provoked to disagree over the degree to which such a new synthesis is possible or even desirable. Dupré's thought calls into question programs for communicative social action or a restoration of traditional moral virtues detached from the quest for a metaphysical synthesis. Modern culture still needs a metaphysical project in order to rethink the loss of "the image of a cosmic order projected unto the plane of human experience."[159]

Yet Louis Dupré's writings offer more than just provocation. Though subtle shifts have been noted, there is a remarkable consistency to the project which began as early as 1952 with a monograph on the historical progress of religion.[160] In all of his writings, Louis Dupré seeks to understand the very foundations of the spiritual predicament of our age in terms of both modern forms and traditional spiritual content. Given their rarity in the present intellectual climate, no theologian today would be advised to dismiss Louis Dupré's search for first principles.

---

157. Cf. Hans Urs von Balthasar, *Theologik* II: *Wahrheit Gottes* (Einsiedeln: Johannes, 1985), pp. 29-32: "Liebeslogik."

158. Dupré, *Metaphysics and Culture*, pp. 7-8.

159. Clifford Geertz, *The Interpretation of Cultures* (New York: Basic Books, 1973), p. 90.

160. Louis Dupré, "Godsdienst en Historische vooriutgang," *Studia Catholica* 27 (1952): 95-99.

CHAPTER 14

Free Expressivity within the Social Whole: Still a Modern Dialectic

PHILIP CHMIELEWSKI, S.J.

Cultures struggle. They are not made through singular events like the Promethean theft of fire. The social critique of Louis Dupré has little room for a trickster Titan like Prometheus. Dupré's analysis turns sharply against the romantic progeny of Prometheus who would in raging isolation carry out assaults against the heights and then lie in noble, futile agony. Dupré rejects rebellion and determinism, for Dupré has appropriated Vico's insights in the *New Science.*

Vico observed the repeated ancient phenomenon whereby a people associated Hercules with its coming to independent self-identification. Similarly, Dupré attends to the channels along which people strive to craft their culture. Vico presents the mythic Hercules in the repeated service of struggling communities; Dupré's social ethic stands alert to their Herculean efforts to accomplish the ordinary, difficult tasks repeatedly. As Vico perspicaciously captured the insight that fables reveal truths of the social world, so Dupré grasps how the figure of Hercules represents the repeated intervention of the transcendent realm in cooperation with human freedom. Through such a freedom persons today are engaged in an historical struggle to achieve a culture both expressive and integral.

Thus, Hercules (not Prometheus) is the symbol which best captures Louis Dupré's analysis of sociocultural activity and the social ethic which follows from it. Dupré accordingly presents a nuanced investigation of values as they are lodged in the varied everyday activities which constitute civil society. By emphasizing the need to locate and denominate those practices that achieve the social and individual benefits which together constitute the common good, he directs attention to the expressive activity of members in a society, based on

311

ongoing traditions, and to the supporting, organic order for this web of activities and citizens. The particular practices of a society articulate its ethics.

Dupré's ethic is comprehensive because he illuminates how the achievement of the common good comes about through varied practices which shelter and develop life, labor, and language. Dupré's social ethic is extensive in its pursuit, ranging from an assessment of sexual activity to the examination of participation on the part of citizens. His ethic requires the investigation of the particulars of institutions. The range of the ethic he offers goes even further than concerns for intermediate associations and political structures, for this social ethic astutely examines the several registers of expression borne by cultural institutions and fashioned by creativity. The alertness to cultural activity enables this social ethic constantly to record how unique, free persons have created a given system. The interpretation of cultural artifacts and practices makes it possible to grasp the significance of historical position and development for the shaping of the goals and values of a given society. Socially created artifacts express communal values, the activity of social institutions, and the actions of individuals. Still more, these artifacts contribute to the constant alteration and revision of a society's ethic.

Now, when Dupré delineates these social processes which take place in history, he keenly examines the interaction of forces which plays itself out between those elements of the world whose strangeness impinge upon and distort the development of persons and those achievements of culture that enable free action and the common good to come about. In this, the breadth of his analysis is so encompassing that it can examine the movement toward liberty, reciprocal self-expression, and the common good even as this movement occurs in the face of resistance and failure. Both his probing of Marxist analysis and his examination of the inconclusive achievement of the baroque indicate that contrasts, dissension, and conflicts are all elements in the shaping of a free and richly harmonious society. While Dupré's work constantly affirms the centrality of the individual free activity that contributes to the processes constituting social structures, his scrutiny of the central texts of the Marxist heritage enables him to consider more particularly the structures which both constrain and enable this activity. His perspective is dialectical in its attention to historical slippage, systemic interaction, and the movement toward reconciliation. Familial, economic, ideological, and aesthetic processes, in a mix of complex effects, both skew personal activity and channel the developing articulation of freedom in society.

In order to discover how freedom manifests itself within social structures and to construct an effective and realistic ethic, Dupré hermeneutically analyzes the forces which drive the systems of Hegel and Marx. He thereby brings to light materials for delineating how persons construct a world whose harmony spans both their own lives and the actions of groups. Dupré's ethic concentrates on that activity of individuals which sets up a reciprocal relation between person and society and which also brings about a functional coordination among social systems.

In his trenchant attention to the exercise of freedom lodged within social systems, Dupré considers the role of creativity as it finds expression in artistic activity. Engagement in art fosters recognition within communities and provides a resonant exercise which joins theory and practice, particularly in terms of social values. Creative activity manifests itself in the various arts and also in the enactment of the institutions which build a culture. Such institutions are key factors in establishing a society. Furthermore, creative activity also constitutes society's life in a complex set of relations to nature.

The transcendent realm is constitutive of a dynamic social order. Dupré's understanding of transcendence permits and, indeed, sustains liberty within the course of events. This transcendence is the foundation for human expressive activity. Creative activity, in turn, signals the presence of the transcendent dimension within a society and culture. It also discloses the need for articulating this dimension within a social order that can achieve the common good.

Creative activity represents, with particular clarity in the arts, the expressive achievement of persons. Beyond the fine arts strictly understood, such expressive action and its results proliferate throughout the realms of personal and social living. Language and customs constitute two familiar loci for the practical exercise of creative activity. This activity provides, through its varied expressions, the avenue for articulating personal freedom along with other persons within the framework of society. Freedom also emerges in the activity of interpreting the artifacts and practices of a culture.

The freedom that emerges in creative and interpretive activities is the basis for an ethic which is capable of undergoing transformation on the way to a desired future. Given the forces which constrain personal freedom and misshape mutuality within today's society, the complete articulation of a social ethic will not be accomplished spontaneously, necessarily, or soon. Nevertheless, hope is expedient because human freedom always reemerges and because, in its recurrent expressivity, it moves to the reestablishment of the common good. Artistic expression consistently directs attention to the domination imposed upon expression. Expressive activity proliferates as it emerges from the extensive, unexpected activity of persons in all the ranges of social interaction. Interpretive skills shape dissent and pose alternatives to present structures. The movement to an ethic that has not yet been achieved is impelled by those very activities of freedom which articulate the life of any society and culture. Expressed in creative and hermeneutic activities, established upon a transcendent base, freedom still works, within complex social structures and in the face of shattering historical conflicts, toward the articulation of a social ethic.

This essay treats the range of Dupré's writings on social ethics in eight sections arranged in sequence of publication. Each of the parts, save two, focus on a single major work. The fourth and sixth, falling on either side of the examination of *Marx's Social Critique of Culture*, each handle a different series of articles related in themes and published in neighboring years.

As his investigations succeed each other, Dupré's ethic presents a refined understanding of the dialectical movement of social institutions and social systems that can advance toward an organic order which is able to pursue the common good. Dupré's progressive inquiries persistently strive to delineate more fully the constant, powerful activity of personal freedom, which manifests itself in reflection and language, in expression and symbols. Furthermore, this social ethic moves forward to achieve a nuanced understanding of transcendence that is integral to social order and cultural life and that emerges within the expressive freedom of persons.

I

Louis Dupré's dissertation examined Marx's youthful critique of Hegel's political philosophy.[1] As Hegel in *Elements of the Philosophy of Right* introduces the unfolding of the ethical life *(Sittlichkeit)* with a treatment of the family, in his early *Contraception and Catholics: A New Appraisal* (hereafter cited as *CC*),[2] Dupré presents several themes that explore the significance of the family structure for the development of the person as a member of society. When an ethical evaluation centers on an appeal to human nature, Dupré insists that this nature be understood as "a principle of development" (*CC*, pp. 44 and 84). Moreover, Dupré views the individual as a body, a person, and a member of society. Although these appear simply as aspects or facets, it is through their interaction that these elements constitute the human individual and impel his or her development.[3] Symbols offer a distinctively human means for development. Even in this early work, Dupré emphasizes that an objective symbol is never simply and completely given. Symbols are received, particularly those whose medium bodily actions constitute; but persons live the symbols and in so doing transform them (*CC*, p. 79). The symbol of the marital act makes manifest the

---

1. Louis Dupré, *Het Vertrekpunt der Marxistische Wijsbegeerte: de kritiek op Hegels Staatsrecht* (Antwerpen: Uitgeversmij. N.V. Standaard-Boekhandel, 1954).

2. Louis Dupré, *Contraception and Catholics: A New Appraisal* (Baltimore: Helicon Press, 1964).

3. He affirms that the primary end of marriage includes the raising of the child to adulthood. The child is not simply a body shielded by the parents; he or she is educated in part through the mutual expression of the parents' love. See Dupré, *Contraception and Catholics*, p. 60.

desire to express love. Indeed, the symbolic expression of love carries its significance more widely than that borne solely by the agent's intention. The sexual expression of love creates a component of society, the family; it creates persons; and it brings the bodies of children into being.[4] The family is a way whereby persons attain freedom.

II

In an early, major publication, "Dialectical Thought: Kant, Fichte, Hegel, Marx, and Engels" (hereafter cited as DT),[5] Dupré sets out the insights in Kant's seminal work and Fichte's understanding of free activity,[6] to which Hegel and Marx respond in establishing their own systems. From Hegel's criticism of Kant's thought, Dupré provides a key to his own requirements for an ethic:

> Law and reason in this view are too far removed from inclination and nature: the opposition between is and ought constantly denies life as it is actually lived. Kant's moral autonomy is in fact a heteronomy of life, far worse than any positive law. (DT, p. 171)

The ethic sought must attend to nature and must provide structures that sustain free actions within the world. Dupré returns with regularity, on the one hand, to the refined analysis of Hegel's dialectic,[7] and, on the other, to the constraining

---

4. Education is a primary form of social expression. It is institutionally situated and transgenerational in its impact. Dupré's later *Marx's Social Critique of Culture* speaks of education as *Bildung* in the context of a discussion of Hegel's *Propädeutik* ([New Haven: Yale University Press, 1983] p. 20 n. 6). Education also harbors the process of learning. Interestingly, in an extended discussion of the force which impels the movement of history, Dupré makes use of Habermas's belief that social progress depends more on learning than on modes of production. See Dupré, *Marx's Social Critique of Culture*, p. 81. In addition, Dupré notes how Habermas explores the combination of kinship lines and learning capacity as key in the development of human society. See p. 101.

5. Louis Dupré, "Dialectical Thought: Kant, Fichte, Hegel, Marx, and Engels," in *Approaches to Morality: Readings in Ethics from Classical Philosophy to Existentialism*, ed. Jesse A. Mann and Gerald F. Kreyche (New York: Harcourt, Brace & World, 1966), pp. 164-282.

6. For Fichte, "[t]he world becomes a reality only insofar as it is an object of man's free activity." See Dupré, "Dialectical Thought," p. 168. Any extended assessment of Fichte disappears in Dupré's later discussions of the particular evolutions within the thinking of Hegel and Marx. The development of each is presented in terms of their respective responses to an array of contemporary movements, e.g., Hegel's to the rise of British economic science and Marx's to the other Young Hegelians.

7. See Dupré's early work along this line in *Het Vertrekpunt der Marxistische Wijsbegeerte*, pt. 2, sec. 1.

capitalist developments in Marx. Both discover how persons can exercise their freedom within society and its structures. Here within the argumentative lode of early idealism, Dupré is mining for materials that can be used in constructing a world where harmony, both personal and social, is possible, as well as in shaping an ethic that can stand in a close relation with that world.

When he gives the contours of Hegel's thought, Dupré describes the articulation of freedom in the juridical, moral, and ethical ranges as well as in the institutions of family, civil society, and state.[8] In terms of the particularly human character of social interaction, the ethical life is freedom *expressing* itself objectively (DT, p. 165). As in his book on contraception, again Dupré holds that the person surpasses the character of an individual. But now, Dupré affirms that such personal life is achieved not simply in the family but insofar as he or she acts, in a concrete actualization "of his universal nature" (p. 182), as a citizen.

Hegel's concern for the movement beyond objective spirit to art, religion, and philosophy as well as his unclarity concerning the relation of this realm to that of absolute spirit (p. 183) establish the field of Dupré's engagement with art and religion in their bearing upon life in society. This engagement is the framework for his effort to bring the advanced achievements of cultures to bear on the delineation of an ethic. Further, Dupré's work attempts to move past the instability of the relation in Hegel's system between the realms of objective and absolute spirit.

In the same piece from 1966, when he arrives at the examination of Marx's work, Dupré directly addresses the question of social ethics:

> [Marx's] criticism of Hegel was directed not against the social nature of ethics but against the asocial character of Hegel's society. Hegel simply took it for granted that the present-day society allows man to lead a truly social life, but this assumption is entirely false according to Marx. (DT, p. 184)

While Hegel's thought requires that an ethic must be integral to society, Marx's critique demands that the actual ramifications of a particular set of social interactions be keenly assessed. The lenses Marx uses for this assessment are an implicit humanism deriving from Greek antiquity and a more explicit, but by no means fully acknowledged, utopian perspective.

Dupré's work scrutinizing Marx's thought provides a major, comprehensive interpretation of Marx's arguments; a charting of their development through the span of his career as philosopher, journalist, economist, and revolutionary; and an acute attention to their unbuttressed assumptions. This

---

8. "Through these institutions he becomes free." See Dupré, "Dialectical Thought," p. 178. For the ranges, see p. 173.

effort on the part of Dupré must be understood as a movement toward a social ethic by way of an evaluation of social life today. Dupré directly assesses contemporary social life in terms of its lack of wholeness. He indirectly contributes to the assessment of contemporary social life by examining the adequacy of Marx's analysis. Marx requires that no one assume that the current social arrangement is the desired basis for a social ethic. Dupré requires that the Marxian project itself submit its presuppositions and claims of coherence to examination. He carefully warns, for example, that the position Marx assumed with respect to the relation between man and nature threatened human freedom. Dupré inquires into the precise unfolding of this relation in Marx's thought in order to maintain both an integrity with nature and the potential of freedom.

III

Dupré's *The Philosophical Foundations of Marxism* (hereafter cited as *PFM*)[9] extends his analysis of Hegelian and Marxian thought through a more nuanced understanding of social structures and of the free activity which takes place within them.

An idealized view of the Greek city-state informed the longing for a total synthesis which Hegel presents in the *Elements of the Philosophy of Right* (*PFM*, p. 3). The holism of the integration between individual and society, as well as between city and nature, springs from the same origin. In fact, Dupré reads Herder and Hegel together in order to speak of the *polis* as a "cultural structure" (p. 5).[10] Significantly, the city-state also nourished its citizens through the creation of art, religion, and wisdom.

Building upon classical humanism, Hegel also provides an armature which can comprehend the more complex structures of modern societies in a social ethic. The good must become real through the existing institutions of the family,[11] civil society, and state. These three spheres of the good are stages of

9. Louis Dupré, *The Philosophical Foundations of Marxism* (New York: Harcourt, Brace & World, 1966).

10. In a later work, Dupré connects this integrative understanding of the *polis* with the modern concern for the common good: "A society such as the Greek polis genuinely unifies private and public interests" (Dupré, *Marx's Social Critique of Culture*, pp. 205-6).

11. The repeated mention of the topos of the family is not merely dutiful. The topic returns at a significant juncture when Dupré discusses how Engels in the *Origin of the Family* radicalizes the historicity of the Marxist project "by showing how even the determinant factor [i.e., production relations] of history had a historical origin" (Dupré, *Marx's Social Critique of Culture*, p. 99).

freedom. A formidable means by which the person as a particular individual progresses toward fulfillment, the state constitutes concrete freedom.[12]

This fulfillment takes place by way of the activities of art, philosophy, and religion. Although Hegel declares the realm of absolute spirit superior to that of society and state, in his early *Realphilosophie* and in his mature *Elements of the Philosophy of Right* he leaves ambiguous the relation between the domains of objective and absolute spirit. In Dupré's exploration of this area, the activities characteristic of Hegel's realm of absolute spirit are those through which particular persons achieve their freedom and through which a given culture can arrive at a concrete freedom. Like the Young Hegelians, Dupré avoids both idealist and materialist threats to freedom and focuses upon the "concrete nature of man, which is both spiritual and material, finite and infinite" (*PFM*, p. 73). This humanist conviction about the problematic freedom of persons impels Dupré to interpret Marxian texts in order to support such a commitment and to assail the determinism too often ascribed to the Marxian system.

What Dupré observes, along with Marx, is that the structures of social and political life are at odds with the real life of persons (*PFM*, pp. 100-103). Dupré indicates his own movement past the conservatism of the later Hegel when he says that in those later years Hegel did not take the process of alienation as seriously, less consistently accounted for struggle as critical to the progress of spirit, and no longer counted surprise as an element of the unfolding of spirit (p. 136).

The root of Dupré's concern for the development of a culture draws its nourishment from Marx's youthful (1844) declaration that work is an expression of the person's being, not merely a means, and that a culture can be more or less genuine, depending on the articulation of this expression (*PFM*, p. 132). Dupré finds this same expression of life in Marx's (and Engels's) subsequent *German Ideology* from 1845-46 (p. 148). In the era of capitalism, the production of cultural expressions has become so deracinated and individuated that it contradicts the conative and axiological demands of both persons and of societies. Marx examines the contradictions between productive forces and social relations as these impasses lead to revolutions (p. 161). Nevertheless, Dupré criticizes the *Communist Manifesto* because social conditions, although they can be the cause of the development and generation of certain aesthetic motifs and concepts, can give "us no information about the creative impulse itself."[13]

---

12. Dupré, *The Philosophical Foundations of Marxism*, pp. 49-50, 47, and 53-54. Concerning the social situation of the family, Dupré notes Marx's depiction of deteriorated family life in newly industrialized Britain (p. 195).

13. Dupré, *The Philosophical Foundations of Marxism*, p. 211. In his later book, as he examines the historical dialectic in culture, Dupré asserts that "However much capitalism invites technical progress, its internal development alone neither explains nor produces it" (Dupré, *Marx's Social Critique of Culture*, p. 79).

Dupré's respect for the power of imagination and creativity proceeds from his attention to their renovating dynamic in struggles. In this way he preserves a space for creative, resolving, socially advancing surprise.

Dupré understands culture in a Marxian mode, that is to say, he sees culture as both the result and the process of an engagement with nature (*PFM*, p. 221). Marx, however, fails, because he economizes this relation: "By restricting the social to the economic sphere Marx makes it subordinate to limited interests. The truly social goes much deeper: it is not subordinate to anything, but rather is that which makes the individual into a person" (p. 227). This parallels the Hegelian move, observed earlier, by which the person emerges beyond the individual. It is central to the requirements of Dupré's ethic.

The concept of the person develops through history. Freedom as it is known at a given stage of history cannot be equated with human freedom as such (*PFM*, p. 202). Even apart from ethical categories, the very constructs of economic analysis have themselves historically evolved (p. 188). Dupré's investment in the hermeneutical study of the historical transformation of concepts is both developmental and genealogical. When he examines *The German Ideology,* Dupré carefully notes how a class rallies other classes "by proposing its own interests as the interests of the entire society." Along with this social process, a conceptual development takes place: "The ideals of a new epoch are always more universal and abstract than those of the previous one" (p. 161).

Dupré's analysis of modern culture similarly illustrates an emergence of standards which in each succeeding age are more comprehensive than those which guided the previous period. In the same section of this interpretation of *The German Ideology,* Dupré implies that freedom and equality are central ideals of capitalist society, that they constitute a certain progress, and that even this will, nevertheless, be surpassed. He repeatedly presents freedom as a central strand which must be available in a social ethic, but he carefully sets it out as an activity which takes place within society. He also carefully stipulates the meaning of the transcendence of freedom; this transcendence is capable of emerging within the web of cultural expression. Because imaginative activity takes place in grids of common understanding, the novel expression achieved by this activity is interpretable by others who inhabit the society.

Dupré conceives the common good as a relation among members of the society sustained by the discursive expression of their needs. According to Marx, the reestablished social world will naturally include a division of tasks, but this division will not be impersonally determined by productive forces (*PFM*, p. 167). The participants in this communist economy will express themselves as they face common needs together.

IV

Subsequent to the pair of books from the years 1964 and 1966, Dupré insists, in an explicitly ethical article, that a satisfactory concept of human nature cannot be static.[14] He maintains his emphasis that freedom realizes itself in the objective world.[15] The free activity of persons pursues an unending search amid concrete challenges for what is right. Indeed, through their free activity, virtues and values are created.[16]

In an article which appears the following year, the theme of marriage is taken up again with an explicit consideration that the goods of marriage include the relation of the spouses, the children's well-being, and also "the good of the society as a whole."[17] Marriage is a framework in which persons exercise their freedom, but it "is also a social institution in which the common good is at stake."[18] Tension and dynamism, rather than subordination and stasis, characterize this goal as a process. The relation of the partners is not a mere contract, it is an institution whose effects and consequences exceed the partners' reciprocal exchange and reach "society as a whole."[19] Personal activity is critical in Dupré's understanding of society; yet the effects of such activity exceed the targets of intention because it necessarily partakes in a societal institution.

Returning to the theme of contraception in another study, Dupré considers freedom once again, but he does this in terms of the moral category of conscience. True to the dialectic, the subjective exercise of conscience becomes a requirement for objective morality. The exercise of this freedom Dupré describes in terms drawn from his study of Hegel's *Phenomenology:* "An extrinsically provided rule . . . must still be recognized by the individual as objectively true, as acceptable."[20] Freedom, considered in terms of the conscience, maintains the possibility of an ethic.

Another article addressing the key ethical issue of abortion presents, a few years later, themes that have already emerged but with a significant, new turn. Once again, a distinction, one grounded deeply in the scholastic tradition, is made

---

14. Louis Dupré, "Situation Ethics and Objective Morality," *Theological Studies* 28 (1967): 245-57, here p. 250.

15. Dupré, "Situation Ethics and Objective Morality," p. 248.

16. Dupré, "Situation Ethics and Objective Morality," p. 255.

17. Louis Dupré and Constance Dupré, "The Indissolubility of Marriage and the Common Good," in *The Bond of Marriage: An Ecumenical and Interdisciplinary Study,* ed. William W. Bassett (Notre Dame: University of Notre Dame Press, 1968), pp. 181-204; originally published in *America* 118 (1968): 224-28.

18. Dupré and Dupré, "Indissolubility of Marriage," p. 191.

19. Dupré and Dupré, "Indissolubility of Marriage," p. 194.

20. Dupré, "Catholicism and Birth Control after *Humanae Vitae*," in *Exploding Humanity: The Crisis of Numbers,* ed. Henry Regier and J. Bruce Falls (Toronto: International Forum Foundation, 1969), pp. 57-63, here p. 60.

between the individual result of procreation and the person.[21] Human life depends upon freedom, here "self-determination." Dupré yokes freedom with "the nature that provides the potential for this achievement" of personhood.[22] The dialectic emerges in the activity of the person. This activity depends on the person's potential, which Dupré, drawing on the ancients, stipulates as a "dynamic combination of presence and absence moving toward ever greater presence."[23] The person depends on a dialectic which moves ahead without limit. Both the absence integral to personal potential — a potential which is itself dynamic, moving, active — and the inarticulable moment in this activity will become deposited through expressive activity in symbols. This absence and the transcendent element indicate the necessity of a hermeneutic. The transmittal and reception of mere signals do not require hermeneutic activity; the communication and interpretation of symbols reflect human existence in its lack and ineffability.

Symbols also mirror experience's continual alteration. "Ethical norms develop gradually and this process cannot be substantially accelerated beyond the pace of the culture in which they originate."[24] When facing the pressing issue of abortion with its array of practical, immediate consequences, Dupré carefully reminds theorists and practitioners that persons, societies, and the norms expressive of their selected goals will all change. The development of ethical standards is an actual, historical process. In addition, this process occurs in symbiosis with the life of a culture. An attention to the interaction between values and the culture which is their matrix is required in order to articulate properly targets for personal behavior and social activity.

Dupré highlights, in an article of the following year, the particular significance of Klaus Hartmann's judgment concerning a pivotal issue in Marx. Marx's project becomes ambiguous as he attempts to maintain a normative anthropology while presenting the dialectical method.[25] Dupré's project for a social ethic is founded upon a resolve to secure the dialectical method within history while at the same time maintaining a domain for a normative but dynamic anthropology. Dupré continues to wield these two instruments. For example, two years later, he reveals his own outlook as he asserts, "A critique

21. Dupré, "A New Approach to the Abortion Problem," *Theological Studies* 34 (1973): 481-88, here p. 483. Also see the parallel passages, placed in a different framework, on pp. 20-23 of Louis Dupré, "Philosophical Discussions," chap. 1 of *Beginnings of Personhood: Inquiries into Medical Ethics. I,* ed. Donald G. McCarthy (Houston: Institute of Religion and Human Development, 1973), pp. 18-25. This is accompanied by "Interdisciplinary Dialogue," chap. 3, pp. 26-44.

22. Dupré, "A New Approach," p. 484.

23. Dupré, "A New Approach," p. 482.

24. Dupré, "A New Approach," p. 485.

25. Louis Dupré, "Recent Literature on Marx and Marxism," *Journal of the History of Ideas* 35 (1974): 703-14, here p. 704.

of the economy such as Marx's *Capital* is not written from a purely economic point of view: it is also, and primarily, a social critique inspired by a specific idea of man." In addition, Dupré criticizes Marx's merely assuming that the dialectic actually bears upon historical development.[26]

In *Transcendent Selfhood*, published at this time, this pair of concerns becomes transformed into the categories found in *Passage to Modernity* and *Metaphysics and Culture:* "Culture originates from a succession of decisions by which we create, refine, and constantly revise a system of values."[27] The dynamic pattern of social structures (here represented by value systems) moving along through history devolves from human persons. Three years later Dupré names the logic of the rational will, not that of economic events and categories, as the actual foundation for Marx's historical vision.[28] Dupré takes up the task of situating the activity of the rational will within history. His particular understanding of will emphasizes its need for and movement toward transcendence.[29] Transcendence is critical for the construction of a "universal and creative" ethical system.[30] The transcendent emerges as a vector within the activities of persons and societies. It is, further, "a moment of absolute and unpredictable novelty."[31]

While Dupré here affirms and will later extend his consideration of the concurrence in which the human will and transcendence participate, he also continues to explore the interaction of the will and social processes. In an article from 1979, Dupré presents the twin elements that establish the basis for a rationality of history:

> One is the intrinsic rationality of all social-economic development, the other the reason which the human will imposes upon those developments. The

26. Dupré, "Religion, Ideology, and Utopia in Marx," *New Scholasticism* 50 (1976): 415-34, here pp. 426 and 431. Also see the relevant pages in Louis Dupré, "Marxist Theory and Religious Faith: A Plea for Ideology and Utopia," in *Faith and the Contemporary Epistemologies* (Ottawa: Éditions de l'Université d'Ottawa, 1978), pp. 55-69.

27. Louis Dupré, *Transcendent Selfhood: The Loss and Rediscovery of the Inner Life* (New York: Seabury Press, 1976), p. 15. Also note the close relation between culture and ethics when the next year Dupré presents this challenge: "Denn was ist eine Kultur anders als ein Wertsystem?" "Die Säkularisierung und die Krisis unserer Kultur," *Kerygma und Mythos VI, Zum Problem der Säkularisierung,* vol. 9 (1977): 92-100, here p. 97.

28. Louis Dupré, "The Idea of Historical Progress in Marx and Marxism," *Yale Review* 94 (1979): 33-43, here p. 40.

29. "Culture requires freedom, but freedom requires spiritual space to act, play, and dream in. Such a space is not provided by leisure alone; leisure itself becomes suffocating without spiritual content. The space for freedom is created by transcendence" (Dupré, *Transcendent Selfhood*, p. 28).

30. Dupré, *Transcendent Selfhood*, p. 40. Here he refers to Bergson's *Two Sources of Morality and Religion*, and on p. 41 he speaks of the paradoxical transcendence required for defining the good life.

31. Dupré, "Religion, Ideology, and Utopia," p. 427.

former without the latter results in economic determinism, the latter without the former is utopianism.[32]

Upon socioeconomic developments with their specific rationality, the human will exerts its prudent force. In addition, he associates this same rational will with a longing that reaches toward utopian goals. Dupré's warning is that a social theory, indeed a social ethic, must discover a dynamic coordination that spans the movements of social systems as well as personal desires and decisions.

In a significant move, Dupré indicates the particular coherence between structural development and the activities and achievements of persons:

> To avoid the connotation of a one-to-one correspondence which is foreign to Marx's thought, Walter Benjamin introduced the term expression. To say: the superstructure expresses the social-economic substructure, means that it articulates it in a symbolization process of its own.[33]

The structures and processes of economic life situate the forms of the society's superstructure; nevertheless, these forms have an independent systemic life. Dupré raises his central concern for symbols so that the realm of human freedom can be preserved conceptually. In addition, because symbolic interaction requires a social embeddedness, this sphere of social activity remains contiguous with the mute and semi-independent forces of society. Symbols constitute a critical means which makes possible the examination of human activity embedded within complex social structures. Symbols constitute the matrix out of which an ethics can be articulated. Dupré declares that the more complicated view — more involved than the bare base-superstructure picture — concerning the relation of the elements of life in common "presents a demand for a more complex hermeneutics."[34] When symbols contribute intrinsically and independently to the social life of expression, interpretation is a key activity in the discovery and maintenance of an ethic congruous with a society and pertinent to its needs.

V

Dupré makes new use of Marx's thought and advances his own reflection in *Marx's Social Critique of Culture* (hereafter cited as *MSCC*). In his statement of the work's thesis, Dupré calls attention once again to the basis of Marxian

32. Dupré, "Idea of Historical Progress," p. 43.
33. Dupré, "Religion, Ideology, and Utopia," p. 422.
34. Dupré, "Religion, Ideology, and Utopia," p. 422.

anthropology in the productive relation to nature, but now the stress in his analysis lies on how Marx's project sought a cultural reintegration. Simultaneously, Dupré criticizes Marx's positions in terms of their internal omissions and contradictions. As he points out, Marx shares the nineteenth-century assumption that socioeconomic activity has a unique priority in the complex process of culture. Here Dupré casts this criticism in ideological terms; that is, he pursues a criticism of the results which reflection produces in a given culture. Marx does not follow the bias toward the subject which other nineteenth-century thinkers displayed, because he emphasizes the social character of praxis. However, this emphasis makes it dangerously likely that no neutral reflection can take place (*MSCC*, p. 13), for there is no independent standpoint which would give purchase to critical thought.

Dupré signals that the goal of a social ethic is to reconcile, to "reintegrate," at a level where complex activities and institutions constitute culture. He takes Marx's project seriously enough both to require that a social ethic be based in the social praxis which shapes persons and to insist that the ethic range even further than the admittedly wide field of the sundry economic activities, a field which by no means ranges broadly enough to cover all the activities through which persons constitute and are constituted by a culture. In fashioning a social ethic, neutral reflection is itself a means of probing and prodding the other culture-formative activities. Dupré's continued and deepened examination of expression and symbolizing is, on the one hand, an attempt to articulate these as cardinal dynamisms in the establishment of culture. His examination of this pair of operations is, on the other hand, an approach toward bringing the activities which characterize absolute spirit into a more immediate relation with the structures and processes of objective spirit. From this perspective, Dupré's insistent protection of disengaged reflection guards the freedom of the person in the face of the structures which stand over against him or her. He thereby preserves a space out of which the creative can emerge. Furthermore, because of this invested allegiance both to independent reflection and to the work of the imagination, Dupré is able to maintain a moment leading toward a cultural integration throughout a society. As they contribute to this cultural integration, the activities of independent thought and creative imagination are ethical.

Dupré calls this work an "essay in hermeneutics." The interpretive analysis concentrates on Marx's critique of culture but does not remain only at the level of the trenchant interpretation of the Marxian corpus. Dupré also pursues the interpretation of the "present ramifications of what he criticized in that culture" (*MSCC*, p. 14). His hermeneutic lays bare the genealogical paths that reveal free activity within a culture's symbols and structures. This also allows him to prepare for an examination of an age more modern than the one Marx knew, an era whose culture devolved, to be sure, from the achievements and discordances Marx witnessed.

One subject for Dupré's hermeneutic is the origin of the modern "desire for unlimited self-assertion." This Promethean desire, which characterized Marx and his contemporaries, continues to characterize the present age, as it colors the entire process by which a society constitutes itself. He locates the origin of this desire in the time far preceding German romanticism. He looks to the early Italian Renaissance (*MSCC*, p. 1), or what he calls in another place "the beginning of the modern age," where the subject becomes the sole source of rationality.[35]

Dupré also submits to hermeneutical assessment Marx's own approach to historical interpretation: "Marx's reading of history is consciously hermeneutical. He interprets the past on the basis of a comparison with the present" (*MSCC*, p. 80). One result of this modern vantage is Marx's insistence that socioeconomic factors are fundamental; this, however, projects modern concerns upon earlier societies (pp. 102-3). Such an approach does not account for the privilege it assigns to its own outlook.

Dupré's own mapping of the origins of modernity traces the movement of history by carrying out his observation from two analytical perspectives. First, he traces the conceptual and practical elements which have worked in the streams of the cultural heritage to bring about the present age. Secondly, he charts the present circumstances exactly as they are problematic, rather than as they are expressive of ever higher levels of progress or an ever more complete determination. This charting acts as a filter on the assessment of the historical unfolding.

His hermeneutic also probes changes in rationality and consciousness. By turning to an examination of consciousness, Dupré conjoins his early work on the *Phenomenology of the Spirit* with the major discovery inherited from Marx: "Thought itself, according to Marx, plunges its roots in the deeper soil of the practical consciousness. A fundamental critique, then, must trace all theory back to its 'practical' source" (*MSCC*, p. 11). One is not to remain at this source — the term "base"[36] is avoided — rather, one proceeds there in order to learn how to interpret a theory and how to assess the social and cultural significance of theory itself.

---

35. Dupré, *Marx's Social Critique of Culture*, p. 7. Still later in the book, Dupré offers a hint of his larger project in *Passage to Modernity*: "Quite possibly, as our own conclusion will suggest, Marx's basis is too narrow for such a general critique of culture. Much even of what he himself attributes to an economic system may stem from tendencies that long antedate this system and of which the capitalist structure itself is only a uniquely powerful manifestation" (p. 50). In addition, Dupré sees that the late medieval shift to objectivism culminates in the modern, extensive economization of life (p. 56).

36. "The base-superstructure scheme tended to isolate the instrumental aspect of the productive act from its total social and cultural context" (Dupré, *Marx's Social Critique of Culture*, p. 213).

His reading of Karl Korsch prompted this development in Dupré's reflection.[37] Sustained by the results of Korsch's work, Dupré writes:

> A critique of society, then, should not be restricted to economic theories and political institutions: it should include the theoretical forms of consciousness as well. In fact, only the active intervention of consciousness can convert a critique of capitalist economy into a theory of social revolution. (*MSCC*, p. 245)

Dupré explores in his subsequent publications the sequence of historical and conceptual shifts that led to the modern form of consciousness. His examination of these advancing stages constitutes a reflective element that contributes to the possibility of altering the present disjointed and alienated state of affairs. Korsch also stimulates Dupré's thinking with respect to the connection between consciousness and expression.[38]

Language is the link between consciousness and expression. "In itself language is neither ideological nor derived: it belongs to the basis of all social relations. Endowed with a structure of its own, it does not 'reflect' reality, it expresses and represents it" (*MSCC*, p. 228). Language is an activity that carries on a symbolizing function with respect to reality. The action of language operates in an independent space: "Language first and foremost conditions itself: it never 'reflects' existing social conditions without providing at the same time a structure for transforming them" (p. 228). Language provides the prime analogate for expressive activity. Language is particularly important for the social ethic toward which Dupré is moving, for it exists by means of the free exercise of its self-conditioning. The twin powers which linguistic activity exercises — namely, the articulation and representation of reality and the transformation of it — are also significant, because, as Dupré criticizes in Engels's work, a unidirectional, causal understanding of linguistic, productive, or other expressive activities both manifests and exacerbates social divisions (p. 234). The unconstrained power of linguistic activity provides a vital force that for both society and culture can lead to their reintegration.

The activity of language provides the basis for culture. "Through language individuals universalize their relations, thus laying the foundation for culture" (*MSCC*, p. 227). Language is the initial moment for both culture and society. Here, Hegel's thought remains as the source, but Hegel himself is making use of Herder, especially in order to stress the connection between culture and

---

37. Dupré already discusses Korsch in "Review Article: Dialectical Philosophy before and after Marx," *New Scholasticism* 46 (1972): 488-511, here see pp. 501-2.

38. "The dynamic core of reality, praxis, includes all forms of consciousness, even the ones more remote from the actual process of production and social structures" (Dupré, *Marx's Social Critique of Culture*, pp. 245-46).

ethical structure (p. 221). Linguistic activity is a privileged field for creating good persons in a good society — not merely good individuals, but persons. The focus on expression enables Dupré to combat an isolated subjectivism which makes the transformation of culture impossible. "Before Hegel, no one attempted to establish the intrinsic necessity of that higher realm of objective expression in which the social as well as the cultural has its roots" (p. 277). The activity of expression is objective in that it moves beyond subjectivity into a world where each person exists along with others; this objective expression redounds upon the subjective center as a channel for its development and shaping. Objective expression is necessary for persons and for society. Expression makes possible a twin cohesion of persons: with the historical achievements of their culture as well as with others through the structures of society.

This treatment of language helps clarify the relation between productive activity and art. Dupré, as did Marx, searches for a cultural integration in society, an integration whose values are aesthetically grounded (*MSCC*, p. 262). Aesthetic activity that follows the prototype of Greek art produces objects, performances, and practices which provide an often implicit criticism of utilitarian production — oriented as it is to problem solution and constrained by narrow time frames — and provides models of the activity that fashions an organic, ethical society.[39] The productive activity of persons brings about social integration within an organic order. That is to say, it is a dynamic and flexible order. This productive activity, commonly occurring on many levels of a community, encompasses the making of objects, ideas, and social systems. Language is the model for production. Language is aesthetic because it strives to communicate in its expression, because agent and audience partake in similar modes of appreciation, and because it strives to make a whole.

Beyond a critique of a capitalist attitude and its effects upon art, "What Marx is saying is more fundamental: art must cease to be one function among others in the social production process. It must cease to be, or at least cease to be limited to, a separate activity in the total productive output of society" (*MSCC*, p. 263). Thus, the organic model of social interaction requires and sustains a world where culture does not stand as some separate range of values (p. 224) and art is not relegated to the position of an isolated industry. Social organizations can become organic where all who take part in productive activity recognize its aesthetic force. The exercise of language is a common activity where persons can recognize and direct this power for social integration.

The good society will be structured to stimulate and foster organic interaction. The base-superstructure model for the origin of ideas militates against even conceiving of the expressive activity requisite for achieving an organic

---

39. Dupré, *Marx's Social Critique of Culture*, p. 261. In this intriguing discussion, Dupré refers to Michael Lifschitz, *Marx und die Ästhetik* (Dresden, 1967).

culture. It also fragments those elements of such a society which may actually exist.[40] At the epistemological, anthropological, and sociological levels, respectively, the scheme of mutual, ongoing influence, expressive activity, and an organic order are three central elements that cohere in Dupré's development of a social ethic. Dupré's approach to knowledge, action, and social order requires criticism as well as transformation.[41]

Dupré's hermeneutic brings an increasingly more complex attention to bear upon the notion of expression. Expression encompasses activity and the deposited results of that activity in artifacts, structures, and operations. Both the activity and its results require interpretation. Dupré moves beyond Marx's understanding, which restricts the causes that shape culture to the varied economic forces; yet he appropriates Marx's insights that religious, philosophical, and artistic activities are situated in a society, rather than in isolated, heroic sensibilities, and that these activities are expressive.[42] Dupré moves past Marx to a more comprehensive idea of culture as a range of social activities. Expression is not restricted to the linguistic or artistic activities of the person. "All economic transactions other than the simplest forms of exchange in a primitive society, constitute mediate or species relations" (*MSCC*, p. 209). Repeatedly, Dupré insists on the pluriform, shifting, multidirectional bonds which constitute and shape persons, products, and society itself. With these intersecting grids and interwoven structures, the significance of expression exceeds the value of the product and producer. At the same time Dupré maintains his Hegelian vantage. Cultural expression proceeds from consciousness which may be prevented from recognizing itself in those artifacts and activities.[43]

In his discussion of Marx's *Grundrisse*, Dupré indicates that "objective expression" is "the very basis of culture" (*MSCC*, p. 37). Now, precisely at this point where he indicates that objective expression occupies a wider field than that of linguistic activity, his discussion analyzes the historical character of alienation. Namely, the critique which focused on alienation as a result of

40. "I do not believe that Marx ever reconciled the architectural-causal interpretation of culture with the more fundamental organic-dialectic one" (Dupré, *Marx's Social Critique of Culture*, p. 238).

41. See Dupré's criticism of the loss of this critical edge in Marx's discussion in *The German Ideology* of the relation between ideas and social structures (Dupré, *Marx's Social Critique of Culture*, pp. 225-26).

42. "Not that Marx simply 'socialized' Hegel's idea of culture. But he incorporated its entire content (including the spheres of Hegel's Absolute Spirit: art, religion, and philosophy) into the wider realm of social expression" (Dupré, *Marx's Social Critique of Culture*, p. 16).

43. Dupré, *Marx's Social Critique of Culture*, pp. 26-27. Lest he be read as a Parisian existentialist, Dupré is careful to assert that such consciousness when alienated cannot be reduced to a state of mind. Alienation "consists in an objective social condition" (Dupré, *Marx's Social Critique of Culture*, p. 26).

property[44] has now become a critique that targets the loss of control over the conditions of one's production.[45] This is doubly historical, for it incorporates Marx's exacting analysis of the peculiar quality and dynamic of modern alienation and it also sets a new stage in the development of Marx's thought. Earlier, Dupré shared an interest with Marx in exposing the historicity of supposedly timeless economic concepts. Both are also interested in the historical conditioning of ethical concepts.[46]

Dupré continues to plot the development of the new stage of thought through those sections of the *Grundrisse* where Marx goes on to probe the workings of technology and of exchange. As the understanding of alienation deepens, sociality becomes recast. The contemporary distortion of sociality is the cultural split not simply of classes but of cultures where representatives of one resent the imposition of cultural artifacts, including values, on the part of the dominant culture (*MSCC*, p. 52).

In pointing ahead to the location where a social ethic might be constituted and to the time when this might take place, Dupré has absorbed from Marx that the terms of the ethic cannot be cast in the form of values or principles that have already been articulated, and that the participants in such an ethic include the analogous agency of social institutions and emblems. Still more weightily, Marx has shown that either traditional patterns of interaction or ordinary artifacts may present goals and guidelines in a deficient form or that received ideals and imperatives may actually distort social expression. The common good is a proper target for a social ethic when it represents the interests of all groups and not just of select economic classes. The common good entails the development of the individual members of a society.

Dupré is careful to observe that an alienating reduction does not result only in a warping of consciousness or a deviation within an ideology. No matter how grave these may be, far more is at stake. Drawing upon Jean-Paul Sartre's *Critique of Dialectical Reason,* Dupré warns, "In adopting a particular form [each society] imposes its own value system even upon those who would prefer not to share it — dependent societies and dissenting members" (*MSCC*, p. 105). Dupré's hermeneutic screens out those constructions of an ethic which would

44. Concerning this early form of social critique in Marx, see Dupré, *Het Vertrekpunt der Marxistische Wijsbegeerte*, pt. 2.

45. Once again, Dupré points out this Marxian effort, here in the context of *The German Ideology.* See Dupré, *Marx's Social Critique of Culture*, p. 31.

46. Dupré refers to the distortion capitalism inflicts upon culture: "In a passage of the much neglected second part of *The German Ideology* he [Marx] shows this alienating effect in the one instance of moral utilitarianism. In the *Phenomenology* Hegel had interpreted the absolutization of the category of usefulness as the final result of the Enlightenment. For Marx, the entire capitalist economy is not more than an application of a theory that subordinates all relations to that of utility" (Dupré, *Marx's Social Critique of Culture*, p. 33).

lead to still more alienation in a culture. An ethic requires society's adoption of nondominating institutions. These structures permit that dissenters and groups can participate in a society's patterns of expression. Dupré's hermeneutic prepares for fashioning an ethic that integrates dissent and fosters independence.

Dupré subjects the dialectic once again to hermeneutical analysis. First he considers the movement of the dialectic in history. When Dupré examines Marx's dialectic, he emphasizes a certain irony; for while Marx denounces Hegel's holding that reality makes sense, he himself assumes this as the basis for trusting the dialectical method. Because Marx rejects any transcendent force that would bring history to its necessary resolution, Dupré can find support for this optimism in the dialectic of history only "in an unshakable faith in man's ability and determination to remake the world in the image of reason" (*MSCC*, pp. 65-66). Marx thus represents the position held by many other enlightened moderns.

Dupré's criticism of the Marxian version of an optimism concerning progress through effort implies that the rational will must be something other than a device for the execution of the results of a utilitarian or Taylorist program. Rather, when he stresses the significance of expression and interpretation within society, he extends the range of the complex interaction of reason and will. Marx fails to indicate why the social structure becomes more rational. Dupré, aware of this critical gap, indicates that transcendent activity operates in the course of events while still allowing for liberty. This is the significant background for Dupré's thinking about expression and symbol.

Dupré turns, secondly, from the analysis of the dialectic in history to the dialectic as it occurs within and through social structures. The structural dialectic takes place through an organic mediation:

> The principal characteristic of this structural dialectic is that it organically connects the various phases of the economic process which classical economy had separated. For Marx, production already contains consumption and distribution itself is a form of producing. This interrelatedness of all economic categories marks a clear innovation in economic thinking made under the direct impact of Hegel's philosophy. (*MSCC*, p. 125)

The sociohistorical human activity which is the center of Dupré's interest mediates between person and society, between system and system, as well as between concept and concept. Dupré goes on to say (with Bertell Ollman) that "Marx uses no 'simple' concepts, only conceptualized relations" (*MSCC*, p. 125). Likewise, Dupré himself pursues an ethic whose terms are conceptualized relations — for example, the common good.

Dupré's allegiance to a nuanced dialectical model both in history and society proceeds from his insight about an encompassing order which will be able to maintain itself precisely because of its fluidity. When Marx discovers that "the abstract form of average labor time constitutes value in a capitalist economy," he simultaneously reveals the characteristics of the activity which shapes a good society. Such creative activity must manifest "its sociocultural quality and its subjective origin" (*MSCC*, p. 177). The activity within society must maintain the culture as a social whole. It cannot undertake this if economics, or any other range of engagement, is cut off as a closed system purportedly on the model of physics or chemistry (p. 197). Unlike the Hegelian schema that assigns parallel fields to civil society and the state, Marx's position maintains that the areas must inform each other in "constituting a vital social order" (p. 209). If the conception of their productive activity holds out an alternative to sectarian, stratified, putatively scientific efforts, persons can maintain the connection between their economic and their other social activities.

Further still, sociocultural activity not only maintains the social whole, but also its source is a uniquely personal vantage and expression. Marx criticizes the thought world of classical economics because it requires an abstract, univocal assessment of temporal change. To assess expression properly one must attend to the varied time plottings for particular individuals within specific societies. "The thorough objectification that rules the capitalist economy totally betrays . . . [the] subjective quality of the producing act by submitting it to objective temporal quantification" (*MSCC*, p. 177). As a consequence of this challenge to capitalist assessment, the proper interpretation of productive and expressive activity must, by implication, be capable of providing a qualitative assessment of the subjective changes borne and created in the course of the activity.[47] The conception of productive activity must accept temporality in its "subjective origin" and personal variation.

The economic and other expressive efforts of individuals shape and alter the form of society. In capitalist society, socialization opposes objectification. Socialization, in Dupré's mind, is the realm of activity which is culture creating, as opposed to the implied destruction of culture which objectification brings with it (*MSCC*, p. 184). This position proceeds from Dupré's examination of Marx, naturally enough; but, in addition, it echoes Dupré's increasing apprehension concerning the cultural forces in the West which lead to the objective point of view.

While Marx smuggles in an assumed positive humanism as the foundation and the direction for his social critique,[48] a humanism, however, that essential-

47. When, in reference to Marx's criticism of the Gotha program, Dupré writes, "Labor cannot be equalized," he points to the varied embodied constraints and potentials that differentiate workers in their activity. Implicit in this differentiation is the variety of times which shape these bodies and their works (Dupré, *Marx's Social Critique of Culture*, p. 184).

48. Dupré, *Marx's Social Critique of Culture*, p. 134. Here Dupré once again utilizes the insights of Klaus Hartmann. Dupré maintains that a humanist measure perdures even in the mature Marx. "The so-called social-economic contradictions described in the three

izes an ahistorical ideal of work (*MSCC*, p. 131), Dupré strives to come to a way of conceiving personal and social activity as it emerges *within history*. This activity takes place in time; it also gives expression to time as this bears upon those who present this activity and upon the society they shape.

Free activity alters in the course of the history it shapes and presses any situation to an unexpected future. Although he continues to move toward an ethic centering on freedom, Dupré is aware of the missteps that others have made in this direction: "For the conflicts resulting from the capitalist system are precisely not the ones of freedom. As Marx presents them they are not created by decisions and attitudes, but by objective modes of production and social structures." It would be inadequate to social and historical processes were an ethic to derive from an anthropological thesis such as static "human nature" (*MSCC*, p. 137). Agreeing with some of the more contemporary adherents of Marxism and appalled by the consequences of state capitalism that posits a dialectic whose completion has already taken place, Dupré highlights the on-going character of the ever unsettling dialectic, so deep is his commitment to a socially integral freedom (p. 163).[49] Even social and cultural conflict proceeds from human decisions, while human nature also alters in the course of these decisions and their consequences. Giving the lie to any pronouncement of a utopian attainment, the freedom of persons is a persistent force in shaping societies.

In his endorsement of the dialectic, Dupré makes another investment which has seldom been noted: "In a unique way, the dialectical method incorporates the negativity of man's social experience and, with it, the need for change, as an essential movement into the analysis itself" (*MSCC*, pp. 163-64). Dupré desires an ethic that is historical enough that it can in its broad reach take evil into account, so humane in its vision that it can bring into careful view the efforts of persons as they and their structures engender negative consequences and also as they combat them, so utopian that it can analyze the movement toward the positive even in the course of the occurrence of the negative results. Dupré assesses the limits even of the merits of Marx's system. Immediately following the previous quotation, he proceeds: "But its ability to do so also defines its limits, for change and negativity are exclusive characteristics of the social experience" (pp. 163-64). Dupré's early examination of the

---

volumes of *Capital* consist mainly, and sometimes exclusively, of situations not so much self-contradictory as conflicting with the fundamental (i.e., human) nature of economic activity" (Dupré, *Marx's Social Critique of Culture*, p. 18).

49. See his praise, a few years later, of another Marxian scholar on this important point: "Raya Dunayevskaya has restored the unsettled, restless, intrinsically dialectical quality of Marx's thought . . ." ("Preface" to Raya Dunayevskaya, *Philosophy and Revolution: From Hegel to Sartre, and from Marx to Mao* [New York: Columbia University Press, 1989], pp. xv-xx, here p. xx).

range of issues connected with family life and contraception served to indicate his awareness of how matters of conscience and ordinary life both generate and combat negative outcomes at the level of persons and their intimate circles. Here he alludes to the ranges of morality that are lacking in Marx's analysis.[50]

In conjoining an approval for the dialectic's capacity to comprehend change and negativity together with his criticism of its omitting the personal and moral, Dupré suggests his concern to fashion a social ethic that comprehends both personal and social workings. Such an ethic would contribute to the reintegration of society and culture, and, further, could test any mode of integration which offered itself for this reinterpretive role. A cogent ethic must confront cultural alienation and provide guides to action against this alienated structure. Dupré has gained doubly where Marx has erroneously interpreted Hegel. Marx is correct in seeing the alienation caused by the separation of theory and practice. Unlike Dupré, however, he fails to acknowledge consciousness and its movements.

VI

Turning now to the articles from the years 1985-92, we see that Dupré continues to grapple with the ideas revealed in his earlier work in order to develop a firm structure for social ethics. Human creativity, culture, and freedom remain central motifs in this conceptual development.

Establishing his understanding of creativity upon the Marxian tenet that persons and nature interact in the making of each other, Dupré recalls that the Marxian ideal postulates a nature that is social.[51] Just as the activity of persons shapes surrounding, environing nature, so too this same activity shapes not only particular individuals but also what human nature is.[52] Dupré returns to this theme two years later, reaffirming the teaching of *Grundrisse:* "Human

---

50. When Marx, "so convinced of society's ethical nature . . . eliminates Hegel's separate sphere of private morality" (Dupré, *The Philosophical Foundations of Marxism*, p. 106), then Dupré sets out another avenue along which he distances himself from Marx.

51. Louis Dupré, "Marx's Moral Ambivalence," review of *Marxism and Morality,* by Steven Lukes, *Review of Politics* 49 (1987): 290-94. "In this respect his [Marx's] ideal stands much closer to Aristotle than to Kant — a fact that becomes less surprising if one regards Marx's entire endeavor as moving toward the restoration of an idea of nature which is (as it was for Aristotle) both social and normative" (p. 293).

52. Taking up Walter Loewith's warning against a univocal understanding of species when applied to humans and the nonreflective living elements of nature, Dupré notes, "A species view of mankind denies precisely its unique capacity to define its own nature" (Louis Dupré, "A Conservative Anarchist: Eric Voegelin — 1901-1985," *Clio* 14 [1985]: 423-31, here p. 428).

nature has ceased to be an abstract ideal a priori: it develops with the social-economic praxis."[53] The development of the human component of nature takes place by way of a social activity, just as nature as a whole is itself social.

Dupré reflects that cultural activity does not remain intrasocial, it constantly (re)establishes the multiple relations of persons to nature. Rather than valorizing a romantic striving for immediacy, Marx argues that through cultural activity relations with nature are mediated.[54] In drawing this distinction, Dupré makes clear the broad range and significance of the creative activity which builds culture. Not only does cultural creativity establish society; it constitutes society's life in a complex set of relations to nature. Integral to the wholeness required in an organic culture is a nondominating, nondistant relation to nature.

Human creative activity fashions and moves society. Dupré realizes the inadequacy of focusing simply on economic activity or a rendering of all other social processes and artifacts to a dependence on it. He derives from Herder the catalyst for conceiving symbolic expression as an organic activity and as an activity which comprehensively characterizes structures throughout a society.[55] Dupré recognizes that symbolic activity can become subverted when the human person loses control of "the conditions of his material production" and — significantly — "as a result, of his cultural creativity."[56] The social fragmentation, understood as fetishism or reification, distorts the conditions for creativity.

Creativity evinces its accomplishment throughout the range of efforts by which actual persons build and maintain societies. The symbolic expression of creativity manifests itself in common, diurnal activity and accomplishment. Language and customs constitute two loci for the practical exercise of creativity. Dante argues that language is the human, creative response to physical and spiritual needs.[57] Suárez recognizes that the customary activities of persons and societies express the *ius gentium* (the law of the people).[58] Such ordinary, resourceful actions express the ethical articulations of a society.

53. Louis Dupré, "Objectivism and the Rise of Cultural Alienation," in *George Lukács and His World: A Reassessment*, ed. Ernest Joós (New York: Peter Lang, 1987), pp. 77-98, here p. 79.

54. Dupré, "Objectivism," p. 87.

55. Louis Dupré, "The Broken Mirror: The Fragmentation of the Symbolic World," *Stanford Literature Review* 5 (1988): 7-24, here p. 17. For Dupré's later use of this stimulus see Dupré, *Metaphysics and Culture*, the Aquinas Lecture, 1994 (Milwaukee: Marquette University Press, 1994), p. 18.

56. Dupré, "Objectivism," p. 78. Also see *Lukács*, in *Sovietica*, ed. Tom Rockmore (Dordrecht/Boston: D. Reidel, 1988), pp. 70-85. One may also consult "Marx's Critique of Objectivism and the Rise of Cultural Alienation," in *Intersovietica Socialita Religione, Archivo di Filosofia* 54 (1986): 653-67.

57. Dupré, "The Broken Mirror," p. 10.

58. Louis Dupré and William O'Neill, S.J., "Social Structures and Structural Ethics," *Review of Politics* 51 (1989): 327-44, here p. 340.

Culture in its actuality is achieved through these ordinary imaginative activities.[59] However, even though the creativity can ideally be liberating or reconciling, it frequently results in constrained or distorted practices. Dupré realizes that the fissioning, isolating, and insulating dynamism of capitalist society skews not only expressive activity but also its position as a structure within society: "The commercial quality of popular culture as well as the reaction of an elite that isolates culture in a different realm follow from the all-determining reification of a commodities economy."[60]

As does Marx, Dupré himself searches for a culturally integrated productivity. The aesthetic world will be the key to grasping what this activity may entail in the modern age.

> Marx' ideal of a culturally integrated productivity holds the potential to rethink the aesthetic object in a manner that removes it from the "aestheticism" introduced in the late eighteenth century and to reconnect it with the Greek *techne* ideal. The German revolutionary knew that all art, regardless of its ideological content, operates as a critical factor in society.[61]

This ideal cultural activity helps find its bearings by looking to the world of art, for art offers its accomplishments not only for admiration, but also as criticism. Aesthetic activity provides a system-inherent vantage for pressing ahead to the utopian. Such activity also indicates the necessity for and the emergence of transcendence within a culture.

The transcendent emerges along with the activity of language. Assertion and affirmation both indicate an implicit desire in the mind itself. This desire signals and requires a ground that makes both language and desiring possible.[62]

The transcendent emerges not only through aesthetic activity and in language; it also emerges in work:

> Leaving the aesthetic attitude out of consideration, we may still assert that human activity is never purely practical. Its universal scope transcends the immediacy of the task at hand. But a truly universal activity requires purely

59. Discussing the variety of activities that constitute culture and their interrelation, Dupré expresses his agreement with George Lukács: ". . . cultural productivity expresses itself in a number of forms. Artistic creation reflects the state of economic production, yet clearly surpasses it" (Dupré, "Objectivism," p. 89).

60. Dupré, "Objectivism," p. 83.

61. Dupré, review of Eugene Lunn, *Marxism and Modernism: An Historical Study of Lukács, Brecht, Benjamin, and Adorno* (Berkeley: University of California Press, 1982), in *Studies in Soviet Thought* 34 (1987): 195-99, here p. 196.

62. Louis Dupré, "The Truth of Religion," in *Morality within the Life and Social World, Analecta Husserlina,* ed. Anna-Teresa Tymieniecka, vol. 22 (Dordrecht: Reidel, 1987), pp. 457-64, here pp. 462-63. Dupré refers to Joseph Maréchal at this point.

theoretical acts. Insofar as all work is a project it presupposes distance, observation, reflection — in short, contemplation.[63]

Ordinary activity, insofar as it is a project, entails not only planning and ideation, but it also depends on a receptive speculation. The creative activity manifested in work is basic to human production and points to the necessary foundation of this effort.

That creativity which expresses and maintains the ethical character of a society both urges the importance of freedom and itself instantiates that freedom. Creativity manifests freedom. As much as did Marx, Dupré too understands freedom (and emancipation) in terms drawn from Fichte, namely, as a self-determination which is not individual but collective.[64] Expressive, creative activity emerges as a primary avenue for personal freedom that carries significance within society. Profoundly humanistic, Dupré's thought resists both determinism and any isolated, capricious voluntarism. He seeks a freedom where persons are responsible alongside others and within traditions.[65] Exactly here, the power of freedom plumbs deeply. Emphasizing the significance of "creative spontaneity," Dupré affirms that "its signal characteristic consists not in the power to ratify pre-established values but in the ability to create them."[66] Nevertheless, the deployment of this freedom requires social cooperation. Consequently, the creation of values is not a series of isolated Promethean triumphs, but rather, an arduous engagement in social development.

Since his early publications Dupré has pointed out that ethical guidelines are limited by the perspective of the age which generates them. One key instance of this restriction was the development of an interest in value during the age of capitalism. Value was ascribed to something or some behavior. The object then became conflated with the ascribed value. That some benefit of persons was the end of the original pursuit of the intermediary valued means was forgotten.[67] Similarly, the subjectivism of the modern period also threatens to upset the construction of a suitable ethic: "To respect the other is precisely not

---

63. Dupré, "Objectivism," p. 96.

64. Dupré, "Marx's Moral Ambivalence," p. 293.

65. Dupré, in addition to his grasp of social interaction according to Hegel's understanding, makes use of a theological model for this cooperation, drawn from Suárez's older contemporary, colleague, and fellow expert in the field of moral theology. Opposing the restrictions on the human will as posed by Bañez and his Thomist allies, Dupré recalls, "To this determinism Molina and his school, anxious to preserve human responsibility, opposed a free human causality next to, and partly in competition with, divine causality" ("Evil — a Religious Mystery: A Plea for a More Inclusive Model of Theodicy," *Faith and Philosophy* 7 [July 1990]: 261-80, here p. 267).

66. Dupré, "Evil — a Religious Mystery," p. 269.

67. Louis Dupré, "Catholic Education and the Predicament of Modern Culture," *Living Light* 23 (June 1987): 295-306, here p. 300.

to draw him into the closed circle of my own subjectivity but to encounter him in the open space where he may be allowed to be what he himself is."[68] The ages which generated the notions of value and respect failed to overcome the bias of subjectivism.

The persons who constitute the cynosure of an ethic that does take free cooperation into account find themselves embedded in a world together. Mutual respect requires a social framework and social traditions because the assessment and regard of the other individual takes place outside the subjectivity of a person. The very sociality of the ethic secures the uniqueness of each person. This "encounter" in the "open space" is not restricted to chance meetings or intentional intimacies. Even more amply than the economic examples he offers, Dupré's ethic seeks "ideal structures of cooperation as the substantive ethical expression of the common good."[69] The structures of cooperation secure the space for the repeated manifestation of respect. Free persons articulate their ethics in the construction of institutions and processes that express their common good.

VII

In his latest major book, *Passage to Modernity: An Essay in the Hermeneutics of Culture* (hereafter cited as *PM*),[70] Dupré builds upon his work from 1985-92 and traces the modern predicament back to its late medieval origins. He also considers the difficulties that the establishment of an ethic in this context entails and studies Baroque art as a model, albeit failed and insufficient, for a cultural endeavor that could stimulate human activity, support a coherent ethic, and stand open toward the transcendent. All of these achievements allow a more supple interpretation of culture through an examination of its inherent conflicts and offer a keen perspective on the interplay between free activity and transcendence.

In the examination of Marx, Dupré made clear that an effective critique of the economy must be undertaken "with constant reference to . . . historical origins" (*MSCC*, p. 120). Now he broadens this analysis as he probes the origins of the modern consciousness in order to develop a comprehensive understanding of cultural activity and social order. The nominalist displacement of the logic of divine

68. Dupré, "Catholic Education," p. 306.

69. Dupré and O'Neill, "Social Structures and Structural Ethics," p. 340. On p. 338 the authors' criticism of Hegel implies their goal of an ethic which enables the creation of structures that reflect both the common good and subsidiarity.

70. Louis Dupré, *Passage to Modernity: An Essay in the Hermeneutics of Nature and Culture* (New Haven: Yale University Press, 1993).

activity into the mysteriousness of God's will transfers God out from an order of cosmos, nature, and persons. "This removal of transcendence fundamentally affected the conveyance of meaning" (*PM*, p. 3). The expressive activity of persons will now articulate itself along profoundly altered paths, as the transcendent is no longer a channel for and the target of meaning and as persons are separated from the world of physical nature. In this world now advanced to a separation from the transcendent, "Freedom henceforth became a self-choice, more than a choice that selects among given alternatives" (*PM*, p. 124). And further, without a transcendent mediation, *homo faber* stands opposed to nature (p. 4).

The very conception which — along with the work of the Italian humanists — dissolves the old cohesive order presents a familiar face for a possible ethic in Dupré's work, namely, freedom. Ockham's God wields a power marked by a freedom so absolute that it exceeds "what we consider ultimate rationality" (*PM*, p. 123). Dupré declares that the initial moment toward modernism required, in addition to the nominalist theology, a compounding with the early humanist understanding of the creativity of persons (p. 3). He indicates that the voluntarism of ethical choice, legal decision, and political theory does not depend on nominalist theology solely. "Its seeds had been planted in Augustine's theology of love, which had been accepted . . . by such decidedly anti-nominalist humanists as Petrarch and Salutati" (p. 124). The twin fonts at the origin of modernity, nominalism and early Italian humanism, share a common source: a theology of love. The interpersonal and social activity of love generates both freedom and creativity.

Dupré thoroughly examines the breakup of the earlier, harmonious order. He then presents the products of the baroque because they indicate a last, though unstable, synthesis that presented active persons, cosmos, and transcendence as a single whole. The baroque synthesis adds a rich but still unsettled sense of the person's novel activity as well as a preliminary grasp of the role of struggle within the constituting of reality. Dupré describes:

> Baroque culture was essentially representational. Each aspect of it may be considered both as it is in itself and as it refers to a higher spiritual reality. In its successful achievements, the horizons of immanence and transcendence become totally fused. The theater serves as a metaphor of the entire culture. (*PM*, p. 240)

Dupré emphasizes the allegorical and (in the most accomplished productions) metaphorical character of the baroque aesthetic achievement. In addition, when he notes that baroque dramas attend to the oscillation between truth and illusion (p. 241), he is examining dialectical movement in another guise.[71] He

---

71. In Dupré, *Marx's Social Critique of Culture*, in a reference to the mannerist stream of baroque art, he notes that A. Hauser sketches how mannerism both expresses an alienated society and reacts against it (p. 260 n. 58).

addresses, moreover, the shape, stresses, and strains of this realm of post-Renaissance aesthetic expression:

> This dual center — human and divine — distinguishes the Baroque world picture from the vertical one of the Middle Ages . . . as well as from the unproblematically horizontal one of later modern culture. . . . The tension between the two centers conveys to the Baroque a complex, restless, and dynamic quality. (p. 237)

Human and divine now participate on a definite plane which joins them, the plane of creative and free action. The plane shared cannot be one of equality, as the later image of a horizontal surface would suggest. But the two parties can interact even to such a degree that they stand in emerging and reconciling tension. The Augustinian theology of love here reappears as the profound orientation of the parties toward each other, each in a unique complexity, each with potentials, each restless.

In this and other attempts at synthesis, voluntarism — offspring of late medieval thought — is problematic because it vigorously dissolves the ordered cosmos of the past. Yet Dupré discovers the paradoxical benefit of exactly the move that enabled voluntarism to emerge. Reconceiving God as a person whose actions are guided simply by utter freedom is an advance toward a comprehensive ethic. Such voluntarism "prepared the modern concept of moral autonomy in presenting the divine lawgiver as a model for the human one" (*PM*, p. 128). Although a concept of such autonomy is a requisite for an ethic which educates and guides contemporary persons, it is insufficient because such an autonomy is exercised by a will whose range of action is uncircumscribed. *Pace* Descartes, Dupré implies how an ethic may be crafted that encompasses personal, moral autonomy since it is articulated within a larger order. He searches with the purpose of locating avenues by which the will can collaborate with the intellect (p. 131). He searches in order to understand how intellect and will, each expressive of the organic order of the person, can together present decisions and actions which reflect, as they unfold within it, a larger, dynamic order. In his cultural analysis, Dupré maintains that aesthetic experience and crafting operate to join will and intellect, both acting in response to a larger world.

The ethical evaluation and direction will be coordinate with the social and, indeed, political life, and will be capable of analyzing this life (*PM*, p. 131).[72] As is more readily understood in terms of education but applies in Dupré's intellectual framework equally to the world of art, the ethic sought will be a social ethic in that it evades any restriction of morality to privatized capsules

---

72. Dupré, of course, criticizes the Machiavellian topography which situates the political life in a separate area, governed merely by the constraints that efficiency dictates.

of living. In its reduction of persons to their will, the modern age has shaped liberated, unstable persons that pronounce mere choices. Stability is attained only through the agreement of wills through a contract. Beyond this, the exercise of language and other expressive activities produces a society whose interindividual structures and processes far exceed the minimal moves of contract. As love exceeds choice, so expression exceeds contract.

The work of Suárez attracts Dupré's interest because of the Spanish scholastic's wide-ranging effort "to incorporate the voluntarist notion of natural law within the traditional one" (*PM*, p. 137), that is to say, to bring into a coherent whole the working of will and reason as they have both personal and social bearing. In terms of crafting an ethic with a social compass, Dupré approves the Spanish scholastic's attempt to steer "a middle course between a preestablished natural hierarchy of authority and a legal positivism" (p. 138). Still, having noted that for Suárez political structures are established upon the social nature of human beings, Dupré points to a portentous lacuna in that theory:

> By giving natural law a content independent of any political structure, he created a rift between a natural law based on abstract reason and the political tradition in which it had to find its concrete expression. This typically modern separation between an abstract idea of human nature and a concrete political realization of it opened a space for an area of "human rights" that existed before and independent of any social structure.[73]

Yet, in accord with Suárez's attention to the customs of nations, one can view these conventions as constituting the concrete activity that instantiates the abstract potential for social life. By a further step, these customs become the matter out of which political traditions are engineered, while they remain the vital force which steers or blocks emergent traditions.

From his study of Herder, Dupré realizes the achievement of a people's

---

73. Dupré, *Passage to Modernity*, p. 139. Suárez developed the earlier work of such outstanding Spaniards as Francisco de Vitoria, who had developed the initial stages in the thinking of human rights. Just as he criticized the interpretation of Suárez which would lead to a chasm between an abstract notion of human nature and actual schemes of the political life, so Dupré brings a similar criticism to bear on the modern representatives of a philosophy of the subject who would isolate "existence" as an abstraction disjoined from cultural expressions (Dupré, *Metaphysics and Culture,* p. 35). In contrast to such an isolated conception of individuals, he also indicates, drawing upon Alexis de Tocqueville, how rights both articulate claims of the common good upon persons and educate them toward dedicating themselves to that common good (Dupré, "The Common Good and the Open Society," in *Catholicism and Liberalism: Contributions to American Public Philosophy,* ed. R. Bruce Douglass and David Hollenbach [Cambridge: Cambridge University Press, 1994], pp. 172-96, here p. 183).

social life derives not only from their political structures but also, in large measure, from their language and other cultural activities. Dupré refers to Herder's great predecessor Giambattista Vico, who reinstated hardworking Hercules as a nonrebellious model of cultural creativity (*PM*, p. 113). Vico depicts three ranges of solemnly celebrated customs which are "eternal and universal," namely, those associated with religion, marriage, and burial.[74] Here Vico, who himself had long studied Suárez, points out patterns of human performance that indicate some features of a natural law *(ius gentium)*. These customs provide a continuity between the abstract idea of social nature and political institutions. In addition, the ritual activities and artifacts connected with these realms of ordinary living proceed from the activity of expression which is so important in Dupré's conception of society. Furthermore, such realms of custom, as is evident with respect to the observances that surround religion and burial, point toward some transcendent, underpinning realm. Linguistic, expressive, and aesthetic activities likewise point toward the transcendent as they contribute to the building of a society. Meaning requires the transcendent:

> Nor can the transcendent factor be omitted from the meaning-giving process: transcendence is not merely what lies beyond the world, but first and foremost what supports its givenness. The achievement of . . . a more comprehensive synthesis remains part of the program of the modern age. (*PM*, p. 251)

This supporting and surpassing transcendence lies within and can emerge from the givenness of ordinary activities. The synthesis that a model of a harmonious cultural activity will offer includes these activities. Such a synthesis will also embrace the conflicts among these varied actions of persons and societies.

A modern social ethic must once again draw upon a legacy that includes the concern for a transcendent foundation which makes freedom possible. When he traces the reductive narrowing of ethics, Dupré spotlights a misstep that must be avoided:

> As science of the good, ethics had always been more than a concern about human perfection. . . . But when modern thought reduced the good to personal or social perfection, independently of and occasionally in opposition to the whole, it deprived it of ontological depth and marginalized morality with respect to the totality of Being. (*PM*, p. 143)

An ethic cannot be comprehensively social if it restricts itself to personal morality or even to models for social living and schemes for political community. The contemporary formulations of an ethic, if the pace and timing of current

---

74. *The New Science of Giambattista Vico,* trans. Thomas Goddard Bergin and Max Harold Fisch (Ithaca: Cornell University Press, 1968), no. 333.

cultural development does not yet allow a finished concept of wholeness, must themselves act as symbols. In terms that Dupré suggests in his subsequent book, these symbolizing elements point toward the whole in its unsettling depth.

A more complex age will require a more complex form for its ethics. From his examination of baroque art, Dupré learns the necessity of moral autonomy and of a complex interaction with the transcendent. Attending to the same source, he gains insight into still other requisites for a social ethic. Speaking of the resolution that baroque drama attained with respect to the dramatic conflicts of individuals, historical forces, and providential governance, Dupré holds:

> The Baroque achieved this balance of harshly contrasting yet interacting forces by means of a more inclusive conception of harmonious form than the Renaissance had possessed. Its complex form could grant the warring components a great deal of independence. (*PM*, p. 247)

An aesthetic sensibility yearns for the appropriate fit between shape and substance. The harmony of such a form, as the baroque shows is possible, includes contrasts, conflicts, and dissension.

VIII

Within a year of the publication of *Passage to Modernity*, Dupré crafts a firmer cohesion among the several elements needed both for cultural analysis and for achieving an encompassing cultural form. In *Metaphysics and Culture* (1994) (hereafter cited as *MC*), Dupré characterizes a metaphysics that would sustain a harmonious, developing society. In this way, his current work makes possible the recognition of a clearer connection between an ethics and the transcendent. At the same time, Dupré develops his earlier thought along a new approach to understanding symbols and symbolizing activity.

Hegel and Dupré share a common search; for both, the "quest for the ground . . . must recollect the various cultural forms in which the Spirit has expressed itself" (*MC*, p. 4). Culture encompasses the activities of objective and absolute spirit (p. 18). In order to delineate their respective means for conveying significance, Dupré probes several ranges of meaning-bearing activity. These interpretive endeavors themselves participate in the work of discovering the transcendent basis for expression. They participate in the required "recollection" of cultural forms. Expression here is clearly linked with the transcendent ground, the activity of the spirit. The culture-formative processes of externalization and internalization are now unmistakably identified with the ranges of activity that bring about expression and the corresponding, interpretive acknowledgment of this expression (p. 3).

Dupré sets out to design a metaphysics that can maintain itself in the variety and the changes of complex cultures. This metaphysical concern still focuses on determining an understanding of the ethical life. Dupré affirms Kant's surprising emphasis on the connection between morality and culture. According to this, free persons who carry out their moral activity within history establish a culture that is a bridge to nature and a morality that draws them to the transcendent (*MC*, p. 17). Dupré has enriched the concept of expressive activity. Not only does the activity of persons — be it linguistic expression, be it artistic creation — move them toward the transcendent; not only is the transcendent the basis of their activity;[75] but more, expressiveness itself is an attribute of the absolute. Here is another indication of the development of Dupré's thought that results from his appropriation of the baroque. Persons and the transcendent cooperate on a plane, for they share this capacity of expressive activity. They are not, of course, equal, for the transcendent expressiveness itself anticipates and enables human language.

Dupré firmly indicates that expressiveness and symbols are linked in his thought world (*MC*, p. 31). Symbols express the personal subject. Because expressiveness ranges within a culture that unites persons and because expressiveness is grounded in the transcendent, such symbolizing is not doomed to messages which are futile because of an intractable solipsism. "Symbols," as Dupré describes their action, "enable the mind to perceive the permanent in the transient, the universal in the particular" (p. 9). Correspondingly, symbols make possible two dynamics critical to Dupré's understanding of a vigorous culture in a society: they point to the perduring transcendent, and they enable the persons to locate themselves within a society. A social ethic, then, requires education in symbolizing activity, in its performance as well as in its interpretation.

Symbolizing activity expresses human freedom in a particular culture. The location in a particular society is determined by historical process. Likewise, apt interpretation must be alert to the cadences directed by historical change. Societies are organic cultural units which incorporate history as ingredient to their particular lives.[76] Dupré situates Hegel as a key figure in the development of this understanding, for with the *Phenomenology* time enters into the absolute (*MC*, p. 27). Dupré introduces this assertion precisely when he recalls "the modern perception of freedom as capable of intrinsically transforming reality" (p. 26). The transcendent emerges within history by dint of the exercise of human freedom. The absolute enters into time as the freedom of persons

75. As their basis the good and the common good require a restoration of "some sense of transcendence" (Dupré, "Common Good," p. 189).

76. At this point, Dupré once again invokes the work of Vico (Dupré, *Metaphysics and Culture*, p. 16).

expresses itself in symbols. Human freedom is specific in terms of person, time, place, and culture. In all their specificity, these symbols imply the profound ground of this freedom. The task of hermeneutics is to interpret such free exercise as it emerges from the produced artifacts and processes. Proper interpretation will also reveal how these cultural expressions are grounded upon the transcendent. The attentive observation and interpretation of these transient, particular expressions help fashion a cultural whole and assist persons in locating the transcendent.

When Dupré's ethic makes use of a hermeneutic and aesthetic understanding of social structures, he returns here to the concern for embodied new human life and the emblems of marital expression in his early works on sexual ethics and marriage. Culture develops in a society through social processes and structures intimate to the family, namely, education. Once again, Dupré distances himself from the modern, Promethean creation of a second nature. He conceives of culture as "fostering and developing an existing nature" (MC, p. 13).[77] Education, paideia, is a set of social structures, beginning in the family, for the shaping of free persons as cooperating citizens who participate in a shared culture. The learning of language assists persons in articulating the primary symbolism of embodiedness. The expressiveness of words draws attention to the body as a symbol of persons both in their immediacy and in their transcendence (p. 7).

Paideia impels rational change in history by the development of persons in historically self-transforming societies. In its incorporation of persons into society, education has over the centuries presented the centrality of virtuousness in the good life. This ethical principle, Aristotelian in its origin, Dupré posits as a cultural principle.[78] Social structures shape persons into ethical individuals; this enables them to become participants in the culture.[79]

Dupré's examination of history makes possible the positing of a contemporary ethic. Dupré seeks out the pattern in history, a pattern that social structures establish and that alters as a result of the interaction of these structures. Through his probing of Marx he has grasped that no one set of antecedents determines the shifts of history, and even "the ultimately determining factors . . . must be understood in their total context" (MSCC, p. 79). The pursuit of patterns is a significant element in the hunt for an all-embracing scheme. Dupré and Marx share the humanist's canon: interpret always within the relevant context and in terms of the pertinent whole. Dupré's aesthetic, humanist judg-

77. Persons must come to know themselves as the active element of reality which transforms the passive element. See Dupré, Passage to Modernity, p. 11.

78. Louis Dupré, The Joys and Responsibilities of Being a Catholic Teacher, Marianist Award Lecture (Dayton: University of Dayton, 1992), p. 12.

79. The principle of subsidiarity directs the formation of the common good so that it does not override the concerns of individuals (Dupré, "Common Good," p. 191).

ment enables him acutely to present the deficiencies in Marx's and Hegel's understanding of the mechanical and organic processes which shape this history. At the same time, this aesthetic acuity seeks a pattern for the sociocultural complex, a configuration whose flexibility can match the processes of social transformation and whose form can match cultural complexity. Pivotal is the requirement that the form of the society and culture must integrate person, the several levels of society, nature, and the anchoring lineaments of meaning so that they together constitute a harmonious whole. This cultural pattern also requires a social anthropology that focuses upon the liberating and producing person. Dupré abjures any Promethean humanism; instead he, along with Vico, regards Hercules as the exemplar, who assiduously accomplishes a series of tasks that make possible life in society.

In the present linguistic and notional circumstances of the postmodern age, the sought personal and social harmony is patently impossible both conceptually and practically. Yet Dupré surveys the currents dating from the time of nominalism which have led to this failure of integral form in society and culture. Dupré's scholarship charts a course while adhering to a stringent discipline: the future harmony must be sought while no future vision must be given — lest one run the dangers either of determinism or wish fulfillment. Nevertheless, one must allow for the utopian and assess the signs that emerge even now as an unaccountable surplus out of present cultural activity in society. His work enables trajectories to be plotted. His efforts provide both warnings of inadvertent errors and clarifications of the age's focal desires. Through his astute and diligent efforts, Dupré's oeuvre illuminates how life, labor, and language mediate the achievement of the common good. His writings will facilitate the task of ethicists significantly. His work will help them to develop the norms, virtues, patterns, and ideals by which these activities in a society remain expressive as well as interpretable. His objective is a social ethic where these activities remain integrated in the community, dynamic over the course of social changes, and, in addition, disclosive of the transcendent.

Major Publications of Louis Dupré

Kierkegaard as Theologian: The Dialectic of Christian Existence. New York: Sheed & Ward, 1963. Reprint, London: Sheed & Ward, 1964.

Contraception and Catholics: A New Appraisal. Baltimore: Helicon Press, 1964.

The Philosophical Foundations of Marxism. New York: Harcourt, Brace & World, 1966.

Contributing editor, with Francis Eterovich and others. *Approaches to Morality: Readings in Ethics from Classical Philosophy to Existentialism.* Jesse Mann and Gerald Kreyche, gen. eds. New York: Harcourt, Brace & World, 1966.

Editor and introduction. *Faith and Reflection* by Henry Duméry. Translated by Stephen McNiernery and M. Benedict Murphy. New York: Herder & Herder, 1968.

The Other Dimension: A Search for the Meaning of Religious Attitudes. New York: Doubleday, 1972. Reprinted in abridged paperback edition, New York: Seabury Press, 1979.

Transcendent Selfhood: The Loss and Rediscovery of the Inner Life. New York: Seabury Press, 1976.

A Dubious Heritage: Studies in the Philosophy of Religion after Kant. New York: Paulist Press, 1977.

The Deeper Life: An Introduction to Christian Mysticism. New York: Crossroad, 1981.

The Common Life: The Origins of Trinitarian Mysticism and Its Development by Jan Ruusbroec. New York: Crossroad, 1984.

Marx's Social Critique of Culture. New Haven: Yale University Press, 1983.

A detailed bibliography up to June 1997 can be found in Paul J. Levesque, *Symbols of Transcendence: Religious Expression in the Thought of Louis Dupré,* Louvain Theological and Pastoral Monographs, vol. 22 (Louvain: Peeters/Grand Rapids: Eerdmans, 1997), pp. 281-367.

Editor, with James Wiseman. *Light from Light: An Anthology of Christian Mysticism.* New York: Paulist Press, 1988.

Editor, with Don Saliers, and introduction. *Christian Spirituality III: Post-Reformation and Modern.* World Spirituality: An Encyclopedic History of the Religious Quest, vol. 18. New York: Crossroad, 1989, 1991; London: SCM, 1990.

Editor and introduction. "Nicholas of Cusa." Special issue of *American Catholic Philosophical Quarterly* 64 (1990). Washington, D.C.: American Catholic Philosophical Association, Catholic University of America, 1990.

Passage to Modernity: An Essay in the Hermeneutics of Nature and Culture. New Haven: Yale University Press, 1993.

Metaphysics and Culture. The Aquinas Lecture, 1994. Milwaukee: Marquette University Press, 1994.

Index